A NEW LABOR MOVEMENT FOR THE NEW CENTURY

A NEW LABOR MOVEMENT FOR THE NEW CENTURY

EDITED BY GREGORY MANTSIOS
AFTERWORD BY JOHN J. SWEENEY

MONTHLY REVIEW PRESS
NEW YORK

Copyright © 1998 by Gregory Mantsios
All rights reserved

Library of Congress Cataloging-in-Publication Data

A new labor movement for the new century : a collection of essays from
the Labor Resource Center, Queens College, City University of New
York / edited by Gregory Mantsios : foreword by Dan Georgakas :
    p.   cm.
    Also published by: New York : Garland Pub., © 1998.
    Includes bibliographical references and index.
    ISBN 0-85345-937-1
    1. Labor movement—United States.   2. Labor policy—United States.
3. Trade-unions—United States.   4. Trade-unions—United States—
Political activity.   I. Mantsios, Gregory.   II. Queens College (New York,
N.Y.). Labor Resource Center.
HD8072.5.N484   1998b
331.88'0973—dc21   98-17905
                                                                CIP

All royalties from this anthology will be used to support student scholarships. These
scholarships will be made available to students enrolled in the Queens College
Bachelor of Applied Social Science Program—a special degree program designed to
prepare students for advocacy work with unions, community organizations, and
government.

Monthly Review Press
122 West 27th Street
New York, NY 10001

Manufactured in the United States of America
10 9 8 7 6 5 4 3 2 1

Contents

CONTENTS

CONTENTS

FOREWORD

For the contributors to this volume, the 1995 contested election for leadership of the AFL-CIO was a watershed event. The victory of the New Voice slate led by John Sweeney is not seen as an automatic fix to all that has troubled the trade union movement, but as an opening of the door to a serious reorganization and reorientation of that movement. They are greatly heartened that the New Voice team candidly acknowledged the movement's shortcomings even as it asserted its desire to reanimate labor's historic mission.

Taking their cue from the myriad of forces which ultimately produced the change in AFL-CIO leadership, the contributors to this volume take up every problem area troubling working class organizations. While hopeful about the prospects for change, they indicate that if trade unions do not transform themselves, then the labor movement as we have known it is probably doomed. Dire as this assumption may be, with the exception of labor's role in international affairs, the changes advocated are rarely a fundamental break with the past and rarely are they entirely novel ideas. Instead, the proposals elaborate on current strategies that have proven effective. In this sense, the authors seek to be catalysts in processes already in motion. If this decreases the drama of what they are proposing, it also increases the possibility that their proposals can indeed be implemented in the near future.

Another characteristic of these authors is that they are not the usual set of outside critics or losers in bureaucratic infighting. As their impressive author identifications indicate, they have labored long and hard in the house of labor, advocating their ideas within trade union structures where the consequences of decision making, good and bad, are felt immediately in daily life. As officials in local and national unions, they have to answer to their memberships for ill-conceived or poorly executed programs. They are also in a position to hear what issues truly concern the membership.

President John Sweeney's contribution to the volume demonstrates the dramatic change in the attitude of the national leadership of the AFL-CIO. Rather than denouncing internal critics as disrupting labor's unity or offering points of attack to enemies, Sweeney actively encourages the public airing of different proposals, whether to his liking or not. He also indicates that in an organization as large as the AFL-CIO, different strategies can be tested in different arenas and that diversity can be a component of strength rather than weakness.

Editor Gregory Mantsios and his contributors are determined to see the trade union movement regain at least as much political weight as it enjoyed during the 1940s and 1950s when a little over a third of all working Americans were unionized. They also have a bolder, longer-range concept of the centrality of working people to the democracy of the coming millennium. They believe that the obituaries for organized labor in America are not only premature, but that if American labor is able to realize the opportunities they outline, the best is yet to come.

This volume caps the "Labor in America" series issued by Garland Publishing for which I have been the general editor. That series has mainly been devoted to exploring the strategies and practices of the labor movement at times when it was growing in strength and influence. The targeted audience for these works was scholarly, whether those scholars were in the academy, the community, or trade unions. Unlike those volumes, *A New Labor Movement for the New Century* focuses on the future, and its authors seek a general audience so that instead of remaining interesting discussion points, their views might materialize into practice. A reasonably priced paperback seemed the best means to reach such an audience. The editors of Monthly Review Press agreed, resulting in the volume in hand.

DAN GEORGAKAS
March 1998

ACKNOWLEDGMENTS

All of us at the Labor Resource Center are grateful to the individuals who made this anthology possible. First, we want to thank each of the contributors for their willingness to devote the time and energy this project required. We invited them to submit essays because we have great admiration for their work: that admiration has grown as we have come to better understand the ideas that inspire and motivate that work. A large measure of our thanks must go to Dan Georgakas, the editor for Garland's labor series, who first suggested the book, served as a reader, and provided suggestions from the very first conceptualization of the book to the finest details of the finished product.

Major contributions to the production of this volume were also made by individuals whose names do not appear in the table of contents. Margarita Colón Ortiz did an enormous amount of work on this project and had the unenviable task of tracking submissions, making corrections, formatting, and proofreading: she did all this while adding her insights, good judgment, and good humor to the process. Laura McClure and Mark Levitan served as readers and provided thoughtful comments and excellent editorial suggestions for each of the essays. In a number of instances, they worked very closely with authors to help them prepare their essays. Deborah D'Amico and Paula Finn also worked extensively with authors to prepare essays: their knowledge of the labor movement and craft for writing made for important additions to the collection. Paula Rothenberg read, re-read, and re-read again a number of sections and provided critical comments and suggestions.

Special thanks are also in order to the following: Andy Banks for suggesting the conference that inspired the book; Len Rodberg for working out of title and keeping our computers humming; Bob Greenwald for providing a continuous stream of business periodicals; Richard Wallis for seeing the hardcover edition through to its completion with Garland Publishing; Christopher Phelps and the people at Monthly Review Press for doing a terrific job of putting the paperback edition on the fast track and providing tender loving care; Dan Ratner, Mitra Behroozi, and Richard Levy for their generous help in securing the release of paperback rights; Barbara Saltz and Deena Turk for their careful reading and copy editing; Matt Schum for copy editing and tracking down obscure citations; David Kusnet for his thoughtful comments on the book; Emily Schnee for proofreading; Kate Bronfenbrenner, Ed Ott, and Nick Unger for commenting on specific essays.

The Center staff would also like to thank all the members of our Labor Advisory Board whose strong support has been indispensable to all of our work. Arthur Cheliotes, who chairs our Advisory Board, has given tirelessly of himself to the labor programs at Queens College for nearly fourteen years and in the course of that time has not only inspired great ideas but has always helped us find the resources to turn these ideas into reality. For ongoing support of the Labor Resource Center, we are also deeply indebted to Cathy Nolan, Brian McLaughlin, Joe McDermott, Larry Mucciolo, Ed Ott, Allen L. Sessoms, Sheldon Silver, Ed Sullivan, John Thorpe, and Hratch Zadoian. When the very survival of the Center and Worker Education was in jeopardy, over 100 national and local union leaders, 100 University colleagues, and 1,000 union member-students came to our aid. We want to thank them not only for their support, but for showing us what solidarity is all about.

On a personal level, I would like to thank Miriam Thompson, Geoffrey Jacques, Tani Takagi, and Suzette Ellington for shouldering a considerable burden as the anthology distracted me from the affairs of the Center. Special thanks are also in order to Susanne Paul, Sean Sweeney, and their respective staffs for doing the same with our Worker Education program. Last, but certainly not least, I would like to thank my family: Paula Rothenberg, Alexi, and Andrea for the love and joy they bring to my life as well as the patience and tolerance they demonstrated as the manuscript increasingly encroached on our living space and our lives in general.   —G.M.

Introduction

Gregory Mantsios

This would be a good time for those interested in the working class and the U.S. labor movement to devote an entire book to questions.

Why, they might ask, has the working class, which is working more and making less in the richest and most powerful nation in history, failed to use its collective force, either in the workplace, the voting booth, or the streets, to demand fundamental changes in the way this country distributes its wealth and resources? This, after all, is a nation where the wages of the middle-incomed have deteriorated for two consecutive decades despite cyclical upturns,[1] previously secure blue- and white-collar workers still live in fear of "downsizing," the threat to life and limb on the job remains perilously high, and the public services that working people depend on are deteriorating rapidly and dramatically.

What, they might ask, has kept the urban ghettos, with their high concentration of people of color, from rebelling to demand racial justice? It is in the U.S. where unemployment and infant mortality among blacks and Latinos are twice that of whites,[2] where one in four African American males in the prime of life is in jail or on parole,[3] where life expectancy among blacks is six years below that of whites,[4] where the median weekly earnings of Latino workers are 64 percent of those of whites and declining,[5] and where thousands of Asian immigrants toil in sweatshops—many living and working under conditions of indentured servitude.

How do we explain the persistence of male domination and a culture which despite advances, still relegates women, especially poor and working class women, to second class citizenship? Women earn $.75 for every $1.00 earned by men,[6] one out of every two women experiences sexual harassment in her work life,[7] and women, abandoned by their mates and trying to raise their children on meager government subsidies, are blamed for the nation's ills.

Why has the nation tolerated the persistence of poverty? Nearly one in four children in America live in poverty,[8] 13.5 million adults still cannot find full-time employment,[9] and more than 27% of those that do not find jobs earn less than the amount it would take to keep a family of four above the poverty line.[10]

All of this is compounded by the fact that the gap between the haves and the have nots has grown to unprecedented levels. For this is also a nation where corporations are reaping record profits, a single CEO can earn more in one year than 65 workers make in a lifetime,[11] and the net worth of the wealthiest one percent of the population exceeds the net worth of the bottom ninety percent combined.[12] This is a nation where Green Tree Financial's CEO makes more than $100 million a year in salary,[13] Microsoft's Bill Gates is worth $35 billion,[14] and financier George Soros made one billion in currency speculation in the space of a few days.[15] The average worker earning $34,000 per year would have to save all of his or her income for the next 30 millennia—29,418 years to be exact—to accumulate just $1 billion.

Life without adequate and equitably apportioned resources can bring extraordinary pain and arouse considerable anger. But rather than turn our anger toward those who gain at our expense, too often we come to idolize the rich and famous, stand in awe of the fortunes and power of corporate giants, and displace our frustration onto those less fortunate. It is in this context that the political and religious right have gained in popularity, and that the efforts to downsize government and turn back policies designed to regulate the abusive power of big business have succeeded.

Many would attribute these setbacks to passivity on the part of the dispossessed. But it is not that simple. Capital has real power not only to influence the way we think, including who we blame for our individual and collective plight, but also to impose serious penalties, through layoffs and plant shut-downs, on workers and communities that might otherwise consider alternatives to corporate rule.

Others would challenge a portrait of passive Americans by pointing to countless examples of workers willing to strike, people of color willing to protest, and communities willing to say no to corporations seeking additional advantage. People resist in spite of the economic and cultural dominance of corporate America. But Americans are no more born activists than they are born robotons. And our willingness and ability to stand up and confront injustice occurs in the context of alternative cultures, visionary leaders, and strong social movements. Without these, there can be little meaningful or effective resistance. This raises another set of questions.

Why did a labor movement that was so vibrant, massive, and capable of bringing about fundamental change in the 1930s and 1940s become virtually moribund in the 1980s and 1990s? In their heyday, unions represented 34 percent of the U.S. workforce, wielded considerable political influence on both the national and local levels, and at times threatened to redistribute both wealth and power in the United States. Fifty years later the mass media described organized labor as impotent and irrelevant.

The last two decades were among the worst in this century for workers and unions, especially those at the lower end of the economic spectrum. Corporate and government assaults have left unions with fewer members and reduced political influence. Unions have been severely weakened in their ability to represent their members, and their numbers have been reduced to a fraction—less than half—of their former strength, leaving nearly six out of every seven workers without union representation or protection. Many critics would place blame for the decline of organized labor squarely on the shoulders of its leaders. They would argue that labor leaders failed to organize the unorganized, mobilize existing members, confront employers, and develop either a new vision or an effective political strategy. Leaders were elitist and exclusionary, purged their most effective and militant activists, and remained too focused on the narrow institutional needs of their organizations. In short, they were too complacent and failed to lead.

But on its own, this explanation for labor's decline is too simplistic. Advances in technology displaced the labor force in manufacturing where unions were strong, new production methods allowed corporations to shift operations to other parts of the world where wages are lower and unions non-existent, and the rise of competitor nations in Western Europe and Asia created an environment where U.S. corporations could use the very real threat of competition to hold workers in check. These changes in the domestic and world economy would have made it difficult—although not impossible—for any labor leader to protect the gains made by the labor movement under more favorable conditions.

Both the failure of the past and the challenge of the future provided the context for the historic convention of the American Federation of Labor-Congress of Industrial Organizations (AFL-CIO) in 1995, the first since the merger of the Federation four decades ago in which top leadership positions were contested. At stake was the leadership of a federation representing 71 national unions and 14 million workers from a broad range of industries and occupations. Both slates of candidates in the 1995 election offered proposals for change. Both expressed a strong commitment to organizing the unorganized and reversing labor's long decline in its membership rolls.

John Sweeney won the presidency of the AFL-CIO at its 1995 convention because delegates believed he and his slate represented a more significant break with the past and the best hope for the future. While the economic factors that allowed corporate America to increase its hold on the lives and livelihoods of working people remain in place, enthusiasm over the leadership change was rooted in the belief that the conditions for working people could be improved, the decline of union membership could be reversed, and the change in leadership marked an end to an era of passive, narrow, and stodgy unionism. As one critic described the change, "Labor has finally awakened from a long, deep sleep."[16]

Not everyone in the labor movement was euphoric. Some, primarily from the old guard, considered the new leadership to be romantics. Others, progressives among them, described the change as a palace coup. Since 1995, many have been asking whether there is a real difference between the labor movement of the past four decades and the one that will usher us into the next century. For those who are deeply committed to social and economic justice the real question is, will this labor movement bring about fundamental change?

While this certainly is a good time to write a book about questions, this is not that book. This is a book in search of answers—not so much to explain why things are the way they are, as much as to suggest how things might be. While this book focuses on the future of the labor movement, it is questions about inequality, injustice, the status quo, and change that have pre-occupied the contributors to this volume.

All of these contributors share a deep commitment to and a long history of activism on behalf of social change. As a diverse group of leaders, activists, and educators, they are thinkers and doers with progressive perspectives, rich experiences, a passion for justice and activism in their blood. They have been critical of the labor establishment, but they are critics who have remained committed to the labor movement, warts and all, for what it has already done to bring justice to workers and for what it is capable of doing in the future. At the same time, these authors all have different, often contradictory, opinions about what needs to be done: their visions, ideas, remedies, strategies, and tactics are distinct from each other. Well respected leaders and activists, they are some of the individuals whose ideas and actions are helping to bring back the vitality the labor movement so desperately needs.

The idea of bringing together such a group grew out of a conference organized by the Queens College Labor Resource Center on the eve of the AFL-CIO convention. That conference brought together 350 participants from around the country—most of them offering sharp critiques of organized labor's establishment. Panelists, and subsequently our contributors, were asked to identify the criteria by which activists should judge the success or failure of the leadership about to be elected. What would it take, we asked, to satisfy those who for so long have been advocating for change? Interestingly, four of the contributors to this volume, who were asked this question in 1995, have since been appointed to high-level positions within the leadership of the Federation.

Perhaps as important as the convention itself were the debates that the contested election stimulated at all levels of the labor movement. With deep divisions within the house of labor and with unprecedented media attention, national and local leaders and union staffers, as well as shop stewards and rank-and-file members, waxed philosophic. Because of the nature and mission of the AFL-CIO, the discussions stimulated by this election were broad and profound: they focused neither on a particular industry nor a particular sector. Instead, labor leaders and activists, reflecting their ideological diversity, made sweeping arguments about the mission, values, structures, strategies, and tactics of organized labor. At stake in these discussions were the future and the direction of the movement.

This anthology attempts to capture that moment, keep it alive, and move it forward in the belief that discussions about the future need to be deepened, widened, and ongoing. We invited these leaders and activists from across the country to present their views of and visions for the labor movement, with the objective of fueling further discussion and debate about the issues confronting workers and the labor movement.

The collection of essays is arranged around five topic areas: Democracy, Ideology, and Change; Organizing the Unorganized; Diversity and Inclusion; Parties and Politics; and International Affairs. In each area, we asked contributors to articulate a vision, specify realizable short-term and long-term goals, and identify the standards and criteria by which they would evaluate the success of the AFL-CIO and the U.S. labor movement. For this task, we asked contributors to think ten years ahead. How must the labor movement see itself in the years to come? What new roles must it adopt? What new methods must it embrace? Most importantly, we asked our contributors to focus on change that is both cultural (involving values and priorities) and structural (involving governance, process, strategy, and tactic).

Several assumptions were made when we undertook this project. The success of the labor movement will depend on its ability to:

1. reach unorganized workers and dramatically reverse membership decline;

2. offer a vision and engage in democratic and inclusive practices that empower workers, especially women and people of color;

3. build political alliances, develop new electoral strategies, inspire more effective political mobilization, and dig deeper roots in communities;

4. respond to the new global economy and overcome the ability of transnational corporations to pit workers in different countries against each other.

In the end, this collection grows out of the belief that a strong and vibrant labor movement is critical to a democracy and to the well-being of its populace. While the last two decades have been dismal for workers and the labor movement, there are good reasons to believe that a new political and economic environment is in the making. The contest for the leadership of the labor movement may indeed turn out to mark a watershed—a turning point—in the everyday lives of workers and the movement itself. A newly revived labor movement which draws on labor's best militant and democratic tradition may in fact represent our nation's best hope for achieving social and economic justice in the twenty-first century.

NOTES

1. Lawrence Mishel, Jared Bernstein, John Schmitt, *The State of Working America 1996-97* (Armonk, N.Y: M.E. Sharpe, 1997), p. 144.

2. World Bank, *World Development Report 1990* (New York: Oxford University Press, 1990), pp. 232-233. Also Andrew Hacker, *Two Nations: Black and White, Separate, Hostile, Unequal* (New York: Scribners and Sons, 1992), pp. 103 and 231.

3. *The Washington Post*, February 27, 1990, sec. A, p. 3, citing Marc Mauer, "Young Black Men and the Criminal Justice System: A Growing National Problem," The Sentencing Project, January 1990. Also see Manning Marable, *Black Liberation in Conservative America* (Boston: South End Press, 1997), pp. 43-47.

4. Hacker, *Two Nations*, p. 231.

5. Nancy Folbre and the Center for Popular Economics, *The New Field Guide to the U.S. Economy* (New York: The New Press, 1995), chapter 4, p. 11.

6. "Women Losing Ground to Men in Widening Income Difference," *The New York Times*, September 15, 1997, sec. A, p. 1.

7. Women's Action Coalition, *Stats: The Facts About Women* (New York: The New Press, 1993), p. 53.

8. Mishel, *State of Working America*, pp. 300-301.

9. Ibid., p. 244. This figure includes involuntary part-time workers.

10. Folbre, *New Field Guide*, chapter 2, p. 9.

11. *The Nation*, April 7, 1997, reported the annual compensation for Sandy Weill, CEO of Travelers Group, as $94.1 million. Average U.S. workers' annual salary is calculated at $34,000.

12. Folbre, *New Field Guide*, chapter 1, p. 2.

13. *Business Week*, April 21, 1997, p. 58.

14. *Fortune*, August 4, 1997, p. 38.

15. *Worth*, November 1996, p. 76.

16. Katha Pollitt, speaker at conference "Fighting for America's Future: A Teach-In with the Labor Movement," held at Columbia University, October 4, 1996.

PART | 1 | DEMOCRACY, IDEOLOGY, AND CHANGE

In this first section, contributors examine the issue of democracy as it is conceived and practiced both inside and outside the labor movement. While all unions are formally governed by democratic principles, specific procedures and organizational practices vary greatly from union to union. As a result, the checkered history of internal union democracy has severely tarnished labor's image. An underlying assumption in these essays is that both the reality and the image will have to be repaired if efforts to mobilize current members, organize new members, and revitalize the labor movement are to succeed. But even when the democratic procedures and practices are in place, fundamental questions about the relationship between leadership and the rank-and-file remain. For example, many contend that unions are more effective when they are driven from the bottom up, by an active rank-and-file, than when driven from above, by a democratically elected leadership and their appointed staff. Similarly, many activists challenge the notion that democracy applies only to internal union governance and national electoral politics. They contend that it is necessary to democratize the U.S. economy so that decisions by and within economic institutions are subject to the democratic process. Labor unions, in the final analysis, are about empowerment and if they are to inspire a broad social movement for change, they must be seen as democratically run organizations fighting for workplace and economic democracy.

In the lead essay, Elaine Bernard argues that unions must place democracy at the heart of labor's agenda. Pointing out that despite the efforts of unions, the workplace remains one of the least democratic environments in our society, she suggests that labor's primary goal ought to be to extend democracy to the workplace and the economic sphere. For this to happen, however, internal union democracy is central, for if unions teach and practice democratic decision-making within their own ranks, they will create a sense of democratic entitlement within society. To achieve that end, Bernard offers a number of specific proposals. She sees the development of a culture within the labor movement that is more open to debate and discussion of controversial issues as key to the democratic growth of organized labor.

Bill Fletcher makes clear how challenging this is. Union democracy is a dead issue he writes, if members believe unions are irrelevant to their principal concerns. While most unions have formal democratic structures, the more fundamental question is, how relevant are unions to the everyday lives of workers and do workers have control over their own organizations? Democratic reform movements appear as abstractions to most rank-and-file members because they are disengaged from the practice of unions altogether and no longer feel the impact of reactionary leadership. Union members will remain disengaged as long as unions are officer or staff driven, place no genuine expectations on members, limit the practical means of participation, and make no great effort to mobilize their membership. Fletcher offers a number of suggestions for getting members to buy into decisions made by unions, ranging from organizing debates and discussions on political endorsements, to organizing sports clubs. Formal democracy, he argues, is less important than member involvement and control, and the strategic direction that evolves from membership participation.

Jeremy Brecher and Tim Costello examine the New Voice program— the platform upon which the current leadership of the AFL-CIO built its successful challenge to the Federation's incumbent leadership. While generally pleased with the platform, they warn that greater militancy and more vigorous organizing alone will not succeed in revitalizing the labor movement. As long as people continue to view unions as undemocratic and bureaucratic institutions, the labor movement will remain impotent. Reversing labor's decline, the authors argue, will require a new organizational culture that values and promotes rank-and-file initiatives in organizing, politics, coalition building, and international solidarity support. They urge the AFL-CIO to avoid bureaucracy, legitimize internal opposition, and develop democratic pluralism at all levels of the movement, arguing that the current leadership of the AFL-CIO will accomplish little unless they encourage those on the ground to empower themselves.

In the final essay of this section, Gregory Mantsios focuses on labor's message and the question, What does labor stand for? He contrasts the ideology of the current leadership with that of the past and identifies a clear shift away from a narrow, Washington-based approach toward a more broadly defined, socially conscious labor movement. At the same time, he suggests that the current ideology remains rooted to a number of outdated assumptions about the socio-economic order. He challenges organized labor's faith in capitalism, its belief that the long term interests of labor and capital are congruent, and its acceptance of the logic of the market economy. These have defined and severely limited labor's vision. He calls for a more class-conscious approach that will, on the one hand, offer a sharp critique of corporate domination, private gain, and class inequity and, on the other, build a popular movement for public control of corporate enterprises and economic institutions. Mantsios urges organized labor to develop a bold vision of democracy and equality that will inspire and unify a broad social movement.

Creating Democratic Communities in the Workplace

Elaine Bernard

The most important challenge for labor and society in the twenty-first century is the question of democracy. Can we build and sustain democratic communities where we live, in the workplace, throughout the country, and globally? The New Right, in the U.S. and internationally, fully understands what is at stake in this battle for democratic control—and they are out to destroy democracy. For the most part, the New Right is not so crass as to come right out and say they are against democracy. Rather, they go about thwarting and rolling back popular control by stealth. Everywhere, they seek to replace democratic institutions with market mechanisms. They are attempting to construct a new political consensus which designates virtually all problems as the responsibility of the individual, whose fate is left to the mercy of market forces. This program of the Right seeks nothing less than the destruction of civil society and community, without which there can be no democracy.

THE MARKET VIEW

How does democracy differ from market relations? In a democracy, the practice is "one person, one vote." The humblest and most distinguished citizens are equal, with each having only one vote. But in the marketplace, it is "one dollar, one vote," which, despite an appearance of neutrality and equality, is an inherently unjust equation that privileges the rich at the expense of the poor. In such statements as "Let the market decide," promoted as principle by the New Right, the market disguises human agency and action and gives the appearance of a natural process, while serving the demands of the wealthy whose dollars have the power to shape the rules of the market.

The elevation of markets as the sole arbiter of value also destroys people's sense of belonging to a community. People feel isolated and powerless, which in turn leads to demoralization. If each of us is on our own, none of us can change very much individually, so we are forced to accept things as they are. No single individual can answer any of the big questions in our society. An individual cannot opt for single-payer health care or rapid transit, or address the problem of declining wages and unemployment. So by default these "big" problems become "unsolvable."

Former British Prime Minister Margaret Thatcher summed up this anti-social, anti-community philosophy of the New Right succinctly when she proclaimed that there is no such thing as society; there are simply individuals and their families. This frightening world view forces people to seek individual solutions and pits people against one another, reducing social responsibility and cohesion. If there is no such thing as society and there are only markets, then government is a waste, and redistributive programs are robbery. With no society, anything that goes from my pocket into the community is a scam. Worse yet, anything that goes from my pocket makes it just that much harder for me and my family to survive. It is a zero-sum view of society where your gain is my loss, and an injury to one is their problem. And this is the view that will ultimately prevail if the New Right succeeds in its attempt to eviscerate democratic institutions—from government to communities to unions.

WORKPLACE RIGHTS AND DEMOCRACY

It is important to place the issue of democracy in the labor movement within the wider context of the New Right's attempt to destroy democracy and inclusive democratic communities throughout society. After all, what is it that unions do? First and foremost, unions are about creating community. Yes, unions improve workers' wages, benefits, and working conditions, and that is an important struggle in the face of growing income inequality. But unions have always done more than simply organize for improved wages and benefits. Unions are vehicles for forging a community of interest among workers, and that is what makes them vital institutions of civil society throughout the world. Unions help workers see that they have common interests with their fellow worker, and unions make possible collective action that can protect the vulnerable and improve conditions for all.

Yet, in spite of the best efforts of unions, the workplace remains one of the least democratic environments in our society. In fact, workplaces should be seen as factories of authoritarianism polluting our democracy. The workplace is a place where workers learn that they actually have few rights to participate in decisions about events of great consequences to their lives. Citizens cannot spend eight or more hours a day obeying orders and accepting that they have no rights, legal or otherwise, to participate in important decisions that affect them, and that they can be fired at will for no cause, and then be expected to engage in robust, critical dialogue about the structure of our society. Eventually, the strain of being deferential servants from nine to five diminishes our after-hours liberty and sense of civic entitlement and responsibility. Put simply, the existing hierarchy of employment relations undermines our democracy.

Many of the rights that we take for granted in other locations simply do not exist in the workplace. For example, a fundamental assumption in our legal system is the presumption of innocence. In the workplace, this presumption is turned on its head. The rule of the workplace is that management dictates and workers obey. If a worker is accused of a transgression by management, there is no presumption of innocence. Even in organized workplaces the rule remains: work first, grieve later. Organized workers protected by a collective agreement with a contractual grievance procedure can at least grieve an unjust practice (or more specifically, one that violates the rights spelled out in a collective agreement). Unorganized workers, however, are left with appealing to their superiors' benevolence or entering the unemployment line. The implied voluntary labor contract—undertaken by workers when they agree to employment—gives management almost total control of the work relationship. "Free labor" entails no rights other than the freedom to quit without penalty. That is one step up from indentured servitude, but still a long distance from democracy.

PRACTICING WORKPLACE DEMOCRACY

To meet the challenge of the New Right and its attempt to destroy democracy and inclusive democratic communities throughout society, labor needs to take the offensive. In particular, that means leadership in the struggle to democratize the workplace, and to make democratic decision-making the norm in all walks of life. Unions need to become schools of democracy for workers who do not find democratic practice or rights in the workplace and increasingly are feeling isolated and powerless both inside and outside of the workplace. Unions, as the self-organization of working people for social and economic justice, need to be models of democratic practice in their activities. Labor needs to teach and practice democratic decision-making and inclusion within its organizations and work to create a sense of democratic entitlement within society.

But what does democratic practice look like? And how do we balance democratic rights with the need for effective, disciplined, mass participatory organizations? At first glance, most of the principles of democratic practice are familiar. Democratic organizations assure members of the right to participate in decisions that affect them, equality of representation, access to information before decisions are made, open debate and discussion about choices, the right to dissent, and procedures to assure that decisions are acted upon and that leaders are accountable. Yet democracy in practice is much more complicated than a series of rules or abstract rights.

Democracy is first and foremost a process, not a rule book. That is, while organizations can adopt structures, rules, practices, and forms to enhance democracy, it will be in the daily practice of organizations that people will judge if there is genuine participation and a real sense of ownership of the organization by the members. Most of us, unfortunately, are all too familiar with organizations that are democratic in "form" but undemocratic in practice. It is for this reason that unions must not only have formal democratic rights for members but also seek to instill a democratic practice and high levels of participation in all their work and organization.

If we look at each of the elements of democratic practice listed earlier, we can see there is no easy formula for the best practice in all circumstances and for all sizes of organizations. For example, how do we put into practice the right to participate in decisions? In some cases, with small local unions or relatively independent components within large organizations, direct democracy is possible. But with very large organizations which may be geographically dispersed, representative democracy is clearly more appropriate than direct participation. That is because with direct democracy while formally everyone can participate, sometimes in practice they cannot. If meetings are held far away from a member's work or home, for example, they cannot participate. So, to assure a balance in representation, members elect delegates to represent them. However, even in these cases, if a union saw its role as primarily to facilitate the creation of a community within the workplace, then it might seek to complement its representative structure to assure some element of direct democracy, maybe by forming workaday sub-units, or by organizing workaday meetings and other attempts at increasing participation.

Equality of representation is another example of a democratic principle which gets complicated in practice. In its simplest form, equality of representation is achieved by assuring that each person has one vote. However, there is often a need to modify structures in order to achieve the principle of equality of representation in practice. Most national and even state organizations, for example, have some formula to assure that there is geographic "balance" of representation on leadership bodies through set-aside positions or some other form of regional structure. Yet it is a sad irony that while many in the labor movement balk at set-asides for women or people of color on leadership bodies, most organizations practice geographic set-asides—as if geography were the most important representational inclusion question before organized labor today.

The right to participate in decision-making, of course, implies informed decision-making. But for informed decision-making, access to information is vital. In addition, the right to participate in decision-making also means that people need to have real choices before them, so they should have the opportunity to participate in the formulation of proposals. Real choice also includes the opportunity to dissent and to formulate alternative proposals and to participate in open debate over options. The right to dissent further implies the right to caucus. Every disagreement or alternative proposal will not necessarily lead to the formation of a caucus—but permitting self-organization of groups within an organization (that is what a caucus is) is certainly in line with democratic practice. After all, the right to stand in opposition, alone, while important, does not really mean very much. But the right to meet with others and to formulate an alternative, that is a serious challenge, and assures that opposition and alternatives will be taken into consideration by the majority.

While democratic organizations are ruled by the majority, the minority's opinion must be heard and taken into consideration. Indeed, the mark of a true democracy is that the minority must have the opportunity to influence and even win majority support. But to assure that the minority really does have a chance to influence the majority, it must be permitted the ability to organize—up to and including its own caucus. After all, the majority is usually well-organized. Dissent or disagreement is not just an abstract right or a luxury permissible only at certain times. In practice, a good discussion about direction or policy helps the majority. It plays an important role in offering choice and even in clarifying and winning people to the merits of the majority position. Vigorous debate is a sign of health in a democratic organization. In the U.S., there is a tendency to see disagreement and argument as a problem, even organizationally disloyal, and certainly not as a necessary part of any democratic process. In Westminster legislative systems (modeled on the British parliamentary system), the "opposition" is often referred to as "Her Majesty's Loyal Opposition" because the concept is that opposition in a democracy is loyal. In fact, it is a disservice to an organization to have grave concerns over policy issues or direction and pretend to agree. Raising objections or concerns, and even formulating alternatives, is the method through which democratic organizations develop and refine positions.

For too long, the dominant view of many labor leaders and even of much of the membership has been to see dissent and disagreement as a problem. It is viewed as at best suspect, and at worst disloyal. There are both good reasons and bad reasons for this attitude. Because solidarity is so important to labor, activists and leaders occasionally forget that the powerful unity that is forged when a decision is made is the product of informed consent, with serious consideration and exploration of various alternatives.

Of course, the right to dissent does not mean that unions should become debating societies. After all, another important aspect of democracy is accountability. Accountability means that if leaders are to be held accountable for decisions, they must also have the power to assure that decisions are implemented. There is a time to debate and there is a time to act. But unity in action is best forged when members have been afforded significant participation in formulating the program of action.

The right to dissent and to form caucuses can, of course, be abused. Occasionally, the majority and a minority harden into "factions" which, rather than informing members of alternatives and facilitating healthy debate on decisions, turn meetings into name-calling and recrimination sessions. Rather than facilitating discussion, caucuses can "factionalize" debate, with members not listening to the merits of an argument but rather judging comments solely by the commentator. The solution to this problem, however, is not to ban caucuses, but rather to try and keep them from becoming "hardened" and exclusive. And to seek to make the forming and dissolving of caucuses a natural part of organizational life, not just for the majority (or the executive) but for all sorts of other concerns and interests. Too often, a minority caucus hardens in response to a hardened and exclusive "administrative" caucus of the current leadership. Two of the most important attributes of a democratic union organization are the right to participate and the accountability of leadership to the membership. These are also the two most difficult processes to structure in practice. Yet, as pointed out earlier, there are structures which tend to inhibit, and structures which tend to facilitate participation and accountability.

EMBRACING DEBATE: THE CANADIAN MODEL

Having observed AFL-CIO national conventions, Canadian Labour Congress (CLC) conventions, and numerous state and provincial federation conventions, I have been struck by the differences in delegate participation between federations in the two countries. The CLC convention and most Canadian provincial labor federation conventions have more delegate participation, and in most cases this is not because of size differences. Rather, in Canada delegates are generally directly elected by their locals to attend the convention—not appointed by the national leadership, as is the case in many U.S. labor federation conventions. The CLC and provincial labor federations each have weighted formulas for determining the number of delegates at their conventions: each affiliated local union receives at least one delegate and additional delegates are allocated to locals depending on their size.

This process of direct delegate election with one delegate, one vote in the convention, seems to have a significant effect on the character of the proceedings. First, the vast majority of delegates at the convention are local union leaders, not union staff or full-time officers. Delegates are expected to report back to their local and therefore tend to be a little more attentive to the proceedings. Second, resolutions at the convention are drafted by locals, and locals expect to hear back about what happened to their resolution and issues. Finally, because delegates are directly elected, they have a "base" of support, and they tend to have a real sense of ownership of the convention and its procedures. Reflecting the fact that the delegates "own" the convention, generally, formal speeches by union leaders, politicians, and invited guests are kept to a minimum when compared to U.S. conventions. Nevertheless, the Canadian delegates still complain about the lack of time for the convention to debate policy.

While CLC and provincial labor federation conventions may not be models of participation, there is much to be said for the direct election of delegates, and for a convention where the delegates decide the outcome on the basis of one delegate, one vote. This method obviously gives significantly more power to the labor councils and to smaller organizations within the federation. While the largest unions still have the majority of votes at convention, they are forced to deliver delegates to the convention, which gives opponents an opportunity to talk with and influence activists. And with each delegate having one vote, caucuses and discussions among delegates tend to be more important. Delegates feel they have more power, because every delegate's vote counts for the same. Generally, it leads to conventions with more debate, more discussion, and fewer guest speakers. From a democracy point of view, it is more participatory and overall it is a more educational experience.

But why this emphasis on debate? What does discussion and debate have to do with democracy? For informed decision-making, people need to fully explore policy positions and alternatives. Debate is useful in permitting participants in decision-making to hear all sides. When decisions are made after carefully weighing alternatives, and after the leadership has advocated its position, delegates go home better armed to explain and defend the position adopted. Having gone through a discussion, they are well-equipped to deal with questions, objections, and challenges to the adopted position. Too often in the labor movement, positions are adopted with little or no discussion, or worse, after only hearing speakers in favor of the decision. Members participating in such proceedings are often ill-equipped to explain and defend the position or policy when faced with opposition.

Developing a critical culture within the labor movement, more open to debate, and more open to discussing controversial issues is central to the democratic growth of organized labor. Again, while we do not want the union to become a club or debating society, we need to recognize that throughout our history we have dealt with, and must continue to deal with very controversial issues, from immigration to affirmative action to political action. Often it is felt that certain public policy issues cannot (or should not) be raised at conventions, or anywhere within the labor movement, because these issues are controversial and divisive. It is as if, by not discussing controversial issues affecting our members, or by keeping these issues "off the floor," the divisions will disappear. But unions, like all democratic organizations, are about constructing a community of interest. And this cannot be achieved by trying to bury controversy or drawing an artificial line between "social and political" issues and "bread and butter" unionism. What problems or issues are central to the "community" of working people has changed over time and will continue to change.

Sometimes, we fear controversial issues so much that we play into the hands of labor's opponents. By not openly confronting our differences and problems ourselves, our opponents are able to exploit both our differences and our failure to address these differences. Yet, sometimes, if issues which we think are divisive are brought to the floor and debated, we can discover that we are much more united than we thought.

A case in point from the Canadian labor movement and many U.S. unions is the hotly controversial issue of abortion. For many years, the Canadian labor leadership was very hesitant about permitting pro-choice resolutions to come to the floor of convention. Surely, this was clearly an issue of individual choice that had little to do with organized labor. The failure to debate this issue at convention in Canada led to some women forming multiunion caucuses and eventually getting the resolution onto the floor of convention. The CLC and most provincial labor federations eventually all voted overwhelmingly for a pro-choice position, and none of the splits, walk-outs, or resignations that leaders had feared took place. Today, the Canadian labor movement is pro-choice and the position is relatively uncontroversial within the movement. This is also true of the few major U.S. unions which have debated and taken a position on this issue.

OPPORTUNITIES FOR THE AMERICAN LABOR MOVEMENT

Debating controversial positions on the floor of a convention can help win people to a majority position, or it can force the majority to reconsider its position, and most important, it can often play an important role in clarifying labor's position. A case in point of an issue which badly needs to be discussed openly is the AFL-CIO's position on political action. The vast majority of unionists in the U.S. believe that the AFL-CIO's political position is to support the Democrats. Yet, the actual position of the labor movement has for decades been non-partisan. In a tradition which spans back to the American Federation of Labor (AFL) founding president, Samuel Gompers, politically labor's stance is "to reward its friends and penalize its enemies." However, in practice, the labor movement has had a very different practice. There has, for many years, been a close and "special" relationship in practice with the Democratic Party and leading Democrats—in spite of the formal non-partisan position. Today, with organizations such as the Labor Party arguing that labor should reconsider its non-partisan position and become more actively engaged in political action, a debate on labor's political stance is clearly needed. Such a debate, regardless of outcome, could assist in educating members on why politics is important for labor and why labor needs to be involved in electoral politics.

It is widely understood that information and access to information facilitates participation in decision-making. That is why openness is a hallmark of democratic organizations. What decisions are taken by an organization and how they are made should be visible to all members. Interested members should be encouraged to sit in on executive meetings, or committees or conferences. There are, of course, some times when a union cannot be completely open about all issues, such as bargaining or strike tactics. But for the most part, the vast majority of things that unions do at all levels of the organization, could and should be open to any interested member. Exclusion should be the exception, not the rule. Openness is also related to access to information. Often privileged access to information by certain members, and exclusion of others, is a method of perpetuating leadership and preventing serious challenges on policy issues.

Another area where openness and improved communications could assist in both strengthening the labor movement and making it more democratic is building links among union activists across organizations. This and support of multiunion/community coalitions, such as Jobs with Justice, are activities to which revitalized central labor councils could certainly contribute. With few exceptions, activists rarely meet with their peers in other organizations.

Linked to both the concept of participation and accountability is the issue of turnover and change of leadership and inclusion. The excitement generated by the 1995 AFL-CIO convention was at least partially related to the fact that there was the possibility (and as it turned out, the fact) of a change in leadership. Accountability in practice is closely related to turnover of leadership, or at least the reasonable possibility of a successful challenge to leadership. For accountability to work, leaders and members both need to feel that leaders can be removed by members, and that their positions can be successfully challenged. Procedures to assure leadership accountability are difficult in practice. Term limits, while assuring turnover, do nothing to assure accountability and, in fact, might even be counter-productive, resulting in a constantly changing elected leadership with a powerful, experienced, non-rotating permanent staff. Rather than methods of assured turnover, such as term limitations, procedures that assure open elections at conventions, that give all candidates access to delegates and, where appropriate, access to the membership to campaign for delegate election, are much better methods. Again, though, they can only work if there is a practice that recognizes the right to caucus, as challengers will need organization to mount a serious challenge, not simply the right to personally dissent.

CONCLUSION

This leads us back to the wider issue of democracy in society as a whole and the goals of a labor movement. What is the ultimate role of labor? Is it merely to lobby power and get a little more for its members? Or is it to transform power in society as a whole by extending democracy to the workplace and the economic sphere and to break up the authoritarian rule of concentrations of power, influence and wealth? If labor's goal is the transformation of power, then it means leading a democratic struggle throughout society. It also means moving beyond a strategy of simply seeking to lobby those in power, whether by militant or cooperative strategies, and instead, building a democratic alternative to the concentration of power and wealth. It means placing democracy at the forefront of labor's agenda and building a labor movement which is larger than the ranks of the current union membership. A movement which can speak for the majority because it is the majority. Majorities are not found. One does not simply go out and look for one; rather, like all social constructions, they are built. It means getting involved in ongoing and disciplined coalitions with labor's allies, other progressive social movements, and constructing an alternative democratic agenda for power.

Seeing unions in this political context is vital to organized labor's success and survival. But understanding how politics is changing and the challenge of the New Right is important in appreciating the ongoing attack on unions and the rights of working people. With 14 million members, the labor movement remains the largest multiracial, multi-issue membership organization in the country. As such, it is a prime target of the political New Right which is attempting to further reduce working people's rights, in and out of the workplace and substitute markets for democratic decision-making. The New Right's program of privatization, deregulation, and free trade is aimed at destroying what democratic control we do have as a community over the economy. To meet the challenge of the New Right and its attempt to destroy democracy and inclusive democratic communities throughout society, labor needs to take the offensive. Labor needs to become the champion of democracy and civil society. The New Right is attempting to undermine all democratic institutions by turning everything into an individual responsibility. We need to respond by creating democratic communities, in the workplace and beyond. But for this to happen, unions themselves must become models of democratic practice.

WHOSE DEMOCRACY? ORGANIZED LABOR AND MEMBER CONTROL

Bill Fletcher, Jr.

Sometimes when I reflect on the question of union democracy, the nineteenth-century abolitionist William Lloyd Garrison comes to mind. Following the Civil War, Garrison argued that his job was completed since the curse of slavery had been ended. Although he lived until 1879, witnessing the crushing of Reconstruction, Garrison thought his role in the struggle for emancipation was limited to eliminating that peculiar institution. The move toward racial justice had only begun, but Garrison and other abolitionists narrowed their vision, so that they could believe that their job was completed. All too often the struggle for union democracy has a similar feel: it becomes an end in itself rather than part of an overall program of economic justice and workers' rights. Without any social context, it is hard to understand the struggle for union democracy, who is fighting for it and why.

This became very clear to me in the 1970s, when I was engaged in a reform effort among shipyard workers. The shipyard where I worked was represented by the now defunct Industrial Union of Marine and Shipbuilding Workers of America (IUMSWA). Although IUMSWA, a union formed in the 1930s as part of the Congress of Industrial Organizations effort, had a proud history of progressivism and commitment to the struggle against racist discrimination, my local was quite the opposite.

The conservative clique of older white men who led the local all but ignored the growing number of workers of color in their ranks. In general, they also ignored the changing and increasingly hostile labor/management scenario that spread across the United States during the seventies.

What many of us in the reform effort discovered was that our calls for union democracy were an abstraction for most rank-and-file members. To most members, the reform effort seemed like one group of workers complaining that they were not in power and that the game was stacked. Although in many ways the game was indeed stacked, the true lack of union democracy was all but irrelevant to the everyday lives of most members.

After all, the union had the trappings of democracy. The members could vote on a contract and elect officers. While many other unions appointed shop stewards, we elected them. Thus, at the empirical level, the situation looked different from those unions most often associated with corruption and tyranny. But the larger obstacle to engaging workers in our struggle was this: the members could, and often did, disengage from the practice of the union altogether. When they did, they no longer felt the impact of the reactionary leadership and its various policies.

The members were encouraged to think of the union as their insurance company and law firm, and so their expectations were limited. Although the officers would talk cynically about the members or even attack them for their failure to attend membership meetings, the local leaders made no great effort to encourage attendance. Union election campaigns, with the exception of those run by the reformers, were essentially popularity contests, and, again, no great effort was made to mobilize members.

The local leaders, like many other sophisticated tyrants and crypto-tyrants, encouraged the members to disengage. By placing no expectations on them and putting limits on the practical means for participation, the leadership sanctioned the members' avoidance of the internal life of the union. Disengagement did not bring about any immediate consequences for the members, and as the members could clearly see, there were unpleasant consequences if they did try to engage in the life of the union. During contract time the members would mobilize, but only for short periods.

Not all struggles for union democracy run into the same problems noted above. The struggles in the United Mine Workers and in the International Brotherhood of Teamsters both represented courageous efforts to rid their respective unions of corruption and tyranny. In far too many struggles, however, the issue of democracy is, in practical terms, separate from the everyday life of the members. As such, their impact, even if successful, is too limited.

FORMAL DEMOCRACY VS. MEMBERS' CONTROL

Most unions have formal institutions of democracy. Obviously there are exceptions, including unions where there is mob influence. But that is not the dominating force in most unions or in union life generally. Whether the members have the right to elect national officers directly or to elect them via convention, there is some kind of formal mechanism to represent the rank-and-file.

If workers only aim to look at whether or not a union has democratic institutions, what I call the "Garrisonian syndrome" takes effect. Organizations established to advance union democracy can run into such a quandary. The more fundamental issue is whether workers have control over their own institutions.

Workers' control over the production process has been a key issue for the Left. During the 1980s, however, the newly arising black trade union movement in South Africa (which preferred to refer to itself as non-racial), raised the issue of workers' control over their unions. This was not a matter of formal democracy, but of institutionalizing member control and involvement at all levels of their movement. This idea confused many U.S. observers because it went beyond matters of formal elections. It was about the relationship of elected leaders to the rank-and-file; the relationship of full-time staff to elected leaders; and the need for member involvement in the larger struggle, including, at that time, the struggle against apartheid.

There are important lessons U.S. unions can draw from the South African experience. The principal issue facing U.S. unions is not formal democracy, but rather member control and involvement. How can we institutionalize the members' role so that we do not rely on spontaneous eruptions of the rank-and-file? This is a relevant question for even some progressively-led unions. For example, a local I am acquainted with and respect recently held a regular election in which ten percent of the membership voted. When asked why the low turnout, the local's leader said that matters of governance did not appear to be relevant to most members. Such a statement, made quite honestly by a sincere union leader, carries an awesome message.

SEARCHING FOR ANSWERS

Many progressives, in attempting to address this problem, have concluded that one or another version of an organizing model or organizing approach to labor unionism is the appropriate course of action. This approach suggests that the crisis in U.S. unionism can, in part, be addressed by increased member involvement in confronting the day-to-day issues which they face. Rather than a reliance on full-time staff to resolve problems, the organizing model suggests activating the membership to address their own questions.[1] While an organizing model/approach might introduce a more progressive practice into U.S. labor unionism, it does not resolve the contradictions surrounding membership involvement and control. What this model can do is increase members' involvement in their own day-to-day struggles in a way that can be personally empowering (to use an abused word). But the "organizing model" does not necessarily change the power relationship between the member and his/her own union. And so, paradoxically, members may get involved in many struggles, but still sit out critical membership meetings and elections, remaining at the margins of the internal life of the union-as-institution.

Confronted by this paradox, some unionists argue that union democracy and workers' control are impossible as long as members are "apathetic." This is just presenting a superficial description of a problem as the explanation. It places the blame for uneven union democracy and lack of members' control on the workers themselves.

"Apathy," as a description, misses the point. Many honest union activists who use this term are actually describing union members who do not share their view of what their priorities should be.[2] If members feel the union is irrelevant to their concerns and if they can disengage from the union without damaging consequences, then members tend to be "apathetic." Of course, there are often structural obstacles to participating that further encourage workers to disengage, but we have to avoid overemphasizing structural obstacles since lack of participation can be found even when the union-as-institution actively encourages membership involvement.

DEMOCRACY, VISION, AND PROGRAM

The argument presented here may, at first glance, appear somewhat heretical. The issue of union democracy, that is, formal democracy, is not presented as paramount. Rather, the central questions revolve around member involvement, control and strategic direction. To put it simply: union democracy is a dead issue if the members believe that the union is irrelevant to their principal concerns. If this is true, we need to think about how the union movement can become relevant again. This is a question for the AFL-CIO, as an institution, and for every local of every U.S. union.

There are several directions unionists can consider. As populist electoral campaigns have demonstrated, from the progressive Jesse Jackson to the reactionary Pat Buchanan, working people are very concerned about their declining living standard. Most feel they lack both someone to champion their interests and a means to struggle successfully for change. The AFL-CIO leadership under John Sweeney has proclaimed that it will speak to these concerns. But speaking to them can only be one part of the equation. We need a mechanism to actually mobilize working people in struggles. They cannot feel that they are passive observers in a larger process going on around them. This is a real danger with populist electoral candidates, who sometimes tend toward paternalism, like Huey Long.

The labor movement can also become more relevant by developing institutions that address various working people's concerns. The union movement created sports clubs and credit unions. But many of these institutions have been allowed to atrophy. In the face of right-wing assaults on our community-based organizations and agencies, the labor movement should begin again to construct and defend such institutions. This is especially important for workers of color, whose communities have suffered disproportionately in the face of the right-wing onslaught.

Another way the labor movement can regain relevance is to better address the issue of unemployment. Labor needs to have a multilayered response to unemployment, promoting community and regional economic development; unemployment assistance; job training and retraining; and direct organizing of the unemployed to fight for jobs. Working people must come to believe that the union movement will address their concerns whether or not they actually have a job.

The labor movement must be seen as a vehicle for furthering struggles that rank-and-file workers believe are relevant to their own futures. These struggles may be large scale such as the South African movement's embrace of the fight against apartheid, or here in the U.S. where some unionists are committed to the fight against societal racist oppression. The struggles may be more localized, like struggles against budget cuts. In either case, the labor movement, through its unions, must offer workers a way to redress their collective grievances.

How then can we begin to address the matters of member control and involvement? Part of the answer is contained in the various tactical initiatives offered in the organizing model/approach to unionism, which emphasizes members' mobilizing to fight for their immediate concerns. But, we must move beyond that. After its 1992 convention, the Service Employees International Union (SEIU) formed the Committee on the Future to offer a direction for the union into the twenty-first century. That committee found that a rank-and-file member's attitude toward the local union tended to gel within their first eighteen months on the job. After that, members tend to have rather fixed notions and expectations about the union. Thus, the way the union approaches new members can be critical in gaining members' support and involvement. New or potential members must understand their union as an institution as well as its relationship to the larger community. As the SEIU committee noted, this necessitates new member programs that are substantive.

Even if the union speaks to issues relevant to the members and engages new and potential members, workers need to be able to buy into the decisions made by the union-as-institution. This applies to a union's political endorsements. Numerous pollsters have concluded that union endorsements of candidates mean less and less in terms of voter turnout. If this is to change, unions must address their members' views on various issues. This is not simply a matter of focus groups and polls, but of actual member involvement in the making of decisions. Unions should engage in debate over endorsing candidates and referenda. A decision by the local union's executive board is not enough to ensure that members agree.

Unions need to clarify members' relationship with union staff. Each union committee should have a corresponding staff person. The staff person should not be there to lead (unless they are an elected union official) but to serve as the organizer for the committee. All too often membership committees serve as rubber stamps for the union staff. They also sometimes serve as micro-managers of the union staff, thereby minimizing their own roles. The alternative is to build a member/staff relationship that lets members decide the actual direction and gives staff the task of presenting policy options and implementing the decisions.

Another way to give members more control over the union is to link it to control over the workplace. While unions must be very careful about various so-called quality programs that are suggested by management, they cannot afford to ignore the workers' desire to have greater control over their jobs. The question for a union is how does it engage in these initiatives in such a way that the members actually gain power?[3] Can the union be a vehicle for changing the shape of the workplace and involving the members in that process? To bring change to the workplace, the union itself will need changing. If the union cannot change, then it will be discarded.

WHERE DOES THE CHANGE START?

Many of the changes suggested here cannot begin at the level of the AFL-CIO. The AFL-CIO is a federation of independent unions. While the AFL-CIO can and should model certain behavior, the bulk of the changes suggested here must take place within individual unions at the local level. Such changes need the support of the leadership, but they must happen at the base.

The October 1995 election of John Sweeney, Richard Trumka, and Linda Chavez-Thompson can be a torch to guide unionists working to rebuild the linkage between working people and the union movement. The federation's emphasis on organizing and political action can set the tone for what a reconstructed labor movement should represent.

Nevertheless, to actually recast the relationship between unions-as-institutions and their members (and potential members), reconstruction has to begin at the base. The suggestions offered here hopefully shed light on the kind of rebuilding effort we need to keep the labor movement from falling into oblivion.

NOTES

The opinions presented in this paper are those of the author and do not necessarily represent those of the AFL-CIO or the Service Employees International Union.

1. The notion of the *organizing model of unionism* was principally advanced by the editors of the journal *Labor Research Review.*

2. There is an exercise which I have often used in union trainings to spark discussion on the question of so-called member apathy. I have asked participants how many would like to join my bridge club. In almost every case, few if any participants have any interest in bridge (the card game). I then go on to berate them for their lack of interest, their unwillingness to learn, their... apathy! By doing this we are able to explore what lies behind this notion of apathy, and that there are many reasons why someone may choose not to unite with the objectives or directions which we offer.

3. I use the term *gain power* as opposed to the term *empowerment* quite consciously. In many workplace settings, the notion of "empowering" workers is suggested as a selling point for various cooperation or participation programs. Empowerment, as a term, tends to be a quasi-psychological notion which more correctly references how someone comes to feel about one's self and one's personal ability to get something done. *Gaining power*, on the other hand, refers to the ability of workers, as a group, to gain a level of control so they can influence what is done. Worker participation strategies need to be grounded in the notion and objective of *gaining power*.

A "NEW LABOR MOVEMENT" IN THE SHELL OF THE OLD?*

Jeremy Brecher and Tim Costello

THE POLITICS OF REFORM

In 1995, an insurgent campaign which dubbed itself "A New Voice for American Workers" captured leadership of the AFL-CIO. It called for a "new labor movement." But any effort to construct a new labor movement was bound to come up against the fabled rigidity of the AFL-CIO, which labor historian David Montgomery once compared to a great snapping turtle, "hiding within its shell." Why did New Voice emerge and what possibilities does it open up for the development of a new labor movement, given its location within the rigid and contorted shell of the old?

The Fall of the House of Labor

A lot has changed since the formation of the AFL-CIO forty years ago. A regulated national economy has been transformed into a global economy—one in which American workers can be put into competition with others anywhere in the world. Corporations have decentralized their activities, downsized their in-house operations, and outsourced their production even

---

*This article is a substantial revision of an essay that appeared in the *Labor Research Review* 24 (Summer 1996).

while concentrating their power around the globe. Large urban industrial complexes like Detroit and Pittsburgh have been replaced by small, highly mobile production units, which can easily be relocated. White men have become the minority of the U.S. workforce and women and people of color the majority.

Meanwhile, no major American institution changed less than the labor movement. At the end of the twentieth century, American unions are as poorly adapted to the economy and society of their time as were the craft unions of iron puddlers and cordwainers to the mass production industries of seventy years ago.

During the 1980s and 1990s, the AFL-CIO executed a stately, slow-motion collapse. Membership plunged to 15.5 percent of wage earners, with only 11.2 percent in the private sector. Major strikes and lockouts, for example Bridgestone, Caterpillar, Staley, and the Detroit newspapers, ended in devastating defeats. Not surprisingly, many workers came to accept almost any concessions rather than strike. In 1995 there were only 385 work stoppages compared with 3,111 in the peak year of 1977, and in 1996 strikes hit a fifty-year low. Real wages declined about 15 percent between 1973 and 1995; real incomes for young families decreased by one-third. And, after its greatest grassroots mobilization in twenty years, labor saw a Democratic president and congress it had worked hard to elect pass the North American Free Trade Agreement (NAFTA) that posed the threat of a personal pink-slip to large numbers of American workers and union officials. Maine AFL-CIO President Charles O'Leary observed that labor's public image was that of "white-haired old men meeting down in Bal Harbor talking about the past." The once powerful AFL-CIO seemed little more than an empty shell.

During labor's "era of stagnation" there emerged a considerable number of reform movements, local activists, leaders, and staff members with progressive political ideas. They were visible in official and insurgent strikes like the Pittston coal strike and the Austin, Minnesota, Hormel strike; the biannual labor convocations held by *Labor Notes*; the militant AFL-CIO Organizing Institute; the transnational and strategic corporate campaigns of the Industrial Union Department; the local coalitions against NAFTA; the cross-union activism and solidarity promoted by Jobs with Justice; and the successful reform movement in the Teamsters union. Until 1995, however, barely an echo of these new forces was audible inside the

AFL-CIO's headquarters in Washington or its council meetings in Bal Harbor.

New Voice

Early in 1995, leaders of the biggest unions—well aware that inertia at the very top of the AFL-CIO was contributing to the decline of their own organizations—attempted a conventional power play. They asked Lane Kirkland, for sixteen years the president of the AFL-CIO, to step down and let his second-in-command, Tom Donahue, take over. When Kirkland said no, they asked Donahue to run against him, but he declined. John Sweeney, head of the large and fast-growing Service Employees International Union, emerged as the insurgents' alternative. Sweeney said he launched his candidacy only because Donahue refused to join the drive to unseat Kirkland. "I decided to run for president of the AFL-CIO because organized labor is the only voice of American workers and their families, and because the silence was deafening."[1]

As Kirkland continued to hang on, the Sweeney campaign dubbed itself "A New Voice for American Labor" and developed a momentum of its own that went far beyond the initial palace power play. To Sweeney, generally regarded as a dynamic but mainstream trade unionist, the New Voice ticket added Richard Trumka of the United Mineworkers, for many a symbol of militancy, and Linda Chavez-Thompson, representing women and people of color, groups notoriously unrepresented in the AFL-CIO's top echelon.

New Voice developed a trenchant critique of two decades of labor movement failure. Sweeney scored the AFL-CIO as a "Washington-based institution concerned primarily with refining policy positions" instead of a "worker-based movement against greed, multinational corporations, race-baiting, and labor-baiting politicians."[2] He charged that the American labor movement is "irrelevant to the vast majority of unorganized workers in our country" and added that he had deep suspicions that "we are becoming irrelevant to our own members."[3] Linda Chavez-Thompson attacked "30 or 40 years of AFL-CIO isolation and inaction."

Further, the national union presidents who initiated New Voice turned to forces from outside the palace. New Voice mobilized thousands of activists and progressives and promoted many of their ideas and programs. By the time Kirkland finally accepted his opponents' original demand and stepped down in favor of Donahue, it was too late—there was no going back for the forces the Sweeney campaign had mobilized. It is symbolic of the new forces at play that the reformers who had taken over the Teamsters provided Sweeney's margin of victory at the October 1995 AFL-CIO convention that elected the New Voice ticket; it is indicative of the continuity in the AFL-CIO's power structure that the presidents of a few large unions called most of the convention's shots.

New Dynamics

New Voice shifted the AFL-CIO's rhetoric from that of business unionism toward that of a social movement and proposed institutional vehicles for making that rhetoric real. But the new AFL-CIO Executive Council was composed primarily of the same officials who had presided over the previous two decades of the labor movement's decline. Few of them had challenged the institutional constraints imposed by labor law, union structure, bureaucratic deadwood, and organizational inertia. While some New Voice leaders had been associated with progressive or reform forces in their unions, others had fought oppositions who advocated the very changes that New Voice now promoted. Some had silenced rank-and-file initiatives and had even broken strikes of their own members. Few had projected an alternative vision for the labor movement, let alone for society.

Nonetheless, even bureaucrats, faced with extinction, have been known to change. Many of the union leaders who initiated the CIO—John L. Lewis in particular—had been politically conservative and heavy handed with their own members. But they came to recognize that the labor movement, and their own organizations in particular, could only be saved by unleashing a rank-and-file initiative that they could not always count on controlling. Those who took over the AFL-CIO face a similar challenge: encourage dramatic change or see their own organizations plunge toward extinction. They might prefer to limit change to a militant business unionism which combines top-down control with more vigorous organizing and a greater willingness to strike. Nevertheless, any substantial revitalization of the labor movement will require a move toward social movement unionism, in which grassroots activism supplants the rigid, bureaucratic character all too typical of American trade unions.

Transcending the Shell

The new leadership established a host of task forces, institutes, centers, and committees to implement the New Voice program. These can provide information, resources, networking, and leadership that will be invaluable to local activists. But they will accomplish little unless they encourage those on the ground level to empower themselves.

Some of the most important recent initiatives of labor movement activists—building local coalitions, conducting their own international outreach, organizing solidarity operations, and supporting rank-and-file insurgencies—have been independent of and at times even opposed to top labor leadership. Activists may well be tempted to abandon such independence for more conventional activities within the framework of a more accepting AFL-CIO mainstream. And the labor mainstream may try, even from the best of motives, to internalize such efforts. (Soon after his election, a top New Voice official told local Jobs with Justice activists that, with New Voice's ascendancy, they should start directing more of their efforts into regular union channels—a position which was actively contested and eventually reversed.)

The unfortunate result could be official coalitions dominated by unions with only paper participation by allies; international linkages limited to top union officials; union solidarity that mobilizes more staff than rank-and-file; and isolation of progressives from the struggle for grassroots democracy within the labor movement. It could also turn progressives into disciplinary agents within the labor movement and leave them no base if conservative forces regain control at the top.

In an earlier era, trade unions were regarded as only one element of a wider labor movement. Tomorrow's "new labor movement," likewise, should be seen less as a reformed AFL-CIO than as a broader constellation of allied forces and institutions. Both AFL-CIO leaders and local activists need to promote institutions allied with, but outside, the shell of the AFL-CIO: occupational safety and health groups, labor education programs such as the Highlander Center, labor history associations, labor arts programs, producer and consumer cooperatives, vehicles for community investment, Jobs with Justice, political coalitions, issue coalitions, local labor centers, and the like. Such initiatives "outside the shell" are one key to putting the "new" in the "new labor movement" and to opening the way for future organizing.

THE FUTURE OF THE REFORM AGENDA

The New Voice campaign issued an election platform with a broad evaluation of the crisis facing American workers and dozens of specific proposals for generating a new labor movement to meet it. Taken as a whole, the New Voice platform represents a serious, comprehensive, and well-thought-out response to labor's current predicament, incorporating a great many of the ideas proposed by reformers over the past few years. It provides both a valuable starting point for a discussion of what changes the labor movement needs and a set of commitments to which the New Voice leadership can be held accountable. We will address in turn each of the seven sections of the New Voice program:

- •Organize at a pace and scale that is unprecedented
- •Build a new and progressive political movement of working people
- •Construct a labor movement that can change workers' lives
- •Create a strong new progressive voice in American life
- •Renew and refocus our commitment to labor around the world
- •Lead a democratic movement that speaks for all American workers
- •Institutionalize the process of change

Organize at a Pace and Scale that is Unprecedented

The New Voice program stated that "the most critical challenge facing unions today is organizing."[4] While previous AFL-CIO strategy concentrated on political efforts to ease organizing by changing labor law, the New Voice platform argued, "We must first organize despite the law if we are ever to organize with the law." It proposed to increase the AFL-CIO organizing budget substantially; create an AFL-CIO organizing department to facilitate multiunion organizing and explore experimental organizing approaches; expand the AFL-CIO Organizing Institute to train and deploy 1,000 new organizers in two years. During its first year in office, the New Voice leadership moved rapidly to meet or even exceed these goals.

Organizing has often been offered as a panacea for what ails the labor movement, but the realities are sobering. One study in 1990 by Gary Chaison and Dileep Dhavale estimates that to maintain present memberships, unions would have to spend $300 million dollars on organizing.[5] The difficulty of conventional organizing—professional organizers handing out union cards and petitioning for National Labor Relations Board elections—has led many labor activists and progressives, including those associated with the AFL-CIO's Organizing Institute, to advocate more radical approaches.

New Voice rhetoric redefined organizing as a movement for human rights, not just a vehicle for economic bargaining. It envisioned a strategy that moves beyond workplace-by-workplace organizing to the creation of a mass movement. In his acceptance speech Sweeney proclaimed, "If anyone denies American workers their constitutional right to freedom of association, we will use old-fashioned mass demonstrations, as well as sophisticated corporate campaigns to make worker rights the civil rights issue of the 1990s."[6]

Organizing strategy would include "training and motivating rank-and-file workers to organize the unorganized," supporting "local coalition-building efforts with community, religious, civil rights, and other organizations," creating a network of "local organizing centers" and community-based Worker Rights Boards.[7] In another speech, Sweeney also emphasized the value of new forms of "community unionism," such as the Los Angeles Manufacturing Action Project, and experiments with "associational unionism" in which workers form "an association that addresses sexual harassment, pay equity, promotional activities" instead of, or prior to, traditional collective bargaining.[8]

Discontent among American workers is at a historic high. If the labor movement can make itself a vehicle for expressing that discontent, people will clamor to join unions or will simply go ahead and organize themselves. But at present, most do not identify joining a union as the solution to their problems. No organizing technique is likely to be effective if people see the labor movement as an undemocratic, toothless bureaucracy representing interests that are different from their own. Ultimately, success in organizing new members will depend on success in transforming the labor movement itself.

BUILD A NEW AND PROGRESSIVE POLITICAL MOVEMENT OF WORKING PEOPLE

The New Voice program emphasized that "our politics must start in the neighborhoods where our members live and vote." It called for a National Labor Political Training Center to train labor activists and political candidates and a Labor Center for Economic and Public Policy to develop policy and support legislative efforts. A new media strategy would establish a media workshop, studio facilities, marketing and distribution teams, and a strategic center. In its first year the new leadership substantially increased spending on electoral campaigns, though the increase was dwarfed by the explosion of corporate spending in the 1996 campaign.

Portraying Central Labor Councils (CLCs) as the stepchildren of the labor movement, New Voice proposed to revitalize them to serve as "the front line of labor's political efforts." (Chavez-Thompson noted, "The AFL-CIO has left the state federations and the central labor councils up the creek and they didn't even lend them a paddle."[9]) They would organize members on a multiunion basis in neighborhoods to "re-energize our base and build bridges with individuals and organizations who share our views."

An apparent contradiction in the New Voice political program has to do with the relation to the Democratic Party and its candidates. Sweeney has said that labor needs to "stop wasting our money on candidates who turn their backs on workers after they are elected."[10] But in spite of its dubious record, he continued the traditional AFL-CIO myopic support for the Democratic Party, saying "President Clinton has done a great job as president and deserves our support."[11]

In his acceptance speech at the AFL-CIO Convention he said, "We will re-elect a president and elect a Democratic Congress committed to the people who 'work hard and play by the rules.'"[12] Sweeney's strategy appeared to be to assert more influence by involving the labor movement more intensively with the Democratic candidates. But labor's support seemed to have little influence either over Clinton's campaign or his second-term agenda.

Such a strategy cannot deal effectively with "candidates who turn their backs on workers after they are elected"—a problem evident on issues ranging from NAFTA to labor law reform. Nor is it likely to "build a progressive political movement." Local labor activists have developed more promising strategies. In many states they have established coalitions with other progressive groups that have, in effect, created their own progressive political machines from the ground up. They have recruited activists from their own ranks, trained them, put resources behind them, and managed their campaigns. This has created a base from which they could challenge Democratic machines in primaries or, when necessary, run independent candidates. If the AFL-CIO wants to build a progressive political movement and hold those it elects accountable, it should direct major support toward such efforts and encourage its local affiliates to participate in them.

Considerable sentiment has also developed in the labor movement for a labor-oriented third party, perhaps modeled on the Canadian New Democrats. Whether or not a third party is ultimately the best political strategy, labor can only benefit from the development of a party with a pro-labor platform. The AFL-CIO should welcome the participation of labor activists in groups like the Labor Party and the New Party, and should support independent and third party candidates where Democratic and Republican candidates are unacceptable.

CONSTRUCT A LABOR MOVEMENT THAT CAN CHANGE WORKERS' LIVES

The New Voice platform declared that "the Federation must be the fulcrum of a vibrant social movement, not simply a federation of constituent organizations." The proposed vehicle for this was a Center for Strategic Campaigns that would coordinate national contract campaigns and establish a national network of resources inside and outside the labor movement for bargaining and organizing campaigns. A strategic campaign fund would provide grants to unions in difficult contract fights. A strike support team of top leaders and staff from international unions would be deployed early to help local leaders with long-running strikes. A modest start was made on this ambitious program during the new leadership's first two years.

Breaking with the past, New Voice leadership tried to stress solidarity and identify the AFL-CIO with militant labor struggles. New Voice candidates joined picket lines around the country (provoking their opponents to do the same). They honored strikers and locked out workers, like Staley hunger-striker Dan Lane, at the convention.

The current AFL-CIO leadership initiated a series of campaigns to build momentum for its efforts. In the spring of 1996 it started holding hearings on falling living standards in communities across the country to "ask working men and women what is happening to their jobs, their paychecks, and their family budgets." "Union Summer" started in June, with 1,000 college students and young workers organizing voter registration and living wage campaigns. "Union Fall" to "organize and mobilize working Americans around the fundamental issue of raising wages and increasing incomes" was essentially a campaign for the Democratic Party ticket.[13]

Some elements of what the labor movement could do to "change workers' lives" were missing from the New Voice program. For example, little attention was given to issues such as shorter hours, rights for contingent workers, resistance to lean production, and other problems of daily work life. Similarly, "capital strategies," which promote employee ownership and community economic development, were not included in the New Voice vision, though they subsequently received attention from the new leadership. Most important, crucial struggles like the A.E. Staley and the Detroit newspapers lockouts have been allowed to go down to devastating defeats; top AFL-CIO officials have joined picket lines and even committed civil disobedience, but have so far not tried to mobilize workers for a major mass struggle.

CREATING A STRONG NEW PROGRESSIVE VOICE IN AMERICAN LIFE

The New Voice program called for an overhaul of the AFL-CIO's public communications and public affairs work to "redefine America's (and many of our own members') perceptions of us." The AFL-CIO should provide a "forceful new voice for working families on national issues." The vehicle would be a revamped Labor Institute for Public Affairs, transformed from "an institutional support organization" into a "pro-active strategic operation" aimed at "creating a pro-worker and pro-union public environment."

Sweeney initiated a highly effective campaign to pressure Congress to raise the minimum wage by making low wages amid high profits a national political issue: "In every speech I give from the Press Club to the picket lines, I try to make this simple point, 'America Needs a Raise.'"[14]

Labor's problems with the public and with its own members go far beyond "communications," however. As a recent study conducted by Peter D. Hart Research Associates for the AFL-CIO observed, "Members generally have little or no ideological orientation that would link economics, government, and politics. So while they know that these are hard economic times for working people, few can articulate any explanation for what has gone wrong, who is responsible, or what should be done about it." The Hart study concludes, "Labor's longer-term strategic mission is to develop an ideological framework among the membership that helps them to make sense of the Brave New Economy they confront in ways that lead to progressive political conclusions. We need to tell a compelling story about the economy, corporate irresponsibility, and the conservative policies that have helped shift even more bargaining power toward capital over labor."[15]

The war of ideas has been crucial to the Right's current dominance. The labor movement needs to provide a distinctive labor interpretation of what has happened to working people, why, and what to do about it. "America Needs a Raise" was a good initial slogan, but it provides no answer to the ideas of the Christian Right, Pat Buchanan, the freemarket Right, New Democrats, corporate globalists, and establishment liberals. Labor needs to explain that the suffering of working Americans is being created by global corporations who are playing workers and communities off each other, and that the solution to our deteriorating conditions of life and environment lies in a new solidarity of working people.

Then it needs to develop a program to address the real problems of working Americans, including local, national, and transnational strategies for countering the effects of globalization; providing jobs and economic security for all; establishing basic democratic rights and a high quality of life in the workplace; giving individuals and families greater control over the time of their lives; reversing the drive toward inequality; and protecting the natural and social environment on which our life and our economy depend. Ultimately, this adds up to an alternative vision of society and the place of workers within it.

Developing an alternative vision of this kind is not something that can or should emerge from a committee or a handful of leaders. But organizational leaders can foster an environment that nurtures such a vision. Toward that end the AFL-CIO should create an equivalent of the Organizing Institute dedicated to popular education for its members and allied groups. It should promote and distribute a wide range of existing models and materials and fund development of new ones. Its goal should not be indoctrination but rather informed debate on the future of work and society. In parallel, activists should create, and the AFL-CIO should support, the development of an independent labor education movement like that which exists in England and many other countries. This movement would include university and college-based programs, like the labor studies and labor extension programs at the University of Massachusetts, where rank-and-file activists from different unions and different backgrounds can come together, and independent centers like the Highlander Center in Tennessee and the Labor Institute in New Jersey.

Renew and Refocus Our Commitment to Labor Around the World

At first glance the New Voice program appeared to support the cold-war-oriented international policy that has been such a dominant feature of the AFL-CIO since its inception. It stated, "we are proud of our accomplishments over the years, culminating in the defeat of apartheid in South Africa and the role of Solidarnosc in leading Poland to democracy." (While many American trade unions provided valuable support to the freedom struggle in South Africa, the AFL-CIO's most notable contribution was its long-running refusal to work with the principal black trade union center because of its alleged Communist ties.)

The program proposed, however, to redirect the AFL-CIO's international work. "In today's global economy we need to see our international efforts much more in terms of the self-interests of American workers." While this formulation may seem to indicate a nationalist or protectionist direction, the contemplated shift seems rather to be from "helping" downtrodden workers abroad to mutual aid for mutual benefit. "We recognize that we need the support of the international free trade union movement because global employers exploit workers wherever quick profits are to be made and because so many of our American employers are corporations that are controlled abroad."

New Voice proposed to create a transnational corporate monitoring project (perhaps as part of the Center for Strategic Campaigns) which would serve as the central resource for information on global, corporate, and labor organizations; support all efforts to achieve international solidarity on behalf of American workers; and monitor international institutions and treaties like the World Bank, the International Monetary Fund, the General Agreement on Tariffs and Trade (GATT), and NAFTA. Such a project could serve as a vehicle for reorienting the AFL-CIO vis-à-vis the global economy, but there are several problems.

One problem has to do with how the AFL-CIO approaches the global economy. In a labor version of economic nationalism, Sweeney told the AFL-CIO Convention, "the problem is American companies that export jobs instead of products."[16] If the AFL-CIO embraces an economic nationalism that promotes the interests of American workers at the expense of those elsewhere, it is hardly likely to find enthusiastic support when American workers need international solidarity. Instead, it needs to develop a global strategy based on raising the labor, social, and environmental standards of workers all over the world. As Richard Trumka put it, we need "an America which doesn't compete around the globe by driving our wages down, when we should be forcing our competitors to pull theirs up."[17]

Another problem is the heritage of the AFL-CIO's international work. During the cold war, the AFL-CIO international operation was virtually an arm of U.S. foreign policy, often lending support to dictatorial regimes around the world. *Business Week* described the AFL-CIO's global operations, such as its International Affairs Department (IAD) in Washington and its American Institute for Free Labor Development in Latin America, as "labor's own version of the Central Intelligence Agency—a trade union network existing in all parts of the world."[18] The AFL-CIO demanded that trade unionists shun all contact with unions tainted by communism; in practice, it often demanded that its affiliates shun even non-aligned unions. The principal funding for AFL-CIO activities overseas has been the U.S. government. This is particularly ironic, since the AFL-CIO defines "free" labor unions with which it will cooperate as those that are not subject to government influence or control. The past role of the IAD and the regional institutes in such countries as South Africa, Brazil, Russia, and Chile forms a serious block to solidarity with the very labor groups with which U.S. workers need to cooperate.

Some national union leaders, as well as many if not most of the activists who supported New Voice, rejected the AFL-CIO's cold war heritage; so do the new staff members Sweeney has appointed to head the International Affairs Department. There is considerable opportunity for both the IAD and for progressive officials and local activists to make change. For instance, they can pick some good fights that symbolize the common interests of workers in different countries and the value of international labor solidarity. When these fights require cooperation with labor organizations the AFL-CIO has previously shunned, they should insist that cooperation is necessary and right. They can use these fights to educate union leaders and members on how workers should deal with the global economy. In these efforts they should utilize the experience of groups like the National Labor Committee in Support of Worker and Human Rights in Central America and the International Labor Rights Research and Education Fund.

The New Voice program noted that "we also have much to learn from unions abroad." The AFL-CIO leadership should encourage tours to learn from unions in Canada (health care, labor law, and international labor cooperation), France (resisting government cuts), Germany (shorter hours and job training), Brazil (alliances of labor with the poor and unemployed), South Africa (transforming racist institutions), and others. If the AFL-CIO will not do it, progressive unions should give some highly visible invitations to some previously "shunned" unions, and let the chips fall where they may. The new institution for transnational corporate monitoring should take as one of its most important tasks to make it possible for workers anywhere to link up with those in the same industry, company, or occupation anywhere in the world.

Lead a Democratic Movement that Speaks for All American Workers

The prevailing image of organized labor is a bureaucracy that primarily represents the special interests of its officials and a privileged sector of the workforce. The New Voice platform proposed to "create a labor movement that speaks for and looks like today's workforce." This involves a redefinition of the role of the labor movement, a new emphasis on racial, ethnic, and gender inclusion, and reforms of organizational structure.

Representing All Workers:

New Voice leaders are trying to position the AFL-CIO as an advocate for all working people, not just the agent of those in unions. The New Voice program stated, "The labor movement must speak forcefully on behalf of all working people." Sweeney proclaimed, "To the more than 13 million workers we represent, and to millions more who are not represented, our commitment is firm and clear. When you struggle for justice, you will not struggle alone."[19] Linda Chavez-Thompson said the labor movement needs to be the voice of those who need us, such as the unemployed, the underemployed, the young, the old, the poor, and children. "We need to be the hopes and dreams of those who can't speak for themselves."[20]

This change of emphasis is essential for creating a new labor movement, but it needs to be implemented concretely. For example, campaigns for rights for contingent workers and laws requiring just-cause for firing would address core problems of workers who are not organized. AFL-CIO support for worker advocacy resource centers and organizations of the unemployed would show commitment to advocating for all working people, not just current union members.

Inclusion:

The New Voice leadership has begun to change the scandalous domination of the AFL-CIO by aging white men. It created a new position of executive vice president and ran Linda Chavez-Thompson, a Latina woman, for the seat; she was then given primary responsibility for outreach to women and minorities. New Voice reserved ten seats on the executive council for women and people of color and negotiated a new executive council with six women, nine African Americans, one Latino, and one Asian American. It proposed establishment of an advisory young workers' task force.

The AFL-CIO has taken steps in the right direction, but there is a long way to go to reach full and equal representation. Prior to the October 1995 convention, black union leaders noted they were not consulted in selecting either candidate. William Burrus, executive vice president of the American Postal Workers Union and a leader of the Coalition of Black Trade Unionists, observed, "Decisions were made without including us. Now, after the fact, they are reaching out to hear our views."[21] The Coalition of Black Trade Unionists drew up eleven demands calling for more minorities and women as delegates, executive council members, and staffers. While both tickets agreed in principle to most of the black unionists' demands, the issue of tokenism remained, according to Burrus: "You can't hold them accountable until they're forced to recognize the political strength of groups like women, African Americans, and Latinos." The look of the executive council will not change "as long as they have the power to anoint with a hand on the shoulder who they want."[22]

The question of inclusion also involves the ways issues are framed. William Lucy, president of the Coalition of Black Trade Unionists, notes that the AFL-CIO opposed NAFTA primarily on the grounds that Americans would lose jobs as companies shifted operations to Mexico. According to Lucy, what should also have been stressed was a civil rights issue: the diversion of investment from urban communities where blacks might have gained employment.[23] Burrus added that, "With a black viewpoint included, the campaign against NAFTA might have been a lot deeper and broader."[24]

Organizational Reform:

The New Voice program proposed to "expand the involvement of our grassroots leaders" and calls for "the top leadership of the Federation" to be "in constant touch with its grassroots leadership." It proposed quarterly executive council meetings, with written agendas circulated in advance, and summaries of council action sent to affiliates; an annual budget; annual general board meetings of all AFL-CIO unions and of all state federation presidents; an annual conference for all central labor council leaders; and sets an age limit of seventy for top officers.

By the very act of contesting the election, New Voice challenged the one-party, party-line norms that have governed the labor movement since the era of Sam Gompers. Sweeney told delegates to the AFL-CIO convention that the secret to protecting the labor movement lies in part in "opening the AFL-CIO to debate. When we do that, the solidarity and unity that are at the core of our movement are tempered and trued and made stronger."[25] Like Pope John XXIII, he has recognized the need to "throw open the windows of the church."

But the New Voice program barely begins to grapple with the depth of the problems created by the lack of democracy in the AFL-CIO, let alone in the labor movement as a whole. For the previous sixteen years, the AFL-CIO executive council was composed of 33 mostly white male international union presidents who were reelected every two years as a group by voice vote without opposition or debate. They met in closed sessions and kept any disagreements secret; council minutes remained closed even to scholars for thirty years! The new executive council was also selected via a back-room negotiation between the two tickets and elected with virtually no opportunity for discussion or alternative nominations. Many national unions function with a similar level of democracy.

This lack of democracy contributes mightily to negative public and member perception of the labor movement. The Hart study noted that many union members often liken the union to "another boss." "Too many members see unions as bureaucratic institutions which have lost sight of the average member's interests."[26]

Sweeney has said that the whole governance and structure of the AFL-CIO needs to be reviewed to "find ways to operate more effectively."[27] But the reforms proposed by New Voice were grossly inadequate to address this in reality.

Unions at every level need to be run more by rank-and-file workers and less by full-time officials; to guarantee freedom of speech and association without the threat of reprisal; to provide direct elections of top union officials by all union members; and to ensure rank-and-file negotiation and ratification of contracts. New AFL-CIO structures should support rank-and-file empowerment, not re-centralization of authority.

While democratic reform will require a grassroots struggle union-by-union, the AFL-CIO can make a significant contribution. It should use the precedent of its first contested presidential election to advocate a new norm of democratic pluralism, rather than single-party rule, for all levels of the labor movement. It should insist that oppositions and insurgencies be regarded as legitimate elements of the labor movement and pursue genuine neutrality toward them. It should welcome those who have been "shunned" because of past support for oppositions and insurgencies back into the fold. Its emerging ethical practices code should require that affiliates provide the basic human rights and democratic practices that we demand of governments throughout the world.

Now, as in the past, conflicts between national union leaders and their own rank-and-file are likely to pose difficult problems for the AFL-CIO leadership. What will the New Voice leaders do when rank-and-file workers reject contracts but are ordered back to work by national union officials? When appointed trustees replace the elected leaders of local unions? Or when workers strike despite the opposition of their union leaders? While it may not be the AFL-CIO's role as a federation to pick sides in such situations, at the least the new leadership should ensure that the AFL-CIO will not function as a de facto strikebreaker. Labor activists who believe in union democracy should continue to support the right of rank-and-file workers to act on their own behalf, whatever national unions or the AFL-CIO may do.

Institutionalize the Process of Change

The New Voice platform emphasized the need "to provide for a process of continual growth and change." To that end it proposed a "Committee 2000" of top union officials to conduct a strategic planning process and submit a report to the 1997 AFL-CIO convention. While such a strategic planning process is undoubtedly a good idea, the proposed form suggests that the process of change will be tightly controlled by those at the top of the labor hierarchy, when what is required most of all for a new labor movement is relaxation of the top-down control to make room for a continuing process of initiatives from below. In shaping the future, the new AFL-CIO leadership needs to pay far more attention to John Sweeney's campaign rhetoric: "We mean more than just changing the leadership of our labor federation at the top. We mean building a strong new movement from the ground up."[28]

The organizational strategy outlined in the New Voice program was essentially to build a new AFL-CIO staff structure that largely by-passes the existing officers and departments. This responded to the need to address a new set of tasks, to avoid entanglement in structures that are poorly adapted to those tasks, and to circumvent the bureaucratic deadwood. While perhaps wise, this strategy risks building not a new labor movement but rather a new bureaucracy in the shell of the old. Labor writer Suzanne Gordon wrote of the New Voice program:

> For every union problem, there's a new Washington solution—an institute, a task force, a monitoring project, a clearinghouse, a policy center, a training center, a center for strategic campaigns, a new organizing department (with an office of strategic planning), a strategic planning process ("Committee 2000"), two or three campaign funds, a labor council advisory committee, and a "strike support team of top people" from various union staffs...This platform proclaims that "we must *institutionalize* the process of change." They will certainly do that if, on top of the AFL-CIO's many existing departments, they establish all these new institutions in and around the AFL-CIO headquarters.[29]

If the new AFL-CIO leaders count on their new committees, task forces, institutes, and centers to create a new labor movement, they will fail. Only if they are able to nurture a new movement culture that values and promotes rank-and-file initiative do they have a chance to succeed. What they can and should do (and what the New Voice program at its best proposed) is encourage and provide resources for a wide range of such initiatives.

After the devastating defeat of the Pullman strike in 1894, Eugene Victor Debs opened the pages of the union's magazine not only to the union's members, but also to the widest possible range of those throughout the country who had proposed new approaches to "the labor question." Such an open discussion, updated for the age of electronic communication, provides a more inspiring model of how to institutionalize the process of change within the labor movement than a committee of top union officials attempting to chart the future for the entire labor movement.

CONCLUSION

Throughout its history, the labor movement's low points have also been its turning points. The same could be true now. But to meet the needs of working people today, the labor movement needs to change at least as radically as the transnational corporations have changed. What needs changing goes far beyond the AFL-CIO as a national union center; the entire definition of the labor movement as a means for particular groups of workers to bargain with particular employers within the framework of a national economy is as outmoded as the vertically-integrated national corporation. Its focus on collective bargaining, its definitions of bargaining units, its divisions among unions, its notions of seniority, its limited repertoire of tactics, its narrow conception of workers' needs and interests, its faith in the beneficence of economic growth, and its embeddedness within a national framework all require drastic change.

In today's globalizing economy, the needs of working people and the goals of the labor movement can only be met through a worldwide coalition of labor and other movements to impose human and ecological interests on transnational corporations and other out-of-control institutions and forces. Within such a coalition, the labor movement can represent the specific needs of workers in the workplace and their organization at work as part of the movement as a whole. In some ways, such a labor movement will more resemble the community-based unions of the nineteenth century than the model we have inherited from Gompers and Meany. Can the emergence of new leadership in the AFL-CIO contribute to such a change, or will it instead help contain the forces of change within the existing shell?

Some shelled animals outgrow their original shells but continue to prosper by adding on new, larger, and differently-shaped chambers; some leave their outgrown shells behind; some die when their shells no longer allow them room to develop. If the AFL-CIO can change enough to let a "new labor movement" emerge, or even if a revitalized labor movement eventually has to escape from its confines, the current attempt to build a new labor movement within the shell of the old will have played a constructive role. But if the AFL-CIO tries to confine the regeneration of the labor movement within its own shell, it risks killing the very forces that might give it a new life.

NOTES

1. *BNA Daily Report*, October 25, 1995.

2. *BNA Daily Report*, October 25, 1995.

3. *BNA Daily Labor Report*, Interview, September 1, 1995.

4. This and all future references to the New Voice program are taken from "A New Voice for American Workers: Rebuilding the American Labor Movement, A Summary of Proposals from the Unions Supporting John J. Sweeney, Richard Trumka, and Linda Chavez-Thompson," June 28, 1995. Available from the AFL-CIO, Pamphlets Division, 815 16 Street, N.W., Washington, D.C., 20006.

5. Gary N. Chaison and Dileep G. Dhavale, "A Note on the Severity of the Decline in Union Organizing Activity," *Industrial and Labor Relations Review*, Volume 43, 1990.

6. *BNA Daily Labor Report*, October 27, 1995.

7. *BNA Daily Labor Report*, October 27, 1995.

8. Sweeney National Press Club speech, December 1995.

9. *BNA Daily Labor Report*, Special Report, October 5, 1995.

10. *BNA Daily Labor Report*, Interview, September 1, 1995.

11. *Milwaukee Journal-Sentinel*, September 4, 1995.

12. *BNA Daily Labor Report*, October 27, 1995.

13. National Press Club, December 1995.

14. National Press Club, December 1995.

15. Memo to AFL-CIO from Geoff Garin and Guy Molyneux, Peter D. Hart Research Associates, Inc., September 19, 1995.

16. *BNA Daily Labor Report*, October 27, 1995.

17. *BNA Daily Labor Report*, October 27, 1995.

18. *Business Week*, May 15, 1966, quoted in Beth Sims, *Workers of the World Undermined: American Labor's Role in U.S. Foreign Policy* (Boston: South End Press, 1992).

19. *BNA Daily Labor Report*, Special Report, October 27, 1995.

20. *BNA Daily Labor Report*, October 27, 1995.

21. Louis Uchitelle, "Blacks See Opening in AFL-CIO Leadership Fight," *The New York Times*, July 15, 1995.

22. Uchitelle, *The New York Times*, July 15, 1995, and Martha Gruelle, "Black Unionists Demand Meat on 'Diversity' Bones," *Labor Notes*, October 1995.

23. Uchitelle, *The New York Times*, July 15, 1995.

24. Uchitelle, *The New York Times*, July 15, 1995.

25. *People's Weekly World*, October 28, 1995.

26. Memo to AFL-CIO from Geoff Garin and Guy Molyneux, Peter D. Hart Research Associates, Inc., September 19, 1995.

27. *BNA Daily Labor Report*, Interview, September 1, 1995.

28. *BNA Daily Labor Report*, October 27, 1995.

29. Suzanne Gordon, "Is Sweeney's 'New Voice' a Choice or an Echo?," *Labor Notes*, October 1995.

WHAT DOES LABOR STAND FOR?

Gregory Mantsios

In response to the question, What does labor want?, Samuel Gompers, the first president of the American Federation of Labor (AFL), replied:

> Labor wants more school houses and less jails; more books and less arsenals; more learning and less vice; more constant work and less crime; more leisure and less greed; more justice and less revenge; in fact, more of the opportunities to cultivate our better natures.[1]

Gompers was articulating not only the breadth of labor's concerns but its vision for a more just and humane society. The question, what does labor want? and its corollary, what do unions stand for? have not always been easy ones to answer. Nor have the answers been easy to communicate—certainly not in the mainstream media.

Since the day Gompers first uttered those eloquent words more than a century ago, the mainstream media has reduced Gompers' message and those of his successors to "labor wants more." As a result, the image of labor that has dominated American culture is one of unions as self-serving, special interest groups narrowly focused on monetary issues.

Organized labor can respond to this predicament by improving the reality upon which its image is based, focussing on how to get its message across in the context of an unsympathetic press, or examining the message itself. To a large extent, labor's success depends on its ability to address all three issues. Unfortunately, not enough attention is given to examining labor's message and the ideological foundation upon which that message rests.

Ideology is important because it is the set of ideas upon which we, consciously or unconsciously, base our decisions, engage in activities, make sense of our past, and justify the course of action we undertake to build a better future. The way the leaders of the AFL-CIO view the world, and the way they present and act on these views is extremely important: it affects labor's ability to serve its members, organize new members, inspire and motivate a broad social movement, and effect change.

The labor movement has never been monolithic in ideology or in practice. Nor does the composition and orientation of labor's national leadership—the AFL-CIO—necessarily reflect the theory and practice of national unions or of regional or local labor bodies. However, since its founding as a merged federation over four decades ago, the AFL-CIO has served as the official voice of organized labor and has been in a position to answer the question, "What does labor want?" more effectively than any single union. When it does its job effectively, the AFL-CIO's response influences the organizational rhetoric of constituent unions. Its views may dominate the national discourse even if these views are not necessarily espoused by its affiliates.

Organized labor's ideological frameworks fall into three paradigms: pragmatism, social contract unionism, and class-conscious unionism. While these paradigms are not mutually exclusive, they do represent profound differences in thinking and emphasis. Moving from one paradigm to another can be perceived either as taking a new road at a critical crossroad or as a step in the evolutionary development of the labor movement's thinking. In either case, organized labor is currently poised for a shift in ideological direction. With new global conditions buffeting workers and the labor movement, and with a leadership that seeks to distinguish itself from its predecessors, now is an ideal time to examine labor's ideology. In order to understand how the AFL-CIO's current ideology differs from that of the past and how it might change in the future, we need to examine the words, ideas, and goals upon which the deeds of organized labor are based.

THE IDEOLOGY OF PRAGMATISM AND THE "OLD" AFL-CIO

Ironically, the old AFL-CIO often denied it had a world view. George Meany, who held the Presidency of the Federation from 1955 to 1979, and Lane Kirkland, who held that position until 1995, liked to distinguish themselves from their labor counterparts in other parts of the world by suggesting that they rejected ideas from both the left and the right. Meany put it this way:

> The American labor movement is not restricted by any dogma or any ideology. It is bound together by one slender thread: the desire of all working people to improve their lot. It exists for no other purpose.[2]

Both Meany and Kirkland argued that they were guided only by the immediate and practical concerns of organized labor. The word that best describes the U.S. labor movement, said Meany, is "practical":

> We deal with one problem or set of problems at a time. We avoid preconceived notions and we do not try to fit our program into some theoretical, all embracing structure. This down to earth, one thing at a time approach is uniquely American.[3]

Pragmatism, the ideology behind what is often referred to as "business unionism," was the dominant theme and mode of the U.S. labor movement during the Meany/Kirkland era. According to this framework, unions exist in order to address the immediate and practical concerns of unionized workers. The objective of unions is to protect their members economically, primarily by negotiating and enforcing the union contract. Unions are seen essentially as service organizations, whose task is to insure fair wages, increase job security, protect against victimization, improve the conditions of work, and provide additional economic benefits.

In the arena of politics, unions are concerned only with those issues that have a direct or indirect impact on unions, their members, and the industries in which they function. Pragmatic unions align themselves with whichever mainstream political party is most likely to support their immediate political agenda—usually, but not always, the Democratic Party. Deliberately avoiding earth shaking perspectives or actions, such unions simply seek a more favorable tip in the balance of power between labor and management.

But, despite Meany and Kirkland's claims to the contrary, the AFL-CIO they led was both ideological and very much involved in issues that went beyond the job and workplace. The belief in business unionism and a pragmatic approach, of course, is itself an ideology. It accepts the fundamental principles of the status quo and views the socio-economic order as fundamentally just. Labor's goal is to obtain what is considered a fair share for workers within the framework of the "free market" economy. Addressing the issue of collective bargaining and a capitalist economy, Meany writes: "Bargains can be reached because each side has the same general objective—a fair share from a prospering enterprise."[4] Several years later, he writes again in *The American Federationist*: "The U.S. worker is banking on the success of the American social order...American workers want a fair share of the abundance they have produced—no more, no less."[5]

According to Meany and Kirkland, the real interests and objectives of workers and employers are congruent because each depends on the other for their prosperity. Both men had a deep faith in the logic of the market economy:

> We think that the American economic system, with its potential for progress, works quite well...American business has prospered through mass markets. Unless the ever-rising tide of goods that American enterprise can produce is matched by the increased real earnings of workers, these goods cannot be sold. Our mass production system must be matched and supported by mass consumption. The higher take home pay that unions seek is indispensable to the sustained growth of production, jobs, and profits in this ever more productive American economy.[6]

Discord and conflict, if any, are considered aberrations, resulting from ethical lapses and greed on the part of management. Meany explains,

> Harsh as it may sound, I believe greed and profiteering are to a great degree responsible for America's unresolved domestic problems. Greed motivates wage chiselers, child labor violators, run away corporations, and foreign labor exploiters. All too often some people turn their backs on their religious ethics and democratic principles when their own small sphere of existence is confronted with opportunity to advance brotherhood and humanity.[7]

The leaders of the federation espoused the virtues of capitalism, which they saw as synonymous with democracy. George Meany perceived the profit motive to be subordinate to democracy:

> The distinguishing feature of the American system is its emphasis on people, on freedom, on free institutions, and on the opportunity for betterment. The Bill of Rights, the Constitution, and our educational system are all integral parts of our economic order and more essential to it than the stock exchange or any corporate board.[8]

The ideological orientation of the Federation was perhaps most blatant on the flip side of its pro-capitalist stance. Meany and Kirkland provided significant rhetorical and organizational support for anti-communist forces throughout the world (including the forces that helped overthrow the democratically elected socialist party of Salvador Allende in Chile).[9] By making capitalism synonymous with democracy and regarding the international interest of U.S. capital and U.S. workers as identical, the Federation maintained a cold-war foreign interventionist position throughout the Meany-Kirkland era. "Suppose we stepped out of Vietnam. What would happen? Two million people would go into slavery immediately," declared Meany. The Communists, if victorious, would not stop there. "I would rather fight the Communists in South Vietnam than fight them down here in the Chesapeake Bay."[10] Not only was the AFL-CIO among the last and most steadfast bastions of support for the Vietnam War, its advocacy of capitalist values and principles in general and its specific desire to promote and protect U.S. economic (read "corporate") interests abroad led it to international interventionist activities jointly funded by the U.S. State Department and the Central Intelligence Agency[11] and, as Meany proudly acknowledged, a large number of U.S. corporations.[12] By working to make the world safe for U.S. business in the 1950s, '60s, and '70s, the AFL-CIO laid the ground for labor's current predicament: the world became all too safe for U.S. corporations interested in cheap labor and unregulated environments.

Despite their view that unions need to remain narrowly focused on getting a "better deal" for workers, the Federation was, for better and for worse, more committed to social and liberal reform than either its rhetoric or reputation often suggested. The Federation was more attentive to social legislation than most of its national affiliates and put its weight behind a number of progressive legislative proposals, providing Meany and Kirkland with the significant role they aspired to within the Washington political establishment. But support for progressive policies occurred in the context of alternative and more radical proposals, giving the Federation's policy positions a reactionary and often hypocritical taint. Meany and Kirkland found a convenient, and not entirely ineffective, ideological and practical niche within the mainstream because of the international threat of communism on the one hand, and what Meany often called the domestic "hotheads" of the sixties, on the other hand. In the arena of civil rights, for example, the Federation's relatively early support for civil rights legislation did not translate into support for the civil rights movement, let alone the Black Power movement. For those who expressed rage over the discriminatory practices of the Federation's affiliates, the AFL-CIO's call for civil rights legislation appeared to be a whitewash that hid the labor movement's shameful acquiescence to racism. Quick to deal with affiliated unions charged with Communist influence, it failed to do so with unions with constitutional bars against black membership, segregated locals, and discriminatory employment practices.[13] The AFL-CIO's political activity was not as narrow as its rhetoric implied, but both its words and its deeds appeared to many as less principled and more opportunistic than the Federation's leaders would have liked everyone to believe.[14]

THE IDEOLOGY OF SOCIAL CONTRACT UNIONISM AND THE CURRENT AFL-CIO

The ideology of today's AFL-CIO is both similar to and significantly different from the ideology of the "old" AFL-CIO. The differences have become apparent in a remarkably short period of time and reflect not only shifts in the policies and practices of the Federation, but changes in how the AFL-CIO and, potentially, unions and their members view themselves and the world.

Gone from most, although not all, aspects of the new ideology, are references to pragmatism. In their place, the AFL-CIO has adopted a more socially conscious orientation, with less emphasis on unions as service organizations and more on unions as organizers of a social movement. It is not that labor's federation is no longer practical, but that it has gone beyond the ideology of pragmatism to embrace a unionism that is more grassroots by nature, broader in scope, and more militant in style.[15]

This shift represents an evolution, rather than a revolution, in thinking and practice and is rooted in changes in the domestic and global economy. "American workers are losing ground as never before," stated the New Voice platform of John Sweeney, Richard Trumka, and Linda Chavez-Thompson, the insurgents who were elected to top AFL-CIO office in 1995. In response, unions must "organize at a pace and scale that is unprecedented, build a new and progressive political movement of working people, . . . [and] lead a movement that speaks for all American workers."[16] But as Sweeney himself points out, his "old guard" opponent, Tom Donahue, shared the view that the labor movement needed an "expanded commitment to organizing, a tougher stance in the political arena, and more diversity."[17] With a declining membership and unprecedented corporate and government assaults, it has become increasingly difficult to negotiate, sign, and administer contracts. If unions are to be successful, they will have to go well beyond addressing the immediate occupational needs and interests of their members at the bargaining table and in Washington. They will have to organize the unorganized and build a movement that will change the environment in which unions operate. Without detracting from the role that the Sweeney team played in pushing the old guard to adopt a more progressive orientation in the face of a leadership challenge, the fact remains that organized labor had to change if it was to be relevant force in American society.

The ideological and practical differences that accompanied the change in leadership are significant in a number of ways.

1. There has been an ideological shift in emphasis and breadth with respect to both the issues to which, and the constituency for which, the AFL-CIO speaks. While the ideology of the old AFL-CIO encouraged unions to focus narrowly on union-negotiated contracts—one activist described the labor movement's self-image as "Contracts Are Us"[18]—the current ideology encourages a broader view of the problems confronting working people and the role unions have to play in resolving those problems. Organized labor, writes John Sweeney, must "reach beyond the workplace and into the entire community and offer working people beyond our ranks the opportunity to improve their lives and livelihoods."[19] In his speeches and writings, Sweeney focuses public attention on the declining income and the lowered aspirations of working people, assails gross inequities in wealth and power, and calls for policies and practices that will re-prioritize our national goals and restore family values, adequate leisure time, and a strong sense of community.

Coupled with a greater emphasis on social issues is a broader definition of organized labor's constituency. Federation leaders have drawn attention to the plight of the unorganized, especially people of color, women, immigrants, and low-wage earners in general. They have, for example, turned a spotlight on working conditions in the nation's agricultural fields, poultry factories, and textile mills and have taken pride in fighting for improvements—such as a higher minimum wage, the extension of health insurance to families without coverage—that are "as beneficial to low wage workers outside our movement as for our current members."[20]

It is not that the previous AFL-CIO leadership did not say much of this before. It is that the current leaders say it more often, more publicly, and more sharply than their predecessors. The difference in emphasis is significant because it changes the way unions and their various constituencies view the world, and it encourages alternative strategies and actions.

2. The ideology of the current AFL-CIO puts more emphasis on grassroots efforts and direct action and less on the Washington-based policy analysis and lobbying so central to the old AFL-CIO. Reflecting on the tenure of his predecessor, Lane Kirkland, Sweeney writes, "The AFL-CIO of the 1980s and early 1990s too often seemed content to generate position papers—thoughtful ones to be sure, but with little effect on workers beyond the Washington Beltway."[21] For Sweeney and his colleagues, revitalizing the labor movement depends on building a grassroots movement. While the old AFL-CIO feared that rank-and-file mobilization and militancy would only marginalize organized labor, the current AFL-CIO believes that building a grassroots organization willing to engage in direct action is essential to organized labor's survival. "Revitalizing the labor movement," writes Sweeney, "is like weaving a seamless garment of activism."[22] Sweeney's own presence on picketlines and in street demonstrations symbolizes the new grassroots approach.

3. The ideology of the current AFL-CIO encourages a shift away from the narrow institutional interests of unions and toward a focus on building coalitions and a broad social movement. The old AFL-CIO focused on the needs of constituent unions and concentrated on protecting the organizational and economic interests of these unions and their members. The current AFL-CIO has shifted emphasis to building a social movement. "The Federation must be the fulcrum of a vibrant social movement, not simply a federation of constituent organizations" stated the New Voice platform.[23]

As part of this effort, federation leaders have stressed the need to build strong and meaningful coalitions which go beyond labor's immediate concerns. Change, they argue, will require a broad-based movement that will turn the tide of public opinion. Again reflecting on the tenure of his predecessor, Sweeney says, "Relationships with natural allies torn apart in the 1960s and 1970s went unrepaired. The labor movement became isolated and introverted, concerned more with our own deepening crisis than with the crisis in the world around us."[24] In contrast, Sweeney argues, "our movement should be opened up and the dialogue should be as wide as we possibly can make it."[25] The current AFL-CIO has demonstrated a commitment to openness and coalition—building by leaving the door open, at least part way, to support for an independent labor party and by organizing town hall meetings, labor-academic conferences, and meetings with organizations such as the National Organization of Women and the Rainbow Coalition. This has been part of an effort to build a coalition and a mass movement.

The AFL-CIO leadership change in 1995 reflected an evolution of thinking within the labor movement and a change from a pragmatic and business oriented ideology toward a more socially conscious and movement oriented ideology. Emphasis shifted from servicing members to organizing new members; from the economic protection of its members to social justice issues; from lobbying for favorable legislation to direct action on the grassroots level; from preserving institutional interests to coalition—and movement building. These changes go beyond intellectual oratory. It has committed significant resources to organizing new members, reached out to new constituencies and potential allies within the progressive movement, advocated on behalf of broad social issues, and encouraged rank-and-file mobilization. Sweeney put it this way, "We shouldn't act as one more special interest group. We need to act as a social movement that represents working people throughout the society—union members and non-union members alike."[26]

In the war of ideas, the current AFL-CIO leadership is providing one of the few progressive, humanistic, populist voices in an ideological arena where political conservatism has experienced a revival, a religious Right has made significant gains among the working class, and the mainstream of the Democratic Party has shifted profoundly to the political right. In this context, it is easy to gloss over the ideological differences that still exist within the labor movement or to neglect the realm of what could be. This would be a mistake.

PERSISTENT BELIEFS

While the AFL-CIO is departing from many of the ideas, policies, and practices of the past, it continues to remain wedded to a number of old assumptions. In fact, it could be argued that the heightened level of activity and sharper, more visible rhetoric mask an ideological foundation that remains fundamentally unchanged. At its core there persists a deep belief in the ability of the U.S. economy and the U.S. socio-economic system to provide a fair and just distribution of resources. This belief assumes that American business will continue to prosper, and that the logic of capitalism requires a well-paid domestic labor force that consumes the goods and services it produces and provides. While other labor federations around the world have embraced anti-capitalist or socialist positions or remained economic agnostics, the AFL-CIO has maintained a pro-capitalist position since its founding. It is a faith in the socio-economic order that has defined and limited organized labor's objectives. Sweeney expresses the logic of the system this way:

> [speaking to business leaders] Labor's victories can be your victories, too. With decent paychecks, we can buy your products and services. (December 6, 1995)[27]

> We want to increase productivity. We want to help American business compete in the world and create new wealth for your shareholders and your employees. We want to work with you to bake a larger pie which all Americans can share—and not just argue with you about how to divide the existing pie. It is time for business and labor to see each other as natural allies, not natural enemies. (October 24, 1996)[28]

> [We seek] a new virtuous circle in which higher wages translate into more sales, new investment, job growth. (April 16, 1997)[29]

The idea that it is in the self-interest of employers to increase pay and thereby increase the buying power of workers has its roots in "Fordism." In 1914, Henry Ford increased the wages of his workers to five dollars a day—doubling the prevailing wage at the time—and tried to persuade other industrialists to do the same in order to enlarge the pool of consumers of mass produced products. Similarly, the AFL-CIO argues that it is in the interest of employers to raise wages in order to stimulate domestic consumption and promote a healthier economy. The effect of this ideology is to emphasize the common interests of employers and employees. According to this way of thinking, while labor and management may be adversaries in the specifics of particular collective bargaining agreements, they remain partners in the broad scheme of such things as economic growth, international competition, and national prosperity.

This is a view of a nation united—a nation comprised of people with a common understanding and with common interests. At a 1996 conference in Rome, John Sweeney observed:

> For a quarter century or more after the end of World War Two there was extraordinary social solidarity in the U.S. and in most other advanced industrial societies. Most people lived by common values and shared understandings—a social compact, if you will.[30]

The notion of a social compact figures prominently in the ideology of the current AFL-CIO. It refers to an unwritten and assumed commitment to mutual respect and fair play amongst disparate players—labor, management, and government. It is based on a strong sense that "we are all in this together" and a deep belief in the cooperative spirit and its value in achieving a fair, equitable, and affluent society. In New York (1995) Sweeney noted:

> When things were good, as they were for almost 30 years after the end
> of World War Two, we all prospered, because we prospered together. We
> were concerned with raising the standard of living for working
> Americans, not just accumulating enormous wealth for a fortunate few.[31]

Herein, according to the AFL-CIO, lies the source of labor's current malaise. The social compact that held our nation together and drew on its tradition of ingenuity, hard work, loyalty, mutual respect, and industrial cooperation has been broken. Faced with a new global order, U.S. corporations chose to pursue short term gain at the expense of the common good. From this perspective, it is short term greed and a betrayal of the public trust that reversed the upward spiral that improved the lot of all Americans:

> The root cause of our problem is that corporate America decided to
> meet these challenges [of high technology and global competition] the
> wrong way. They didn't do it by building on America's traditional
> strengths: the know how and love of experimentation that helped us
> develop the advanced technologies and the teamwork we displayed
> during World War Two and the next three decades when business,
> labor, and government worked together to help all Americans move
> forward. Instead, corporate America decided to break the post-war
> social contract.[32]

The vision that has endured in the AFL-CIO since its founding is one of a partnership between labor and capital. In this partnership, workers provide corporate America with their labor, loyalty, expertise, and the means for increased profitability and in exchange, receive a fair share of these profits. In this scenario, the economic interests of labor and management are, if not identical, closely linked so that each partner's prosperity is dependent on the others. Economic enterprises remain in private, rather than in public hands and labor's objective is to tilt the balance of power toward receiving a more favorable share of the profits.

In sum, the AFL-CIO sees things this way. An unwritten social compact preserved a partnership between labor and capital for nearly three decades following the end of World War II. In this compact management agreed to increase wages and benefits for workers, thereby stimulating mass consumption and increasing corporate profits. It was this compact that made America great—providing prosperity to all Americans. It is the breaking of this compact that has led to economic inequality and a decline in the wages and working conditions of the U.S. labor force. When management, in the pursuit of short-term profitability, chose to break the social compact, it led to a decline in wages, attacks on unions, deteriorating working conditions, and increased inequality in America.

WHAT'S WRONG WITH THIS PICTURE?

There are a number of fundamental problems with the views that currently permeate the labor movement. First, it promotes a romanticized view of the post-WW II period. While the standard of living for most Americans increased during this period, the prosperity masked racial and gender discrimination, urban blight, environmental degradation, job alienation, and a significant urban and rural population that lacked adequate food, shelter, and decent medical care. As Michael Harrington reminded the rest of the nation with the publication in 1962 of *The Other America*, 45 million Americans were living in poverty during those "affluent" years. What some union leaders characterized as a period of labor-management cooperation, partnership, and teamwork, was characterized by others as co-optation and complacency. The post-war period left a much more ambiguous legacy than many in the labor movement are currently suggesting.

Second, it assumes continued growth for the U.S. economy and ignores changes in economic reality that make it impossible to return to the past. The post-WW II economic boom in the U.S. occurred in the context of an industrial base that had been destroyed in Europe and Japan, and a period of U.S. exploitation of the third world largely unhindered by competition from other Western nations. But the economic supremacy that allowed U.S. workers to advance during that period no longer exists. Instead, new technologies and new markets have made it easier, and new competitors have made it more important for U.S. corporations to cut their labor costs. In this context, we should be seeking new solutions and new ways of distributing the nation's resources, rather than calling for a return to the past.

Third, it suggests that corporate leaders are mismanaging, when in fact they are simply following the dictates of the market. Similarly, it suggests that specific corporations that are particularly egregious be targeted, instead of recognizing that it is the nature of the "free" market system that short shrifts workers. Corporations exist for the sole purpose of returning a profit and maximizing that profit. Corporate executives are not wrong to pursue cheap labor abroad, break unions, or lay off as many employees as they can. This is what they are paid, quite handsomely, to do. Corporate owners and managers are motivated not simply by greed, although there is certainly plenty of that, but rather by economic imperatives. They will resist unions and union demands unless union force, not persuasion, makes them do otherwise. Maximizing profit in an era of intense market competition requires that corporations do whatever they can to reduce costs both in the short term and the long term. In this context, we should be addressing systemic and structural issues rather than moral ones.

The AFL-CIO calls for a return to an economy where "a rising tide lifts all ships." But those days, to whatever extent they ever existed, may well be gone. The logic of "Fordism" worked when U.S. monopolies could control consumer markets. Today, better paid workers in the U.S. are just as likely to buy products from foreign companies as they are from domestic ones. And with the emergence of new global markets, U.S. corporations have demonstrated that they can increase productivity and profits without increasing the buying power of the domestic workforce. Unless unions force change or there is a temporary labor shortage (which corporate America would quickly seek to reverse), economic growth and self-interest will not lead to everyone having more. It is in this context that corporate America declared open class war, engaging in anti-union campaigns, deregulating industries, privatizing the public sector while dismantling the welfare state, and reversing the hard won reforms of the past. Appeals to common sense or moral responsibility will not lead to a bigger piece of the pie for labor: on the contrary, self-interest dictates greater inequality. In many ways, we are living in a zero sum society, where the increase in the relative income of corporate America and the wealthy decreases the relative income of the poor and working class.[33] It is no accident that CEO salaries and stock dividends go up when companies cut wages and lay off workers. Rather than being misguided, representatives of corporate America are showing their true face: this is simply capitalism in its cruder form. While the current AFL-CIO's more socially conscious unionism is a long overdue improvement over the "pragmatism" of the past, a class-conscious perspective would be more accurate and effective for the changing reality as we move into the twenty-first century. The interests of capital and labor are clearly opposed, and clinging to the faith that the structure of the U.S. economy is fundamentally just is self-defeating. We need to acknowledge the fundamental changes in labor's circumstances and reject the logic of partnership with corporate America.

WHAT SHOULD LABOR STAND FOR?

On the eve of his 1992 nomination as the Democratic candidate for the Presidency, Bill Clinton remarked to his speech writer, "I agree with you about populism. But we can't lead with class struggle. We have to be pro-growth populists."[34] Clinton's comment suggests that he understood the significance of class in dividing the nation, but chose a more politically expedient message to define both his campaign and his presidency. Pro-growth, after all, suggests that "we are all in this together," while class struggle suggests a "them" and "us" dichotomy. Notions of class and struggle, especially from a populist perspective, would pose a serious ideological challenge to the wealthy and to corporate America, on whom Clinton relied for support. Four years earlier, Clinton's predecessor, George Bush said, "[Class is] for European democracies or something else—it isn't for the United States of America. We are not going to be divided by class."[35] Not surprisingly, Bush rejected the notion of class altogether.

The United States, however, is divided by class and these classes are engaged in a struggle. While politicians are ideologically constrained from acknowledging this reality by their own class background and their financial dependence on the wealthy, labor is not. Organized labor is free to develop its own independent ideological paradigm. But to adopt a class-conscious ideology, labor will have to jettison its old assumptions about the virtues of capitalism, and break from the "pro-growth" ideological framework promoted by the Democratic Party.

How might the labor movement shape a class-conscious response to the current challenges facing working people? It would project a bold vision for economic and political democracy; offer a sharp critique both of corporate domination of society and of class, racial, and gender inequality, and propose a set of creative initiatives to bring about incremental change toward a more egalitarian and just society.

Labor's critique would challenge upper class lifestyles and class privileges, and focus public attention on how these privileges impact on our occupational opportunities, educational experiences, leisure, health, safety, and life chances in general. It would suggest that ending class privileges would allow us to lead freer, more creative, and more meaningful lives. In this context, a class-conscious labor movement would propose progressive tax reform, guaranteed income, a maximum income cap, and similar measures that not only raise the income of the poor and working class but lower the income and unfair privileges of the wealthy.

The critique would also focus attention on those who own and control corporate America and their ability to dominate politics and government by influencing public officials, shaping public discourse through control of the media, and leveraging their economic power by threatening to wreak economic havoc when communities do not meet their demands. Organized labor would lead the fight for political reform, champion legislation that prohibits for-profit corporations from any activity intended to influence the political process,[36] and advocate campaign spending limits, public campaign financing, and the prohibition of lobbying by for-profit corporations.[37] Like many of its counterparts in other parts of the world, the labor movement would run its own candidates with an overt labor message, seeking power—not just influence—on behalf of the working class and their communities.

Advocating greater democracy, however, needs to go beyond the realm of politics and government. For contrary to George Meany's claim, politics and government in the U.S. are subordinate to the economic forces that dominate American society. These economic forces have reduced the political terrain to a contest between the conservative and liberal wings of capital and their respective strategies for preserving the economic health and strength of corporate America. If, however, we are to put people first and pursue a more equitable distribution of power and wealth, we will have to broaden our vision and goals.

A class-conscious labor movement would provide a vision of economic democracy that gives workers and communities greater control over economic enterprises. Such a framework would allow labor to demand that economic decisions, like political decisions, be subject to public discourse and the democratic process so that workers and communities can decide not only what, how, and under what circumstances goods are produced and services rendered, but how our technologies are utilized, our resources developed and invested, and our goods and services marketed in the global economy.

Labor would transform "regulation" from a dirty word into a battle cry, serving as a public watchdog to expose profit margins, tax loopholes, environmental violations, and corporate irresponsibility. It would call for a national economic development strategy based on creating jobs and meeting social needs—including full employment, rewards for socially useful production, and public works projects.

While Americans have long been ideologically committed to democracy, the notion of economic democracy has not been part of our culture or tradition. The labor movement needs to engage in political education that underscores the inconsistency between American democratic ideals and capitalist economic organization. It must address the nature of class power in America: who has it, how they use it, how class domination can be reversed.

Rather than suggesting that "we are all in this together," such a movement would recognize that the interests of the wealthy and the rest of us are not only different, but are for the most part diametrically opposed, and that the colossal wealth and privilege of the elite are acquired at the *expense* of the rest of us. It would argue that the plight of working America is due not to circumstance nor to greedy, short-sighted, or unenlightened corporate leaders, but to corporate executives who have an interest in and a mandate to minimize labor costs and maximize profits. It would go beyond submitting that America needs a raise (the costs of which can be passed on to the consumer), and call for strict limits on wealth, income, and profit.

Overall, the labor movement's vision would be neither pro-growth nor anti-growth, but rather pro-people, pro-democracy, and pro-equality. The vision would draw on moral values and principles of equality and justice that would motivate and mobilize people to take action. The vision would be original, realizable, and capable of capturing the imagination of the young as well as the old. It would neither resurrect outmoded models nor have a static, absolute, or doctrinaire quality to it. Rather than merely offering a nostalgic call for a return to the earlier days of glory, it would be new and forward thinking.

With a clearly articulated vision of democracy and a bold approach to achieving it, organized labor could inspire the broad-based social movement it currently seeks to build. But labor could not realize this vision alone. Nor can a movement for greater equality and democracy be limited to class issues. It must challenge privileges based on race and gender as well. Such a movement would highlight the role racism and sexism play, both in oppressing people and in dividing them from each other. It would express an absolute intolerance for discrimination—and tokenism—including within its own ranks. It would enter into coalitions with other organizations that seek to end privilege and redistribute power and wealth, and lead a movement for economic democracy.

WOULD A CLASS-BASED APPROACH NARROW THE LABOR MOVEMENT'S APPEAL?

Many activists who are sympathetic to the notion of a class-conscious labor movement would argue that the language of a class ideology is permanently and hopelessly associated with the political fringe, and that adopting it would therefore reduce the labor movement's appeal to workers. But two important changes in American society have made a class-conscious movement more viable. First, the cold war is over making it much more difficult today to associate class terminology with foreign and traitorous conspiracies. Secondly, the American dream has lost its hold on large segments of the population. The myth that we live in a classless society where hard work, sacrifice, and perseverance will lead to success is no longer as credible as it once was. Nor is the myth that we are all getting richer. Working people are more conscious than ever of both the widening gap between the rich and everyone else and the inverse relationship between workers' well-being and the well-being of stockholders and corporate executives.

Not only is a class-based approach more realistic and viable today than ever before, it may be the only way for organized labor to transform itself into a social movement. Providing a broad social vision, developing non-rhetorical language to support it, and finding ways to move toward that vision, while empowering workers and communities each step of the way, can revitalize not only the labor movement, but a populist, progressive movement. In the tradition of Martin Luther King Jr., visions and dreams can inspire a movement.

THE CLASS-CONSCIOUS PARADIGM

A class-conscious ideological paradigm would differ from both a pragmatic and a socially conscious ideology in a number of ways: it would shift emphasis from the articulation of common interests and toward articulation of opposing class interests; from focusing on the issues of economic protection and social justice and toward focusing on the broader issues of economic democracy and equality; from viewing labor management conflict as an aberration and toward viewing it as systemic; from support for the liberal wing of capitalism and toward independent class politics; from an ideology of reform and toward a ideology of transformation.

Since the AFL-CIO leadership was elected in 1995, change has come more quickly than almost anyone expected. Organized labor, however, has rapidly arrived at another crossroad. It can seek to integrate labor and unions into the status quo and assume that this is both possible and desirable in the current context, or it can seek to transform both the economy and polity of society to reflect more egalitarian and democratic principles. If the leadership continues to assume that the interests of labor and capital run parallel, then it will inevitably buy into the profit-oriented decisions of management—at least as long as labor gets its cut. In the past, labor's decision to be part of the status quo led it to support militarism and foreign intervention, and to accept, albeit reluctantly, two-tiered wage systems, contracting out, shoddy products, and destruction of our environment and communities—all in the name of profit. We need to examine the validity of a message that asks poor and working people to buy into the notion that together labor and capital can build a just and prosperous society.

A social movement will emerge in the U.S. because people are bound together by a set of ideas and are willing to confront an institutionalized system of social injustice and economic inequality. While it may be a long time before the labor movement is unified enough to establish a clear set of ultimate goals, it can establish an ideological framework which mobilizes poor and working people around egalitarian values and democratic principles.

What would a class-conscious labor movement look like ten years from now? Imagine a labor movement that evokes intense passion and deep commitment from the grassroots on up because it stands for economic and social equality. Rather than being a loose amalgam of organizations whose strength is built on personal loyalties or patronage, such a movement would coalesce around ideas and actions. It would be as much a social cause as an organization. This is a labor movement that serves as a powerful moral force and the conscience of the nation.

Imagine a labor movement that mobilizes its members not for politicians endorsed by labor, but for labor candidates who are unabashed about serving as representatives of workers. This is a labor movement whose representatives in government develop policies that criminalize capital flight, restrict corporate profit, and prevent corporations from marketing and selling their products unless certain standards of employment are met.

Imagine a labor movement that is completely integrated into the life of our communities and uses its resources to develop and implement policy initiatives designed to improve these communities. This is a labor movement that goes beyond its own narrow institutional interests to propose changes in education, housing, transportation, and social services, so that government better serves the needs of the poor and working class. This is a labor movement that demonstrates leadership, earns the support of non-union members, builds alliances with community organizations concerned with the disadvantaged, and makes a real difference in the life of the community.

Imagine a labor movement that transforms our culture and changes the way we think about ourselves and others. This is a labor movement that sensitizes the nation to class bigotry that is expressed in our language, humor, television, news media, film, and literature.[38] It is a movement that makes us more confident and assertive and teaches us not to misdirect our anger towards those who have less, but to focus that anger on class privilege and a class system. This is a movement that has an impact on social consciousness, not unlike the impact that the civil rights movement and the women's movement had on the race and gender consciousness of the nation.

Imagine a labor movement that has the power not only to win concessions, but to help bring about fundamental change in the way our nation allocates resources and power. This is a labor movement with its eyes on both short term and long term goals. This is a movement that targets not only specific corporations but corporate America. And it is a movement that demands and wins democratic control of workplaces and industries.

Imagine a society where labor and community rule.[39]

NOTES

The views of the author expressed in this essay, are not necessarily those of the Labor Resource Center.

1. "What Does Labor Want?" speech delivered in September 1893, *The Samuel Gompers Papers,* Volume 3, Stuart Kaufman and Peter Albert, eds. (Chicago: University of Illinois Press, 1989).

2. *The American Federationist,* October 1966, p. 12.

3. Ibid., p. 6. See also Lane Kirkland, *The American Federationist,* September 1972, p. 11.

4. *The American Federationist,* October 1966, p. 7.

5. *The American Federationist,* September 1972, p. 8.

6. George Meany in *The American Federationist,* December 1966, p. 2.

7. *The American Federationist,* September 1969, pp. 14-15.

8. George Meany in *The American Federationist,* December 1966, p. 1.

9. Edy Kaufman, *Crisis in Allende's Chile* (New York: Praeger, 1988), p. 81.

10. Comment made to the AFL-CIO Executive Council, quoted in Robert Zieger, *American Workers, American Unions, 1920-1985* (Baltimore: John Hopkins University Press, 1986), p. 172.

11. Kathy Sawyer, "AFL-CIO Toils in Foreign Vineyards," *Washington Post,* November 19, 1983, sec. A, p. 2.

12. *The American Federationist,* June 1972, p. 21.

13. Zieger, *American Workers,* p. 174.

14. In large part, lobbying legislators was one of the few roles the Federation believed it could claim for itself. Leaving contract negotiations and enforcement as well as union organizing to its affiliates, the Federation focused on politics and public relations.

15. One area where the current AFL-CIO has departed from the past by adapting a more pragmatic approach to its work is in international affairs. Rather than espousing an anti-communist ideology to justify its international activities, the current Federation is underscoring the self-interest of U.S. workers in developing an international strategy that will protect its economic interests at the workplace.

16. "A New Voice for American Workers: Rebuilding the American Labor Movement, A Summary of Proposals from the Unions Supporting John J. Sweeney, Richard Trumka, and Linda Chavez-Thompson," June 28, 1995, p. 3. Available from AFL-CIO, Pamphlets Division, 815 16 Street, N.W., Washington, D.C., 20006.

17. John Sweeney, *America Needs a Raise* (Boston: Houghton Mifflin, 1996), p. 95.

18. Elaine Bernard at conference, "Fighting for America's Future: A Teach-In with the Labor Movement," held at Columbia University, October 4, 1996.

19. Sweeney, *America Needs a Raise*, p. 123.

20. From speech delivered to the Pontifical Council for Justice and Peace, Rome, Italy, December 2, 1996.

21. Sweeney, *America Needs a Raise*, p. 90.

22. Ibid., p. 99.

23. "A New Voice"

24. Remarks by John Sweeney at the AFL-CIO IRRA 50th Anniversary Meeting in New York City, April 17, 1997.

25. AFL-CIO News, November 6, 1995, quoting Sweeney at the AFL-CIO Convention.

26. Sweeney, *America Needs a Raise*, p. 106.

27. Remarks to the Association for a Better New York, New York, December 6, 1995.

28. Remarks to "Business for Social Responsibility," New York, October 24, 1996.

29. Remarks to the Economic Strategy Institute, Washington, D.C., April 16, 1997.

30. From speech delivered to the Pontifical Council for Justice and Peace, Rome, Italy, December 2, 1996.

31. Presentation at the Association for a Better New York, New York, December 6, 1995.

32. Sweeney, *America Needs a Raise*, p. 56.

33. Lester C. Thurow, *Zero Sum Society* (New York: Basic Books, 1980).

34. David Kusnet, "Feeling His Way," *Mother Jones,* Jan./Feb. 1997, p. 47. Kusnet, who was Clinton's speech writer, went on to co-author *America Needs A Raise* with John Sweeney.

35. Quoted by George Will in "A Case for Dukakis," *The Washington Post,* November 13, 1988, sec. A, p. 27.

36. David C. Korten, *When Corporations Rule the World* (West Hartford, Conn.: Kumarian Press, 1995), pp. 307-320.

37. Corporations claim this violates their free speech. But as David Korten and others point out, corporations are public entities and chartered by law, not natural born persons to which our Constitution guarantees rights of free speech. By giving them the ability to lobby and carry out public campaigns, corporations achieve precisely what the Constitution intended to prevent: domination of public thought and discourse.

38. Michael Parenti, *Land of Idols: Political Mythology in America* (New York: St. Martin's Press, 1994), p. 55.

39. For more discussion of some of the proposals identified in this essay, see Sam Pizzigati, *The Maximum Wage* (New York: The Apex Press, 1992); The Labor Institute, Corporate Power and the American Dream (New York: Labor Institute, 1995); David Korten, *When Corporations Rule the World* (West Hartford, Conn.: Kumarian Press, 1995)

PART | 2 | ORGANIZING THE UNORGANIZED

Union membership has been in a tailspin for forty years. From an all-time high of 35 percent in 1954, unions now represent only 14.5 percent of the labor force. With the workforce growing by nearly two million workers a year, unions would have to organize 300,000 new members each year just to stay even, and a total of 15 million to return to the previous high. The dramatic decline in membership can be attributed in part to a number of external factors: capital flight, globalization of the economy, technology, the growth of part-time employment and the service industries, hostile employers, and unfair labor laws. There were, however, internal factors as well. Some union leaders became complacent, satisfied with servicing existing members; others feared risking a serious drain on resources in protracted struggles if they lost and a shift in internal union politics with a changed constituency if they won; still others chose to focus on changing labor law to create a more favorable climate for organizing. Whatever the reasoning, organizing, with few exceptions, had atrophied. In large measure, the shake-up in the AFL-CIO was a reaction to this atrophy. The New Voice candidates called for a massive organizing effort, and one of their first initiatives, after being elected to office, was to train and deploy one thousand college students to organize the unorganized. This program, called "Union Summer," received favorable press coverage and was generally welcomed as an exciting new initiative for the waning labor movement. Union Summer, however, also raised a number of questions about whom to organize and how. Should organizing efforts shift from white-collar professionals to low wage workers who are largely immigrants, women, and people of color? What is the role of community organizations? Should unions re-think their relationship to the legal system? Should every union be encouraged to organize whoever they can, or should specific workers be targeted and organized along industrial lines, where they can be more effective? To what extent should organizing efforts be centralized (where the resources are) and to what extent decentralized (where the initiative can percolate from the bottom up)? In this section, contributors offer a range of views. One point they agree on: unions have to stop the hemorrhaging and build a mass movement.

All of organized labor's work, writes Stephen Lerner, must be judged by how it helps the movement grow in numbers and power. Lerner underscores the depth of labor's decline, rejects both familiar explanations and conventional remedies, and proposes a new set of objectives. He draws on his own experience in organizing campaigns, to urge the labor movement to engage in direct action and civil disobedience, and to conduct massive organizing drives by industry, geography, and markets. He emphasizes the importance of industry-wide organizing in order to remove wages from the competitive strategy of employers. Lerner calls for a broad-based movement for economic and social justice in order to motivate a massive response. Rather than making labor less confrontational, as some would suggest, he urges a more vocal, aggressive, militant, and creative approach to organizing. Unions and union leaders, Lerner writes, must take risks to advance the cause of justice.

Steve Early is highly critical of what he describes as the AFL-CIO's effort to "parachute Peace Corps–type cadre into workplace campaigns after a crash course in organizing." He warns that campus recruits, like those deployed during the union summer programs, lack work experience, ties to local communities, and any meaningful connection to the internal life of the unions they serve. Nor does he favor the use of full-time functionaries as professional organizers. He doubts these efforts will lead to an organizing upsurge and suggests that even when successful, this approach to organizing is likely to lead to local unions that are dependent on and dominated by outside staff. In contrast to this approach, Early urges organized labor to build a new organizing culture within unions that encourages a worker-to-worker approach to recruiting new members. He suggests that unions train rank-and-file members and organize them into committees based on the job experience and ethnic, regional, or community ties they share with unorganized workers. These committees can share personal experiences and information, and help build long-term local leadership and activity that brings the union to life on the shop floor. Early describes a number of cases where a worker-to-worker approach to organizing was successful and where the AFL-CIO's current approach would have failed. He argues that the AFL-CIO would better serve the cause of organizing by helping affiliates develop organizing campaigns that are membership based.

Josephine LeBeau and Kevin Lynch argue that the labor movement needs to provide greater support for local level organizing, use rank-and-file workers as organizers, and develop an aggressive organizing strategy that builds on commonalities among workers. While recognizing the importance of organizing at the federation and international union level, especially in new industries, they contend that concentrating additional organizing resources at the local level will meet two important objectives. It will be effective in bringing new members to unions because it encourages the use of rank-and-file organizers who are closer to the daily experience and concerns of workers and better positioned to establish links to community-based allies and resources. Moreover, it will promote good unionism because it empowers members, encourages democratic practices, increases involvement in union affairs, and develops new leadership. Furthermore, organizing campaigns driven by ethnically and racially diverse union locals are more likely to result in a more inclusive labor movement—one whose members and leaders more accurately reflect the race, gender, and class composition of the workforce. LeBeau and Lynch outline the components of their successful experience with organizing on the local level. They urge the current leadership of the AFL-CIO to continue its organizing efforts at the national level while simultaneously directing funds down to the local level to support grassroots organizing efforts by locals with good organizing prospects and proven track records.

Janice Fine provides a number of valuable examples of how unions have re-examined past practices and developed new ways of thinking and organizing. In these new initiatives, unions have variously disregarded traditions of exclusion, top-down organizing, employer-based collective bargaining, and politics divorced from economics. In their place, unions have experimented with "living wage" campaigns, workers' rights centers for recent immigrants, and coalition efforts at economic development. These experiments, suggests Fine, have been successful because they respond to the need to combine labor market and community-based strategies. While a labor market strategy establishes a loose monopoly over the labor supply and takes wages out of competition across a city or industry, a community-oriented strategy addresses broader community concerns, and establishes the union as central to people's lives and as a key institution in the community. Fine urges labor to move these innovations to the center of its strategy in its effort to revitalize the movement.

Taking the Offensive, Turning the Tide

Stephen Lerner

This is a terrible time for workers. Our jobs, rights and security are threatened by seemingly unstoppable economic forces. Until recently, unions—traditionally the primary weapon at workers' disposal—have felt increasingly powerless to challenge corporate power and its political allies. For a generation we have been losing membership, influence, self-confidence and strategic direction. This slide is reflected in diminished power and a sense of futility—a sense that our best hope is merely to slow the rate of decline.

By the year 2000, unions may represent only five percent of the private sector workforce. Despite increased emphasis by some unions on organizing, no union is consistently organizing large private sector units. This is true throughout the country, including regions and industries of traditional labor strength. Even if labor's hemorrhaging among currently organized workers is stopped, there is no reason to believe our current level of activity in organizing will stop labor's slide into irrelevance. In fact, we would need to organize millions of people to increase the percentage of people represented by unions. In order to get back where we were in 1955, we would have to organize fifteen million people tomorrow.

The consensus at every level, from rank-and-file workers to local officers and union presidents, is that our current efforts are not working. We are not successfully organizing the unorganized or protecting the living standards of current members through collective bargaining. The 1996 election saw the first concerted effort at advancing a compelling political and legislative program. Yet, even as the lives of our members deteriorate, unions often seem determined to commit suicide rather than fight back. The political right may be offering simplistic solutions, but until recently unions were not offering anything—no analysis, no program, no strategy, no vision.

More than our own interests are at stake. A just, democratic society depends on a powerful workers' movement. For workers, economic and political strength comes from collective organization, not individual wealth. Without such organization we are bound to lose in the labor market and the political arena. And when we lose, democracy is replaced with corporate oligarchy. Over the past generation these elementary truths have disappeared from political debate, even among progressives. Recovering them is a first step in restoring life to the American labor movement, in rebuilding unions and transforming them into the leaders of a new movement for economic and social justice.

But it is only a first step. Frustrated workers, union activists, and elected union officers can all agree that the situation is bad, and that unions need to do something new, something different. Yet, opinion is sharply divided over what should be done. Given our grim situation, how can we, as individuals, as institutions, as a movement change the way we mobilize our members, engage employers, and fight back against corporate attack? According to some trade unionists, we must give up on unions' traditional adversarial posture; in a competitive international economy, workers need to cooperate in ensuring the competitiveness of their firms, hoping in exchange to win greater job security and training. Others emphasize that workers need their own representation, but that current circumstances require a shift in organizational form: from traditional unions, with their role as collective wage-bargainers, to non-union forms of worker representation, such as works councils, or "new age" unions, that would focus less on compensation than on administering internal labor markets. A third view proposes to arrest the decline of labor through a more aggressive strategy of organizing focused on individual "hot shops" (work sites) where workers are especially dissatisfied and angry. A fourth focuses on the state, arguing that unions should lobby politically to improve both conditions for organizing and standards of living.

Each of these four strategies—cooperativist, non-collective bargaining, "hot shop" organizing, and political lobbying—has serious deficiencies. We have tried cooperation and been rewarded with wage decline and job insecurity. Non-collective bargaining solutions, such as works councils, developed as an outgrowth of strong unions and political movements in countries where union power is not dependent on individual firms. But in the United States, a weaker overall union movement means such solutions are unlikely to advance workers' interests. In any case, we cannot give up our role in collective bargaining. In addition, aggressive organizing of individual work sites without addressing real competitive pressures ensures implacable opposition from employers and limits our ability to make substantive long-term economic improvements. Finally, an exclusively political strategy under our current conditions of weakness at best promises minor victories, at worst another round of public humiliation.

Labor's response thus far has been defensive and conciliatory. While employers seek to destroy us, we try to convince them we can help make them more profitable. Rather than advocating unions as the only way for workers to win economic and social justice, we have allowed the question of whether unions make companies and the economy more competitive to define the debate on the importance of unions.

Two broad assumptions underlie this response. First, we have been seduced into believing that a shift to a more global, service and information-based economy has altered the basic relationship between employers and workers. According to this position, no one is to blame for the impoverishment of workers because the global economy is beyond the control of people, countries, and politicians. Markets and technology are presented as inevitable economic forces; to do battle with them is to hold back history and progress. As a result, workers have been convinced that it is hopeless to organize, protest, or change the distribution of wealth and power in the United States. In fact, if you look at where wages have plummeted the most, factors other than global competition are involved. For example, it was deregulation and declining unionization that drove truckers' wages down, not trucks coming over the border from Mexico or Canada.

The second assumption underlying the weak response of unions to deteriorating wages and conditions is that we continue to operate, in most of our work, as if unions are accepted and valued as part of this country's economic and political life—a partner in a system of industrial relations. If we continue down this track, we can only expect more of the same, but with diminishing success. A consequence of this assumption is that we approach organizing in the narrow, mechanical way structured by the National Labor Relations Act (NLRA). Organizing is done in a vacuum, rather than as part of a larger movement. The campaign is conducted on the narrow issues of which is more credible, the union's position or the company's threats. The union is defined by our ability to win more than fifty percent of the vote on a given day. Even when we are successful, organizing strictly under the terms of the NLRA is so limiting that even if we keep winning some elections, we will continue to die as a movement. Under the National Labor Relations Board (NLRB) less than 100,000 people are organized in the entire country each year. In order to increase our power and the percentage of people represented by unions, we would need to organize more workers than jobs created every year. By this definition of successful organizing, despite temporary increases in total workers represented, labor has been unsuccessful in its organizing for nearly four decades.

While a hostile political climate is often blamed for the decline of organized labor, it is a myth that prior to the Reagan era and before the growth of union-busting management consultants, unions were consistently growing in numbers and power. In fact, union membership as a percentage of the workforce peaked in 1954 at 35%. With a little more than 17 million union workers then, the number of union members did increase by more than 3 million from 1954 to 1980. But in 1980 these 20 million workers represented just 23% of the workforce. *Although our absolute numbers were growing, union power had actually been declining for 26 years before Reagan took office.* In the 20-year period from 1934 to 1954, the percentage of the workforce organized grew from 12% to nearly 35%, while in the years since, the percentage has dropped to barely 16%. It is true that our decline has been faster since Reagan and that organizing is more difficult now than in the mid-1960s. But if we did not organize at the peak of our strength, what makes us think we can be successful using the same failed model of organizing in more difficult economic and political times? Rather than simply blaming others for our problems, we need to face difficult questions concerning our failure to organize even in friendlier times. We need to meet the challenges posed by the demographics of the new workforce—immigrants, people of color, and women. We need to understand the shift to a service economy built on low-wage jobs and how this affects organizing and bargaining. We need to figure out how we use our remaining power to organize now. We need to relearn how to capture imaginations, generate excitement and articulate a vision that can mobilize union and non-union workers. Something has to change—maybe it is us.

NEW ORIENTATION, NEW GOALS

Our first step must be a fundamental change of orientation. We have to stop thinking that unions are one half of a "labor-management partnership" or part of a "system of industrial relations." There is no partnership, and the only relation is hostility. We are now a movement in opposition. Hindered and hurt by our country's laws, we face a life and death struggle with the very corporations, politicians and government with whom we have spent a lifetime building relationships.

We did not choose opposition; we have been forced into it. And now we have no alternative but to focus our time, energy and resources on a radically different approach to rebuilding labor's power. That approach must draw on our principal strength, which is not the good will of employers enthusiastic about cooperative labor relations but the millions of union workers who believe in their hearts that strong unions are essential to a better future. We need to mobilize those forces around a set of goals animated by the sense of justice and injustice that has guided the labor movement since its inception. Consider four such goals:

1. Organize millions of workers, by industry, geography and markets, by making the case that unions remain essential to economic justice for workers, security for our children, and a democracy in which our voice counts.

There are a number of successful examples of union struggles that built "mini-movements" within specific industries. The Justice for Janitors campaign targeted the building service industry nationally for organizing while focusing on key geographic markets where the union could take wages out of competition by organizing the majority of workers, cleaning contractors and office buildings. Key to the campaign's strategy and tactics is an understanding that the real power in the industry is not the legal employer, the cleaning contractor. The so called "secondary employers," the building owners, are the real power who controls labor costs, even though they have decided to hide behind the cleaning contractors to avoid the legal and moral responsibility for the horrendous conditions of the janitors who clean their offices.

This analysis of the industry and who has power in it means a dramatic shift in how the union organizes on every level. In the first Justice for Janitors campaign in Denver, many workers opposed the union when we were organizing one building at a time through the NLRB. They were won over by management's logic that increasing labor costs in just their building would raise their contractors' prices, allow a non-union contractor to bid the work at a lower rate and put them all out of work. The same group of workers became union supporters and activists when they learned that the union's goal was to organize the entire industry in Denver; the result of unionization then would not be unemployment but higher wages and more stability for all janitors, because all contractors would be forced to pay the same rate. Because this strategy is based on market realities rather than narrow NLRB definitions of bargaining units, it makes logical sense to workers. They are thus more likely to fight for it.

In Washington, D.C. we developed a comprehensive strategy based on understanding 1) the power of the real estate industry and its role in the city's economy; 2) relationships between building owners and cleaning contractors; and 3) what changes needed to be made to improve the lives of low-wage workers at work and in their communities. We targeted the 80 buildings (out of 500) with the highest rents and largest offices, the prestige buildings of the city. These buildings drove the market for tenants and cleaning services. By targeting these buildings, we could maximize our influence on the market while minimizing the universe of buildings we had to organize initially. We forced double-breasted contractors to become 100% union in a citywide agreement for the District of Columbia, by striking them in D.C. and honoring picket lines in other cities around the country where they operated. We passed a law called the "Displaced Workers Act" that requires a private sector contractor who takes work from another contractor to keep employing workers from the original contractor. This provides real job security in an industry where workers face replacement every time a new contractor is hired while also protecting union bargaining rights. We won a ballot initiative, with seventy-eight percent of the vote, that called for fairer taxation of commercial office buildings, which should produce more revenue for city services. A combination of these kinds of tactics helps to create a climate where workers are more likely to take the risk of organizing, where community support for organizing increases and where the real estate industry has a powerful disincentive to fight the union.

The Justice for Janitors campaign looks to identify the various levels of power within the industry and to develop appropriate tactics for each of those levels. Because we understood the industry locally and nationally, we could turn industry characteristics traditionally seen as disadvantages into advantages. We took advantage of the monopolization and increasing concentration of ownership in the cleaning contracting industry by developing the capacity to strike contractors in unionized markets in support of unionization in weaker markets. We became powerful advocates and built public support for underpaid immigrant workers, thus helping create an environment where immigrants went from being less likely to organize to more likely to do so. In this industry, janitorial companies and their workers can be kicked out of a building with a 30-day cancellation notice. This, too, we turned on its head—instead of our workers losing their jobs, we learned how to cause non-union contractors to lose their jobs in thirty days.

We have found that we can move low-wage workers very quickly into action against huge, powerful corporations when we have an analysis of corporate power and a strategy and tactics for overcoming it in a particular industry. The very reorganization of the economy that has made it difficult to organize can be turned on its head to create new weapons to fight back and achieve organizing success. When we truly understand the work of the industries we are organizing, we open up a whole new arsenal of actions that can totally change the balance of power.

2. Improve our bargaining position by taking wages out of competition.

We cannot ensure decent wages if we pursue single-facility organizing and bargaining—current competitive conditions rule that out. By taking on whole corporations, industries and regions we can regain contracts that force employers to compete with each other over the quality of their products and services, not by driving wages down. Though much discussion of wage depression has focused on international competition, the majority of U.S. workers are in firms competing in regional or national markets. Their wages have been driven down not by foreign competition but by pressure from non-union firms vying for the same market. Janitors, hotel workers, health care workers, truckers, warehouse workers and many others face relentless wage pressure precisely because unions no longer represent the majority of workers within their industries. Workers, quite rationally, will not organize if the risks to their jobs far exceed expected benefits. They know from experience that organizing one shop at a time is a prescription for bad contracts and lost jobs.

We need to look at where we have stable industries and do what labor unions have done historically, which is to take wages out of competition by organizing the majority of an industry and letting employers compete on the strength of the quality of their product, rather than on reduced labor costs. How do we develop power to force employers to recognize the unions and sign good contracts? How do we demonstrate power so non-union workers want to join the union? By asking these questions, we set the stage to free ourselves from a failed model of organizing and to fight employers on our terms, not theirs. As the example from Denver illustrates, the logical response of employers to single-site organizing makes sense to workers, while this logic falls before an industry-wide approach. At bottom, the problem with single-site organizing is that unions will fail if employers correctly believe that signing a contract is tantamount to committing economic suicide, nor will workers engage in large scale organizing if it means less security instead of more. Even where a single shop is unionized, we must accept minimal contracts to avoid making the employer non-competitive. By targeting industries and taking wages out of competition, we can rationalize wages and tame market forces.

3. Through the power of our actions and force of our principles, create conditions that require politicians and courts to protect and expand workers' rights—not because they love us but because they see such protection and expansion as the only rational remedy to the escalating conflict between labor and management.

As we seek to revive the labor movement we should take history to heart. Rather than making ourselves less confrontational, we need to become more vocal, aggressive, militant and creative in how we lead the fight for workers' rights. Virtually every great non-violent movement of the twentieth century has been built around direct action and mass civil disobedience. From India's struggle for independence to the anti-apartheid struggle in South Africa, effective social movements have stood for something so important that large numbers of people have taken tremendous risks to support them. It is hard to imagine successful organizing and bargaining in the 1930s without sit-down strikes, or a successful civil rights movement without mass civil disobedience. More recently the health care workers of the National Health and Human Service Employees Union (1199), the United Farm Workers, and public employee unions won critical victories only because they were willing to break the law. The biggest organizing gains in the private sector in the last thirty years have come in occupations not governed by the National Labor Relations Act. Likewise, to overcome current obstacles, mobilizing our members through mass civil disobedience is the strategy with the best chance of success.

Civil disobedience—planned and open violations of laws that interfere with the ability to win justice—means different things to different people. Some think of symbolic, choreographed arrests, others of huge demonstrations. Non-violent civil disobedience can play many different tactical and organizational roles, depending on purpose and level of mobilization. Beyond the impact of the action itself, civil disobedience draws power from the image of people voluntarily getting arrested; it says that their cause is so just, it is worth the risk of going to jail.

The need for non-violent direct action flows from the same source as civil disobedience: an inability to win within a framework of unfair laws. In direct action, the goal is to maximize the level of disruption without necessarily engaging in symbolic arrests. Embracing civil disobedience and direct action is a practical and moral choice, based on the conviction that it is our responsibility to take risks, both individually and institutionally, to advance the cause of justice. These methods have an impact on corporations and employers that is more effective than tactics that stay within the law. The idea is to escalate the scale of conflict, beyond that of narrow individual fights and isolated workplaces, until we create the level of crisis necessary to settle disputes. We spread the "strike" to whole companies, industries and cities, engaging those in the political/corporate community who support and tolerate unjust treatment of workers.

Discussion of direct action often relegates such tactics to the past, citing the fear of legal and financial repercussions that threaten the resources that unions have accumulated since the use of these strategies was common in the labor movement. However, if we continue on our present course, we may preserve union buildings and investments but lose our ability to fulfill our mission and fail in our responsibilities to members and to workers. Moreover, we have control over when we take risks, and we can find creative ways to minimize financial risks. Our rule should be: expand the scope of conflict, limit the scope of our liability.

The decision to use civil disobedience and direct action as basic weapons in labor's arsenal has significance far beyond its immediate impact on our ability to bargain and organize. Concerted, militant action puts unions on a moral high ground. It says to workers and the country that unions believe the labor movement is worth fighting for, that it stands for values so important to workers and the country that they are worth going to jail for. It says we are assuming leadership not just for the future of unions but for the whole country. In so doing we will be defining ourselves not as victims of an onslaught, but as agents of a more just society.

To the extent that unions have employed these tactics, they have largely worked. Examples include the Pittston miners' strike, the public challenge by health care workers to Proposition 187 in California, the Los Angeles Justice for Janitors victory over Century City and the arrests of janitors in Washington, D.C. These examples demonstrate that civil disobedience and direct action will strengthen our hand in achieving our basic goals—organizing the unorganized, bargaining with employers, mobilizing our base and advancing a legislative program.

Workers will not fight for a union, go on strike, or take other risks to win the union unless they believe they have a reasonable chance of success. That is the reason for industry-wide organizing and the reason for campaigns that involve large numbers of union members, non-union workers, and allies in the direct action to defend workers' rights. Such battles fundamentally change both the reality and perceptions of power.

It is difficult to activate members when we ask them to do something that will have little impact. By building a campaign around activities designed to engage and beat our enemies, we give our members reason to be involved. We can challenge them to deepen that involvement and take risks that bind them to the movement in new ways. Instead of lowering the definition of what it means to be a union member—cheap benefits, another credit card—we are saying that what we have is so valuable that it commands greater commitment.

We would not expect a majority of members to immediately get arrested in support of the union. We are trying to win victories that inspire members through the actions of those most committed. Members who are not ready or willing to get arrested can still support the actions of those who do. We should begin by doing more with the most active members. If one percent of labor's membership, 160,000 people, could be organized into an army of activists ready to risk arrest to support organizing, bargaining and strikes, we would have the potential to bring whole cities to a standstill. Through this kind of activity we can demonstrate power that will increase the number of members willing to take risks. After all, the auto plants were shut down by a militant minority and the bold actions of relatively small groups with the civil rights and anti-apartheid movements in the U.S. sparked national movements.

4. Move beyond wages and working conditions to lead a broad-based movement for economic and social justice, and against a spiritual and moral poverty that tolerates racism and sexism and scapegoats society's most vulnerable members.

Apart from strengthening its position in organizing and bargaining, the labor movement has an opportunity to champion the rights of all workers—organized and unorganized, employed and unemployed, working and retired—in the political arena. How we articulate and fight for our beliefs politically can mirror, expand and build on our direct battles with individual companies. By clearly stating our interests as workers versus the interests of corporate America, we can define who the enemy is, who we represent and what we are trying to accomplish, and thus force politicians to choose sides. We cannot cooperate with politicians who are anti-union any more than we can with corporations who want to eradicate unions.

Our legislative and political program must be linked to our day-to-day struggles. As long as we approach legislative and political work as a sterile exercise of getting people to vote every few years, we cannot expect mass involvement of members. In contrast, if we, for example, speak the truth that Occupational Safety and Health Act (OSHA) reform will mean more workers murdered on the job, we set the stage to confront politicians in the same way we confront employers who endanger our lives. We can disrupt their offices, hearings, lives, and businesses, holding them personally accountable for supporting the right of employers to kill workers on the job. By targeting the business operations of companies advocating the "right to work" or "regulatory reform," we can involve members in fighting the people responsible for funding the politicians who oppose us. Unions force companies to do things they do not want to do. We use the threat of greater economic damage to get them to agree to changes in wages and benefits. We need to apply the same kind of economic pressure to neutralize them and their allies in the political arena.

The "living wage" campaigns recently launched in a number of cities and states are a good example of such a political strategy. Aiming to address declining wages and increasing income inequality, living wage regulations require employers that contract with a city or state to pay wages above the current minimum. But living wage campaigns are not substitutes for organizing and collective bargaining. Raising the minimum wage typically does not provide a living wage, only a higher poverty wage. With a weak labor movement, it is hard to imagine winning a living wage legislatively on a broad scale. Instead, political campaigns should serve as tools in helping to build a movement that organizes, wins contracts and improves workers' lives. These campaigns can drive public debate about the causes and consequences of declining wages, activate workers and give them hope by winning concrete victories and by building coalitions dedicated to workers' rights.

STEPS TO A REVITALIZED LABOR MOVEMENT

In support of the goals elaborated above, we must do the following:

1. *Go on the offensive and act powerfully on our moral convictions.* To fight for economic and social justice we must build the organizational capacity to conduct ongoing, escalating actions to promote organizing, bargaining and legislative goals. The overlay of all our work must be a growing ability to interfere with the operations of companies, communities, cities and governments unless they help settle disputes that stem from anti-worker action.

2. *Launch the largest organizing drives in our history.* All of our work must be judged and evaluated on how it concretely helps us to grow in numbers and power.

3. *Mobilize our own base.* We need to mobilize and organize union activists to support a broad fight for workers' rights and to rebuild the labor movement. These activists must be trained and committed to engaging in mass actions that physically interfere with and shut down the operations of labor's enemies. When anti-labor laws, injunctions, and court orders limit unions' ability to fight, progressives and community activists must step forward to fill the void.

4. *Restore the link between organizing and bargaining.* Bargaining needs to be used as a key component in mobilizing members to win union recognition in non-union parts of their company and to support labor's larger program.

5. *Commit our resources to the struggle.* At every level of the labor movement, we must shift resources away from servicing a declining base to supporting offensive organizing and bargaining. What better way to change our image and capacity to challenge corporate America than to change how we spend our money and allocate our resources?

6. *Refuse to divorce our political and legislative agenda from our basic principles.* Unions must refuse to support any candidate who does not actively support workers' rights. The litmus test for every politician and piece of legislation must be how it impacts our ability to organize and bargain. Our political work must mirror our life and death fight in the workplace.

7. *We need an approach to movement building that encompasses all of labor.* The AFL-CIO can be the moral, strategic, and logistical center of a campaign to build a national movement dedicated to fighting for the rights of workers, defending democracy, and improving the lives of the ever increasing numbers of people forced into poverty.

Changes at the AFL-CIO, combined with mounting worker anger over declining standards of living, offer us a historic opportunity to rebuild the labor movement at every level. There is a window of opportunity now for this kind of organizing, an increasing recognition of the depth of labor's crisis, combined with a willingness to hear new ideas. We still have enough power to directly impact our ability to organize. But if we do not use these opportunities now, it may soon be too late. By dedicating ourselves to fighting for the rights of all workers, organizing the unorganized, engaging in civil disobedience and direct action, and defeating corporate power, we can breathe life into an old saying: "Bring to birth a new world from the ashes of the old—for the union makes us strong."

NOTES

The views of the author expressed in this essay are not necessarily those of the AFL-CIO. Parts of this essay have previously appeared in *Boston Review* (May 1996).

MEMBERSHIP-BASED ORGANIZING

Steve Early

Few initiatives undertaken by the current AFL-CIO have received as much publicity as recruiting students to work as union organizers. In 1996, the Federation's "Union Summer" program deployed over 1,000 campus recruits in campaigns around the country. "Union Summer" symbolized a youth movement that actually began in the early 1990s, when the AFL-CIO Organizing Institute (OI) first opened its doors to college graduates seeking jobs with unions. By 1995, 50 percent of the OI's $2.5 million budget was devoted to corporate-style campus recruitment. Reflecting this focus, half of all OI trainees seeking internships, apprenticeships, and job placements with Federation affiliates now come from academia, rather than local unions. After John Sweeney was elected president of the AFL-CIO, he named OI founder Richard Bensinger as the Federation's organizing director and promised to spend up to $20 million a year on organizing. As a result, labor's utilization of staffers hired through the OI and from outside its ranks increased even further.

Interestingly enough, this is one AFL-CIO program that was little debated during the fall 1995 leadership contest between Sweeney and incumbent, Tom Donahue. Both candidates fervently embraced the OI and engaged in a kind of bidding war over who was going to spend more money on organizer training and recruitment. Few public criticisms of the OI have been aired for understandable reasons. First, any efforts to rebuild union membership are viewed as better than none at all. Second, the media image of idealistic young people "looking to unions for careers in social change"— which has been actively promoted by the OI—is far more appealing than the old stereotype of union staffers as tired, overpaid hacks. "Union leaders and university professors, many of them veterans of the civil rights and anti-war movements, are delighted to see these students sign on with labor," *The New York Times*[1] reported in early 1996. Another *Times*[2] article during the same period predicted this would "inject new energy into the long-torpid labor movement."

A more critical analysis of the OI's role is needed. That is because union revitalization and membership growth are not going to occur as a result of parachuting Peace Corps-type cadre into workplace campaigns after a crash-course in organizing. OI campus recruits who lack local ties, union experience, or any organizational context for their work are a poor substitute for rank-and-file organizers recruited from and working off a base of existing members in targeted areas or industries. Union overreliance on OI-trained college grads often goes hand-in-hand with underutilization of workers themselves, both organized and unorganized. It avoids the hard, politically challenging work of creating a new organizing culture rooted in local unions and their communities. It also perpetuates the technocratic notion that the "leadership" of union professionals is essential to reviving labor's fortunes in organizing and other fields.

The cause of organizing would be far better served if the AFL-CIO instead helped its affiliates develop a much larger network of "organizing locals" committed to doing systematic outreach to non-union workers on a long-term basis. Expanded OI training and support of activists from such locals could contribute to the growth of a viable and effective organizing infrastructure. In contrast, the OI's current orientation toward transforming ex-college students into transient, disposable "mobile organizers" encourages unions to recruit new members in a dysfunctional way.

THE "WORKER-STUDENT ALLIANCE": THEN AND NOW

Many "forty something" professors and college-educated labor officials are enthusiastic about union recruitment of students because they believe it represents a great change in institutional attitudes. When they had just graduated from college in the late sixties and early seventies, it was not so easy to move directly from the campus to a union payroll unless you were related to a labor leader or acquired the technical skills—in law, journalism, or economics—necessary for a headquarters job. Almost no one in unions was rolling out the red carpet for college students, in large part because most labor-oriented students were themselves various shades of Red! Instead, the AFL-CIO warned its affiliates about the danger of infiltration through the summer "work-in" sponsored by Students for a Democratic Society (SDS) in 1969 and other radical attempts to create a "worker-student alliance."

One of the few unions that did try to tap the energy, idealism, and organizing abilities of "new leftists" was the decidedly "old leftist" United Electrical Workers (UE).[3] But the UE believed its field organizers should learn the ropes the old way: by first getting a blue-collar job in a unionized or preferably non-union workplace.[4] This form of "on-the-job" training in rank-and-file activism had historical roots; it is how an earlier generation of labor-oriented intellectuals, with socialist or communist views, often got involved in union struggles in the 1930s. "Colonizing" by former student radicals thirty to forty years later reflected a similar commitment to bottom-up organizing and an adversarial stance toward the "labor establishment." It became the main method of student migration into the contemporary labor movement—in the absence, until recently, of job offers from AFL-CIO campus recruiters. However, in many locals of the United Auto Workers, Steel Workers, Teamsters, and other industrial unions, the presence of such radical "troublemakers" was hardly welcomed or encouraged as a UE-type career path to a full-time organizer's job. Even in "progressive unions"—the UE, District 1199, or District 65—there was often considerable tension between younger leftists in the ranks and older ones in the leadership of organizing drives and strikes. Some veterans of the anti-war, civil rights, and feminist movements became so disenchanted with mainstream union methods of membership recruitment that they launched their own, independent vehicles for workplace organizing. Among these were 9 to 5, the Rhode Island Workers Association, and the United Labor Unions, an offshoot of the community organization, Association of Community Organizations for Reform Now (ACORN).

All three of these brave 1970s experiments ended up as affiliates of the Service Employees International Union. But whatever accommodations their founders ultimately made to the realities of union administration and financing—in a period of extreme employer hostility to unions of any sort—they at least tried to create an alternative model for organizing workers. Each organization emphasized worker empowerment, community involvement, direct action, and the development of indigenous rank-and-file leaders.

Today's crop of campus recruits may be personally sympathetic to such ideas and equally motivated by strongly-held ideals about social justice. But, as one former colonizer notes, "they don't bring to their union commitments a political analysis and collective method of work that was true of the 1970s generation of colonizers. They usually lack either the experience or intellectual tools for a critical analysis of the movement into which they are throwing themselves." They are not likely to question what it is they are trying to organize workers into, because trade unionism is, for most of them, as much a career as a cause. Advancement in these careers is not dependent on the traditional process of building a political base in a unionized shop and then getting elected to office at the local level. Nor is it usually related to organizing one's own non-union workplace, winning a first contract, and then assuming a local union leadership position as a result of those efforts. The recent college graduates recruited and trained by the OI are, instead, hired by various international unions and then deployed around the country in whatever manner the latter see fit. Through no fault of their own, OI grads often become rootless, mobile cadre with little connection to the internal life of the institutions they serve. This arms-length arrangement may serve the interests of unions not committed to organizing as a membership activity or unions leery of membership participation in any form. But it is not a formula for successful organizing nor does it lead to healthy relationships between full-time organizers and rank-and-file workers.

ROOTS IN THE COMMUNITY OR NIGHTS IN THE HOLIDAY INN?

At a recent national conference of labor activists, I chaired a panel discussion on organizing strategies. It featured an exchange between Michael Laslett, an organizer for Teamsters Local 174 in Seattle, and Mo Fitzsimons, a Detroit-based administrator and trainer employed by the Organizing Institute. Their respective presentations highlighted the dramatic difference between the "mobile organizer" approach associated with the OI and the membership-oriented, community-based recruitment efforts of a reform-minded local union. Four thousand-member Local 174 had recently overhauled its organizing program after the election of new officers affiliated with Teamsters for a Democratic Union (TDU). Laslett, the local's new full-time organizing director, is a former TDU staffer who, along with the Local 174 leadership, supported Ron Carey for Teamster president in 1991.

He described Local 174's efforts to apply the same techniques to external organizing that TDU has used so successfully—in Seattle and elsewhere—to promote rank-and-file participation in the Teamster's internal reform struggle. Under its new leadership the local did extensive membership education about the need to organize non-union trucking and warehouse workers to shore up Teamster bargaining. The officers then won support for a special two-dollar per member monthly assessment earmarked for organizing. To assist the two full-time organizers it hired, Local 174 formed an organizing committee composed of volunteers. This group was drawn from stewards and active members at companies like United Parcel Service, Safeway, and Yellow Freight. Committee members were given training and worked alongside the more experienced full-time staffers. They helped develop organizing leads among friends, neighbors, and relatives in non-union shops. They made initial contacts, assisted in-plant committees, and participated in union card-signing, house visiting, phone-banking, and pre-election rallies.

The local's organizing program had been relatively moribund under the old leadership. Organizing was the exclusive function of full-time business agents—when they had time—or international organizers, when they were in the area. Existing dues-payers had little or no say about the direction of new membership recruitment. They were never even asked to rebut anti-Teamster propaganda with personal testimonials on behalf of the union that might have swayed some non-union workers. Just as Carey's "new Teamsters" have done elsewhere in large-scale campaigns directed at employers like Overnite, Local 174 has used its volunteer organizers to tell the compelling story of how their union has been cleaned up in recent years through membership action and democratic elections. When union-busting consultants draw on the ample supply of Teamster corruption horror stories, the local's response is worker-to-worker; Local 174 organizers can now argue, with great credibility, that the union's past history does not reflect its current reality, or hopefully, future direction. The organizers' credibility is also enhanced by the fact that most are still working union members, not full-time union functionaries paid to persuade workers to join the Teamsters.

Within the local, the fifty or more members who have served on the organizing committee over the last six years have become an influential constituency in support of the local's stepped-up organizing activity. Opponents of the local leadership (and Carey) tried to repeal the special organizing assessment at a membership meeting in 1995 on the grounds that too much time and money was being devoted to organizing as opposed to servicing. Organizing committee members helped persuade others in the local to maintain the two-dollar per month financing mechanism. To win this vote they were able to point to positive results. In the three years prior to the creation of their committee, Local 174 won elections covering 130 workers; in the following three years, the local won bargaining rights for three times as many new members.

Like many other unions, Local 174 has also utilized the Organizing Institute to provide basic training for many of its rank-and-file volunteers. But, as indicated above, they were then utilized in a manner far different from the way that OI campus recruits are often used by other unions. At the conference where Local 174's organizing was described, OI staffer Fitzsimons boasted about the Institute cadre who are being recruited and trained for a "Peace Corps–type experience." They had to be willing, she said, to go anywhere, work endless hours, under any conditions. If necessary, they must be ready to spend "200 nights a year in a Holiday Inn" to achieve labor's goal of organizing the unorganized. Her entire presentation revolved around organizing technique and the tactical deployment of self-sacrificing, full-time staff. She did not address at all the question that Local 174 is grappling with, namely, how to create a culture of organizing that makes this work an integral part of local union life.

Nowhere has the weakness of the OI model been more apparent than in a January 21, 1996, *New York Times Magazine* cover story entitled "The Union Kids."[5] Written by journalist Lisa Belkin, with the apparent cooperation of OI publicists (who later used the *Times* cover as a recruiting poster for Union Summer), the article described a representation election campaign at an auto parts plant in Yazoo, Mississippi. The drive was led by three young OI alumnae—all recent college graduates now employed on the organizing staff of the Laborers' International Union of North America (LIUNA). Even without unhelpful hype like the author's description of these "kids" as "the last best hope of the labor movement," the magazine's account of their activities would have been embarrassing.

The focus of the piece—and apparently, the campaign—is not worker activity in the plant. Instead, it is the daily routine of full-time staffers frantically handing out leaflets, ringing doorbells, and driving around with rental cars and expense accounts "looking for workers." Although the union got interested in this particular shop because of a spontaneous walk-out over wages that occurred before the drive even began, there is no evidence of an in-plant committee on the eve of the election. Instead, there are house calls in which the lead organizer, from Massachusetts, adopts "a down-home Mississippi drawl" rather than a "college accent" because the latter "just doesn't play right at all" with the largely black, female, rural workforce. Organizing is depicted as just "talking": going door-to-door with a sales pitch like any other peddler of a product. The company, of course, accuses the union of being "a third party, an outsider, a business." In the *Times* account, it certainly looks that way—even if the organizers involved are young, multicultural women who do not fit the traditional stereotype of middle-aged, white male union reps.

The functioning of LIUNA's nearest affiliate—in Jackson, Mississippi— becomes a campaign issue when management distributes the local's financial statement, highlighting union salaries, cars, expenses, and other items in the usual misleading fashion. LIUNA, like the International Brotherhood of Teamsters (IBT), has a history that lends itself to employer propaganda about "union corruption" and "dues rip-offs." But in Yazoo City, there is no sign of any LIUNA members who might be able to address such issues, one-on-one, with their fellow Mississippians. Not surprisingly, the union loses the Labor Board election. The very next day, the outside organizers pack up and leave town (just like in the movie Norma Rae, which had a happier ending). There is no reason for them to stay around. According to the article—and the OI— a real union organizer is constantly on the move, leading "a life only someone with few other obligations can lead. Home is whatever hotel room they are in." In Yazoo, however, the contrast between the union staffers' apparent job security and mobility—and the plight of the eleven workers fired during the drive—is painfully obvious and was even an issue during the vote. ("If you get distracted on dealing with the terminations, it takes away from the campaign," one organizer explains to the *Times*.)

THE WORKER-EMPOWERMENT MODEL: SOME CWA CASE STUDIES

Unions should reject the notion that this is how "organizers" must live and work (until they burn out and get replaced by more 23-year-old, OI-trained cannon fodder). Throwing "union kids" into the fray on their own, Yazoo-style, is a formula for failure. It does not build workers' power on the job—before or after a representation election. It reinforces some of the worst stereotypes about how and why unions seek new members. Even where this approach does succeed, the new bargaining units that result from it tend to be dependent on and dominated by outside staff. As former UE Organizer Mike Eisenscher has observed, "activism and empowerment must be wed if unions are to be transformed." A "staff-run, top-down organizing strategy," he writes, may utilize the "considerable creative energy and enthusiasm of young college-educated and community activists." But it rarely results in a post-election shift of power to workers in the unit. Instead, writes Eisenscher, "the political center of power remains far from the ranks of the union's members," and strategic decisions are made in the union's upper echelons." Even if there are later "staff-directed mobilizations around contract issues," the traditional "servicing model of unionism remains largely intact."6

Contrast this approach and its results with the attempt by some national unions to create "organizing locals," like Local 174 in Seattle, which are committed to doing systematic outreach to non-union workers in the same community or industry as their existing members. As in Local 174, this invariably requires a major shift in union orientation. Officers, stewards, and members must embrace the idea that organizing is just as important as grievance handling and contract negotiations—and not a responsibility that can be left to "professionals" on the international staff.7

Rank-and-filers—even older ones with families—can then be trained and deployed as volunteers, on a lost-time basis, or in full-time local organizer positions. As in the Seattle Teamsters, they can develop organizing leads, make contacts, and help build in-plant committees based on the job experiences and ethnic, regional or community ties that they share with unorganized workers. In campaigns, the emphasis is on worker empowerment and "ownership" of the drive, not the charismatic role of outside organizers. The latter must concentrate on fostering in-plant leadership and activity that brings the union to life on the shop floor and helps sustain worker organization regardless of whether an NLRB election is won or lost or is even an immediate possibility. As Cornell University researcher Kate Bronfenbrenner has found, "Union success in certification elections and first contracts depends on using a grassroots, rank-and-file intensive strategy, building a union and acting like one from the very beginning of the drive...Unions can overcome even the most intense opposition when they run aggressive bottom-up campaigns."8

A worker-to-worker approach can be utilized even in organizing efforts which involve larger, regional or national targets with multiple work locations and a need for coordination among many different locals. Such drives are usually longer-term strategic efforts rather than an opportunity for single-site card-signing "blitzes." Nonetheless, the greater staffing needs of larger campaigns can still be met by creating organizing teams, which mix younger "project organizers"—who fit the OI campus recruit mold—with more experienced staffers, local officers, and rank-and-file volunteers.

Spurred on by its organizing director, Larry Cohen, the Communications Workers of America (CWA) has created a framework for doing both "hot shop" and strategic organizing through its national "Organizing Network." This network consists of more than 100 local unions committed to signing up at least 100 new members per year. Like Teamsters Local 174, many of these locals have shifted significant resources from bargaining and servicing to organizing new members. They have created full-time organizer positions and volunteer organizing committees. Most of these local organizers were once volunteer organizers themselves in the same local where they have now joined the staff.

Currently, there are about eighty local organizers throughout the union who receive significant funding from its organizing department. The national union has also paid to have 400 CWA members attend the OI's three-day basic training program. In 1996, CWA convention delegates voted to require that at least ten percent of the national union's resources be committed to organizing—thereby insuring a bigger annual budget to subsidize local organizing activity. Within each of CWA's eight geographical districts, national staff members who serve as "organizing coordinators" assist local union campaigns. They also convene periodic meetings and "retreats" for local activists involved in organizing so they can share experiences, develop new skills, and support each other in the often frustrating and difficult work of membership recruitment. Every year, locals which recruit at least 100 new members receive special recognition at the national convention. Since the Organizing Network was formed nine years ago, CWA has organized more than 75,000 new members.

In CWA, there is usually a direct relationship between a local's internal mobilization efforts around workplace issues and bargaining and its development of volunteer organizers and, eventually, full-time organizers as well. By no coincidence, many organizing locals also play an active role in

Jobs With Justice (JWJ). JWJ is a national network of thirty community-labor coalitions formed to defend workers' rights in organizing and bargaining.[9] Its local affiliates include civil rights, consumer, feminist, environmental, student, and political organizations. For the last nine years, JWJ activists have organized fundraising events, rallies, picket lines, and civil disobedience actions on behalf of strikers and workers fired in organizing drives. In 1993, JWJ coordinated demonstrations at National Labor Relations Board (NLRB) regional offices around the country to protest the failure of federal law enforcement. More than 7,000 union members participated and 400 were arrested. A major follow-up project of JWJ has been to establish local "Workers' Rights Boards," composed of community representatives, which can conduct independent investigations of labor law violators and generate adverse publicity about them.[10] JWJ seeks to change the current climate for organizing— for the benefit of all unions. It also provides a militant and effective vehicle for making workers' rights struggles the object of greater public sympathy and understanding rather than just "special interest" lobbying by unions.

In CWA locals like the ones cited below, recruitment techniques were not perfected overnight. It sometimes takes years—and considerable staff time, training and money—to develop an in-house cadre of organizers who are confident, experienced, and committed. They often learn by trial and error, as much through false starts and defeats as from election victories (which tend to be small at first). What distinguishes CWA's worker-organizers from the OI's college grads is their staying power, workplace ties, and community roots. If, as in the case of Local 9410, an NLRB campaign turns into a larger fight for workers' rights that requires political work, community organizing, and international labor solidarity, there is already a foundation for it in place. "Mobile organizers" cannot easily create this from scratch— particularly when they are shifted from one campaign to another, regardless of the election outcome.

OUTLASTING THE UNION-BUSTERS: CWA LOCAL 9410

CWA Local 9410 has about 2,000 members in the San Francisco Bay Area, primarily office and technical workers at Pacific Bell and AT&T. Headed by President Marie Malliett, the local has long been a "community-minded union," active in progressive politics and coalition lobbying on a variety of issues. Its members, for example, led the fight for the first municipal legislation anywhere in the country regulating the use of video display terminals. Like many CWA locals, Local 9410 has lost members due to deregulation and downsizing in its traditional telephone company units. Utilizing full-time local organizers and rank-and-file volunteers, it has made a determined effort to recruit other white-collar workers.

Non-union workplaces in the "information industry" are not easy targets, however. AT&T's main long-distance competitors—like Sprint and MCI—operate 100% union-free. When workers similar to Local 9410 members attempt to unionize in cable and broadcast television, at newspapers, publishing houses, computer firms, or telemarketing companies, the employer reaction is fierce. Several groups of workers assisted by the Local have suffered severe repression in the form of massive unfair labor practices. At the San Francisco office of HarperCollins, Inc., an outpost of Rupert Murdoch's global media empire, and at Sprint Corporation's now closed Bay Area telemarketing center for Spanish-speaking customers, Local 9410 organizers helped in-plant activists build strong union majorities. Management then completely destroyed the possibility of CWA election victories by laying off all or part of the workforce, after systematically harassing, threatening, and intimidating dozens of union supporters. National Labor Board complaints were issued against both companies, but proceedings against them have dragged on for years.

In the Sprint situation, the casualties included 177 Latino workers who lost their jobs when management shut down La Conexion Familiar (LCF) one week before a scheduled NLRB vote in 1994. Local 9410 responded not just with the usual legal counter-measures, but with an all-out local, national, and international protest campaign aimed at making the LCF workers a labor cause célèbre. Eighty of the workers marched on a meeting of the San Francisco Board of Supervisors and secured a resolution censuring Sprint and demanding full reinstatement. The fired workers conducted a round-the-clock vigil in front of Sprint's downtown office building. They set up tents on the sidewalk, gave press interviews, and hosted visiting delegations from churches and other unions. In the city's mission district, LCF workers and their families went door-to-door to persuade Latino-owned businesses to display signs supporting the solidarity campaign. Dozens of Congressmen signed a joint letter to Sprint's Chief Executive Officer, William Esrey, condemning the company's behavior. Bay Area community groups were also enlisted to bombard the company with angry mail. JWJ coalitions in other cities joined the fray by picketing Sprint locations elsewhere.

Telephone workers in Canada, Western Europe, and Mexico were contacted and asked to raise, in their countries, the issue of Sprint union-busting. Members of the British Columbia Telephone Union, for example, confronted Sprint spokesperson Candice Bergen, of "Murphy Brown" fame, when she made a public appearance in Vancouver. The Sindicato de Telefonistas de la Republica Mexicana (STRM) went further than any union abroad when it filed an unprecedented complaint over the LCF dismissals under procedures established by the North American Free Trade Agreement (NAFTA). The STRM complaint cited the "ineffectiveness of U.S. law" in securing Sprint's compliance with workers' rights principles contained in the labor side agreements to NAFTA. The union also sought to bar the company from operating in Mexico, where it is entering the long distance market as a partner of Telmex, until all LCF workers are rehired. In February 1996, representatives of the labor secretaries of Mexico, Canada, and the U.S. convened a formal hearing on the STRM complaint. Among those testifying in favor of sanctions against Sprint were Local 9410 members, their Mexican union allies, leading community figures, and politicians.[11]

Throughout this continuing struggle, the Local has also supported the fired LCF workers by aiding their search for other jobs; by arranging classes for them in basic computer skills and English (many were not bilingual); and by keeping them informed and involved. Key activists in the group teamed up with Local 9410 members to do press work, make contact with potential backers or speak before a variety of audiences here and abroad. Victory—in any conventional sense—is still a long way off. But both the local and the LCF workers are committed to making Sprint pay the highest possible price for its anti-unionism.

ORGANIZING PUBLIC EMPLOYEES: CWA LOCAL 9119

Organizing public employees—unlike workers at Sprint—used to be relatively easy. In states with full collective bargaining laws, the main competition was often between rival unions. Government agencies for the most part remained neutral and did not hire union-busting consultants or wage anti-union campaigns.[12]

Now, however, many public entities—particularly state universities—are behaving more like private industry. Representation elections have become labor-management battles. To win, unions can no longer just sign up workers and then run "beauty contest" campaigns, heavily dependent on outside staff, mass mailings, and advertising. Overcoming stiff management opposition requires building strong workplace organization. The University of California (U.C.), for example, has been resisting CWA-backed organizing efforts among its 18,000 technical and administrative employees since 1991. That is when a 400-member group called the University Professional and Technical Employees (UPTE), which had no bargaining rights, voted to affiliate with CWA as Local 9119.

In representation elections held in 1994 and 1996, U.C. administrators attacked the union as a "third party" run by "outsiders" seeking to "disturb the collegial atmosphere" of the university. Their tax-supported, anti-union campaign failed, in part, because the UPTE-CWA partnership engendered a high level of "worker ownership" of the organizing process. Rather than flood the unit with full-time staffers from elsewhere, CWA devoted significant financial resources to developing indigenous leadership and recruiting organizers from within the University system. UPTE President Libby Sayre initially took a year's leave from her job as a counselor in the history department at Berkeley to lead the organizing effort. The organization's elected vice president reduced his schedule as a researcher so he could spend more than three years working for the union on a part-time basis. The eight remaining full-time UPTE organizer slots were filled by other unit members, formed U.C. student activists, and rank-and-file organizers on loan from other CWA locals. Staffers who were not UPTE members worked closely with those who were to develop strong internal leadership committees on each of the nine campuses involved. Support for the drive was also provided by several national union reps from CWA's west coast district.

This membership-led team has won representation elections in a unit of 4,000 technical workers and another 3,700 professionals. While contract negotiations were still in progress for these groups, UPTE began organizing a third statewide unit composed of 2,000 professional employees at U.C. medical centers. The union has waged active campaigns against staff cuts and contracting out. It has won big back-pay settlements for thousands of workers denied proper overtime and merit pay. As a result, more than 1,200 UPTE members are already paying dues voluntarily, through payroll deduction. "Our success," says one UPTE policy statement, "is due to the high level of interest and activism among our members. We are a rank-and-file organization....We don't depend on outside experts. We set our own agenda."

UNITING THE PORT TRUCKERS: CWA LOCAL 9400

The newest would-be members of CWA Local 9400 have also been setting their own agenda for years. They are the 6,000 truck drivers who move shipboard containers in and out of the ports of Los Angeles and Long Beach. Mainly immigrants from Mexico and Central America, these owner-operators staged work stoppages in 1984, 1988 and again in 1993 without any strike benefits or outside backing. Thanks to deregulation of port trucking, which eliminated the Teamsters from the scene fifteen years ago, drivers are now paid by the load at rates that work out to be a little better than the minimum wage. To get a load, they must wait in line for many hours—without any compensation. Then many are forced to haul containers which are legally overweight. If the cargo inside suddenly shifts on the highway, the driver's tractor, trailer, and container can all tip over—endangering the lives of other motorists as well. Harbor trucking companies used to pay for drivers' gasoline, repairs, pensions, health insurance, workers' compensation and unemployment insurance. Now, with the backing of the National Labor Relations Board, the bosses have declared that their drivers are all "independent contractors." The burden of these costs is no longer a management responsibility.

The 10,000-member Local 9400 is an amalgamated local composed mostly of telephone workers. (Its longtime president, Tony Bixler, was recently elected to the CWA Executive Board.) The Local's first contact with the truckers came through a Latino member who brought food to a picket line set up by wives and children of the drivers during their first strike. Local 9400 supported that walk-out and another over fuel price increases five years later. The Local developed a close relationship with leaders of an existing drivers' group called the Latin American Truckers Association (LATA). To work with LATA members, the local recruited volunteers from among its own activists employed at an AT&T center for Spanish-speaking customers. In 1994, the local's six full-time organizers—four of them Latinos—helped the drivers create a mobilization structure to conduct a mass CWA card-signing drive. With the assistance of 50 to 100 rank-and-filers from the local, almost all of the 6,000 workers eligible signed up. Hundreds of drivers began attending weekly meetings at the Union hall to strategize and organize militant protests directed at the trucking companies, shipping lines, and port authorities. In October 1995, more than 3,000 participated in a truck "Convoy for Justice" that stretched for thirty miles from the L.A.

harbor area to city hall. A delegation went inside to secure passage of a city council resolution backing Local 9400's "efforts to alleviate the stressful conditions associated with the work of the container haulers." Several months later, a second tractor-trailer caravan made its way to Long Beach City Hall where the drivers again publicized their demands for a dispatch and hiring hall system under union control, closer inspection of cargo loads to prevent overweight hauling, and payment for time spent waiting to load cargo.

By May 1996, the local was ready to back another shutdown—this one supported by $100,000 a week in CWA strike benefits. The goal was union recognition. After a rally so large that it had to be held outside in a community college stadium, 5,000 drivers parked their trucks and set up picket lines. At its peak, the work stoppage cut traffic through the harbor to ten percent of normal. At one container terminal, CWA supporters were briefly joined by members of the International Longshoremen's and Warehousemen's Union (ILWU) before an arbitrator ruled that the drivers did not have a bona fide picket line and ordered the dockers back to work. At this writing, the struggle to challenge and change the drivers' independent contractor status is again taking the form of intermittent protests—vigils, public fasts, mobile picketing, truck caravans, and community rallies.

According to West Coast labor journalist Dave Bacon, this seemingly unusual organizing drive is actually part of a wider "immigrant labor upsurge that is reshaping southern California's union movement." In recent years, he notes, drywallers and framers, janitors, farm workers, hotel workers, and factory workers have all gone on strike and won union contracts.[13] Like many union movements linked to the Great Migration of Europeans (1880-1924), this upsurge is as much social protest as it is classic workers' movement. Now, as in the past, rank-and-file initiative and indigenous leadership are key ingredients.

REACHING OUT TO TOUCH SOMEONE: CWA LOCAL 1400

Whether a unit is blue- or white-collar, co-workers—not outside "hired hands"—are often the only ones capable of overcoming internal resistance to unionization. In 1994-95, CWA Local 1400 increased its largely female membership from 200 to 2,000 by using a worker-to-worker approach that gradually changed long-standing anti-union attitudes.

In 1989, the original group of customer service representatives who formed Local 1400 took part in a bitter four-month strike against NYNEX.

One indirect result of this successful anti-concessions struggle was an agreement with the company two years later on new ground rules for union recruitment of unrepresented employees at the regional telephone company's subsidiaries in New York and New England. Under the terms of this deal, NYNEX agreed to remain neutral during any NLRB election campaign. In an arrangement rare outside the public sector, it also granted organizers access to non-work areas of non-union offices so they could meet with prospective members during break time and lunch hours.

Since 1970, both the International Brotherhood of Electrical Workers (IBEW) and CWA had relied heavily on "outside organizers" in their numerous attempts to recruit New England Tel's hundreds of service reps. With the exception of the 1980 CWA election victory that created Local 1400 in New Hampshire, all of these efforts had failed—even when the "outsiders" who tried to sign up the reps were clerks, technicians, or telephone operators from departments of the same company. Many of the service reps had a strong white-collar sense of themselves as being different from these union members. Some were quite company-oriented, and viewed their "commercial-marketing" jobs as entry-level management positions. Others had prior union experience but it was often unfavorable because they had belonged to IBEW locals preoccupied with the concerns of predominantly male technicians and installers. During the 1989 strike, 3,000 non-union service reps had crossed picket lines. Many were subjected to verbal abuse (or worse) at the hands of strikers. After the strike was settled, the unrepresented reps, as usual, got wage and benefit adjustments equal to those received by union members—without having to pay dues or lose four months' pay in a fight over health care co-payments.

In the early 1990s, this added to the difficulty of unionizing the group—even under the improved conditions of employer neutrality. Local 1400 and its president, Melissa Morin, nevertheless decided to make use of the new recruitment rules and deploy organizing teams almost exclusively composed of service reps. The national union provided training for fifteen of the local's existing New Hampshire members—ten percent of its original bargaining unit. These reps then began making contacts in twenty non-union offices located in fourteen towns and cities in three other New England states. For reinforcements, Local 1400 also called upon its sister CWA local in New York City, which represents 6,000 business and residential customer service reps at NYNEX in that area. Four experienced reps, who also had volunteer organizing experience, were taken off the job for varying periods of time to visit non-union offices in New England, along with the Local 1400 organizing committee members.

Over many months, one-on-one conversations in break rooms and lounges gradually began to erode some of the apathy, elitism, and anti-union sentiment that had thwarted so many earlier organizing attempts. CWA's message was delivered, not by full-time union officials or NYNEX employees from other departments who were unfamiliar with service rep issues and problems. It was communicated via "shop talk" among reps themselves—the sharing of personal work experiences and information about how office practices differed between union and non-union locations. Initial contacts became, in some cases, active CWA committee members. Then, meetings were held that linked union supporters in different offices and states. Card signing was systematically tracked and coordinated by outside union staffers who also handled literature production for the campaign. However, almost all the face-to-face work of signing workers up was handled by "insiders," on part-time or full-time union leaves from their regular jobs as service reps.

The big issue in the campaign was ultimately job security—after NYNEX announced plans to cut its regional workforce by twenty percent and consolidate all of its smaller New England customer service locations into three regional "megacenters." In the wake of this bombshell, both IBEW and CWA were, for the first time, able to negotiate job security guarantees that were not automatically extended to the company's management and unrepresented workforce. Many reps—even when informed of this contract protection through leaflets or mailings—would still not have embraced the union in the absence of the personal relationships and CWA committee contacts that had been developed in their offices.

Two rounds of NLRB balloting took place at NYNEX in 1994. In the first, the IBEW—which had pursued service reps in "traditional outsider" fashion—placed third and was eliminated from the ballot. In the November 1994, run-off between CWA Local 1400 and "no union," 670 reps voted in favor of unionization, while 512 remained opposed to it. With 1,500 eligible voters in all, this was the largest representation election conducted in New England in many years and one of the largest white-collar votes held anywhere in the U.S. that year. By June of 1995, after six months of negotiations, Local 1400 succeeded in extending CWA's regional agreement with NYNEX to the new unit, which now numbers over 1,800 workers.

CONCLUSION: ORGANIZING MUST BE PART OF A BROADER WORKERS' RIGHTS MOVEMENT

As Cornell researcher Bronfenbrenner recommends in her study of union organizing strategies, CWA has made a "serious commitment to the training, recruitment, and effective utilization of rank-and-file volunteers from already existing units."[14] A significant minority of its locals have succeeded in developing a "culture of organizing that permeates every activity and structure of the union." This approach has paid off repeatedly because "professional organizers" alone cannot do the outreach, build the personal relationships, or sustain the long-term campaigns necessary to overcome determined employer opposition, legal barriers, and other obstacles to union recognition.

The number of local unions actually engaged in organizing—in CWA or any other AFL-CIO affiliate—is still only a small percentage of the total. Most union members in long-established bargaining units have never had any personal experience with membership recruitment, unless it involved signing up non-members in their own unit in an open shop or agency shop situation. The vast majority of local officers, stewards, and executive board members have never been involved in organizing either—although they are much more familiar with all the official exhortations about the need to organize. No matter how many times they have heard that speech or voted for convention resolutions in favor of organizing, they still tend to view this work as the responsibility of specialists on the full-time staff.[15]

The increasing use of college educated "mobile organizers," newly minted by the Organizing Institute, is one way to jump-start national union organizing programs that are severely limited by their lack of local union involvement, membership participation, and, thus widespread organizing expertise. But it is a quick fix, not a long-term solution. By itself, unleashing waves of professional recruiters is not going to trigger any great new upsurge of worker organizing. Meanwhile, it just reinforces the mind-set that organizing is a job for specialists—for highly trained zealots—rather than ordinary union activists. The vision of union renewal that organized labor needs to project should be based instead on rank-and-file activism. Making dramatic gains in union membership is not just a matter of putting younger, more energetic people on the payroll. It will require greatly expanding the number of working members willing and able to participate not only in organizing, but in contract fights, strikes, and Jobs With Justice-type solidarity campaigns. The new leadership of the AFL-CIO could make a real contribution to improving the climate for organizing by putting far greater resources into Jobs With Justice. If only a fraction of the money that is now being budgeted for the OI was spent on building Jobs With Justice around the country, all the organizers trained by the Institute would have a much greater chance of success.[16] Like the CWA "organizing network," local JWJ coalitions provide a place where activists can meet and learn from each other, support each others' struggles, and fight for workers' rights more effectively. The larger JWJ groups—in Atlanta, Cleveland, Boston, New York, Seattle, and other cities—do rely to some degree on full-time staffers to maintain their Workers' Rights Boards and Worker Hot Lines. Nevertheless, it is grassroots volunteerism, not a handful of payrollers, which propels JWJ activity at the local level. The main energy for rallies, demonstrations, and other forms of direct action in support of organizing and bargaining comes from working union members who sign pledge cards inspired by the old IWW principle that "an injury to one is an injury to all." The card commits everyone who signs it to "be there" at least five times a year "for someone else's fight as well as my own." This simple, concrete and personal promise is elicited through one-on-one contacts at picket lines, workplaces, and union meetings. When needed later on, pledge card-signers are reached through telephone trees, fax networks, and other emergency mobilization tools. JWJ thus succeeds in drawing rank-and-filers into the fray in a manner still foreign to many central labor bodies, which rely heavily on their affiliates' ability to turn out a crowd composed of full-time officials who have been directed to attend.

As Eisenscher notes, JWJ coalitions also "expand the realm of solidarity beyond the labor movement to the community. In building labor-community solidarity movements, JWJ creates new levels of mutual obligation that compel unions to broaden their horizons beyond workplace, craft, or industry to incorporate the needs of entire communities, including traditionally non-union elements within them."[17] JWJ is a natural vehicle for doing more with the AFL-CIO's new focus on students. In Massachusetts, for example, Jobs With Justice has developed an on-going relationship with labor-oriented student groups throughout the area. It has sponsored several "student-labor solidarity" conferences attended by hundreds of campus activists and coordinated the activity of 100 Union Summer participants in Boston. Under JWJ sponsorship, summer interns worked together on multiunion organizing drives, contract fights, and issue-oriented campaigns, rather than being each assigned to a different union. They combined this work with an intensive training program that covered labor history, politics, and basic trade union skills. Interns worked "as much as possible with rank-and-file workers" (although a top Union Summer operative from Washington at first questioned whether Massachusetts JWJ was an appropriate sponsor for the program because its director is a factory worker at General Electric, rather than a union staffer!).[18]

Membership-based organizing—which is the real "best hope" for union revitalization and growth—goes hand-in-hand with the grassroots approach of JWJ. Through JWJ, labor can effectively highlight the absence of justice on the job for the vast majority of American workers who need to be organized. By using their own members as recruiters, unions can put a "new face" on the labor movement that is more than a public relations ploy (which student recruitment has often been). Worker-to-worker organizing encourages local unions to re-invent themselves as membership organizations.[19] It helps them resist the dominant tendency of American unions to function like insurance plans, bureaucratic and staff-run, that dispense services for a fee. The empowering experience that workers have when they beat the boss and form a new union is directly linked to empowering people who have been unionized for years. Rank-and-file outreach to non-union shops thus becomes an integral part of activating labor's existing base for many other purposes as well.

NOTES

1. Steven Greenhouse, "Labor Uses an Old Idea to Recruit the Young," *The New York Times*, February 25, 1996, p. 25.

2. Steven Greenhouse, "Students Looking to Unions for Careers in Social Change," *The New York Times*, March 11, 1996, sec. B, pp. 1 and 4.

3. Another was the United Farm Workers (UFW) which, in the mid-1970s, hired both young, white organizers from the cities and Chicano farm workers fresh out of the fields. One former student radical who worked for the UFW during this period argues that the "professional organizer approach" of the OI has "ideological roots" in the Farm Workers. According to David Bacon, now a California labor journalist, the UFW embodied both ideas, "organizing as a military campaign waged by professional organizers and organizing as a movement and upsurge among workers themselves. Sometimes these approaches were in great conflict with each other."

4. Former UE staffer Mike Eisenscher recalls that the union wanted "young organizers to first learn to be workers and face the conditions that prompt workers to organize...It also sought to inculcate its young staff with the culture of rank-and-file unionism. It was critical that they understand that the maxim, 'the members run this union,' is not just an advertising slogan; it is an organizing principle and way of operating the union."

5. *Sunday Times Magazine*, pp. 26-31.

6. See Eisenscher's "Critical Juncture: Unionism at the Crossroads," in *Which Direction for Labor? Strategic Options Facing the U.S. Labor Movement*, Bruce Nissen, ed. (forthcoming).

7. "Organizing's New Face," in the May-June 1996 *UMW Journal* describes how the United Mine Workers is using rank-and-file organizers. Almost every issue of the UNITE national newspaper also contains vivid accounts of that union's volunteer organizing committee activity, especially in the South. According to a May 13, 1996, *In These Times* account of the Service Employees International Union convention that elected Andy Stern president, "Stern hopes to recruit and train 5,000 'member organizers'" in SEIU over the next four years.

8. See Bronfenbrenner and Tom Juravitch, "It Takes More than Housecalls: Organizing to Win with a Comprehensive Union-Building Strategy," a paper presented in April 1996 at the AFL-CIO/Cornell Joint Union/University Research Conference on Organizing in Washington, D.C.

9. Steve Early and Larry Cohen, "Jobs with Justice: Building a Broad-Based Movement for Workers' Rights," *Social Policy*, Winter 1994. See also Steve Early and Rand Wilson, "Jobs With Justice: Health Care Reform From the Bottom Up," *New Politics*, Winter 1992.

10. See "Community Leaders Stand Up for Workers," the 1995 report of JWJ's Cleveland Area Workers' Rights Board. Available from Cleveland JWJ, 709 Brookpark Road, Cleveland, Ohio 44109, (216) 749-0500.

11. For more on CWA's alliance with the STRM (and other overseas telephone worker unions), see Larry Cohen and Steve Early, "Defending Workers' Rights in the Global Economy: The CWA Experience," in *Which Direction for Labor*, Nissen, ed. (forthcoming).

12. Kate Bronfenbrenner and Tom Juravitch, "Union Organizing in the Public Sector: An Analysis of State and Local Elections," Cornell ILR School Bulletin, 1995.

13. David Bacon, "Big Rig Drivers in L.A. Challenge Their Owner-Operator Status," *Labor Notes*, April 1996, p. 16.

14. Bronfenbrenner and Juravitch, "It Takes More Than House Calls," p. 6.

15. SEIU, for example, is generally regarded as one of the leading "organizing unions." But as Dave Moberg reported in "Service With a Smile," *In These Times*, May 13, 1996, "most of the union's members and local leaders are not active participants in the union's main projects. In a 1993 union survey, only a third of SEIU members supported the union's organizing program. Now, only about 60 out of 400 locals are actively organizing.

Sometimes successful organizing campaigns, such as the heralded Los Angeles Justice for Janitors effort, have been grafted onto locals without changing the structure of the local union or the outlook of its leaders or previous members." According to Moberg, the union's new president, former organizing director Andy Stern, wants more members to view "organizing as the key to their own power to improve their lives."

16. AFL-CIO Organizing Director Richard Bensinger attended his first national Jobs With Justice conference in June 1996, and met with local coalition leaders to discuss ways that the AFL-CIO could work more closely with JWJ on new organizing ventures. As Eisenscher notes in "Critical Juncture," the AFL-CIO's stance toward JWJ, under Lane Kirkland's administration, "ranged from distant tolerance to cool disdain to outright unfriendliness." The Sweeney leadership has adopted "a more friendly and supportive attitude."

17. Eisenscher, "Critical Juncture," pp. 32-33.

18. Russ Davis, "Union Summer Welcomes Students to Try Labor Activism," *Labor Notes*, July 1996, p. 1.

19. Membership participation in organizing was strongly endorsed in a 1996 report by the AFL-CIO's "Elected Leader Task Force on Organizing," chaired by UNITE Executive Vice President Bruce Raynor. For a copy of the Task Force Report, entitled "Organizing for Change—Changing to Organize," contact the AFL-CIO Organizing Department, 815 16 Street, N.W., Washington, D.C., 20006.

SUCCESSFUL ORGANIZING AT THE LOCAL LEVEL:
The Experience of AFSCME
District Council 1707

Josephine LeBeau and Kevin Lynch

As union members and activists have watched the decline in labor's numbers
and power over the past several decades, many have called for the development
of a "culture of organizing" that would focus labor's resources on organizing
and establish it as the central purpose of the labor movement. The new
leadership of the AFL-CIO has brought not only a culture of organizing to
the labor movement, but also the commitment to provide resources to
sustain organizing at many levels and in many places. Clearly, this leadership
sees organizing as a major component of its strategy to rebuild the labor
movement, and has visibly demonstrated its support in a number of nationally
prominent campaigns. Less well-known are efforts to increase organizing at
the local level, the strategies such efforts have utilized, and the ways in which
the AFL-CIO can support these campaigns.

An emphasis on rank-and-file workers as organizers and a concentration
of organizing resources at the local level will help accomplish many of the
key tasks facing the labor movement. These include not only vigorous
organizing, but also fostering a more democratic practice and a more inclusive
leadership and rank-and-file. Local level organizing provides opportunities
for the emergence of new leaders, including more women, people of color,

and immigrants. Drawing from the ranks empowers the membership; relying on our own builds pride and confidence. Rank-and-file organizers are also more likely to be effective because they are closer to the daily experiences and concerns of workers.

The experience of the American Federation of State, County and Municipal Employees (AFSCME) District Council 1707 (DC 1707) provides a window on the issues involved in organizing at the local level within a union led by women of color. This experience offers a number of important strategies for revitalizing the labor movement as well as evidence of the effectiveness of directing resources for organizing to the local level.

BUILDING A CULTURE OF ORGANIZING: THE NATIONAL AND HISTORICAL CONTEXT

Union organizing takes place in an economic and political context. As the national political arm of organized labor, the AFL-CIO has a responsibility to create a favorable organizing environment, a responsibility unfulfilled by the previous generation of AFL-CIO leaders. These leaders, along with many American workers, were hypnotized by the false notion that the prosperity of the 1950s and 1960s was a normal state of affairs to which the country would soon return. The hard times beginning in the 1970s seemed a temporary aberration. Labor leaders were lulled into this false sense of security in part because they had experienced decades of post-war economic expansion and plenty, when it was relatively easy to negotiate contracts, win improvements, and grow the membership. As a result, organizing budgets shriveled and the title "organizer" became synonymous with "sinecure" in many unions, a post given to a loyal member of the leadership team. Organizing was more alive in the professional and service sectors where the leadership was newer and unburdened by nostalgia for labor's "good old days."

As hindsight makes clear, we were never to return to the post-World War II years, when the industrial base of Germany, Japan, Britain, France, and the former Soviet Union lay completely in ruins. Those years were, in reality, the aberration. Normal conditions returned with a vengeance as we watched the living standards of other industrial countries surpass our own, in part because they focused their resources on education, machinery and technology. In recent years, conditions for U.S. workers have deteriorated further, as the policies of global financial institutions and our own government have created conditions favorable to corporate exploitation, including sweatshop labor, child labor, prison labor, unsafe and polluting production practices, and union-free environments in former agricultural regions of the world.

All of these developments have led to an inevitable decline in union membership. When a unionized company leaves to take advantage of such conditions in another country, no amount of strategic planning on the part of a union will keep our members working. Labor's failure to use its political power to prevent corporate flight has created a tremendous insecurity in the American labor force, which has made organizing much more difficult. This insecurity, a response to corporate relocation and downsizing, the growth of contingent jobs, and the erosion of the safety net for the unemployed, was largely responsible for the election of new leadership for labor.

In addition to these economic and political trends, the following factors within the labor movement contributed to the watershed election of a new AFL-CIO leadership and a new emphasis on organizing:

1. The labor movement's current leadership includes people whose political perspective was honed during the Vietnam War years, not those of World War II. Whether they were soldiers or protestors, workers and labor leaders from this era share a resistance to the notion of government infallibility. While the previous generation might have failed to question the trade and economic policies of Democrats and Republicans, the current generation of labor tends to be more critical of both parties. Thus, they seek leadership who will question politicians and demand accountability on behalf of workers.

2. The reawakening of the powerful industrial unions, rich in resources and union experience, occurred as a somewhat belated reaction to the closing of so many huge industrial enterprises. Industrial workers can no longer deceive themselves into believing that the plant is merely closing for retooling. They have no choice but to think the unthinkable: the plant is gone and gone for good. These unions now seem ready to begin organizing sectors which have never before been unionized. They are truly the sleeping giants of labor.

3. The dramatic influx of women into the workforce has led to the emergence of a whole new corps of women leaders who are ready to organize. This is the case particularly in the many fields where women workers are the majority. At a time when it takes two incomes to equal the income of one family member years ago, and when many men work at jobs with few benefits, women are quick to join and

fight for unions. This is especially true of women who are single parents—for them, a union is a life saver.

4. Emerging labor leaders of color, particularly African Americans, also bring new strength and militancy to organized labor. The experiences of these leaders in the civil rights movement, community struggles, and daily battles against racism have steeled them against the tactics of the wiliest bosses, attorneys, and public officials. In the case of DC 1707, our opponents learned long ago that a picket line of women of color is probably the labor movement's most awesome weapon.

All of these factors influenced the unprecedented election of a new AFL-CIO leadership and a new emphasis on organizing and inclusion. The Federation's leadership team is now carrying out these campaign commitments. Early on in their administration, they convened an organizing conference in St. Louis which established the goal of a commitment by every union to devote thirty percent of its dues to new organizing. While only a few unions have yet reached that goal, for the first time in many decades organizing has returned to the very core of union work. The example of top leadership traveling the country to stand shoulder to shoulder with rank-and-file workers engaged in organizing testifies to their commitment, as do their efforts to strengthen the AFL-CIO Organizing Institute.

The AFL-CIO is also focusing serious attention on labor laws that undermine organizing. The Washington legal staff is busy fighting for union rights for millions of so-called independent contractors and temp workers. The political arm is battling the Teamwork for Employees Management Act which could block union organizing drives through the reintroduction of company unions, as well as threats to overtime pay which would cost jobs.

Finally, the election of Linda Chavez-Thompson and the inclusion on the executive council of more women and people of color sends a clear message that all workers are truly valued and welcome in the house of labor. Within the ranks of labor, old divisions along racial, national, gender, craft, age, and political lines are challenged by the influence and style of the new leadership. As a result, the sense of solidarity between older and younger workers, men and women, public and private sector workers, and those with blue-, pink-, or white-collars is stronger, and appeals to unorganized workers of many kinds.

Several international unions, including AFSCME, have committed their resources to organizing as a top priority, and have undertaken high-profile campaigns in trucking, building services, airlines, health professions, among public employees, and other groups of workers. Some internationals have developed highly effective tactics and trained teams of professional organizers for these large scale campaigns. Thus, at the level of AFL-CIO leadership and of the internationals, a culture of organizing is clearly operating. To further expand organizing efforts, development of organizers and tactics at the regional and local levels is the next strategic step.

THE KEY ROLE OF DISTRICT AND LOCAL UNIONS

Organizing at the local level is critical to the growth of the labor movement for the following reasons:

1. Local unions are more likely to use rank-and-file members to supplement the efforts of paid staff.

2. Local organizers have an easier time relating to workers in their home communities, and establishing links to community-based allies and resources.

3. Directing resources to the local level and using rank-and-file members is likely to have the effect of increasing the involvement and membership of people of color and women in the labor movement.

4. Most of today's unorganized workers are employed in units too small to merit the deployment of international reps; the use of lower-paid local organizers eliminates housing and transportation costs, and renders longer, more difficult campaigns affordable and possible.

Concentrating more of labor's resources at the regional and local level will create a more inclusive, grassroots "organizing culture" among American workers. Unions have organized a variety of workers through affiliations and the expansion of collective bargaining rights in the public sector, but the hard core organizing of new workers has generally been done by locals, who very aggressively went out and scoured their communities for workers who needed a union. It is a task best left at the local level. International unions should go after new industries, such as banking.

This orientation has implications for how resources are allocated by the AFL-CIO. There are many locals who have organizing experience already, but lack the funds to pay organizers. Why not identify those locals and provide the resources to field one or more organizers? There are other locals that already have both the funds and the will to organize, but lack experienced and trained organizers. In such cases, the AFL-CIO could offer in-depth training for rank-and-file workers who then return to organize for their locals.

Finally, there is no way to turn millions of rank-and-file trade unionists into the eyes, ears, and mouths of a huge organizing effort without mobilizing the locals. If the AFL-CIO or the international unions create the impression that organizing is a high tech profession best left in the hands of shock battalions of trained cadre, the rank-and-file are relegated to the role of spectators. Instead, the AFL-CIO and the internationals should provide assistance to locals who want to organize and thereby create rank-and-file labor activists.

LOCAL ORGANIZING: THE DISTRICT COUNCIL 1707 EXPERIENCE

A review of DC 1707's organizing program in 1995 revealed that success would require a major commitment of time and attention by the union's top leadership, the re-establishment of an active organizing department, and the development of leadership among organizers. Our direct experience in the communities of metropolitan New York convinced us that there were countless unorganized workers ready to be unionized. A quick survey confirmed this belief, and we soon assembled a solid target list of thousands of workers. We kept the same organizing team in place, but our new leadership provided an important source of strength and strategies necessary for organizing. The leadership of the union was now composed entirely of African American and Latina women, including an executive director who had many years of organizing experience. The professional council staff, drawn from all racial and national backgrounds, was rich with individuals who had proven their commitment to the empowerment of communities and workers.

We also received a contribution of $10,000 monthly from the international union to support our organizing efforts. This, along with our deep roots among local workers and their communities, provided the base for our successful organizing drives. We knew the targeted workers and understood their need for union protection and benefits. Over the next two years, we organized more workers than we had in the past ten.

CREATING EFFECTIVE ORGANIZERS

Our organizing victories are due in large part to our strategies for selecting, recruiting, and training individuals to take on the difficult job of organizing. We believe that if we recruit the right people as organizers and train them well, the number of workers organized will be in direct proportion to the number of organizers in the field. When selecting organizers, we are guided by the following principles:

1. Organizers should be rank-and-file workers who share the kinds of work and life experiences that resonate with the people being organized.

Although our union participated actively in Union Summer, and we support efforts to bring the message of labor to college campuses, our hiring preference is for organizers who are also workers. They may not necessarily have the same job titles or work in the same industry as those they are organizing, but they should be people who have had some experience in the world of work. Because of this belief, we look for good stewards, for people who have worked in their shops, defended their fellow workers, and demonstrated that they can do these things in a competent manner. We look for people who have handled problems common to workers, not only grievances, but also health and benefits issues, and for those who have shown enthusiasm for the union by working with communities and volunteer groups within the union. This is our profile for an organizer.

What is important is the organizer's ability to empathize with fellow workers. They must also be trustworthy and of good character. What organizing involves is taking good workers, who are at a very vulnerable period in their career, workers who are not yet getting any of the protection of a union contract, and moving them from powerlessness to power. During that period of time, the most precious thing in their lives are the jobs which support their families. They put their faith in the union, represented by the organizer, even though they know this jeopardizes their jobs. Thus, organizers must engender confidence as they encourage workers to stand up for themselves.

The organizer has to be a person who functions primarily as a leader; that is the essential ingredient. We have found, for the most part, that rank-and-file workers, whose lives reflect the working class experience and who have a history of speaking up for workers' rights, make the best leaders and therefore the best organizers. They are not visiting the working class, they are not helping the working class, they are of the working class; fellow workers empowering their friends, neighbors, and relatives. If you do not come from the struggle of workers resisting insults and employer arrogance, it is very difficult to express that struggle for the dignity of workers. You cannot read about it in a book or imagine it. In the end, you either are defending your class and your family and where you came from, or you are not.

Of course, there are people who can learn how workers feel and imagine how they are treated, and there are daughters and sons of the wealthy who can bring us skills that we do not have. We should welcome them to the house of labor. But our union prefers to select organizers that emerge from the struggle of working people.

Organizers must be willing to work extremely hard, and to practice a range of organizing tactics and strategies. Organizing requires both discipline and flexibility. For example, last summer, we had three ongoing campaigns. Our organizers were out in 101 degree weather, and we had to send bottles of cold water out with them. Organizers must also turn out when there are inches of ice on the ground, and they must be conscious of the fact that the bus drivers they are organizing have had to drive children to day-care centers on that ice all day. Organizing may require waking up at 5:00 in the morning and working on into the night, but organizers must be ready to endure the same tough conditions that the workers they are organizing live with every day. We recognize that this can be hard on those with family obligations. One of our most successful organizers has seven children. Good organizers have to struggle to balance these competing commitments, and the union has to support them as they do so.

2. Unions must provide training that prepares organizers for their work.

Once an organizing director selects rank-and-file workers with the qualities described above, it is his/her responsibility to ensure that organizers have the skills, knowledge, and resources necessary to function as leaders of unorganized workers. Each organizer must understand how workers are currently surviving in a hostile workplace and how conditions would improve under a union contract. One cannot assume that new organizers understand how unions empower workers, nor can new organizers be expected to develop this understanding without training and education from their union. Although our union tries to choose organizers from rank-and-file workers, we are often surprised by some of the notions even these members hold regarding what unions are and what they do. After all, even dedicated union members get their information to some degree from anti-union media, anti-union local culture. Because of such misconceptions about unions, organizing departments have to provide programs that teach organizers that a union is not an insurance company, or merely an organization to handle grievances, nor is a union a top-down machine.

Organizers must also understand that the union is not a miracle worker, and that the struggle to improve people's lives does not happen in a weekend. Union campaigns are won primarily because organizers understand how a union empowers workers, and because workers understand that they are stronger when they are acting together. For this reason, organizers need to be familiar with all the relevant practical information, including state and federal labor laws, and all other laws and regulations that have an impact on working people. They need to understand their union's contracts, bylaws, and constitution as well as the history of their international union, district, and local.

Training for organizers is critical because everything an organizer does must be infused with a sense of the power of the union. It is the organizer's job to do away with all distortions, lies, obstacles, and fears that stand between workers and their decision to participate in the struggle for union representation.

SUCCESSFUL ORGANIZING TACTICS

Although the union has had an organizing grant from the international for four years, our initial use of the grant was ineffectual. In 1993, the union only organized twenty-seven people in two workplaces during the entire year. In 1995-96 under a new director of organization, we organized 1,800 workers from twenty-three different workplaces. Clearly, we needed something other than more organizing dollars. We had to change the organizing tactics we employed as well as the philosophy and strategy underpinning our organizing effort.

Prior to 1995, our strategy was to look for "hot" places where the workers were angry. Worker anger was considered the essential requisite for a target. Our organizers would go in, sign up a few angry workers, and turn the job of organizing over to a designated committee of workers. They would then meet with the committee every few weeks and review the progress of the organizing campaign. If the committee in the workplace collected enough union cards, they would file for a National Labor Relations Board (NLRB) election. Usually, they did not do very well. Unorganized workers with little experience in unions, when left on their own with minimum contact with the organizers, were no match for union-busting attorneys.

In 1995, the union decided that if this practice were continued, the committee of workers doing the actual organizing should be paid, and the organizers paid by the union should go back to their shops. We are now insisting that our organizers get to know every worker who has put their faith in this union, and actively help lead them to a better place. If that requires meeting with them at the worksite, near the worksite, visiting their house, or at least calling them on the phone, we are going to know the people who are involved in our elections. Of course, we still form committees of workers among those we are trying to organize, because this engages them in organizing themselves. But our organizers now support them actively and constantly.

This approach, which is based on building strong relationships with workers in targeted shops, works best with rank-and-file organizers. Anyone can run an arms-length campaign of dropping cards and leaflets, or a high tech polling and mailing campaign. Our approach, however, requires organizers who can quickly get close to workers.

Some of the organizers adopted this new approach and some resisted it. Those who adopted a one-on-one personal style were successful; those who did not were not. Now, the union runs survey sheets on everybody involved in a campaign. Every ten days, our staff is expected to fill out a form reporting in detail on one-on-one discussions with each worker preparing for a union election. As a result, we know how opinion is leaning in the course of the campaign. A frequent phone poll tells us, on almost a daily basis, whether or not the management message is reaching people, and whether our ideas are moving people. We also spend time learning the social relations of the workplace. For example, we have organized people on the basis that we know four or five of the workers watch "Melrose Place" together, and we show up that night with pizza.

The organizer must be prepared to respond honestly and clearly to the variety of issues that emerge in an organizing campaign. The organizer's response must be bold and aggressive, but responsible. The organizer must understand the true extent and limits of union power. We will not tolerate the organizer who suddenly becomes very militant and says, for instance, "We will manage to achieve a twenty-five percent increase in your salary next year!"

There is a tendency for young organizers, who are good, working people, to sometimes forget that the worker out there is just a person like their aunt, their uncle, their neighbor, their friend, the woman down the block, the man around the corner. Organizers need to be calmed down and encouraged to talk with people as if they were talking to their own brother and sister—in a rational, common sense, confident fashion.

We try to sign up workers, collect home addresses, and form a shop committee before the boss knows we are there. Once we believe the boss knows a union campaign is underway, we encourage our organizers to act boldly. One organizer, a former shop steward, would only approach workers out of sight of the employer who knew a campaign was underway. When the workers would come by, he would whisper and flash a union card as if it were dangerous or pornographic. He would tell the workers, from the shadow of trees or bushes, that they had a right to join a union and need not be afraid. Ironically, his whole approach broadcast fear! The more he hid, the more he tried to protect the workers, the more the workers got the message that there was something fearful about this union business. We convinced him to try another approach. The union provided a folding table, a union hat, piles of union literature, and sat him as legally close to the door of the place as possible—with balloons on his table! The union's approach was to present a bold and aggressive strategy in terms that this organizer, who happened to be very religious, would understand. His role was compared to that of a preacher bringing good news to people, telling them they are finally going to be free of everyday worries, such as whether the supervisor is going to arbitrarily make their life miserable or transfer them, or lay them off for a younger worker. The union would now defend them and empower them so that they could defend themselves. The organizer was encouraged to see his work as lawful, and as a mission to proclaim the rights of working people. In this way, the training that organizers receive encourages them to see the labor movement as part of the larger movement for social justice, and to project this message to other workers.

When the organizer in question took this approach, he got a majority and won the election. Because he exhibited confidence and courage, the workers showed confidence and courage. Of course, to sustain this confidence, a union must be prepared to mount an effective legal and job-action defense if any lead worker is fired. Unions must offer such workers jobs in union shops or even temporary jobs on staff; this is part of the covenant a union makes with workers fighting for the union. We write to the employer listing our key committee people in the shop (with their approval), warning the employer not to take action against them. This gives us a strong NLRB position if an unfair labor practice occurs.

It is common practice now for employers to hire union-busting law firms; our union has had to develop a strategy for responding to such tactics and overcoming them. Our organizers try to demystify the power of authority that the combination of bosses and their lawyers represent. For example, we sometimes take advantage of the general distrust of lawyers to demonize them in workers' eyes. We may point out features of the lawyer's lifestyle that emphasize his shared class interest with management. In an organizing campaign, lawyers and management will always bring up the issue of dues: "The union is a business, the business is to collect dues from you." That is why it is so essential that organizers know the difference between the union and a business. They have got to have that difference in their heart. They cannot recruit people to the union movement if they have the vision of an insurance company. Organizing should always be a fight over the worth of workers, not the cost of dues. Organizers should talk about the substandard pay in terms of humane values: "The boss must think that is all you are worth, because that is all he is paying you." In this way, they demonstrate how management undervalues the contribution of workers to the enterprise. Unions, on the other hand, place the highest value on each worker. So we ask workers: "What happens when you take your kid to the doctor?" We emphasize that workers should not have to worry about the bills, because we know that it is difficult enough to be worrying about a sick son, daughter, or spouse. In this way, we demonstrate that we have different priorities than the boss who could not care less. We show that unions have a culture that emphasizes a human movement as opposed to a business view. We have a different vision of what people are worth.

Finally, while there is no right formula for organizing successfully, many unions' practices are rooted in a demoralizing and unwarranted lack of confidence in labor's own ranks. Within the collective experience of our rank-and-file workers lies the base on which successful organizing rests. The drive to organize comes from workers, workers in our shops, workers in our organizing drives, workers who are related to union members. They share the experience and the needs of working people; this gives them the motivation to act on their power and to defend their own interests.

Successful organizing in the labor movement involves a commitment to and identification with workers—the ability to create a sense of teamwork. The key is that unions keep close to their own members. Above all tactical or philosophical positions is this question: Does the leader see himself or herself primarily as a fellow worker? It is only logical that it takes a rank-and-file union to develop a corps of rank-and-file organizers. Therefore, only a democratic and activist union can expect to expand its membership.

When workers feel a sense of ownership about their union, they are more likely to become involved in all aspects of union work, including organizing.

If workers feel a strong sense of solidarity with their union and its members, if they experience what the union means in their own workplaces and their own lives, they are likely to want to build the union and to spread its message to friends, neighbors, and co-workers. DC 1707, through its newspaper, weekend events, education programs, and special conferences, tries to connect its members to the struggles of other unions, to community concerns, and to international issues relevant to our members. For example, we have hosted dignitaries and activists from South Africa's anti-apartheid movement, held conferences on women's health, and provided meeting space for welfare recipients who are organizing. As women of color who care for the children of the poor and working class of New York, our members tend to express solidarity with single mothers on welfare. Through our involvement in these kinds of movements, the members see the union as their voice and as the site for struggles around issues that concern them. They can become involved in union activities through participation in these efforts, as well as through more traditional union channels. Another vehicle for increasing the voice of members in DC 1707 has been the borough meetings held periodically in each of the five boroughs of the city. We have been surprised at the turnout, even in bad weather, of members who respond to our effort to come to their neighborhoods and meet with them close to home. By increasing the places, times, and ways of being involved in its activities, the union fosters greater opportunity for participation and involvement. This, in turn, creates more potential rank-and-file organizers for our campaigns.

Union activists often lament that it is difficult to get people to union meetings; all of the arguments about long travel, and people's busy schedules, their second jobs are true. But the struggle remains. Unions must encourage and sustain rank-and-file leadership if they are to be successful in organizing at the local level. The scheduling and timing of union events and activities must reflect the needs, interest, and participation of rank-and-file members. The labor movement must continue to struggle to involve members, and must find the ways to do it. For example, if unions assemble workers and then an official lectures them for an hour, never asking for their opinions, and never giving them a chance to vote on anything, it is going to be hard to get them back to the next meeting. If union meetings take the form of broadcasting to members, rather than engaging them in dialogue, then union meetings are competing with more entertaining TV networks. If workers are called to a meeting where they have no opportunity to voice an opinion, they will not come back very often, if at all. If unions become more inclusive and democratic, we can become the one place in society where members can have a voice.

Union members who participate in making decisions are more likely to attend meetings and take responsibility for carrying out the decisions. Working people, in general, do not like to waste time on philosophical arguments, but do appreciate an opportunity to let their opinion be known and to vote a matter up or down. This is why when DC 1707 goes into negotiating a contract, we practice democracy on the negotiating committee. We do not submit the contract to the membership until the rank-and-file negotiating committee is satisfied with it. Then it is sent to the membership, all of whom get to vote on the contract. This practice, while it lengthens the negotiating process, is essential because it tells workers that we, as union leaders, feel this is their contract, their union.

HOW THE AFL-CIO CAN SUPPORT ORGANIZING, INCLUSION AND A POLITICAL AGENDA THAT BUILDS UNIONS

The new leadership of the AFL-CIO ought to initiate a drive to get organizing money down to the local level as quickly and directly as possible, and to support this increased funding with technical assistance for training and research. There are some large locals within internationals that already have the requisite experience and ability to organize; they only need an infusion of funds to begin. The $10,000 a month that our union receives from the international has allowed us to put five more organizers out on the street and, as a result, to achieve significant victories. There are many other locals in the AFL-CIO that may have substantial organizing leads but are too small to field even one part-time organizer. The AFL-CIO has access to experienced people who are able to analyze the potential of a targeted workplace, and could dispatch or make small grants to assist locals who lack personnel, experience, or money. It does not matter whether 500 workers get organized by a local of 20,000 or a local of 700; rather, it is essential to utilize this network of thousands of locals who could have an immediate role in organizing. Currently, such locals are discouraged from pursuing organizing opportunities because they lack funds, expertise, or staff. The consequence is that such targets languish, unorganized, year after year after year.

There is no contradiction between the strategies of targeted efforts by smaller locals, on the one hand, and industry-wide drives by large unions, on the other. The labor movement needs to be involved in both kinds of efforts.

Locals that need to be actively organizing must have resources to do this. This is particularly important if we want to see the leadership composition of DC 1707 replicated in more unions, so that it reflects the rank-and-file in the ways essential for building the labor movement. By giving resources to unions at the local level, people of color can be offered opportunities to become organizers in their communities and workplaces. This can provide a path to active union leadership for women and people of color, and help build not only larger unions but also more inclusive ones.

In addition to decentralizing funding, it is imperative that unions and the AFL-CIO project a political agenda that changes the public perception of unions. The government is heavily involved in the workplace. It is empowering to workers to know that they can have an impact on the political system. The real impact of political work must be a major change in the climate within which bargaining and organizing takes place. For instance, our union managed to get through the state legislature a bill which blocks state-funded agencies from using public money to fund anti-union drives. The majority of taxpayers do not want their taxes used to bash unions, but that is unfortunately how their money is sometimes spent. We also helped the Living Wage bill through the New York City Council. Although this does not bring people into our union, it raises the standards for thousands of unorganized workers. Among these 10,000 people now getting a living wage, whose lot has been improved by the political efforts of the labor movement, are those who will find their way into various unions. Our political action ought to be in defense of all working people; if we succeed, we create conditions in which workers get the courage and the means to handle themselves in the workplace, to challenge management, and to join and build unions.

CONCLUSION

The experience of DC 1707 demonstrates that the use of rank-and-file workers as organizers, the development of aggressive organizing strategies that build on commonalities among workers, and greater support of local-level organizing can achieve the goals of a revitalized labor movement. Such an approach not only increases membership, but can result in a more democratic and inclusive labor movement, and one whose leadership more accurately reflects the race, gender, and class composition of the workforce.

MOVING INNOVATION FROM THE MARGINS TO THE CENTER

Janice Fine

These are dark times for labor unions in America. To become the powerful vehicle for the economic interests of working people that it has been in the past, the labor movement must reinvent itself[1] once again. But not by reinventing the wheel. Rather, it must hone existing forms and add new ones to its repertoire of union models. There are abundant signs that it is doing exactly this. The change in leadership of the AFL-CIO in 1995 came during an era of remarkable experimentation in local and international unions. And so today—as well as historically—we can find ideas and models for labor's future growth. To ensure that innovative practices move from the margins to the center of daily practice in union halls and international headquarters across the country, the challenge for the AFL-CIO's leadership and staff is to take a close look at the rich array of experiments now taking place—and then to pass them on.

At the core of innovations taking place in the labor movement today are two ideas: labor market unionism and community unionism. Labor market unionism is the result of labor's rethinking economics. It boils down to the realization that in an economy that is overwhelmingly unorganized it is not enough to organize firm-by-firm. Instead, unions have to craft strategies to organize whole regions or industrial sectors if they are to take wages out of competition across a city or an industry. Rethinking economics leads to a rethinking of politics as well. Community unionism is the political corollary of labor market unionism: If, increasingly, the community has become the fundamental economic entity that connects people, then taking wages out of competition across a city or industry is a community organizing project where public policy is often the central battleground.

RECLAIMING INDUSTRIAL AND CRAFT ORGANIZING MODELS AND LABOR MARKET UNIONISM

Revitalizing the labor movement begins with questioning the traditional stories we have been telling about the reasons for labor's decline and what can be done to reverse it. Rather than seeing labor's decline as the inevitable consequence of overarching trends in the economy or society, it is time to identify the institutional factors inside unions that have contributed to the decline—that are easiest for labor to do something about. Every union can cite a host of external reasons for their decline, from globalization to technological change or rising anti-union sentiment. But seldom do unions analyze the internal factors that may have contributed just as much to their failure and over which they have a great deal more control.

By carefully reexamining its own history, a union can find new strategies for organizing. Unions must recover the effective practice of craft and industrial unionism and perfect new practices that can succeed in today's economic context. When industrial and craft organizing models are practiced at their best, many of the new labor market union strategies are not such major departures.[2]

IBEW'S HISTORY LESSON[3]

The leadership of the International Brotherhood of Electrical Workers (IBEW) has dramatically changed its view of the root causes of the union's decline. Instead of attributing the decline of the trades largely to outside forces—rising anti-unionism, economic recession and technological changes—the new thinking locates the problem within the unions themselves. Today, IBEW's leaders believe that their own exclusionary practices contributed decisively to the rise of the non-union sector in their trade.

Early in their history, the trades recruited all those employed in a given trade—the original "bottom-up" organizing approach. Organizers went out and "sold the union idea, the union spirit, the union principle...there were no applicants for membership knocking on the door and wanting in...."[4] Organizers were not selling jobs—they were approaching employed tradesmen and selling them on unionism itself. Tradesmen were not joining the union because they expected it to find them work, but because they wanted to be part of a community of mechanics.

After years of hardscrabble organizing, many of the construction unions were able to create a "loose monopoly of qualified tradesmen." Advocates of industrial unionism within the IBEW successfully argued against high initiation fees and dues. And so, admission fees were either non-existent or quite low, and "the only test of a tradesman's qualifications for union membership was his ability to secure and retain employment....If a worker held a job in the building and construction industry, he belonged in the trades unions."[5]

The union monopoly never became absolute, so there *was* an enduring need to continue bottom-up organizing. But there was enough of a monopoly established for local unions to become quite powerful. As bottom-up organizing continued to diminish the supply of qualified non-union tradespeople in the labor market, employers found that they had to use union craftspeople to complete projects. Mike Lucas, former organizing director of the IBEW and key thinker on the topic of organizing in the building trades, points to this period as the beginning of a shift to "top-down organizing" or "the securing of work by selling owners, users, and employers on the advantages of operating under union agreements"—as opposed to bottom-up organizing, which relies on maintaining a loose monopoly of qualified tradespeople to control the work. The trade unions, initially at the behest of employers and later on their own initiative, began to sign exclusive collective bargaining agreements that assured a reliable supply of skilled tradespeople. The system worked well for contractors who wanted to restrict competition for jobs and knew they could accomplish this if only a small number of contractors had access to large numbers of qualified craftspeople.

Essentially, the employers offered the unions a quid-pro-quo—the contractor associations would deal only with the union locals if the union locals would deal only with the contractor associations. One of the results of this arrangement was that signatory contractors became less and less interested in smaller jobs with lower profit-margins. In the short term, union members benefited from this strategy because they were able to earn top dollar while the contractors simply passed along wage costs to their customers—who had no other choice but to use these contractors, since they had a loose monopoly on skilled labor.

Thus, in the post-war period, from the 1950s through the 1970s, top-down organizing—which was always dependent for its strength on bottom up organizing—came to predominate in the trades. What was a logical complementary strategy at the time—that unions would take steps to reinforce their loose monopoly over the labor supply by requiring that workers refuse to work for any contractor who had not signed a collective bargaining agreement—came to replace bottom-up organizing of tradespersons.

Three major mistakes contributed to the decline of the building trades. The first mistake was limiting contractor access to the hiring hall. Excluding some contractors from access to the labor supply created an enormous demand on their part for another source of labor. The second mistake was limiting union membership more and more over the years—"country club unionism." These first two mistakes created a dangerous synergy: employers in search of a labor force and a labor force in search of employers. Finally, during peak years of demand for union labor, locals actually temporarily brought on "white ticket hands"—tradespeople who were trained by members and worked alongside them but were denied membership in the unions. The first two mistakes yielded a set of non-union employers on the one hand and a force of non-union workers seeking employment on the other. Then, by creating a cadre of skilled tradespersons and refusing them access to membership, the unions themselves helped to build the competitive capacity of non-union employers. These white ticketers became the nucleus of a skilled workforce for non-union employers who could now oversee bigger and bigger jobs that had always been the unions' exclusive domain.

While the local unions and the large contractors enjoyed the fruits of their collusion, contractors who had been frozen out of the hiring hall worked hard to break the union's monopoly over skilled labor. Beginning with smaller jobs, over time non-union contractors brought on white ticket hands and developed other strategies for training their own employees on the job and became increasingly competitive with union contractors. They eventually expanded to larger jobs and formed associations of non-union contractors, pledging to working together to destroy labor's monopoly.

Today, Jim Rudicil, director of construction organizing, travels the country encouraging a complete departure from past practice: "One rule we threw away after 1947 was organizing... But what rule did we keep enforcing? No union workers working on non-union jobs...What did we do? We ensured full employment for the non-union worker! Has anybody been teaching non-union workers their rights, has anybody been turning in non-union contractors for violations? No—because we don't let our people go on to these jobs!"[6]

Rudicil argues that instead of banning members from working non-union, locals must tell members it is their sacred duty to actually take these jobs. In the process, unemployed workers are off the bench and earning a paycheck—while they are organizing the unorganized on these jobsites! Rudicil argues that instead of putting up picketlines at jobsites where some trades are union and others are not, forcing trades that are union to leave the job, unions should encourage the union trades to stay on the job and help organize non-union workers.[7]

This "revisionist history" of the trades has led to a return to first principles: a focus on re-establishing a loose monopoly over the labor market by organizing all non-union electricians into the IBEW—bottom-up organizing. This is the essential leverage that unions need to turn a non-union market around. And it is this analysis that is now informing organizing strategies across the country in the IBEW and across the building trades.

SEIU: GETTING OUTSIDE THE PRIVATIZATION BOX

Public sector unions are facing state revenue shortfalls, budget cutting and a growing ideological shift toward the privatization of public services. Service Employees International Union (SEIU), like all public sector unions, has waged bitter battles against privatization in state legislatures and city halls across the country. The union has also responded by building progressive statewide tax and budget coalitions and by launching public relations campaigns to improve the image of public employees.

But privatization continues to loom as a major threat to public employee unions. There is growing awareness in the international and in SEIU's public sector locals that privatization cannot be viewed as the end—as something to be fought until the horse leaves the barn and then the battle is over. SEIU now has a pilot project in which the union will follow their work to the private sector, still targeting the state as the ultimate employer—and in the process, take on the whole notion of what is public and what is private. SEIU Local 509 represents workers in Massachusetts' mental hospitals. As these hospitals have closed or ceased to accept new patients, and mental health care has become decentralized in small community-based centers, the union lost many members. And so, over the past two years, the union has embarked on a campaign to organize the 16,000 workers who are now in the private sector delivering community-based mental health care.

In the old days, the union would have gone out and tried to organize each individual site and company, but now the union views the companies as contractors and the "owner" or true employer as the state. Sandy Felder, former president of 509 explained:

> If our workers were in the public sector now, we would have one employer, but now we have 600 different ones. The union would have dealt with one employer and 10 bargaining units, now we would have 600 bargaining units. To go out and organize one by one, these workers would never be represented, you don't have the resources to get power for that many people, that is why we have to do it differently, we are not going to do it one at a time....We have with all of these little companies, all serving the mentally ill and retarded, all on contracts.... But who is paying the contracts? The state...We in 509 have been in the forefront of opposing privatization—we've sponsored legislation and demonstrated in order to save our workers' jobs. But now there is this unorganized, unrepresented workforce that in many cases used to work for the state. They may be a threat to my workers because they work for less, but they deserve a voice, too; they need to be organized. So we have an intensive campaign to get our members to change their attitudes toward the private sector workers—I have to tell them that a lot of these workers used to be our members. They are us, or they used to be us....[8]

Local 509's plan is to talk to workers in the small private worksites about the union and hopefully over time to get a majority to sign cards. The union will engage in coordinated campaigns across worksites and bring public pressure to bear on the state. The ultimate goal is to get the state to acknowledge itself as the ultimate employer and grant voluntary recognition to the union, thus avoiding innumerable long drawn out National Labor Relations Board elections. Local 509 then hopes that they will win not only voluntary recognition by the state, but acceptance of a first across-the-board contract.

The other part of Local 509's campaign is to approach employers directly. Some of the community-based centers are not particularly open to a partnership with the union yet and so will require a more straight union organizing approach. But others are run by employers who are potential allies in the fight for high quality care and increased funding from the state. By viewing the state as the ultimate employer, Local 509 now has a new way of looking at these providers. This new view is reflected in the language of a new compact that a group of employers signed on December 12, 1995:

> ...The need for a more powerful alliance to secure appropriate government support for publicly funded mental health and mental retardation services prompted the parties to explore the concept of a new labor/management relationship. The parties will continue to focus some of their efforts on influencing both the state administration, the legislature, and the public towards that end. All parties acknowledge that the choice to be represented by a union rests with employees. Together we pledge to foster an atmosphere in which that choice may be freely exercised by all.[9]

Once the union has demonstrated majority support among employees at each agency, the providers will recognize the union and undertake to negotiate a joint, multiemployer, collective bargaining agreement.

Both the IBEW and the SEIU 509 stories point to the importance of recovering historical practices and reclaiming models of craft and industrial unionism that work. To sharpen its strategy and revitalize its model of craft unionism, the IBEW went back to the organizing philosophy and practice of its founders. SEIU 509 adapted to the radically changed structure of industry by drawing upon the early lessons and practices of industrial unionism to forge new approaches to labor market unionism.[10] As we saw in the IBEW example, craft unionism organized workers by occupation and was premised upon controlling access to training, setting and enforcing standards, and limiting the labor supply in a particular occupation. Employers signed exclusive agreements with unions, and craftspeople were not allowed to work for non-signatory employers. Collective bargaining agreements and benefits were not tied to specific firms but directly to the union. The union operated a hiring hall and administered health insurance and other benefits which were portable from employer to employer and financed by employers who had signed the collective bargaining agreement. Today, many craft unions have lost their loose monopoly over the labor market and are struggling to recapture it.[11]

Industrial unionism organized workers based upon their employment in a specific industry. In the past, the union negotiated industry-wide agreements with an association of industry firms at the regional and national level. Through the mid-seventies, this "pattern bargaining" created de facto industry-level wage and benefit standards. But over the past twenty years, the number of industries engaging in industrial-level collective bargaining has dramatically declined.

Both forms of unionism focused on labor markets—occupational, industrial, or territorial. Labor market unionism—taking wages out of competition by re-establishing a loose monopoly over the labor supply— necessitates a strategic approach to organizing. Craft unionism makes local (territorial) labor markets the strategic and organizational focus. Industrial unionism makes industrial labor markets the strategic and organizational focus, and works toward master agreements at the highest level appropriate to the industry. Both approaches go beyond the worksite and firm levels.

Union organizing today must be more strategic than ever before. In an economy that is overwhelmingly unorganized, unions have to concentrate on sectoral and territorial strategies that succeed in taking wages out of competition across a city or an industry. There are few examples of where organizing one company in isolation can succeed. And organizing across firms takes away one of management's most powerful arguments—loss of competitiveness.

As relationships between workers and firms become more temporary and workers are less and less able to rely on a single employer to supply training, benefits, and upward mobility, unions may come to serve this function. In fact, unions could become the only fixed point in the changing universe of work. But unions cannot organize, bargain, and provide benefits one firm at a time. They have to target an entire labor market.

THE MILWAUKEE CENTRAL LABOR COUNCIL

Labor market unionism is being practiced by central labor councils as well as by local unions. Central councils lend themselves especially well to multiunion organizing and organizing across different sectors of the local economy, because they bring together a range of unions, and because they have historically acted as political centers of the local labor movement. Thus they are especially qualified to analyze the labor market as a whole, to devise economic development and organizing strategies, and to mobilize elected officials, government agencies, and local firms to support a cooperative strategy.[12]

Like many rustbelt cities, Milwaukee experienced severe deindustrialization over the past decades. The service-sector jobs that now dominate pay much less than the blue-collar jobs workers lost, and even so, there are not enough of them to go around. Bruce Colburn, president of the

Milwaukee Central Labor Council, working with Joel Rogers and an economic think tank Rogers runs out of the University of Wisconsin, recently organized the Campaign for Sustainable Milwaukee, an economic development and organizing plan for the city. Campaign organizers began by researching the state of Milwaukee's economy, and then developed a strategy for creating jobs—at "family-supporting wages." The organization brought unions and community organizations together with economic development and social service agencies to create a comprehensive blueprint for democratic local economic development that addresses four areas: jobs and training, credit, transportation and the environment and education. Representatives from a broad spectrum of the community served on task forces to develop goals and public policies for each area. The campaign recently received a Casey Foundation grant for several million dollars to carry out these plans.

The jobs and training task force concluded that Milwaukee had the potential to become a "prime location for advanced manufacturing." To get there, "Milwaukee needs to use government and community power to promote high-wage jobs while discouraging the growth of low wage ones. At the same time, it needs to support firms willing to take the high-wage path—to enable them to remain competitive, directly build community capacity to help steer the economy; and make sure that low-wage workers are not left behind in the transition."[13] Specific policy recommendations included:

- an industry training partnership between local government, schools, and firms to prepare a more highly skilled workforce trained for jobs for which there is demand in the local labor market;

- community-based training businesses where community people learn and develop new small businesses;

- an industrial extension program that provides technical assistance to local firms to continually expose them to cutting edge product development, marketing, technology choice, work organization, and quality control techniques;

- corporate accountability through the "Milwaukee Accord," which would hold government contractors and recipients of public resources accountable to minimal standards regarding workers' rights, equal opportunity, living wages, benefits, working conditions, environmental compliance, and "clawback" legislation to recover public funds from companies that violated community standards; and,

- pro-union policies including non-interference in union elections and working in full partnerships with unions inside and outside of firms.

COMMUNITY UNIONISM[14]

As people move from employer to employer more frequently, the community—as opposed to the plant or craft—becomes our fundamental economic and social base. To succeed, labor unions must combine "labor market unionism" with its political or civic corollary—"community unionism." The definition of community unionism is union organizing that takes place across territorial and industrial communities much larger than a single workplace. Community unionism recognizes that a worker's identities and interests are much broader than just who they work for or what they do. Workers have different identities, some that are connected to occupation or employer, some that are not—but most of which are relevant to organizing.

Because so many enterprises that are prime organizing targets have high turnover, unions need to reach workers *before* they are even employed there. That way, workers associate the union with their interests before they even get the job. By fighting for broader community concerns and establishing itself as a key institution in the community, the union can immediately gain the support of workers in a local organizing drive—because the union is already important to people's lives.

Community organizations, traditionally viewed as supportive allies of labor—good to have as part of labor/community coalitions when the chips are down—should instead be seen as partners. Community support and community participation are different. Too often, labor builds and enters into coalitions exclusively on its own terms and solicits organizations, late in the game, to support something it has already decided to do.

In Baltimore's newly redeveloped inner harbor area, where service-sector jobs run the gamut from janitorial to fast food to retail sales, the community is the cohesive economic unit for low-wage workers. Thus, fighting to enact a living wage that benefited low-income workers across a range of employers, Baltimoreans United In Leadership Development (BUILD) has succeeded in winning something that low-income workers across the city would value.

Climbing Jacob's Ladder to a Living Wage—BUILD's Living Wage Effort

> "Contractors wiped their feet on us and we just had to take it,
> because we had no voice....And the tax money we paid based on the
> wages we earned funded the contractors who were paying us below
> the poverty-line wages....That's why we could sign up 70 percent of
> workers in this bus yard for Solidarity."

> —Macon Jones, Bus Driver, Gladney Transportation

> "People didn't know or realize how a person really lived off such a
> low wage. A lot of our building's tenants thought this was just spending
> money and that we were not trying to make a living. People did have
> other jobs, but you had to have it just to pay the bills."

> —Renee Brown, Janitor, World Trade Center (earned $170.00
> biweekly before the living wage, now earns $296.00)

More and more community and labor activists are organizing locally around jobs and the economy. Ground-breaking campaigns to pass living wage ordinances have been mounted in dozens of localities across the United States by labor and community organizations and coalitions. The Industrial Areas Foundation (IAF) pioneered the living wage strategy with the first in the nation campaign in Baltimore. The neighborhood activist Association of Community Organizations for Reform Now (ACORN), working in concert with the New Party and Sustainable America, has organized many campaigns across the country. On the labor side, the American Federation of State, County, and Municipal Employees (AFSCME), the Service Employees International Union (SEIU), Jobs with Justice, and some central labor councils have been quite involved.

Essentially, a "living wage campaign" is an effort to pass a law at the city and state level that aims to raise wages for the lowest paid workers by setting a higher minimum wage for all employees of city or state service contractors. Unlike city, state, or federal minimum wage laws, living wage campaigns do not cover employees of private companies not under contract with the government. Often organizers of living wage campaigns see extending the wage into the private sector as the next step, and there are campaigns to raise the general minimum wage afoot in a number of states and municipalities. In addition to setting a higher minimum, these proposals often contain various other provisions such as "right of first refusal" (the right of workers to retain their jobs even if the contractor for whom they work is replaced), and creation of community hiring halls. Some proposals would require that service contracts be bid on the basis of forty hour work weeks for service workers.

Living wage campaigns do more than raise wages. Just the idea of a living wage is empowering to low-income workers because it validates their realities and gives them a powerful shorthand way to express their real needs. These campaigns also put a human face on the working poor and give organizers an opportunity to talk to people about issues like contingent work.

Living wage campaigns change the public discourse about the economy by framing a public solution to what has come to be perceived by so many as their private problem—low wages. The campaigns also demonstrate to people that they can fight for laws that will have a direct impact on wages and corporate practices. The idea that taxpayer money—including that which comes from the working poor—should be used to establish and reinforce decent community wage standards is one that has broad appeal. One very powerful reason for that broad appeal is that so many people (about sixty percent of all American workers) have worked for minimum wage at some point in their lives. Another is that as more and more laid off workers find themselves faced with the prospect of taking jobs for half of their previous salaries, empathy may well transform into identification.

Three years ago, BUILD, a Baltimore IAF affiliate composed of church congregations mainly in the black community, entered into a partnership with AFSCME to organize the low-income service workers of Baltimore's burgeoning service economy. The most tangible result of that effort, so far, is the passage of the country's first municipal living-wage ordinance, which raised the hourly wage for the approximately 4,000 employees of Baltimore city service contractors forty-four percent, from $4.25 to $6.10 an hour. It was passed by the city council in December 1994, and took effect in July 1995. The campaign also galvanized the BUILD organization and established the Solidarity Sponsoring Committee (SSC), an organization of about 700 low-income service workers. The ordinance has built in annual wage adjustments, but they are not automatic—BUILD and the SSC must wage a campaign each year to get the Baltimore Board of Estimates to raise the wage. In the fall of 1995 they mounted a successful campaign to get the board to raise the wage from $6.10 to $6.60.

The Baltimore living-wage campaign is explicitly using the campaign to build an organization of low-income service workers that is intended to occupy the borderland between union and church. Jonathan Lange, lead organizer on the campaign, describes the SSC as "a little bit of church, a little bit of union, a little bit of social service and a whole lot of politics." Organizers believe that this description, combined with their intensive, one-on-one recruitment style, will help counteract any negative images or experiences black workers might have had with unions. Workers become members of the SSC by paying $10 per month in dues—$5 goes to "building the organization" and $5 goes to a modest benefit plan that includes life insurance and discounts on dental care and eyeglasses. SSC is currently looking into how to create a health benefit plan for its members.

BUILD takes leadership development seriously. To recruit people, BUILD organizers always begin with a one-on-one meeting focused upon getting to know the person and their "foundational stories." The organization has a learning and teaching culture—engaging in frequent actions that provide organizers many "teachable moments." Afterwards, organizers engage SSC members in a debriefing to draw out broad lessons about organizing strategy.[15]

BUILD has four main objectives for the immediate future. First, they are reaching out to the workers who are now covered by the living-wage law to ensure its enforcement and regular increases, as well as to build SSC's membership. Second, they plan to extend the wage to workers in the private sector by getting those employers to sign agreements, either individually or in groups. BUILD already has efforts underway at a number of private sector employers. Third, BUILD plans to address the growth of one segment of the contingent workforce—temporary workers—by starting a worker-owned temporary-employment agency which pays the living wage and provides health benefits. Fourth, BUILD is challenging the new federal "welfare reform" law passed in the summer of 1996. BUILD is demanding a moratorium on implementation of the law in Maryland until the state can find a way to use the block grant it receives from the federal government under the new law to create living-wage jobs for welfare recipients who join the workforce. Welfare recipients would be phased in only as new jobs are created.

The most striking feature of the BUILD living-wage effort is the extraordinary partnership that it reflects between the black church and the labor movement. Because of this partnership, the SSC is politically powerful and has enhanced legitimacy among rank-and-file black workers.

The labor intensive nature of the organizing outreach is a major part of what makes BUILD's work so good, but the difficulties of hand collection of dues make it difficult to "get to scale" in terms of absolute numbers of workers organized into the organization. By community organizing standards, a 700-person membership is quite respectable—especially when several hundred can be mobilized for an action. By labor union standards, it is still a modest size. If organizers want to spotlight the SSC as a promising new organizing model, it needs to be able to demonstrate larger numbers. To grow, efforts like the SSC will require both new models of membership—which they are working on—and a more serious financial commitment from the labor movement.

SSC recently won the right to dues check-off with all contractors doing work for the city of Baltimore. This is an important step, but it will require Solidarity to continually hold (and win) elections in many scattered worksites where there is high turnover. BUILD is now exploring the option of a check-off that would not require the union to have a majority in a workplace in order for an employee to choose to be a member—a new twist on the "minority unionism" puzzle. This worker-sponsored benefits plan would then contract with Solidarity to administer benefits to members.[16]

Baltimore's living-wage ordinance and the related check-off victory exemplifies a key component of community unionism—organizing strategies that are placed in the context of broader societal concerns and are often much more directly connected to politics and policy than traditional approaches. Most importantly, "worker issues" and organizing campaigns are wrapped inside *larger* issues, like asserting the right of living wages for all who work, and new paradigms of service delivery in elder care, mental health care, child care and education. A union's participation in politics—electing and targeting elected officials or fighting to pass laws—is instrumental to its organizing goals. But the political issues unions address as part of a community unionism strategy are broad, general interest issues. As a consequence, the "friends" labor is rewarding, and the "enemies" labor is punishing must be judged on the basis of broad criteria which reflect labor's view of what is in the general interest of all Americans—not one union local.

Certainly, there are union locals—like those in IBEW discussed earlier—that are pioneering labor market union approaches while not pursuing community unionism at the same time. But ultimately, labor market organizing is about re-imposing a set of community standards on wage and benefit levels in a community. It will never be possible to establish the kind of absolute monopoly over the labor supply that will result in permanently taking wages out of competition—there will always be efforts to come in and undercut local standards. Thus, it is the community that must enforce standards.

NEW IMMIGRANT ORGANIZING

From New York to Los Angeles, immigrant workers are a growing presence in everything from agricultural and landscaping work to garment production. These workers are often exploited by largely non-union employers, who take advantage of the lack of enforcement of labor standards for immigrant workers, and play on workers' fears of deportation. Historically, immigrant workers have had no place to go when they are arbitrarily dismissed, not paid for their work, paid significantly less than "native" workers, sexually harassed, or injured on the job.

But over the past few years, immigrant worker centers have cropped up in Texas, Florida, New York, California, Virginia, North Carolina, and Massachusetts. While several of the centers provide services including legal representation, all of them aim to change the conditions under which immigrants work through collective action. While in some cases, these centers have a direct relationship to the labor movement (such as the Union of Needletrades, Industrial, and Textile Employees' centers in Manhattan's garment district and Sunset Park, Brooklyn), the vast majority began and continue to operate outside of it.

The Workplace Project is a workers' center, located in Hempstead, Long Island, in the heart of a burgeoning Latino (largely Salvadoran) community. Since it opened in 1992, over 1,200 immigrant workers— mostly factory, restaurant, and landscaping workers—have walked through its doors seeking assistance with employment-related problems like firings and unpaid wages. Understanding that the key to achieving justice is building power, the Workplace Project agrees to provide legal representation to individual workers, but only if they sign a contract in which they commit to taking a workers' rights course focusing on solidarity-building and participating on one of the Workplace Project's organizing committees.

There are about ten street corners in the area where Salvadoran, Guatemalan, Honduran, and Mexican men gather every weekday morning to wait for contractors to hire them as day-laborers. The men who gather on these corners in the early morning hours comprise a significant portion of

Long Island's landscaping workforce. In the past, these workers took what wages they could get. But over the last two years, contractors who rolled down the windows of their trucks to offer a daily wage encountered something new—an effort to establish a "corner-wide" minimum wage.

Every day, thousands of women go to work as domestics in the homes of middle and upper class Long Islanders. These women are enormously isolated due to the nature of their employment. They have next to no recourse when they are mistreated by their employers. Recently, after a domestic worker was fired by an employer and sent away without several weeks' wages, the employer got a knock on the door. There stood an organizer and the domestic worker, with workers and news reporters in tow. A half hour and one police visit later, the group left triumphant. Not only had the domestic worker been given her back wages, but the police had intervened on her behalf.

The Workplace Project also organizes roving picketlines in front of the homes and workplaces of employers who are refusing to pay workers' wages, despite court orders to do so. In addition, the project casts an image of Long Island's immigrant workers as hard workers who deserve to be treated with dignity and respect.

Workers' centers challenge established categories of organization. They are not quite unions, although they mobilize workers around employment concerns. They are not quite community organizations, although they are involved in community issues. And they are not quite legal services or social service agencies, although they provide some legal representation as well as training and education. They grew out of the enormous unmet needs of immigrant workers who had no organization or representation as they faced tremendous problems in their workplaces. Some workers' centers are directly affiliated with unions, but the bulk of them are independent. Many of them are pro-union in the abstract but their experiences with local unions have been mixed. Eight percent of the Workplace Project's cases are immigrant workers who are having trouble with their unions. In some cases, the union representative looked the other way when the employers had failed to apply the terms of the contract to immigrant workers. In others, the union did not represent workers when they had grievances. Overwhelmingly, the unions had no bilingual staff or capacity.

When an immigrant worker who is a union member comes into the Workplace Project with a grievance, the staff usually tries to get in touch with a union representative to see if they can explain the situation and get the union to take action. Sometimes this is a struggle. The project's most stalwart volunteer, Jeanette Katz, a retired teacher and union activist, puts it this way:

> I was very pro-union—more so than I am now, because of my dealings [with unions in the course of her work]. Many times I have to write six letters, call ten or twelve times, before they [the union staff] call....We almost always have to threaten them. Sometimes they don't act much different than working with an employer.... Everybody laughs around here...(they say) "You are going to write another one of your letters."...I sign the letters "fraternally," and I think I understand union culture, but it doesn't seem to make the unions respond any more quickly.[17]

A key lesson of the Workplace Project and the SSC is the importance of leadership development and a high level of ownership over the organization by those it seeks to organize. While basing organizing drives on sound labor-market strategies is necessary, it is not sufficient. Some organizers have expressed the concern that if some major industry-wide campaigns fail, international unions and the AFL-CIO may draw the wrong conclusions about the reasons—blaming the concept of industry-wide organizing itself as opposed to the quality of the organizing that is done. Strong participation on the part of worker committees has been shown to be a key element of winning organizing drives, especially in countering aggressive anti-union campaigns by management, and in keeping the organization together through a first contract.[18] This is a key point when it comes to the constituents of the new labor movement—women and people of color. There are simply too few of them in leadership positions at all levels in unions. Yet these are precisely the groups that are working in industries most likely to unionize and who are found to be most open to unionization. It is common sense that an organization that does not have the people it seeks to organize playing a genuine leadership role will not reach many potential adherents because it will find it difficult to win and sustain their trust and is also likely to fail to address their needs and concerns.

The Workplace Project is embedded in the culture of the Salvadoran community in Long Island—but not because it is solely led by Latino workers—in fact, Jennifer Gordon, the founder and director, is a young Jewish Harvard-educated lawyer. However, Latino workers make up the entire board of directors, all of the organizing committees, and the staff.

If the labor movement is to organize the new immigrant workforce, it must support mediating institutions like the Workplace Project. But it must also transform the union culture—especially with staff at the local union level. The workers at Davis Optical should not have had to fight so hard to get their union's attention. Local union leaders and staff must be better equipped to work with immigrant members. They need bilingual staffpeople, they need to be sensitized to particular problems these workers encounter on the job—and to their own biases. Of course, some union locals across the country are more than aware of these issues—but they are still the exception. The challenge for the new AFL-CIO is to bring innovative practice from the margins to the center, to spotlight these locals, and to encourage others to follow suit. Immigrant worker centers have much to teach the labor movement.

UNIFYING VISIONS OF WHO WE ARE

Just as work is a universal element in people's lives, so too is the desire to feel we are doing something meaningful and to be valued for the work we do. These are the first principles of the labor movement. Why is it then, that even though organized labor in America has championed broad issues of social welfare and social justice, fought consistently for the underprivileged, and often succeeded in passing laws that chiefly benefited workers not covered under collective bargaining agreements, labor is still perceived as a special interest group by many? No matter how hard labor fights for the minimum wage in Congress, or the living wage in city councils, if unions define their issues narrowly at contract time, they contradict their own broader messages. The entire labor movement, the AFL-CIO and international and local unions, must frame issues in general interest or social justice terms as opposed to narrow, special interest terms—not only when organizing or doing politics but also during collective bargaining.

Today, broad and narrow unionism are shouting each other down in the public space. And that often prevents labor from projecting a single, powerful voice for economic justice in American society. Labor does this in a thousand small ways every year because it does not make sure to frame every public issue in the broadest possible way. The BUILD experience should be a model: It shows labor moving beyond the politics of particularism and fighting on behalf of the general interest of low-wage workers.

Coordinating the messages we are sending as we bargain, do politics, and organize will do more than a thousand "Union Yes" campaigns to reestablish the labor movement as the foremost institution championing the dignity of American workers. This is what is so powerful about the work of SEIU Local 509: The union's campaign includes union organizing, collective bargaining and politics as part of a broad interest: concern about how society cares for the mentally ill.

In *Success While Others Fail*, Paul Johnston argues that public sector unions are compelled to frame their agendas in general interest terms: "For better or worse...they are involved in public issues: because they confront them face to face....Thus, they are participants in a never-ending argument over "what is the public good" and join—and increasingly organize—coalitions on behalf of politically defined public goals associated with their work."[19]

Health care and education issues in the private sector are also adaptable to general interest arguments. But what about other types of service work in the private sector? Justice for Janitors, in arguing for a decent standard of living for private-sector janitorial workforces, projected a "social justice" message: Los Angeles should work for everyone. In the midst of a real estate boom, three out of four janitors who cleaned commercial office buildings still fell below the poverty line—despite working full-time. J for J organized the "A Penny for Justice" campaign which dramatized the fact that the cost to building owners of providing a living wage and family health insurance would be only a penny on every rental dollar.

THE DIVISION OF LABOR

Labor is making new strategic moves to labor market and community unionism. But for innovation to take hold, structure matters. To make sure that innovative practices percolate up—and are disseminated—international unions and the AFL-CIO will have to facilitate a process of practice, strategic reflection, and refinement. But to do so, they must overcome institutional obstacles.

THE AFL-CIO

Historically, unions have pursued their organizing and collective bargaining campaigns quite separately from their broader political goals—so separately that unions bemoan their members' political independence. While the ideology of "business unionism" explains much of this separation, the structure of the American labor movement has historically reinforced it. Organizing and collective bargaining are the domain of international unions and their local affiliates; politics is the mission of the much weaker AFL-CIO and its affiliated state federations and central labor councils. Of course there is always a tension between representing existing membership and advancing the broader interests of workers, but the current set-up exacerbates this problem: the international and local unions with more resources are driven by the need to service existing members.

Although the national AFL-CIO has now invested substantially more resources into its organizing department, it still possesses only a tiny fraction of the total resources of the labor movement. To succeed in increasing labor's power, it will have to catalyze the internationals to spend a much higher percentage of their money on organizing. The AFL-CIO organizing department is pursuing this approach with its emphasis on labor market-wide multiunion drives.[20] Nevertheless, there are two separate structures for organizing: one, the internationals with enormous resources and a direct line to local unions; and the other, the federation with much more limited resources and a direct line only to those local unions that choose to affiliate and participate in AFL-CIO central bodies. In addition, inside of internationals and locals, this same bifurcation is repeated: organizing is too often pursued separately from collective bargaining. Politics are often pursued separately as well.

There are clear signs that things will be more coordinated under the new AFL-CIO leadership. For example, the field mobilization department (the field services department), which is responsible for working with the central labor councils and state federations, is now working closely with the organizing department and the United Farm Workers on a new drive to organize strawberry workers in California. The new director of field mobilization, Marilyn Sneiderman, is a long-time believer in the potential power of central labor councils to play an important role in both organizing drives and community organizing and coalition-building. At a summer 1996 conference of central labor councils, Sneiderman unveiled a mission statement for the AFL-CIO central labor councils that takes a broad view of unionism: "Organizing for justice in our community." Still, finessing relationships on the local level and having central councils play more of a role in supporting local organizing campaigns will be much more challenging.

Central labor councils have always been linchpins of labor's electoral work, and clearly the new AFL-CIO political director, Steve Rosenthal, and others in his department, have already dramatically improved the quality of the Federation's electoral work. They have conducted unprecedented analyses of the voting behavior of union members, developed and targeted persuasion messages, and made a dramatic difference in how union members, especially white males, voted. Some solid progress was made in reinvigorating the Federation's political program, but considerably more needs to be done in getting the political program to return to first principles: building power through organized people, developing leadership, and fighting for the general interest.

A case in point is the Labor '96 effort to take back the House of Representatives. Building on the momentum of the highly publicized leadership contest at the top, the new team at the AFL-CIO clearly wanted to use its first election year effort to send a "labor is back" message. A more sophisticated targeting and voter identification strategy, coupled with a greater number of political organizers out in the field, and increased rank-and-file participation, yielded some impressive results. The Federation's deft use of television advertising stunned incumbents across the country who were suddenly faced with a powerful foe demanding that they answer for their sins.

Labor's "express advocacy ads," however, were a clever new tactic with a significant down-side. In the final weeks of the campaign, business counter-attack ads, featuring cigar-chomping denizens of "big labor," took a toll on labor-backed candidates. Dramatically increased political action on the part of labor (spending a lot more, running these ads) is almost certain to incite a reaction, and labor must anticipate this when it plans strategies, and be better prepared when that reaction comes. Would the reaction have been as wounding if the ads—and the entire campaign—had been run by a coalition of organizations and not just the Federation? Might there have been a way of presenting a different image of labor in the initial ads—as the faces of grassroots amateurs—that would have appealed to the general public more than slickness? Would the strategy have been different if it had as its clear goal the long-term rebuilding of labor's base and organizing the unorganized—and not solely the outcome of this one election?

The Federation is planning to create a political skills training academy within the AFL-CIO to recruit, train, and field local candidates for office as well as campaign managers. As this takes shape over the next few years, the AFL-CIO's legislative and government affairs departments must also work to help these candidates and elected officials formulate and move progressive policy through legislative bodies. The evolution of a new politics is most likely to come through this process of training and recruiting candidates, winning elections, and then dealing with the challenge of sending progressives into legislative institutions to move an agenda and maintain accountability to a base. These experiences are likely to catalyze more fruitful debate over labor's future role in coalitions and political parties than the way that the current "Democratic Party vs. third party" conundrum is debated.

While the AFL-CIO's organizing, field mobilization, political and legislative departments will continue to pursue distinct activities, the Federation still needs to coordinate an over-all vision and agenda, to make sure that each department consciously works to interweave general interest and social justice messages in their bread and butter activities. This is happening between the different departments of the AFL-CIO, the more difficult task is achieving the same level of coordination *between* the AFL-CIO and international unions, and *inside the internationals* themselves.

As labor market organizing becomes more closely connected to political organizing, the hard distinctions between departments might prove less useful. Circulating staff between departments might help develop more generalists with a broader vision of what organizing is.

Internationals

Beefing up local capacity to organize must be the priority. Internationals have been instrumental to increased organizing on the ground in four ways:

1. they have told locals that they have to do it;

2. they have developed innovative new strategies, training programs, and resources to carry out the organizing;

3. they have changed national rules and structures and created new ones that facilitate organizing;

4. they have opened up two-way communication so that information and ideas flow efficiently from the international to the locals, locals to the international, and local to local.

The greatest challenge before internationals today is to create a culture of organizing. Ten years ago, Marshall Ganz and Scott Washburn spent a year interviewing 130 union organizers, staff and leaders across the state of California. Of 7,500 full-time union personnel, 26.8 percent were general officers, 26.9 percent were business agents, 31.8 percent were clericals, 12.1

percent were listed as miscellaneous or other, and 2.4 percent, or 180, were organizers. Almost half of these organizers were in the already represented public sector. This left ninety-six organizers for 6,750,000 unorganized private sector workers in California. Ganz and Washburn concluded that the resources that unions were committing to organizing were not being used strategically. They found that organizing was not seen as a craft—but as something anyone can do if they are given the right marketing pitch to make to unorganized workers. They found that there was too little training and development of organizers. Most damning of all, they concluded that: "Organizing is seen as the least important activity in most unions. It is not 'a way up,' top leaders do not identify as organizers, it is the lowest paid and least esteemed work reserved for the novice or political crony, while becoming a business agent is considered 'making it.'"[21]

Ganz and Washburn's conclusions could just as easily apply to most unions today. Internationals must not only commit greater resources—they must change the internal culture of their unions such that organizing is seen and rewarded as prestigious, high priority work. The SEIU and the IBEW have both taken steps to begin to create a culture of organizing and an organizational structure that facilitates it. Below is a quick synopsis of some of these changes.

In IBEW, President J.J. Barry mandated that every local hire staff organizers. He also moved to open up new lines of communication. Before, local unions were forbidden from communicating directly with one another, and instead had to go through district level representatives. But following the organizational change of the late 1980s, locals engaged in increased contact and coordination. Relations between the international headquarters and locals—as well as between the local leadership and rank-and-file members—became more open and less hierarchical. Increased communication and coordination within the union has been further enhanced by the massive training efforts promoted through the Construction Organizing Membership and Education Training (COMET) program. COMET training helps union members redefine the nature of their problems, learn about new tactics/solutions to these problems, learn how to communicate these new ideas to members and potential members, and to develop their own strategies. This is key given that the new thrust on organizing the unorganized depends upon the ability of rank-and-file members to understand the interests they share with non-union workers. In other words, they had to transform their conception of themselves and their organization from a "country club" to a "brotherhood." COMET training also increases the supply of rank-and-file organizers.

Over the past several years, SEIU has created five industry-based divisions: building services, health care, clerical, public employees, and allied and industrial. These divisions are chaired by international vice presidents and directed by boards comprised of local unions. The division structure has allowed the union to "see itself" more clearly. Membership analysis by division spotlighted which parts of the union were growing and which were contracting. These analyses became the basis for developing new strategies for each division. They provided the impetus for the big locals in the building services to see clearly that they were headed for extinction if they did not change. The divisions also created new spaces for talented staff to be hired, and for strong local leaders to be recognized, and give resources to organize. As Michael Piore has noted, SEIU, unlike a number of other international unions, has built its in-house capacity in bargaining, researching, and organizing, as opposed to relying on outside consultants.[22]

Another extremely important result of SEIU's planning process was the discovery that 100 of SEIU's 300 locals contained only about three percent of the total membership, and that the top twenty-five locals had more than seventy percent of the membership. Because the smallest locals usually could not afford a staffperson, and so needed the most help, a number of staffpersons often spent a lot of time servicing small locals and contracts. Negotiating an agreement for twenty or thirty members in a school district or janitorial firm can take as much time as negotiating for several hundred or a thousand members. The international also saw it needed to focus its organizing efforts on a limited number of industries and occupations, reinforcing the need for industry-wide strategies. In the end, the international engaged in a planning process which led to the targeted distribution of resources in accord with an over-all program, rather than through patronage. SEIU has also expanded its executive board to incorporate a large number of local leaders into high-level decision-making positions.

While many important ideas and strategies have come through international staff, local application of them (as well as their own ideas) has yielded important insights and further innovations. It is also important to note that a lot of the innovators within SEIU came from other unions, from community organizations, and from the locals themselves (at the time that SEIU began doing it, hiring staff and chartering locals from ACORN, Fair Share, and the Woodcutters in Mississippi was seldom done). SEIU President Andy Stern and a number of other international staff came from Local 668 in Pennsylvania, Nancy Mills from Local 285, and Tom Woodruff from 1199 in West Virginia.[23]

CONCLUSION

So long as there is a bifurcation between labor's economic and political agendas, it will be very difficult to achieve the moral transformation of the labor movement—to construct and project a movement that represents the general interests of working people, that speaks and acts on behalf of an entire class, and not only a particular group of workers. The idea of community unionism is to renegotiate this separation and meld economics and politics together into a new model of labor market unionism.

The change in AFL-CIO leadership in 1995 has given the labor movement a renewed sense of purpose. It could not have come a moment too soon—for it is *still labor*, and in truth, only labor, that has the institutional strength to define and do battle on behalf of all working people. This vision must unify the spheres of organizing, politics, bargaining, and internal organization—for without it, *we will drown our own voices out.*

NOTES

The research for this paper was compiled over a period of years with support from the Massachusetts Institute of Technology (MIT) departments of political science and industrial relations as well as a generous fellowship from the Industrial Performance Center. The unifying themes of this essay were suggested by Michael Piore and Richard Locke. A version of this paper is forthcoming as an Industrial Performance Center Working Paper.

1. For an excellent treatment of the history of labor union structures and approaches to organizing skilled and unskilled workforces, see Chapter 2 of *The New Unionism: Employee Involvement in the Changing Corporation*, by Charles C. Heckscher (New York: Basic Books, 1988). Heckscher reminds us that the history of labor unions in America has been one of continuing struggle for survival, legitimacy, and legal, and organizational frameworks appropriate to an evolving American economy—to survive, organized labor has had to keep evolving too.

2. Michael Piore made this point to me in an earlier draft of this paper.

3. This next session is drawn from a paper I co-authored with Richard Locke, "Everything Old is New Again: Organizational Innovation in the American Union

Movement: The Case of the International Brotherhood of Electrical Workers." Mark Erlich, Jeff Grabelsky, Mike Lucas, and Jim Rudicil were invaluable resources in talking through the dynamics of the building trades industries and unions.

4. From "Union Organization in the Construction Industry," a pamphlet by Mike Lucas, 1994.

5. From Grace Palladino, *Dreams of Dignity, Workers of Vision* (Washington, D.C.: IBEW, 1991).

6. Interviews with author for ongoing dissertation research, 1995-1997.

7. Interviews with author for ongoing dissertation research, 1995-1997.

8. Interviews with author for ongoing dissertation research, 1995-1997.

9. Available from SEIU Local 509, Massachusetts.

10. The original janitors union, the Building Service Employees International Union, was an AFL union. By calling it "industrial unionism," I am simply referencing the approach that it took to achieving a labor market-wide industrial agreement.

11. For an excellent description of types of unionism, see Howard Wial, "Unionism in Low Wage Services," *Rutgers Law Review*, 45 (1993), p. 671.

12. For an in-depth look at the Milwaukee Central Labor Council (CLC) and the role of CLCs in the labor movement, see Stuart Eimer, "The Milwaukee County Central Labor Council: From 'Pure and Simple' Unionism to 'Social Movement Unionism,'" draft paper for presentation at the Milwaukee Sociological Society, April 1996.

13. See "Rebuilding Milwaukee From the Ground Up," a report of The Campaign for Sustainable Milwaukee, October 22, 1994, 1001 E. Keefe Avenue, Milwaukee, WI.

14. This notion of community unionism has been developed through a series of discussions with Michael Piore and Richard Locke as well as through a few key articles of theirs. Piore's are: "The Future of Unions," in *The State of the Unions*, Strauss, Gallagher, and Fiorito, eds., (Wisconsin: Industrial Relations Research Association Series, 1991), and "Unions and Politics," a paper presented for the Conference on the Future of Unionism in Manufacturing, 1978. Locke's is: "The Demise of the National Union in Italy: Lessons for Comparative Industrial Relations Theory," Industrial and Labor Relations Review, Vol. 45, No. 2 (January 1992), Cornell University.

15. I have had the good fortune to observe several Solidarity actions and debriefings carried out by IAF organizer Kerry Miciotto, a talented organizer who interned with Solidarity as part of her Master of Social Work training and subsequently joined the staff.

16. These ideas are Jonathan Lange's, lead organizer of the Industrial Areas Foundation for the Solidarity Sponsoring Committee. Jonathan has been experimenting with community organizing approaches to labor organizing for more than a dozen years, first on the staff of Amalgamated Clothing and Textile Workers Union (ACTWU) and then the IAF. He has been working on the "puzzles" of providing health benefits for low income employees and minority unionism for the past several years. We discussed them during site visits in November and December of 1996. Solidarity is still exploring legal

issues with its lawyer and is not yet certain of whether this arrangement can be implemented under existing law.

17. Interviews with author for ongoing dissertation research, 1995-1997.

18. See Steve Early's chapter on this topic in this volume as well as Bronfenbrenner and Juravitch, "It takes more than Housecalls: Organizing to Win with a Comprehensive Union-Building Strategy," paper presented at AFL-CIO/Cornell University Joint Conference on Organizing, 1996, available through authors. Also see, Wade Rathke, "Letting More Flowers Bloom Under the Setting Sun," available through author. For a longer argument on the importance of union democracy to organizing, see Michael Eisenscher, "Critical Juncture: Unionism at the Crossroads" in *Which Direction for Labor? Strategic Options Facing the U.S. Labor Movement*, Bruce Nissen, ed., (forthcoming).

19. Paul Johnston, "The Richness of Its Possibilities" in *Success While Others Fail: Social Movement Unionism and the Public Workplace* (Ithaca, N.Y.: ILR Press, 1994), p. 13.

20. How to engage in multiunion drives that don't get caught up in jurisdictional fights and that build a sense of movement is a key challenge the organizing department faces. Although it has not so far succeeded in getting a roster of internationals to buy in, LAMAP (the Los Angeles Manufacturing Action Project) has done some excellent thinking about this. Essentially, all participating unions would be asked to agree that when new members are organized, they also become members of LAMAP, and would be encouraged to participate in LAMAP-wide meetings and actions, not just their individual union. For more details, see various strategy documents by Peter Olney and Joel Ochoa, available through LAMAP.

21. See Marshall Ganz and Scott Washburn, "Organizing and Unions: A Challenge of the 80s: An Organizer's Perspective," October 1985, available through authors.

22. See Michael J. Piore, "Administrative Failure: An Hypothesis About the Decline of U.S. Union Movement in the 1980s," Department of Economics, MIT, 1989, available through author. Or, see Michael J. Piore, "Unions: A Reorientation to Survive," in Clark Kerr and Paul D. Staudoher, eds., *Labor Economics and Industrial Relations: Market and Institutions* (Cambridge: Harvard University Press, 1994), pp. 512-41.

23. This section was informed by interviews with Andy Stern, president of SEIU, and other international staff.

PART | 3 | DIVERSITY AND INCLUSION

Organized labor in the U.S. has long been the largest, most diverse organization for social change that this country has ever seen. It has organized countless women and people of color, providing them with a vehicle to attain dignity and upward mobility where previously there was none. At the same time, organized labor's history of discriminatory policies and practices has been appalling. Competition for jobs led some unions to bar non-whites in their constitutions, others to exclude women from their ranks. As for the AFL-CIO, it failed to compel its affiliates to integrate when it was founded in 1955, and years later knowingly admitted new unions with constitutional bars to integration in place. Among women and people of color, this historical paradox has prompted a variety of contradictory responses: allegiance, enthusiasm, hope, indifference, and hostility. At the center of these tensions is the fact that employers are the ones who ultimately benefit from a workforce divided and competing for jobs. While great strides have been made, large divisions still remain. If organized labor is to revitalize itself as a movement for social justice that unifies working people around issues of class, it will have to overcome these divisions and come to terms with such issues as affirmative action, identity politics, and inclusive leadership. The labor movement's success will ultimately depend on its ability both to meet the specific needs of an increasingly diverse workforce and to develop a leadership and culture that reflects this diverse workforce.

In the lead essay, Ruth Needleman argues that the future of the labor movement will depend on its ability to organize women in massive numbers, bring women into important leadership positions, and learn from the way women activists approach problems and union work. She points out that in addition to blatant impediments, a number of structural obstacles, often subtle and unintentional, have hindered the advancement of women to top leadership positions. The centralization of union authority and function, the relatively small number of leadership openings available, as well as a distinctly male culture of unions and persistent gender stereotyping have all played a negative role. Change, according to Needleman, will require power sharing and structured opportunity as well as independent space, away from the dominant culture and controlled structures of the union, where women and people of color can identify issues, articulate concerns, validate their experience, and strategize for change. She suggests a number of specific measures including the legitimation of caucuses, changing the demands and styles of leadership, and internship and mentoring programs.

Latinos will comprise one-quarter of the U.S. population by the year 2050. Beginning with this premise, José La Luz and Paula Finn point out that in order to survive, unions will have to organize large numbers of Latinos and immigrants and, at the same time, change institutionally to accommodate these new members. Unions, they write, will have to learn to "organize immigrant workers without asking them to check their language and culture at the union door." Without a change in power relations, the authors argue, these constituencies will turn against the union and even worse, will become cynical about taking future action. La Luz and Finn identify a number of obstacles and how they can be overcome, drawing on the early experiences of the clothing workers union—which organized nationality-based unions—as well as the more recent experience of the Justice for Janitors campaign. They suggest that unions need to view diversity and inclusion as operating principles, not only to build a powerful labor movement, but to radically alter racial and ethnic divisions in the nation—a goal it should assume in and of itself. They call on the labor movement to organize a major national conference for the purpose of developing a comprehensive plan for organizational change from the bottom up, and suggest several strategies that would bring about institutional reform.

May Chen and Kent Wong describe the record of the U.S. labor movement, with regard to people of color and women, as "a source of collective embarrassment." They outline the history of exclusionary practices and sketch the impact of the civil rights movement on unions. While they praise some of the recent changes in the AFL-CIO, they also point out that very few people of color have been appointed to leadership jobs within the AFL-CIO, and that the white male power structures within national unions remain intact. Although some of the ethnic and women's committees that emerged within the labor movement in recent decades have played a positive role, all too often these constituent organizations have been marginalized and reduced to the status of tokens. Failing to provide meaningful political representation for excluded constituents, these organizations have served as social organizations, providing perks and rewards for obedient minority group members who support the union agenda without criticism. These constituent groups, however, have a critical role to play as forceful advocates for change. On the one hand, they must press unions and the AFL-CIO to provide meaningful representation and equal treatment. On the other hand, they can provide a strategic bridge between unions and communities of color. Focusing on the experience of their own organization, the Asian Pacific American Labor Alliance, Chen and Wong examine efforts to organize in immigrant communities (rather than workplaces), by addressing immigrant workers' needs for such services as English classes and help with family and immigration issues, as a way of building a base for union organizing.

Larry Adams ends this section by suggesting that if unions become irrelevant because they do not meet the needs of their members, the poor and the working class will find other vehicles to advance their interests. Drawing on his own experience as an African American, a worker, and union leader, Adams describes the anger and frustration felt by many people of color and reflects on what is wrong with the labor movement. Discussing both the reasons for and the difficulties of moving from a rank-and-file militant to an officer with day-to-day responsibilities for the union, he suggests a number of constitutional and structural changes that would increase rank-and-file involvement in decision making. Adams highlights the tension between rank-and-file democracy and local autonomy on the one hand, and the need for centralized authority to insure local democracy and adequate resources for targeted campaigns. He also suggests ways in which unions can change their relationship to workers and communities of color, arguing for affirmative action, setting numerical goals for diversity in leadership, organizing in localities (such as the South) which are particularly oppressive for people of color, and advocating on behalf of social justice issues that have particular impact on communities of color.

WOMEN WORKERS:
Strategies for Inclusion and Rebuilding

Ruth Needleman

The increased presence and activism of women at the grassroots and local union level have brought about innovative and significant changes in organized labor over recent decades. Pressure from women has extended labor's demands at the bargaining table, enhanced the effectiveness of its political action work and pioneered new approaches in organizing. The creation of 9 to 5, the National Association of Working Women, the development of community-based organizations like Asian Immigrant Women's Advocates or La Mujer Obrera, the expansion of public sector and health care unionism, and the organizing campaigns among home-care workers and support staff at Harvard and Yale Universities, are just a few examples of women's contributions.

The influx of a million women a year into the paid labor force since the 1960s coincided with the dramatic growth in public sector and service occupations and the decline in manufacturing jobs and living standards. Department of Labor statistics report that women make up sixty percent of new workers each year, account for over forty-eight percent of the labor force, represent sixty percent of new unionists, and thirty-eight percent of union membership nationally. In addition, the fastest growing sectors of the labor market today are predominantly and traditionally female: low-wage health care, service, and contingent work. These sectors and occupational groups are where unions must make headway, organizing in order to arrest their own declining numbers and influence. To succeed, unions need not just a few more women members, organizers, and accomplished women leaders, but many more women, ordinary as well as extraordinary, at all levels of leadership.

Since the 1970s, thousands of rank-and-file union women have attended regional summer schools sponsored by the University and College Labor Education Association (UCLEA), the AFL-CIO, and the Coalition of Labor Union Women (CLUW) for leadership training. Many more have participated in women's and civil rights conferences and activities, lobbied for new legislative protections, and worked to build coalitions among women and with women's groups.[1] In doing so, working women have changed themselves as much or more than they have changed their unions. They have gained more confidence in their abilities, and have, in turn, commanded more respect from their union brothers. But thick glass ceilings have continued to block their rise to top leadership positions. Over the past decades, women have gradually infiltrated national leadership bodies in unions and government, but it has been possible to count their numbers on one hand. In places where the most important decisions are made, having the greatest impact on women and workers generally, women continue to have token representation. The surge of participation among union women has not yet been sufficient to alter the traditional structures, hierarchies, methods, and cultures of unions, which to a large degree remain male-dominated and resistant to newcomers and new ways of doing things. Given the appointments and directions of the current AFL-CIO leadership, however, organized labor is better positioned today than ever before to carry out the kind of internal organizational change necessary for it to become the democratic, militant, socially-conscious, and inclusive movement workers need. A central challenge will be the integration of the highest echelons of labor leadership. Up to now, women have been more like invited guests than homeowners in the house of labor, carefully selected and screened, welcomed in small numbers, and shown to their appropriate place. Welcoming women as equal partners in labor leadership means more than adding chairs at the table. Current leadership must open lots of room at the top for diverse women and men, and allow a more far-reaching make-over in union culture.

In leadership positions, women make a difference in tackling some of the thornier problems unions face. For example, to bring unionization to more women, unions have to figure out more effective ways of reaching workers crowded into low-wage, service, and contingent jobs, stressed by balancing family and work, and exhausted from battling daily discrimination. More women leaders are needed as role models, organizers and mentors, and their experiences, perspectives, and knowledge are critical for shaping new strategies and practices. Women unionists and community-based organizers have already made progress in helping unions understand that women in temporary labor markets, moving on and off welfare, or holding multiple part-time jobs, need support systems at home and in their communities as well as at work. To involve more women, experience demonstrates, union activity will have to be structured to favor family commitments, not downplay them. To accommodate women's schedules and responsibilities, unions will need to drop the 24-hour-a-day model for leadership and look to job-sharing, flextime, and other similar work practices that they advocate in bargaining. Such changes would make leadership accessible to more workers and greatly enhance labor's organizing capacity.

Furthermore, if the goal is expansion, what is good for most working women is also good for unions. The changes necessary to include poor, single- parent, minority, and immigrant women will strengthen the position of those within organized labor who have advocated greater rank-and-file participation, greater internal democracy, more collective and community-oriented practices, and more progressive stands on national and international issues.[2] The attitudes, style of work, scope of concerns, and political preferences of today's women union activists can help rekindle a social unionism that integrates workplace rights with civil rights, job issues with family issues, and workplace with communities. If past experience is any indication, women will conscientiously take on a lion's share of the day-to-day organizational work required to rebuild this movement.

OBSTACLES TO WOMEN'S LEADERSHIP IN UNIONS

Women candidates for office still face smear campaigns and ballot box tampering in local elections, if they run against one of the "guys." Although these tactics are often used to protect incumbents, incumbents are much more likely to be men than women. Even more important, the rumors and insults take on a decidedly sexist character, which promotes the more backward and mean-spirited side of unions. This conduct affects all women in the workplace because it exacerbates an illegal, hostile environment. So if women do not "wait their turn," they are labeled "ball-busters" or "bitches." If they win, they "slept their way to the top." And if they organize effectively to win, that is taken as proof that women are not team players. Stereotypes, rumor campaigns, sabotage, isolation, harassment: a few old dogs keep using the old tricks.

The more difficult barriers, however, are more subtle, more structural than individual, and very often *unintentional*. In many cases male leaders express a commitment to inclusion and make efforts in that direction, but fail because they do not understand the inherent bias of their union organization and procedures. Traditional hiring, slating, appointment, training, and promotional practices perpetuate discrimination in a union just as they do in any other workplace.[3] Communication systems in unions which rely on existing networks, word-of-mouth, and informal gatherings to relay information, favor insiders and severely disadvantage outsiders and newcomers. Officers look for leadership potential in those most like themselves, and have trouble recognizing qualities and strengths different from their own. Good intentions and isolated, individual efforts cannot restructure a system originally built by and for male workers.

Union and non-union women alike are checking out labor's 'walk,' not their 'talk,' and while they recognize the advances, they see major shortcomings. Union leaders have not stood up to peers or members who continue to act as if the union were a men's locker room. They have not argued openly against those who blame women, welfare recipients, immigrants, or workers in other countries for job loss at home. Unions have not practiced affirmative action internally, even when they endorse affirmative action policies. No numerical goals, written plans, and oversight exist to make sure women are hired and promoted in numbers proportional to their percentages in the workforce. Furthermore, women and people of color are still the ones who bear the burden of speaking out in the face of racist, sexist or homophobic comments and actions. Women have raised the ante; they not only want men to share authority and decision-making, they want unions to educate and encourage men to share equally in family responsibilities, top leaders included.

Well-publicized and widespread sexual harassment cases like the one at the Mitsubishi plant in rural Illinois make it hard for union women to convince others that unions are as committed to women's issues as they say.

Management and bargaining-unit employees at Mitsubishi engaged in a wide array of harassing behaviors, from on-site physical advances to off-site parties with naked dancers, followed by the circulation of photos from those events throughout the plant. It took dozens of complaints filed by women at the Equal Employment Opportunity Commission (EEOC) and outrageous pressure tactics by the company to isolate those women (bringing masses of workers on work time in buses to demonstrate in front of the EEOC against those complaints) to get the union's attention. It is understandable that international unions have to be guarded in how they intervene in local unions, but they do it readily for problems less damaging to the union movement.

If union women pressed charges against their unions for hostile-environment harassment every time it occurred, unions would be overwhelmed with complaints. Double standards together with harassment greatly disadvantage women in union work. As a result, the people who most easily succeed in unions—unfortunately—look and act very much like those who have succeeded in the past; they are still primarily white and male, more often skilled than unskilled, and increasingly from outside the ranks of labor, energetic college graduates and professionals rather than rank-and-file activists.

The barriers to women's advancement in leadership are systemic rather than individual. Labor organizations developed historically in response to specific circumstances, labor markets, technologies, and workforces. Placing "blame" is irrelevant to remedying the situation. Unions have tried to make accommodations in their organization and leadership bodies. But these efforts are insufficient to bring about the mass organizing and growth identified as essential by the AFL-CIO to secure its future. So far most changes have come through addition: women added to the executive council; hired as organizers; slated for positions; and issues added to legislative and bargaining agendas. But it has mainly been the men doing the adding, hiring, selecting, and promoting, and women doing the adjusting, in order to fit into existing cultures. The next level of change will be harder. So many more women are stepping forward that they cannot so easily be assimilated or pressured to conform. The shift from token voice to equal voice at the decision-making table will mean everyone has to get up and move. All players will have to learn new rules to be effective.

MAIN BARRIERS

1. Centralization of Union Operations and Functions

To deal with corporations at the bargaining table and comply with complex laws, procedures and reporting requirements, unions increased their already centralized operations in the 1950s, shifting decision-making away from the local level. The CIO unions were highly centralized from the beginning in order to organize the mass production industries and to entice corporations like U.S. Steel to negotiate by promising a "disciplined" workforce. The cold war, including the Taft-Hartley Act, the CIO union expulsions, and the red-baiting and race-baiting that it entailed, placed a premium on union centralization. Reliance on lengthy arbitration procedures to deal with work problems also tended to disempower workers on the shop floor. Large legal, research, and benefits departments staffed with professionals took over critical areas of union administration, reinforcing the view that unions are service rather than membership organizations. Rank-and-file influence dwindled. More and more, at the local level, leaders complained of decreasing participation and apathy. Union centralization and bureaucracy had helped to put out the fire of activism.

Understanding or working through the bureaucracy and hierarchical structures required—and still requires—inside knowledge and a helping hand, rarely available to women. Centralization also favors incumbents and reduces the likelihood of turnover. For the most part, women have lacked information and access to the top, which served to reinforce the belief that men were best equipped to handle the responsibilities of "labor statesmanship."

The debate on the advantages and disadvantages of centralization still rages. International unions intent on organizing vacillate on whether to build bigger organizing departments (continued centralization) or allocate more resources to locals to organize (de-centralization); run top-down big campaigns or local ones. To run multiunion campaigns, as in Las Vegas, requires coordination at a national level. To develop a strategic approach by industry, sector, area or occupation, leadership must also come from the top. Even where unions push for decentralization and more local union involvement, they are pushing top-down. To maximize resources locally, they are amalgamating locals and merging unions. While favorable for organizing in many ways, this move to amalgamate is very often unfavorable for women and people of color aspiring to leadership. Again, the incumbents carry the advantage of name recognition, access to resources, and staff and international backing.

Centralization carries additional problems. Decisions to start or stop campaigns or to amalgamate locals or local federations tend to be top-down. From the perspective of grassroots organizers, hierarchical decision-making is undemocratic, discourages or devalues local initiatives and misconstrues them as disruptive, because they may not fit the plan or the time-line. Decisions that leave out the rank-and-file organizer and the workers in a campaign can have the same effect on morale, involvement, and commitment that bureaucratization of union administration had in the 1950s and after. Even as many campaigns are targeting women workers and deploying women organizers in the field, women activists view top-down decisions as sexist, racist, and undemocratic.[4] Used to having their experience and knowledge devalued, women take it very personally—and see it as discrimination—when their voices are not taken into account.

Union reliance on crisis decision-making—in the name of the urgency of organizing—has been used to justify cutting corners and ignoring input. At some point, many women and community-based organizers argue, unions must acknowledge the Pyrrhic character of the victories that bypass the crucial, long-term goals of worker empowerment and leadership development, so central to involving and promoting women.

2. Small Number of Leadership Openings

A further discouragement to involvement is the apparent lack of leadership openings. Although turnover rates vary dramatically from local to local, they are lower at the top than at the bottom. Union leadership has become a lifetime career for many officers. Moreover, with the decline in membership in many unions, the number of top leadership and senior staff positions is contracting. In the name of a "balanced slate," top leadership puts forward a list, selecting people based on long-term service, past support, and proven team spirit. Too often the list ends up with the proverbial token African American and/or woman, individuals who can be relied on to fit into the current team.

Token numbers of women in leadership lack support systems, are overloaded with committee assignments, paraded out for diversity's sake, but not necessarily taken seriously on critical issues.[5] Because of the overload, they get overlooked for the really important assignments.

Competition for the shrinking number of positions exacerbates resentment toward women and strengthens male territoriality in the leadership. Perceived as interlopers, the first generation of women leaders faced a good deal of hostility. Token spots and isolation shaped much of their behavior and attitudes. To be slated, they had to demonstrate their loyalty and their willingness to fit in. Women leaders, like African American men before them, were expected to represent the views and policies of the leadership to their constituencies and not to serve as their advocates. As a result, many of the first women to gain positions of leadership lost the trust of their former peer group who saw them as sell-outs. The small number of openings set the ambitious and talented women into competition with each other for one or two spots. Since men hold the power of selection, women find themselves auditioning for the part, playing the role of "good" woman, and finding fault with their sisters. This approach has caused serious problems among women, exacerbated race and class divisions, and led to resentment against women.[6] Moreover, it has produced burn-out for the chosen few. Looking from the outside in/up, many women have concluded that working in union leadership is for the "superstar," not for them.

The pressure on women and people of color to conform poses a serious dilemma for new leaders, as is clear in the words of this woman union leader: "I'm not sure what the rules of the game are, so I'm always breaking them. Do I care about it? I have to make a conscious decision all the time: be me or be who I think they want me to be. Say my point of view or just ask a question? Act like the new kid on the block and ask them to take care of me, because that's easier for them?"[7] Women and people of color grapple with such decisions every day, and they must weigh the impact of their behavior on their white male colleagues, and decide consciously when to compromise, when to walk away from a struggle, and when to take a stand.

3. Women are "Outsiders" in the Male Culture of Unionism

Studies on local union participation argue that members tend to get involved if they have adequate information about the union, are given concrete ways of contributing, know someone in office, socialize with current leaders, experience relative job satisfaction, and feel that their effort will accomplish something. Otherwise, workers do their job and go home.[8] While all workers have to contend with these factors, they present greater difficulties for women and sometimes insurmountable obstacles for workers of color.

Women, ethnic minorities, and immigrants are less likely to know someone in office, to be part of the in-leadership crowd, to socialize within that circle, or for that matter, to be satisfied with their job. Moreover, women have less access to union information, because family and home responsibilities keep them from "hanging around" the union hall. As outsiders, they most often lack the key ingredient for success in moving up the union career ladder: a mentor, someone to steer them through the minefields.

The male, white cultures of some unions are alienating for outsiders. The minority of men who do not want women invading their space send a message by exaggerating male styles, languages or preferences. They may select meeting places or times to appeal to traditional groups within the union; they may increase informal decision-making in bars, on golf courses, or on fishing/hunting trips. But most leaders do not want to be exclusive. The cultural barriers—traditions, customs, ways of doing things—are holdovers from earlier periods, when discrimination was widely practiced. Why do pictures of top leaders line the walls of union offices? Why are most executive board and leadership meetings held far from home, over extended weekends, with lots of down time? Why is child care frequently regarded as problematic but open bars, less so? Because the model trade unionist, after all, is a man with a wife at home, someone who can commit twenty-four hours, travel easily and on weekends, and who receives praise for putting the union first—not the family. When polled, women unionists preferred week-day meetings, close to home, and down time with the family, not the union. A study of stewards showed that *married* men were the most successful in fulfilling union responsibilities, while *single* women functioned better than married ones in that position. The male stewards received enormous support from their wives and were not expected to take on home responsibilities. In fact, they often canceled out of family events to attend to union business. The women stewards rarely received more than moral support from family, and, more often than not, were criticized by husbands for neglecting the home. Single and divorced women, in contrast, had the ability to juggle and plan their lives to include union work. To do so, however, they gave up sleep, leisure, and personal life.[9] Even if women are provided with equal opportunities and encouragement in the union, they would still have to work twice as hard, unless or until their male counterparts take on equal responsibility for home and family.

Unions like most institutions in our society give recognition and promotions to individual go-getters and often overlook collective work. There are cultures that encourage collective action over individual. Studies of African American women's organizing, for example, indicates a strong preference for collective leadership and shared responsibilities.[10] But what is different or preferred in another culture may not be valued within a white and/or male-dominated union culture. Those who agree with current leadership, work like them, and think like them receive the attention; those who do not or who raise criticisms or recommend trying different ways of doing things receive attention as well, but it is often negative and increases their marginalization.

4. Persistence of Gender and Race Stereotypes

Inseparable in many ways from issues of union culture, and an equally difficult barrier to surmount, is that of gender and race stereotypes—sexism and racism—which play a major role in shaping attitudes and voting preferences within unions. Stereotypes attribute traits dealing with competence to men, and those relating to care-giving and emotions to women. Male stereotypes are valued within the world of work and generally coincide with accepted leadership qualities; female stereotypes have been viewed as an impediment to being an effective leader.[11] For women and people of color to overcome these cultural stereotypes, they must usually meet higher standards of skill and knowledge and work twice as hard. They have to put up with inappropriate language and behaviors, silence themselves to maintain relationships, and sometimes in the name of protecting the union, they have to set aside their beliefs and commitments. It is accepted practice, but it is not acceptable.

Corporations gain profits and control by resorting to racism and sexism. Unions, in contrast, lose members, lose trust, jeopardize unity, and relinquish the power that comes through solidarity. Unions have a tremendous stake in challenging the "isms." Women should not have to prove they are as good as men. Women should not have to tolerate sexual harassment at union conferences or from union organizers. Women should not have to belittle other women to be accepted. Standards for evaluation and measurements of good union work have been socially constructed to reflect the values and priorities of a white, professional, male-dominated society. To promote women and enable them to succeed, unions need to root out racist and sexist attitudes, leaders, and practices, implement far-reaching affirmative action plans, and develop mandatory educational programs.

STRATEGIES FOR INCREASING WOMEN'S INVOLVEMENT AND LEADERSHIP

Individual and union experiences suggest that changing the face of leadership and the union's culture requires personal courage, independent organization among the rank-and-file members, an activist approach to union work, and strategic support from existing leadership. While individuals do need to change, organizational change will make the real difference. Change occurs in response to pressure, and in this case, the pressure comes internally from below and from above in union structures, as well as externally from mass movements.

I have conducted interviews with dozens of leading activists who confirm the importance of both *independent space* and *structured opportunities* in changing union organization and culture.[12] *Independent space* is space away from the dominant culture and the controlled structures of the union. This self-organized space provides room for women to identify what in that culture excludes them or makes them uncomfortable; it also provides room for them to create a different kind of culture or work environment, to explore more familiar styles of doing things. In this space, women can safely articulate grievances, validate feelings, and strategize about how to engage and change the dominant culture.

The consciousness-raising groups of the women's movement represented such a space, as did the black power caucuses within the unions. Joe Crump, who headed the Minority Coalition of the United Food and Commercial Workers' Union (UFCW) for many years, stated that what makes a difference is the existence of caucuses and networks, independent self-organization.[13] The Minority Coalition grew out of informal discussions and networks among African Americans in 1972 and maintains its independent status. The same is true for the minority caucuses in the Communications Workers of America (CWA); they decline official status within the union but welcome the opportunity to meet with executive boards and top leaders of their international.

Workers carve out independent space all the time, by building informal peer networks and ad hoc committees, or by taking storytelling breaks at lunch, after work, or in the hall. The Coalition of Black Trade Unionists provides that space for workers from many unions. The regional summer schools for union women offer a unique space for rank-and-file women from different unions and locals to exchange information, success as well as horror stories, and to identify strategies that work. The community, church, and local organizations that were the backbone of the civil rights movement were all examples of independent space in the dominant white society. Such groups have proliferated in recent decades, not only for women and people of color, but also for deaf, gay, and handicapped workers, among others.

Structured opportunity represents the pressure from above, the support and efforts by those in leadership to open doors, and to provide education and experience as well as vehicles for sharing responsibility and power. The establishment of women's and civil rights departments and conferences, the development of special training programs, internships or apprenticeships, mentoring programs, and also the conscious inclusion of women and people of color in visible and critical leadership positions constitute structured opportunities. These affirmative action measures specifically address the problems of exclusion resulting from the biases of the dominant culture.

In the upcoming unification among the United Steel Workers of America (USWA), the United Auto Workers (UAW), and the International Association of Machinists (IAM), structured opportunity is playing a role. Although the decision to work toward a merger was hammered out in the traditionally top-down fashion, and the executive boards of all three international unions are predominantly white and overwhelmingly male, the leadership recognized the problem of exclusion. Each union has set up an eighteen-member committee of local leaders, more diverse in sex, race, skill, industry, and experience than the board. The USWA and the IAM have included six women each; the UAW, five. While it is unclear how much authority has been delegated or what actual impact their deliberations will have, this structured opportunity will inevitably create independent spaces for discussion and raise issues which might not have otherwise surfaced. Even though the top leadership handpicked the representatives, the body will create a dynamic of its own and help broaden member involvement in the unification process.

Affirmative action, of course, entails more than putting a woman or person of color in the mix. It requires sufficient numbers to allow members of under-represented groups to form their own support networks—independent space—so that they feel encouraged to speak out and speak honestly. Authority and responsibility must be delegated and respected. Effective inclusion involves a commitment to a long-term process of organizational change in priorities, programs, and policies. The USWA's Women of Steel program is an excellent example of a structured opportunity that has trained dozens of rank-and-file women in leadership skills and enabled them to network nationally and independently.[14] Adopted from a week-long education program developed by Canadian women, Women of Steel enables women steelworkers the opportunity to train their sisters in every district of the union.

The Service Employees International Union's (SEIU) Leadership Program was developed through a whole set of structured opportunities to secure the participation of rank-and-file members, local leaders, and top leadership. The union held women's conferences and civil rights conferences which provided space and feedback from rank-and-file members. SEIU also convened special task forces to allow women and people of color to identify barriers and make recommendations for change. As part of the program adopted at their 1992 convention, the union set up mentoring programs, internships, leadership roundtables, regular regional women's and civil rights conferences, and recognized caucuses as a legitimate part of the union's structure.[15] The Communications Workers of America (CWA) has been holding a special two-week Minority Leadership Program for over a decade to provide special training, support, and opportunity for African American and other under-represented groups.

The creative tensions between the official voice of labor and the newer voices of women and people of color play out at the annual meetings of the AFL-CIO organizations set up to foster inclusion and address sexism and racism. These organizations, the Coalition of Labor Union Women (CLUW), the A. Philip Randolph Institute (APRI), the Labor Council for Latin American Advancement (LACLAA), and the Asian Pacific American Labor Alliance (APALA), have official AFL-CIO status and, to a degree, are expected to promote AFL-CIO policies and priorities. At the same time their meetings provide significant independent space for activists to network and organize for their own positions. The strength of independent pressure accounts, for example, for CLUW's support of women's right to reproductive choice which differs from the official AFL-CIO position.

To be effective, structured opportunities must accommodate or allow for the emergence of independent space. The challenge is to overcome policies and practices that favor the "insider," the person who looks like the current leaders and understands their values and their ways of doing things. "Affirmative action works," commented a SEIU local union president, Celia Wcislo. "You see faces like your own, and people identify and develop people who look like them." Yet, she added, "you have to allow women and people of color space away from the world of white men, allow them to be different and not have to act like white men."[16] If the "structured opportunity" requires participants to learn to think or behave like those in power, then those who "succeed" will be those who are willing or able to adapt to the status quo—at great personal cost.

What helps newcomers the most, according to almost every person I interviewed, are two things: a mentor, a supportive person in high places, and a support group of people like themselves. "A feminist insider in a powerful position is important," stressed Karen Nussbaum, former executive director of an almost entirely female organization, 9 to 5. As current director of the new AFL-CIO Working Women's Department, Nussbaum understands the role of a strategically placed female advocate. "In the early days," she noted, "there weren't people who fit that description."[17] According to Joyce Miller, a vice president of the Amalgamated Clothing and Textile Workers Union (ACTWU) and president of CLUW at the time of the interview, "One of the most important things to me, as is true of both men and women, was gaining a mentor." Miller added, "It was important to have good relationships with elected officers to gain expertise that was necessary and fit in with the political goals of the union. I also worked harder than most of my male colleagues."[18] With the help of mentors, Gloria Johnson, director of the Department of Social Action for the International Union of Electrical Workers (IUE), and currently president of CLUW, became one of the leading African American unionists in the country. In turn, Johnson has mentored countless others. "I love the union for what it has done, but more important, what it can do," Johnson commented. "I love being able to play some small role in moving people, sisters and brothers, up in the ranks."[19]

The AFL-CIO's creation of a new vice-presidency, its appointment of women to important leadership positions, has increased their national visibility, their decision-making authority, and their ability to inspire new generations of women activists. The fact that Executive Vice President Linda Chavez-Thompson has made a priority of attending the regional women's schools and other women's programs has made a difference to the activists in the field. Her own supportive style and sisterly words have encouraged many local women unionists to fight another day. The new leadership in the AFL-CIO's Field Mobilization Department also represents a wealth of talent, experience, and diversity. In education, organizing, and political action, women have gained a significant presence, where they serve as models and mentors. Under President John Sweeney, the AFL-CIO has promoted important structured opportunities and used its power of appointment to diversify union staff. It is, of course, critical to emphasize that the advances in elected leadership—where it counts the most—lag seriously behind, and it is here where the AFL-CIO needs to exert more initiative. The "autonomy" of the affiliates will otherwise prove to be the Achilles heel of labor.

Without mentors or connections within the union's decision-making circles, independent space can lead to isolation and intensify alienation. Many of the early black power and women's caucuses were either refused access or were reluctant to use it, which heightened distrust and delayed change. Structured opportunities help to ensure dialogue and joint action for change. "You need to create and control the space for discussion of race and discrimination among yourselves," emphasized Gerry Hudson, executive vice president of New York Local 1199, "but then you can't forget the necessity of joining the larger discussion. Let us think outside the structure but be sure we know we have to think within it."[20]

Promoting organizational change poses problems for leaders as well. When leaders step forward to advocate special measures to develop and promote women and people of color, they, too, face resistance and endanger their own position. Therefore, they will often pressure for a consensus for limited change, for a carefully monitored process that will yield predictable outcomes. But when formerly disenfranchised people are brought together, they seize the moment to create their own space and make their own demands. A couple of years ago the president of an Oil, Chemical, and Atomic Workers (OCAW) local recounted how he had finally made it possible for four women from his local to attend a national women's conference—a first for the local. He then showed me a letter the four had written him afterwards, demanding to know why more women were not sent and why women had not been sent sooner. He was angry and hurt, because he expected 'thank you's,' not recrimination. Often, as in this case, the leader goes for a small step and gets a compromise from his executive board that represents an advance over prior practice. From the women's standpoint, however, the opening unlocks the floodgates. As a result, the leader ends up feeling "attacked" by the very people he set out to support. The dynamics of organizational change release pent-up anger and frustration on all sides, upset the status quo, and cause a heightening of tensions at the same time that progress is being made. Those who seek to maintain comfort in the midst of change, however, become themselves impediments to change.

MOVING INTO THE TWENTY-FIRST CENTURY

From a purely survival standpoint, labor must organize women workers— to rebuild its numbers and prevent further erosion of living standards and working conditions through the use of cheaper female labor, here as well as abroad, and through the expansion of contingent work. To meet this organizing challenge, unions must train, promote, and welcome women into leadership and rely on their skills and judgment.

Current structures and procedures limit access and opportunity for women, and they must be transformed. It would be unrealistic and self-defeating for unions to halt their activities until they can figure out how to change their culture and procedures. Grievances must be filed, contracts negotiated, cards signed, and votes taken. It would, however, be even more damaging to labor's future to postpone radical change until some elusive point when labor is strong and secure enough to withstand the risks inherent in organizational change. Unions urgently need a strategic plan with immediate and consistent steps to eliminate racism, sexism, and the many discriminatory attitudes and practices which have become institutionalized. What this means is that every plan, campaign, and decision must address discrimination, and evaluate the impact of the work on female and minority participation. A strategic plan would include the following components:

- For hiring, promotions, assignments, and slating, establish an affirmative action plan with numerical goals and quotas. The Canadian Labor Congress, for example, sets aside six seats minimally on the executive council for women and people of color.

- Design new descriptions, workloads, and expectations for union jobs so that an ideal unionist can also be a working parent and responsible family member. The very policies unions bargain with employers— flextime, job sharing, on-site child care, paid education leaves, and more—should be available within the union.

- Expand committee structures with increased responsibilities and authority, so that members participate not as passive or isolated individuals but as part of a group with specific tasks.

- Develop a greater range of structured opportunities: schools, internships, mentors, positions of responsibility with financial resources, and room to take risks, fail, and try again.

- Increase support for independent spaces and networking among previously marginalized workers.

- Curb the addiction to crisis management that privileges short-term gains over long-term goals. The process by which unions carry forward their work directly affects the degree of involvement and commitment of workers. More democratic decision-making builds a stronger, more dynamic union.

The ability to implement a plan successfully depends, above all, on the union's commitment to oppose racism, sexism, and other forms of discrimination within the house of labor. Top leaders must enforce existing policies with consequences for violations. There must be support for providing, and resources for attending, anti-racism and anti-sexism programs. Instead of tolerating racist, sexist, homophobic, and other offensive remarks, unions must challenge them. They have so much more to gain by acknowledging the connections among all oppressions, by upholding an injury to one as an injury to all, and by helping members understand the inseparable fate that joins blue-collar craftsmen to welfare mothers.

Finally, unions can expand their support for non-union workers. The Oregon AFL-CIO sponsors a week-long summer school for high school students. Participation at union conferences dealing with women's issues and civil rights in general should be open to non-union grassroots activists rather than limiting the participation of these groups to speaking invitations. The UCLEA/AFL-CIO women's schools could offer scholarships to community-based organizations and individual activists to interact with their highly motivated sisters. Above all, labor's influence is sure to increase if it intensifies its fight for national health care, higher minimum wage, paid family and medical leaves—needs that bring immediate and direct relief to millions of women without union protection.

Labor's future depends on its ability to learn from its women activists, from their style of work and their approach to problems. Women will do more than add numbers to the ranks of labor. Their leadership and commitment will create a better, stronger, more inclusive movement.

NOTES

This article benefitted from the helpful suggestions of Ellen Bravo, Nancy Lessin, Dotti Jones, and the editors of the volume.

1. For further information on women and unions, see: Dorothy Sue Cobble, *Women and Unions: Forging a Partnership* (Ithaca, N.Y.: ILR Press, 1993); Susan Eaton, "Union Leadership in the 1990's and Beyond" (Center for Science and International Affairs, Kennedy School of Government, Harvard University, Occasional Paper), pp. 92-105; Ruth Milkman, "Union Responses to Workforce Feminization in the U.S.," in *The Challenge of Restructuring: North American Labor Movements Respond*, edited by Jane Jenson and Rianne Mahon (Philadelphia: Temple University Press, 1993); Ruth Needleman, "Women Workers: A Force for Rebuilding Unionism," in *Labor Research Review*, VII (1), 1988; Ruth Needleman and Lucretia Tanner, "Women in Unions: Current Issues," in *Working Women: Past, Present, Future*, edited by Karen Koziara, Michael Moskow and Lucretia Tanner (IRRA, 1987); Brigid O'Farrell and Joyce Kornbluh, eds., *Rocking the Boat: Union Women's Voices, 1915-1975* (New Brunswick: Rutgers University Press, 1996); Cheryl Gooding, *Women and the Labor Movement in Massachusetts: Analysis of Issues and Proposed Solutions* (The Labor Research Center, College of Public and Community Service, University of Massachusetts-Boston, 1997); Sharon Kurtz, "All Kinds of Justice: Labor and Identity Politics" (Ph.D. dissertation, Boston College, 1994); and from a Canadian perspective, Linda Briskin and Patricia McDermott, eds., *Women Challenging Unions: Feminism, Democracy and Militancy* (Toronto: University of Toronto Press, 1993).

2. Although research on union women's views is limited, the regional women's summer schools co-sponsored by the UCLEA, AFL-CIO and CLUW have provided anecdotal as well as quantitative data. See, for example, Judith Catlett, "After the Good-byes: A Long-Term Look at the Southern School for Union Women," *Labor Studies Journal* 10 (Winter 1986), pp. 300-311; and Joyce Kornbluh and Mary Frederickson, eds., *Sisterhood and Solidarity: Workers' Education for Women, 1914-1984* (Philadelphia: Temple University Press, 1984).

3. See Cynthia Cockburn, *In the Way of Women: Men's Resistance to Sex Equality in Organizations* (Ithaca, N.Y.: ILR Press, 1991); and Briskin and McDermott, op. cit.

4. Given the importance placed today on organizing low-wage and service workers, and the preference for women and minority organizers at the grassroots, top-down decision-making has been experienced acutely as racist and sexist. Recent studies on how labor in the U.S. has been socially constructed as white and male are critical readings for those struggling to transform organized labor. Consider, for example: Patricia Hill Collins, *Black Feminist Thought: Knowledge, Consciousness and the Politics of Empowerment* (Boston: Unwin Hyman, 1990); Maxine Baca Zinn and Bonnie Thornton Dill, *Women of Color in U.S. Society* (Philadelphia: Temple University Press, 1994); David Roediger, *Towards the Abolition of Whiteness: Essays on Race, Politics and Working Class History*

(London: Verso, 1994); David Roediger, *The Wages of Whiteness: Race and the Making of the American Working Class* (London: Verso, 1991); Alexander Saxton, *The Rise and Fall of the White Republic: Class Politics and Mass Culture in Nineteenth-Century America* (London: Verson, 1991); Robin D.G. Kelley, "Identity Politics and Class Struggle," *New Politics* VI (2) (Winter 1997), pp. 84-96; and David Roediger, "What If Labor Were Not White and Male? Re-Centering Working Class History and Reconstructing Debate on the Unions and Race," *International Labor and Working Class History*, 51 (Spring 1997), pp. 72-95.

5. Rosabeth Moss Kanter's writings on the importance of numbers ("tokenism") most clearly delineate the problems faced by minority groups in organizations. See, for example, "The Impact of Hierarchical Structures on the Work Behavior of Women and Men," in *Women and Work*, edited by Rachel Kahn-Hut, Arlene Kaplan Daniels and Richard Colvard (London: Oxford University Press, 1982) and *Men and Women of the Corporation* (New York: Basic Books, 1977).

6. Tensions among women are often attributed to "women's nature," rather than to the organizational structures and male domination that limit women's access and encourage women to compete with each other. The divisions along race lines have been particularly serious and undermine needed solidarity. Too many studies of women workers address the issues as if all the women were white or as if being a woman were a universal experience. For additional information on differences among women and the experiences of women of different backgrounds, see: Esther Ngan-Ling Chow, Doris Wilkerson and Maxine Baca Zinn, *Race, Class and Gender: Common Bonds, Different Voices* (Thousand Oaks, CA: Sage Publications, 1996); Bernice Reagon Johnson, "Coalition Politics: Turning the Century," *Race, Class and Gender: An Anthology*, edited by Margaret Anderson and Patricia Hill Collins (Belmont, CA: Wadsworth Publishing Company, 1995); Ruth Needleman, *Raising Visibility, Reducing Marginality: A Labor Law Reform Agenda for Working Women of Color* (Women's Bureau, Department of Labor, 1993); Betty Woody, *Black Women in the Workplace: Impacts of Structural Change in the Economy* (Westport, CT: Greenwood Press, 1992); Cheryl Gooding, "Building a Multicultural Union Women's Organization: Lessons from the WILD Experience," *New Solutions* (forthcoming, 1997); Audre Lorde, "Age, Race, Class and Sex: Women Redefining Difference," in *Race, Class and Gender: An Anthology*; Theresa Amott and Julie Matthei, *Race, Gender and Work* (Boston: South End Press, 1991); and Julianne Malveaux, "The Political Economy of Black Women," *Social Policy* 25 (2), 1987.

7. SEIU Executive Board member, interviewed by author, April 1992.

8. For a summary of the research on women and labor union participation, see Needleman and Tanner, op. cit., pp. 211-214.

9. Pamela Roby and Lynet Uttal, "Putting It All Together: The Dilemmas of Rank-and-File Union Leaders," in Cobble, op. cit., pp. 363-377.

10. See, for example, Carol Stack, *All Our Kin* (New York: Basic Books, 1997); Karen Brodkin Sacks, "Gender and Grassroots Leadership," and Patricia Zavella, "The Politics of Race and Gender: Organizing Chicana Workers in Northern California," in *Women and the Politics of Empowerment,* edited by Ann Bookman and Sandra Morgen (Philadelphia: Temple University Press, 1988); Marya Muñoz-Vazquez, "Gender and Politics: Grassroots Leadership among Puerto Rican Women in a Health Struggle," in *Puerto Rican Women and Work,* edited by Altagracia Ortiz (Philadelphia: Temple University Press, 1996).

11. See Barbara Reskin and Irene Padavic, *Women and Men at Work* (Thousand Oaks, CA: Pine Forge Press, 1994); Cynthia Cockburn, op. cit.; Carl Cuneo, "Trade Union Leadership: Sexism and Affirmative Action," in Briskin and McDermott, pp. 109-136; and Needleman and Tanner.

12. An earlier version of this discussion appears in Ruth Needleman, "Space and Opportunities: Developing new leaders to meet labor's future," *Labor Research Review* XII (1), Summer 1993, pp. 5-20.

13. Joe Crump, phone interview by author, September 1992.

14. I worked with the USWA Education Department in evaluating the curriculum and have participated in the week-long program as well. This information is based on numerous discussions with USWA women leaders.

15. From 1990-92, I served as the education director for SEIU in Washington, D.C. and helped to develop this leadership program.

16. Celia Wcislo, interview by author, March 1991, Boston, MA.

17. Karen Nussbaum, interview by author, December 1991, Austin, TX.

18. Joyce Miller, interview by author, April 1991, Washington, D.C.

19. Gloria Johnson, interview by author, April 1991, Washington, D.C.

20. Gerry Hudson, interview by author, January 1993, New York, N.Y.

Getting Serious about Inclusion:
A Comprehensive Approach

José La Luz and Paula Finn

Labor unions remain the only large multiracial, multiethnic democratic institutions in our society. In a nation as racked by racism and sexism, and diminished by the poverty of its efforts toward a meaningful, robust democracy, the union movement holds a crucial responsibility to become a bastion for propagating inclusion and democracy. The institutions of labor are the only institutions in our society adequate to the task of bringing about this sort of change. In order to accomplish this, unions themselves must more fully practice their commitment to these principles.

For the most part, unions remain multiracial and multiethnic as a result of the diversity present in the industries and sectors which they organize. Most unions have not taken up diversity as a principle for shaping their internal structures or cultures, or for building a visionary and powerful labor movement, much less radically altering the country's racial and ethnic divisions. In reality, unions often target women workers or workers of color for organizing campaigns because they are present in a particular industry or geographic location in large numbers, but not because they will help create the kind of unions needed to build the labor movement and connect with other movements for social change. Many union leaders and staff speak of workers who are "difficult to organize"—often "difficult" due to ineffective organizing methods or the current reputation and culture of the union, rather than any inherent qualities of the workers themselves—and they skip the discussion about the kind of union they seek to build. Often the primary concern for numbers—which dominates many unions' organizing strategies —frequently makes the issues of union-building and movement-building seem superfluous.

THE CRITICAL CHALLENGE OF INCLUSION AND DEMOCRACY

Many unions have not sufficiently embraced the difficult and promising work of creating real, profound democratic structures capable of inspiring new members and, by example, expanding workers' demands for more democracy in the larger society. Even the notion that high levels of internal democracy weaken us vis-à-vis the boss still prevails in some circles of the labor movement. Yet it is our inability to engage with different perspectives and solutions, and then take disciplined action, which sometimes make our decisions less defensible and always makes us less able to defend those decisions. Democracy also makes real inclusion meaningful; it helps protect against tokenism, as well as against allegations of tokenism; and it is vital to recreating unions to respond to the cultures and concerns of the members.

Women, people of color, and immigrants—whose voices, for the most part, remain excluded from the strategic decision-making processes within their unions—need to have a sense of ownership and leadership in unions. Women today make up forty-five percent of the workforce. Latinos, African Americans, as well as Asian and other immigrant workers, also constitute a large part of the call for the transformation of unions into organizations capable of championing the interests of all workers, and of inspiring and joining with other social justice movements.

LATINO WORKERS AND THE NEED FOR INCLUSION

Although the Latino workforce in the United States has increased by nearly two-thirds over the past ten years—to its present size of over ten million— Latinos today actually make up a lesser percentage of unionized workers. In 1989, Latino workers accounted for one in ten union members; they now amount to about one in twelve. This is true, despite studies which show that their presence in organizing drives contributes to the likelihood of union success. The decrease in unionization rates for Latinos is higher than those of the overall workforce. Not surprisingly, the real wages of Latinos have plummeted by almost twice as much as those of the average U.S. worker.[1]

What happens to Latino workers will hold profound implications for the entire society, and for the strength of the labor movement, in particular. A recent census bureau report indicates "explosive growth" in the country's Latino population. By the year 2050, the report documents, Latinos will account for a quarter of the U.S. population, up from a current 10.7 percent.[2] In the past, when certain unions have proven unwilling or unable to include new immigrants, women, and African Americans, they grew weaker. Such was the case in the mostly craft unions that existed in the basic industries, like steel, auto, and electronics. Today, as women and people of color increasingly make up the majority of the workforce, this reality becomes essential to all of labor's strategic planning.

OBSTACLES TO INCLUSION FACED BY LATINO WORKERS

Many of the obstacles to inclusion within unions which Latino workers confront are identical to those of other ethnic and racial minorities. However, three problems which Latinos (and other immigrant groups) in particular face are: first, the tendency of non-Latino unionists to be insensitive to, or entirely unaware of, national differences among Latinos, which include linguistic, racial, cultural, and political differences, as well as disparate national experiences with trade unionism. This blindness becomes apparent when, for example, at a national meeting, a union leader has a Dominican staffer from New York translate for a group of Mexican workers from Texas. In spite of the fact that they all speak Spanish, the idioms and regionalisms in their use of the language may become significant barriers in the communication process.

Secondly, there is a widespread tendency to overlook the sometimes considerable political experiences and skills which many Latino workers bring with them from their involvement in political and social struggles, which have been waged for decades throughout Latin America. Sometimes these skills and experiences have been honed in trade union struggles, but frequently they grow out of radical grassroots movements. Overlooking or undervaluing these experiences can prove demoralizing for workers and tragic for the need to develop rank-and-file leadership.

Thirdly, the exclusive use of English in many unions amounts to a paramount obstacle to fostering participation and leadership among Latino members. The unwillingness to create forums which enable Latinos to listen, communicate, or read about union matters in their dominant (or, in many cases, their only) language, distances and alienates Latino and other immigrant workers from their unions. It sends a message which says, "This is not your union until you speak our language."

EARLY EXPERIMENTS IN INCLUSION

The notion that unions should invent new organizational forms to accommodate immigrant workers is not unprecedented in United States history. At the beginning of this century, the immigrant leaders and founders of the Amalgamated Clothing Workers of America (ACWA) wrestled with what today might appear extreme strategies for winning the loyalties of and developing a sense of ownership among a diverse workforce. In centers of clothing manufacturing like Chicago, New York, Baltimore, and Philadelphia the new union supported the creation of nationality and language-based locals; it published union newspapers in six foreign languages; and it established on-going, long-term alliances with a variety of ethnic, social, and political organizations.[3] These strategies were not without short-comings or detractors among the leadership of the union. Union leaders worried, as they do today, about allowing diversity to thrive at the expense of unity. Most leaders viewed these strategies as short-term measures toward what they hoped would lead to a more homogenous union culture. Whatever the perspectives regarding these strategies, they indicate a boldness and a willingness to take risks toward the inclusion of what the leadership deemed a workforce potentially alienated from the then current union structures and culture, yet absolutely vital to building a powerful union.

Significantly, many of these strategies sought to organize new immigrant workers without asking them to check their languages and cultures at the union door. Further, they allowed—indeed, encouraged—disparate immigrants to develop union identity through ethnic identity, rather than in spite of it. The promotion of the nationality-based locals, in particular, hints of a willingness to permit new immigrant groups to recreate their unions in their own languages and cultures in an effort to organize, and then to mobilize large numbers of ethnically and linguistically diverse workers.

CONTEMPORARY UNION STRUGGLES WITH ETHNIC IDENTITY

These strategies became less and less common in unions starting with World War II and beyond, when, in the country as a whole, the thrust toward "Americanization" became emulation. Of course, today many progressive trade unionists continue to counterpoise ethnic identity with class identity, fearing ethnic identity's potential for disunity. However, in the United States, workers of color, women, and immigrants do not have the option of choosing one identity or the other. Forcing this choice not only alienates workers who desperately need union protection—and upon whom the future of the labor movement depends; it also keeps the labor movement from developing alliances with other movements for social change, and from appreciating the variety of motivations that bring women, workers of color, and immigrants—potential union members—to fight against injustice. This variety of experiences and motivations, in fact, accounts for the greater success rate in union organizing struggles which involve people of color and women workers.

ORGANIZING NEW WORKERS IS NOT ENOUGH

Unions organize for several reasons: 1) in order to represent a greater percentage of workers in a given industry, and thus to strengthen the union's hand at the bargaining table; 2) to expand political power as a result of representing greater numbers; and, 3) to bring the benefits of union voice and union contracts to workers who toil without them. In addition, unions must also organize in order to build a political movement capable of representing all workers, and therefore, transforming fundamental power relations within our society. In order to do this, unions must prepare for the internal changes which will make this possible.

Organizing Latinos, women, and other people of color in large numbers into unions does not equal inclusion, although it paves the way and creates the conditions for it to happen. Unions themselves must change as a result of successful organizing drives. Newly organized and inspired workers will seek, and must find, a voice within their unions. Not making opportunities for voice and leadership available to newly organized workers often has the tragic effect of alienating and turning them against their unions, or worse, it makes many workers cynical about taking any further action for social change.

When trade unionists think about organizing thousands of new workers—and to survive we must—we must plan for institutional transformation. This implies changes in power relations. Sometimes it also requires new methods of education; changes in the times, locations, languages, and even the styles of union meetings; and variations in the faces, perspectives, and languages which appear in union newspapers and leaflets. While many leaders and staff have developed outstanding abilities to target and organize new workers, fewer are prepared to accept the transformation of power relations and union culture required for new members to develop ownership and remain active within their unions.

Inevitably, the majority of newly organized workers will increasingly consist of women, people of color, and new immigrants. These groups hold the least power in our society. Unions can ill afford to reproduce those unequal power relations internally. In fact, disenfranchised groups look to unionization, in large part, to ameliorate conditions of injustice.

The Service Employees International Union's (SEIU) Justice for Janitors campaign in Los Angeles has been the most successful large-scale organizing campaign involving Latino workers in the past two decades. As such, it presents significant strengths, as well as shortcomings, vital to understand in order to improve labor's efforts to reach out to and develop union ownership and leadership among Latino workers. SEIU began the Justice for Janitors campaign in the late 1980s, organizing the largely Central American and Mexican workers who cleaned L.A.'s office buildings at night as employees of the burgeoning janitorial service contractors. With few illusions about the likelihood of success through an election campaign organized in response to the considerable hurdles created by the National Labor Relations Board, the organizers devised a strategy which relied on direct action, public pressure, aggressive worker mobilization, community support, legal tactics, and corporate strategies. At the outset of the campaign, Local 399 of SEIU represented health care workers and a dwindling number of janitors, due to the union busting efforts of the office building managements and their use of the janitorial service contractors. As a result of these union busting tactics and Local 399's ineffective efforts to defend its building service workers, the union's membership had plummeted from seventy percent representation in 1980 to only thirty percent in 1987. The campaign, an attempt to recapture the majority of workers in this sector, would end up surpassing even the period prior to the influx of the service contractors, achieving a full ninety percent union representation of Los Angeles and neighboring Century City's janitors.

SEIU's Justice for Janitors campaign is one among a few contemporary campaigns that has drawn a good portion of its power and character from the culture and prior experiences of the workers it has targeted for organizing. A report by David Bacon on the campaign published in the *LA Weekly* makes this point exactly:

> The janitors' tactics relied on the militancy of immigrant workers. Local 399's organizers mobilized them again and again, bringing them into the street to win contracts. They drew on the traditions and experiences of workers who faced down terror in El Salvador and Guatemala. They appealed to workers who had learned as children in Mexico, that while they have a right to a fair share of the wealth of society, they have to fight to get it.[4]

The article cites Eliseo Medina, SEIU's international executive vice president for the Western U.S., who adds:

> When you come from a country where they shoot you for being a unionist or a striker, getting fired from your job doesn't seem so bad. Immigrants from Central America have a much more militant history as unionists than we do, and the more militant workers are, the more unions can do.[5]

The organizers' commitment to draw on these experiences contributed, in large part, to the energy and impressive achievements of the Justice for Janitors campaign.

The Justice for Janitors campaign tells a story of creative organizing; of commitment to fostering authentic community alliances, particularly among immigrant organizations; and of the necessity for unions to permit and plan for the inclusion of a diverse new membership as a result of successful organizing.

According to several Latino officials and activists in SEIU with whom we have spoken, insufficient planning for institutional transition became a serious problem in the wake of the Justice for Janitors campaign, leading the international union to put Local 399 in trusteeship in 1995. The local, representing 25,000 workers—12,000 health care workers at Kaiser Permanente of Southern California, 8,000 janitors, and the rest workers in related industries—would have been expected to undergo growing pains related to the diversity of its membership and their division into different professions and industries. Although not all of the upheaval was related to problems of inclusion, much of the members' frustration was certainly articulated in racial and ethnic terms.

Rodolfo Acuña, a noted historian of Mexican American workers' struggles in California, writes that a group of dissidents, calling themselves reformistas, and originally composed of health care workers, became discontented with the local's allocation of revenues and energies for the expansion of the union and its facilities, rather than for the maintenance of existing contracts and fighting work speed-ups at Kaiser. These workers gained the sympathies of the janitors, who lodged complaints about the bureaucratization of the leadership, symbolized by the locked door in the union's office anteroom that separated the members from their representatives. The reformistas also claimed that the local's top leadership remained dominated by Americans of European descent, leaving little room for upward mobility of Latino and Mexican rank-and-filers.[6] As Acuña puts it in his book on Latinos and the U.S. labor movement,

> As in similar struggles within progressive movements, there is plenty of blame to go around. There is no doubt that there are some opportunists within the ranks of the reformistas. On the other hand, Zellers [president of Local 399] should have handled the situation by taking assertive steps to deal with the problems raised by the Local 399's rapid expansion, rather than taking the membership's support for granted. It was necessary to improve communication with the rank-and-file, to tear down walls rather than to build them to suit the convenience of the bureaucracy.[7]

According to Mike Garcia and Rodolfo Acuña, the reformistas raised several objections to the leadership's handling of the local. Those objections included: 1) a perception by the newly organized, largely Latino members, that the predominantly white leadership was content to use them as soldiers in campaigns and demonstrations, but resistant to encouraging or allowing their inclusion in decision-making and leadership roles; 2) complaints by Kaiser workers and the janitors that the leadership was neglecting the day-to-day needs of the membership in the interest of organizing new workers; 3) a frustrated desire on behalf of the newly organized janitors to assume staff positions, concomitant with a sense that their skills, experiences, and commitment were being undervalued; and 4) a charge that the leadership maintained a distance from the membership, symbolized by the locked door in the union office anteroom and the infrequency of leadership visits to members' worksites.[8] Some of these complaints overtly raised the issue of lack of inclusion based on ethnicity, and other objections focus on problems of a different nature. However, given the broader social context of pervasive racism and ethnic discrimination, the members saw the conflict largely in terms of ethnic divisions. Had the union leadership foreseen this reality and been willing to take bold and thoughtful steps to include the new members in positions of greater authority and leadership, perhaps those problems which had less to do with inclusion might have proven easier to resolve.

The union and its members weathered these difficulties, but not without serious expense of resources and energies that might have been more effectively spent. At present, the building services division of Local 399 has joined with Local 1877, headed by Mike Garcia and consisting of janitors in Silicon Valley, Oakland, and Sacramento, to form one of the largest building service locals in the country. Garcia believes that this move holds the possibility of allowing janitors to gain much greater leverage through unified bargaining and campaign tactics.

THE NEED FOR A COMPREHENSIVE NATIONAL PLAN

Unions which give up on—or fail to take up—the experiment with inclusion and democracy will inevitably become weaker and irrelevant. Worse still, they distance those workers and the movements and organizations which represent them from the rest of the labor movement.

The new leadership of the AFL-CIO has a crucial role to play in ensuring that unions, and the labor movement as a whole, avoid this fate. Remedies to racial, ethnic, and gender-based exclusion from voice and power within unions must be comprehensive. A piece-meal approach has not and will not work.

To begin with, there is a need to redefine the mission of the constituent groups—the A. Philip Randolph Institute, the Coalition of Black Trade Unionists, the Asian Pacific American Labor Alliance, the Labor Council for Latin American Advancement, the Coalition of Labor Union Women, and Front Lash—which have historically sought to play the role of representing the interests of African Americans, Asians, Latinos, women, and young workers within the official trade union movement. The earliest of these groups—the A. Philip Randolph Institute, the Coalition of Black Trade Unionists and the Coalition of Labor Union Women—were formed in response to the progressive social movements of the 1960s and 1970s, and sought to bring the call for racial and gender justice and equality into the mainstream of the labor movement. Until now, these groups have not played a prominent role in shaping a comprehensive strategy for inclusion.

In order to enable the constituent groups to become more effective promoters of institutional transformation, they should be redefined as "organizing groups"; and the labor movement should seek to broaden and clarify their scope of activities, while making specific plans for their strategic development. Whenever possible, they must also play a vital role in promoting and facilitating organizational changes towards inclusion within unions.

In order to delineate the obstacles to inclusion and democracy, and to begin a process for planning effective strategies for overcoming the obstacles, the new AFL-CIO leadership could call a major, national conference. This conference should certainly include the AFL-CIO's organizing, education, field mobilization, and civil rights departments. The so-called constituency groups should play a major role in shaping the agenda and overall strategy for the conference. The purpose of the conference should be to develop a program for organizational and cultural change, that is, a program for inclusion. A conference like this would produce a comprehensive and systematic plan that combines organizing, education, and coalition-building. These efforts would lead to the selection of targets for both new organizing, as well as union-building, in which the constituent groups play a leading role.

Furthermore, the following three major proposals should be considered: the first proposal would address the transformation of the missions and roles of the constituent groups; the second proposal would focus on large-scale, collaboratively developed and collaboratively led pilot organizing projects employing a community unionism campaign strategy; the third proposal would address the need to encourage and assist unions in developing and meeting clear goals to transform their leaderships to reflect the demographic make-up of their memberships.

Many activists among the constituent groups share the perspective that these groups are in need of serious redefinition of their missions, as was expressed in the conference of the constituent groups prior to the 1995 AFL-CIO convention. We insisted at that time that these organizations have historically played a role of supporting and upholding, rather than helping to shape and guide, the tenets and programs of organized labor. This has often robbed the labor movement of the ability to transform itself to adequately meet the social and political challenges of the moment.

Sometimes it has put the constituent groups at awkward and untenable distances from their respective communities, thus yielding them less than effective champions for those communities within labor.

Many activists within the constituent groups also believe that their primary mission should concern organizing. The constituent groups represent the fastest growing sectors of the workforce, as well as those most in need of organizing, due to a higher incidence of poor working conditions and substandard pay.

The organizing proposal would argue for an innovative and ambitious plan to target and develop seven large-scale community-based organizing projects. These projects should proceed under the collaborative leadership of the constituent groups, the AFL-CIO, the appropriate affiliated unions, and the Organizing Institute. Los Angeles, Atlanta, New York, Miami, Chicago, San Francisco, and Dallas would serve as promising sites for these pilot organizing projects. The constituent groups maintain chapters in these cities, and these cities are home to highly diverse workforces, and as such, they would provide the opportunity for the constituent groups to work in-depth with their respective communities to develop the relationships and requisite support for successful organizing.

To carry out this organizing role, the constituent groups must be granted sufficient autonomy and collaborative decision-making power. They must be seen as strategic partners in the development of a revitalized, democratic, and inclusive labor movement. This means that they must also be given adequate resources to develop deep roots within their communities and the respective movements which have grown out of those communities.

Much has been said of the community-based approach to union organizing. When combined with an industry-wide and/or regional strategy for organizing, this approach holds the possibility not only for increasing union power, but for building crucial alliances with other movements and organizations in order to strengthen local (and ultimately, national) progressive politics. Community-based organizing has been described as adhering to the following six features:

1. Important non-labor groups in the community have some sort of ownership of the unionization effort.

2. Great efforts are made to actively involve non-union workers and others of the communities from which the workers come. This is

done, in particular, to develop a more diverse and representative leadership group.

3. Campaign strategy is not defined by the narrow provisions of the National Labor Relations Act, or, in the case of public employees, the state labor relations laws.

4. A significant up-front commitment of resources must be made to develop the necessary base of community support, even before workplace-oriented organizing begins.

5. An emphasis is placed on finding ways to involve other unions with no direct immediate self-interest in the campaign.

6. Organizing strategy focuses heavily on waging an effective campaign in the court of public opinion.[9]

Most of these features speak to community unionism's need to move the sympathies of and develop genuine alliances with people and communities beyond the normal reach of organized labor. The constituent groups ought to play an essential role in these efforts.

An organizing program such as this would enable a vital, two-way learning experience for the constituent groups, and the AFL-CIO, and its unions. Due to the collaborative nature of the targeting and leadership of the campaigns, an excellent chance would exist for drawing on the considerable strengths and understandings of each of the parties. The constituent groups would gain the important experience of direct involvement in organizing drives. This experience should include a thorough organizing education program for members of the constituent groups, thus permitting them to acquire sufficient expertise to make their new role a meaningful one.

On the other hand, the AFL-CIO and the unions involved would gain the necessary understandings of some of the crucial concerns which the constituent groups share with unorganized women, immigrants, and workers of color. The constituent groups would, of course, bring to the projects their ideas regarding cultural approaches to organizing and vital connections with their respective communities.

Finally, while union memberships increasingly consist of women and people of color, the top leadership does not reflect these demographic changes. This is not labor's secret; it is, in fact, the public image that the New Voice leadership of John Sweeney, Linda Chavez-Thompson, and Richard

Trumka has pledged to change. Sister Chavez has been given the task of developing a program that includes a role for the constituent organizations. Constituent groups should play a role in helping unions to develop clear goals and programs for transforming their leadership to reflect the demographics of their memberships.

Rather than promoting universal quotas, an effort to change the face of organized labor should engage unions in reviewing the gender and ethnic make-up of their memberships—an important task in and of itself. It is precisely this information which many unions fail to study or disclose. Ending this silence should bring obvious benefits. Leadership development goals would then be based on these demographics and attached to timelines and education programs to promote those groups currently underrepresented in the strategic decision-making processes within many unions.

This effort to promote a new, more diverse leadership should give rise to the critical discussion within the labor movement of the qualities and characteristics we seek when identifying new leadership in general. Some of the qualities which many unions have undervalued are: the ability of new leaders to make thoughtful, independent judgements; innovation and creativity; effective listening skills; and consensus and group-building skills. Discussions and efforts such as these hold the promise of not only changing the face, but also improving the nature of leadership within unions.

Education programs geared toward promoting new leadership must also build upon sound decisions regarding leadership qualities that unions hope to promote. The style, as well as the content of union education should reflect these goals. If membership participation and consensus-building are important leadership values, then the education programs themselves should, among other things, encourage active participation and team work. Union leadership education for transformation must also be treated with strategic importance as critical to institutional change, rather than the common, ad hoc, or as-the-need-arises approach which most union leaders often allow union education to take on.

In summary, all of us active in trade unions have a stake in promoting inclusion and democratic participation as part of an overall strategy to revitalize and put the movement back in labor. Those of us whose commitment is to empower all workers know the importance as well as the difficulties of this challenge.

NOTES

1. Héctor Figueroa, "The Growing Force of Latino Labor," *NACLA Report on the Americas*, November/December 1996, pp. 20-21.

2. Katherine Q. Seelye in *The New York Times*, March 27, 1997, sec. B, p. 16.

3. Steve Fraser, "Landslayt and Paesani: Ethnic Conflict and Cooperation in the Amalgamated Clothing Workers of America," in *Struggle a Hard Battle*, Dirk Hoerder, ed. (DeKalb, IL: Northern Illinois University Press, 1986), pp. 292-294.

4. *The LA Weekly*, February 28, 1997, p. 12.

5. Ibid., p. 12.

6. Rodolfo Acuña, *Anything But Mexican: Chicanos in Contemporary Los Angeles* (New York: Verso, 1996), p. 188.

7. Ibid.

8. Author interview, 1997.

9. Andy Banks, "The Power and Promise of Community Unionism," *Labor Research Review*, Volume 18, pp. 18-20.

The Challenge of
Diversity and Inclusion
in the AFL-CIO

May Chen and Kent Wong

Together, we are forging a common agenda to build the U.S. labor movement, to strengthen coalitions between unions and communities of color, to organize the unorganized, to promote voter registration and voter participation, to advance civil rights, to defend affirmative action and immigrant rights, and to build a better future for all working people. Now more than ever, people of color, women, and young people must stand together and organize.

Women and people of color are increasingly the growing majority in the workplace today. We are gathered today to pledge our support to build a labor movement that embraces diversity as its strength. Women, people of color and young people represent the future and hope of the U.S. labor movement. While we are committed to defend affirmative action in the workplace, we are also committed to promote affirmative action within the labor movement.

(Joint Statement of the "Full Participation Conference," October 1995)

In October 1995, for the first time ever, people of color and women within the U.S. labor movement gathered together to promote diversity and inclusion within the ranks of labor. The conference immediately preceded the 1995 AFL-CIO convention, which was to elect the most diverse leadership the AFL-CIO has ever had.

Women, people of color, and immigrants comprise the vast majority of new workers, and studies of union elections reflect that these same people are also more likely to join unions than other workers. Diversity is essential to the growth of the labor movement. The new officers of the AFL-CIO have appointed very few people of color to leadership jobs. Within national unions, the white male power structures are still intact. The leadership and staff of unions must change to reflect the new workforce.

In a period when unions represent less than fifteen percent of the workforce, it is essential that they build alliances with community organizations and groups; these alliances will also help ensure that unions are reaching out to more diverse communities. Churches, students, immigrants' rights groups, disability rights groups, gay and lesbian organizations, advocates for housing, health care, and the homeless, and other community-based organizations are all potential allies of labor. The labor movement needs to spend time, attention, and resources to develop and expand these relationships, and to forge a common agenda.

Unions must take the lead in representing the interests of the vast majority within this country—not just union members. In this era of corporate greed and take-backs, unions need to defend the standard of living of all workers and demand universal health care. In this era of renewed and escalating racism and anti-immigrant hysteria, unions must be out ahead in building multiracial unity and defending immigrant rights. In this era, when right wing fanatics are attacking family planning clinics and the rights of gays and lesbians, unions must take the lead in defending the right of choice and in opposing all forms of discrimination.

If unions are to actively involve a broad cross-section of our population, they must move away from the culture of business unionism, in which unions collect dues and provide services, and towards a culture that invites workers' activism and leadership. An organizing union advances a culture in which everything the union undertakes and represents is directed towards organizing its members and reaching out to the unorganized. In this context, workers become motivated to work for social change. The United Farm Workers' slogan "Every worker is an organizer!" captures the essence of that union's organizing culture.

HISTORICAL OVERVIEW OF LABOR UNIONS AND DIVERSITY

The U.S. labor movement's record with regard to people of color and women has been a source of collective embarrassment. The Executive Council, the highest leadership body within the AFL-CIO, has been the almost exclusive domain of older white men for generations. Of the thirty-five members of the council who presided over the 1995 convention, thirty-one were white men, and most were over sixty. However, the 1995 convention brought some change. The debate over diversity held just before the convention was symbolically acknowledged by both sides in the first contested election for AFL-CIO leadership that took place at the 1995 convention. Each slate included a woman: President Tom Donahue selected Barbara Easterling as his running mate, while Service Employees International Union President John Sweeney, the victor, chose Richard Trumka as secretary-treasurer and Linda Chavez-Thompson for a newly established executive vice president position. In addition, the Executive Council was expanded from thirty-five to fifty-four, and the convention resolved that at least ten seats be set aside for people of color. The new executive council includes nine African Americans, two Latinos, the first Asian American, and seven women. While these changes were positive first steps, the struggle for inclusion and democracy continues.

This struggle is rooted in the history of the U.S. labor movement and of the AFL-CIO. In the labor movement's early days, European immigrants were essential in establishing and building unions in mines, mills, and factories. To successfully organize these workers, unions had to bridge cultural and language barriers among various European immigrant communities. For example, the garment industry unions translated their publications into many European languages to ensure that immigrant workers were included. But the recognition of cultural diversity did not usually extend to African Americans or immigrants of color.

At its 1890 convention, the American Federation of Labor publicly opposed union provisions that excluded people because of their race or color. However, because the federation structure allowed considerable autonomy to affiliate unions, individual unions could still explicitly bar African Americans and other workers of color from membership.

In fact, despite the 1890 resolution, many AFL and union leaders opposed organizing and including workers of color. Samuel Gompers, who founded the AFL and was its leader for several decades, steadfastly refused to allow Asian workers to join AFL unions. In 1905, he denied a charter to a multiracial farm workers union from Oxnard, California, because the union included Japanese Americans. In 1905, a period of anti-Asian hysteria, labor unions provided a solid base in San Francisco for formation of the "Japanese and Korean Exclusion League," later renamed the "Asiatic Exclusion League." During the early part of the twentieth century, the federation adopted a policy that explicitly supported organizing African Americans into separate unions.

Despite these policies, workers of color were part of the tremendous surge in union organizing that took place throughout the country during the 1930s. African Americans called for an end to policies of exclusion. At the 1934 AFL convention, A. Philip Randolph, president of the Brotherhood of Sleeping Car Porters, demanded that "any union maintaining the color bar" be expelled from the federation. This resolution was defeated on the grounds that the AFL could not interfere with the autonomy of national and international unions.

Unions in the building trades industry were particularly notorious for excluding workers of color. Many building trades unions functioned as close-knit fraternal clubs, within which jobs and apprenticeships were handed down from father to son, and among relatives and friends. African Americans were excluded for generations before they were able to break down some of these barriers. In contrast, the Congress of Industrial Organizations, established in the thirties, stated in its constitution that one of its main objectives was "to bring about the effective organization of the working men and women of America without regard to race, color, creed or nationality."[1] Unlike AFL craft unions, the CIO advocated industrial unionism to open union ranks to all workers in an industry. The CIO embraced a militant approach to organizing and advanced an agenda opposing racism and segregation within unions.

Despite the more inclusive stance of the CIO, its merger with the AFL in 1955 did not end policies of racial discrimination and segregation within the labor movement. At the AFL-CIO convention in 1959, A. Philip Randolph and other African American unionists again raised their voices to denounce racism and segregation within the labor movement. In response, AFL-CIO President George Meany claimed that segregation existed in unions in part because black workers supported it. The debate escalated, with Meany challenging Randolph's right to speak for African Americans.

Many of the explicit racial barriers enacted by unions remained in place until the civil rights movement and the passage of the 1964 Civil Rights Act.

LABOR AND THE CIVIL RIGHTS MOVEMENT

As the civil rights movement gained momentum throughout the country, support from labor unions grew. The historic March on Washington in 1963 brought together civil rights and union activists in unprecedented numbers to demand racial and economic justice. The civil rights movement, in turn, was a catalyst for changes in the labor movement, in part because it targeted the workplace as a major arena for the struggle for equality. As a result, the 1964 Civil Rights Act included a provision that addressed problems of employment discrimination. In 1968, Dr. Martin Luther King Jr., widely acknowledged as the leader of the civil rights movement, was assassinated while supporting African American sanitation workers in Memphis. His presence there signified the shared struggles of civil rights and labor, symbolized in the slogan of the sanitation workers: "I am a man." This linking of the civil rights and labor movements challenged and transformed unions, as workers of color and women workers increasingly demanded their rights.

In the late 1960s, black workers began organizing caucuses within unions to challenge established union leaders. Caucuses of black teachers were active in unions in New York City and Chicago. Black postal workers and other government workers also set up caucuses to oppose racism. Black workers in basic industries, particularly auto, transportation, and steel, were among the most militant in advancing an agenda for action. In May 1968, black workers at Dodge Main launched a wildcat strike to protest speed-ups. When five black workers were fired, the Dodge Revolutionary Union Movement (DRUM) was organized to pressure both the employer and leaders within the United Auto Workers Union. The civil rights, anti-war, women's, and other progressive social movements of the 1960s and 1970s also encouraged this new generation of labor activists. Some college educated participants in these movements were drawn into workplace organizing.

The United Farm Workers Union (UFWU), led by Cesar Chavez in the 1960s, represented a significant coalition between labor and community-based organizing. Cesar Chavez began organizing through the Community Service Organization, galvanizing broad-based support from the Chicano and Latino communities. The farm workers union gave many Latinos their first exposure to organized labor. The farm workers' movement combined direct union organizing in the fields with support from urban and rural community-based organizations, churches, and students. Thousands of college students and community activists joined the grape boycott and other campaigns designed to pressure growers to sign contracts with farm workers. In the process, a new generation of labor activists was recruited and trained.

The struggles of the farm workers presented a starting point for linking Asian American activists of the 1960s and 1970s with the labor movement. This allowed Asian American students and activists to become acquainted with some of the earliest pioneers of farm worker organizing in California such as Philip Veracruz, a Filipino founder of the Farm Workers Organizing Committee. In the 1970s, the UFWU began a construction project to build retirement homes for Filipino farm workers, and volunteer work crews of students and community activists from the Asian Pacific American communities spent weekends in Delano, California building the Agbayani Village. This project touched and inspired the lives of thousands of young Asian Pacific Americans.

In the Pacific Northwest, Filipino cannery workers, members of the International Longshoremen's and Warehousemen's Union, linked up with community legal advocacy groups and began a series of class action lawsuits challenging the disparate treatment of workers of color in the canneries. Living in bunkhouses segregated from white workers, with inferior food, inferior working conditions, and no opportunities for advancement, these workers challenged the deeply entrenched employment discrimination of the cannery companies. While many of these actions successfully ended discriminatory employment practices, the most infamous case against Wards Cove Packing Company went all the way to the Supreme Court and resulted in a terrible decision which undermined the most fundamental civil rights protections in the workplace. Legislation in the Civil Rights Act of 1964 specifically excluded the Wards Cove workers from its corrective remedies.

Events of the 1970s and 1980s forced Asian Pacific American activists to confront labor's anti-Asian sentiment. The International Ladies' Garment Workers' Union's support for the Vietnam War and its nativist "Buy America" campaign repelled community activists from established labor unions. The brutal beating and murder of Vincent Chin by unemployed auto workers in Detroit in 1982 also pointed out the tremendous dangers of

Japan-bashing by leaders in organized labor. As they joined the workforce and became union members, Asian Pacific American activists put most of their organizing energies into community issues, civil rights and political empowerment, and the fight against workplace discrimination.

THE GROWTH OF CONSTITUENT GROUPS WITHIN ORGANIZED LABOR

One lesson of the civil rights movement was the importance of racial, ethnic, or women's caucuses to focus demands, train and develop leadership, and pressure institutions to change. As the progressive movements of the 1960s and 1970s inspired a new generation of labor organizers, constituent groups representing the particular interests of people of color and women also emerged within the established labor movement during this time. These included the A. Philip Randolph Institute (APRI), the Coalition of Black Trade Unionists (CBTU), the Labor Council for Latin American Advancement (LACLAA), and the Coalition of Labor Union Women (CLUW). These constituent organizations were created to challenge the exclusion of people of color from leadership and participation in AFL-CIO unions. However, some were formed under the initiative and control of the AFL-CIO in response to an insurgent population of rank-and-file workers, or to new communities unfamiliar with the established labor movement.

These groups have had mixed success. Where they have played a strong role as forums for discussion, mutual support and leadership development, they have produced committed and effective new leaders to diversify the AFL-CIO, and they have informed and changed the union's usual mode of business. On the other hand, where they have been marginalized and reduced to the status of tokens within the wider labor movement, they have simply provided perks and rewards for obedient minority-group members of organized labor.

In addition to these organizations within the AFL-CIO, ethnic and women's committees have been established within many unions. Again, the track record is mixed. Some have failed to provide meaningful political representation for the excluded groups, or have served only as social organizations, supporting the union agenda without criticism. In other instances, they have advocated forcefully for change within the union, criticizing exclusion, racism, and sexism, but at no small cost to the committee activists.

Often, established local or national labor leaders have attacked these committees and their outspoken activists as divisive troublemakers or worse.

The most important measure of the effectiveness of these constituency organizations lies in the content of their character and leadership. Even as token organizations, they have existed as a statement of the need for organized labor to respond to all of its diverse members in the patchwork quilt of union democracy. The most important challenge to the leaders of these constituency groups is two-fold: 1) to press labor unions and the AFL-CIO to provide meaningful representation and equal treatment; and 2) to build solidarity across diverse communities within the labor movement, breaking beyond the specific agendas of particular groups.

THE EXPERIENCE OF APALA

In 1992, Asian labor organizers founded the Asian Pacific American Labor Alliance (APALA), the first such organization in AFL-CIO history. This national structure was the outgrowth of committees of local Asian American activists in New York, San Francisco, and Los Angeles who met to encourage greater participation of Asian Americans within unions, and to support stronger relations between the labor movement and the Asian American community.

All three local Asian labor support committees were led by committed activists, with extensive experience both in labor and community organizing. Many of these activists were veterans of the civil rights, student, and anti-war movements, who envisioned their role within the labor movement as part of a broader commitment to social and economic justice. They also hoped that APALA could be used as a progressive voice in the national labor movement.

The strategic vision of APALA from its inception included both base building and coalition building. The vast majority of the membership are rank-and-file workers, and the organization is chapter-based. The day-to-day work of the organization is conducted almost exclusively by volunteers within the chapters, drawing resources from a national office with a small paid staff supported by the AFL-CIO.

At the national level, coalition efforts have attempted to unite other labor organizations and Asian American advocacy groups around a common agenda for civil rights and workers' rights. Within the labor movement, APALA has aggressively forged links with other constituency organizations and the AFL-CIO civil and human rights department to advance the interests of workers of color and women workers. Within the Asian American community, APALA has worked closely with other national organizations on issues such as immigrant rights, affirmative action, and political empowerment.

Since its formation, APALA activists have played an important role in the labor movement by translating union campaign literature into Asian languages, bridging cultural barriers, and challenging the bosses' divide and conquer tactics. In so doing, they have succeeded in bringing Asian Pacific workers into the labor movement. By standing up for workers in the business-dominated Asian Pacific communities and in union organizing campaigns, APALA organizers are often the sole voice for the needs of Asians, immigrants, and newcomers in the workplace.

While APALA is a relatively young organization with a small national staff, its leaders realize that to embrace a culture of organizing means that all existing resources must support an organizing agenda. National Executive Board meetings have been used as strategic planning sessions. National conferences and conventions have been used as training grounds for future organizing. At these gatherings, union caucuses have met to support an organizing agenda within their respective unions. For the first time caucuses of Korean, Filipino, Vietnamese, and South Asian union activists have met one another, and developed informal support networks.

The number of union staffers of Asian Pacific nationalities around the country is still relatively small. As a consequence, rank-and-file members dominate APALA. Because this has the advantages of ensuring a grassroots base, APALA will have to work hard to continue to recruit and train new rank-and-file union members as more Asian union activists move into staff positions.

One of the critical challenges for APALA is to include and involve all Asian Pacific American communities. Asian Pacific Americans represent diverse nationalities and cultures, with distinct languages and immigration histories. APALA's leadership and its strategies have to reflect inclusion of people of different nationalities, genders, unions, and regions.

APALA's leaders chose to concentrate on organizing the large and growing unorganized Asian Pacific workforce. Although Asian Pacific Americans are the fastest growing ethnic community in the country, there are woefully few Asian union organizers, and very few labor unions have committed resources to organize the unorganized, especially immigrants.

APALA leaders realized that the first charge would be to recruit and train a new generation of Asian American labor organizers.

One of APALA's first initiatives was to work with the AFL-CIO Organizing Institute to design a program to recruit and train new Asian labor organizers. The first training was held in fall 1992, just a few months after APALA was founded. Since then, over 150 people have graduated from this program, and many have gone on to work as organizers for unions throughout the country. In 1995, Myung Soo Seuck, a graduate of the APALA/Organizing Institute program, became the first Asian American field staff organizer ever hired by the AFL-CIO.

In summer 1996, APALA's organizers drew together 250 people, including dozens of graduates of the APALA/Organizing Institute program, to develop a strategy for organizing Asian Pacific workers throughout the U.S. Organizing directors from major unions joined with APALA leaders to draft an agreement entitled "A Partnership for Organizing." Under the terms of this agreement, APALA will continue to assist unions who want to organize Asian Pacific workers, recruit Asian Pacific organizers, and forge labor and community alliances that support organizing campaigns. In return, the unions who are party to the agreement pledge to recruit and hire Asian Pacific organizers, to allocate resources to organize Asian workers, and to identify and recruit Asian members into APALA.

In addition to organizing, APALA focuses on civil rights for Asian Pacific Americans. In fact, APALA has become one of the most visible national organizations in that community, and has emerged as an important voice for progressive social change. With its national office in Washington, D.C., APALA has been a focal point for Asian Pacific American legislative and political action.

APALA's broader vision has been to work in coalition with other communities of color for a common civil rights agenda. Its roots in the labor movement and the legislative resources of the AFL-CIO unions have enabled APALA to be an effective voice and political force at the national level. This is especially important because the role of Asian Pacific Americans has not been well publicized and has even been misunderstood within the civil rights movement. Although Asians have been stereotyped as the model minority, harsh discrimination exists in housing, education, voting rights, employment, and other areas. Since its founding, APALA has been involved in the Wards Cove case discussed earlier. APALA has been at the forefront of defending immigrant rights by building labor and community alliances to lobby against anti-immigrant legislation in California. As scapegoats of anti-immigrant hysteria, Asians have pressed for fair immigration policies as part of a broad civil rights agenda. APALA has worked closely with the AFL-CIO Civil Rights Department to advocate for immigrant workers in the labor movement. Most recently, APALA has been involved in the campaign to defend affirmative action, as well as in combating attempts to separate the Asian American community from other communities of color on this difficult issue. As a result of these activities in support of civil rights, APALA has promoted increased political activism for Asian Pacific American workers in their communities and unions on the municipal, state, and national levels through marches and rallies, lobbying and letter-writing.

APALA's joint focus on organizing and promoting civil rights, on speaking for labor in the Asian Pacific community and for that community in the house of labor, serves as a model for addressing issues of inclusion within the AFL-CIO. APALA's community-based organizing and advocacy for immigrants strengthen unions and community coalitions as they bring new workers into the labor movement. Nonetheless, within the broader context of the future direction of the AFL-CIO, the role of constituent groups like APALA is still uncertain. These groups have reached out to communities of color, immigrants, and women, in ways that the labor movement has failed to do in the past. The issues facing these groups cannot just be relegated to small constituent organizations; the whole labor movement needs to integrate them into its organizing, education, political action, and union administration. Thus, while APALA is hopeful about changes within the AFL-CIO, its leaders recognize that fundamental change is still needed. The challenges that still exist within the labor movement include the need to embrace diversity, build labor and community alliances, and foster a culture of organizing.

COMMUNITY-BASED ORGANIZING: LINKING LABOR AND IMMIGRANT ISSUES

In order to organize, in order to build political clout, and in order to realize itself as a significant social force for all workers, unions and the "new" AFL-CIO must find ways to link up with diverse communities and social movements. Both the New Otani Hotel organizing campaign in Los Angeles and the Sunset Park Workers Center in Brooklyn, New York, are examples of strategies that achieve the aims of disenfranchised workers who desire a stronger, more vibrant and inclusive labor movement. In their efforts to link workers' issues with those of communities, in their use of strategies that foster unity among different cultural groups, and in their global tactics for mobilizing support, these struggles give shape to the vision of a revitalized labor movement.

Boycott of the New Otani Hotel

A recent example of a labor and community alliance that supports organizing comes from the hotel industry—the campaign by Hotel and Restaurant Employees (HERE) Local 11 in support of workers at the New Otani Hotel in downtown Los Angeles. The hotel is owned by the Kajima Corporation, one of the largest construction companies in the world, with headquarters in Japan. The New Otani workers are demanding better wages, job security, affordable health care, and fair treatment. Three housekeepers at the hotel were illegally fired for their union activities. Most of the workers are Latino immigrants, and management has consciously attempted to divide Latinos and Asians by paying Latinos slightly better wages and by offering them better work assignments. However, HERE and APALA have forged multiracial and community alliances to countermand this effort to divide workers.

The leadership of HERE Local 11 has been exemplary in diversifying its own staff to reflect the changing workforce of Los Angeles. Not only do they have a talented team of Spanish-speaking organizers, but they have also hired Japanese, Filipino, Korean, Vietnamese, and Asian Indian organizers. This diversity has been a great strength in organizing in the Los Angeles area, with the largest and most diverse Asian immigrant workforce in the country.

APALA and HERE reached out to Asian Pacific community organizations. Many of these groups joined the boycott of the New Otani launched in January 1996, pledging not to "eat, drink or sleep" in the hotel. The Japanese American Bar Association, which had previously held its annual banquet at the hotel, announced that they would stay away for the duration of the boycott. The Japanese National Museum, which was scheduled to sign a $22 million contract with Kajima for a major expansion of the Little Tokyo Museum, chose not to go forward with contract negotiations. All these actions, the direct result of APALA's mobilization, were both embarrassing and costly for Kajima.

As the New Otani Hotel boycott entered its second year, the campaign began to develop an international dimension, with HERE members traveling to Japan to organize support there. APALA has pledged to actively support the New Otani campaign until it succeeds.

In February 1997, the AFL-CIO Executive Council met in Los Angeles, breaking with a long-standing tradition of gathering in Florida for their annual winter meeting. To demonstrate their new emphasis on organizing, the council focused on the New Otani during the week's activities. John Sweeney, Richard Trumka, and Linda Chavez-Thompson participated in a march with 2,000 people on the New Otani Hotel. At the rally in front of the hotel, President John Sweeney pledged to travel to Japan to meet with the New Otani management. In this campaign, the combined strength of HERE's basic commitment to organizing diverse workers, APALA's mobilization of community support, and the AFL-CIO leadership's pledge to organize the unorganized have come together to support Otani workers and to exemplify a new direction for labor.

The Sunset Park Workers Center

The task of organizing Asian immigrant workers in the "dying" domestic garment industry—which has been written off by government, economists, and many in the labor movement—is a tremendously difficult challenge. As sweatshop labor rears its ugly head not only in free trade zones and poor countries in the Third World, but in American communities from El Monte, California to Brooklyn, New York, a test of the "new" labor movement stands before us.

Asian immigrants are creating new ethnic communities in Brooklyn, spilling over from the tenements of the lower east side of Manhattan and Chinatown to settle along the routes of subway lines that link Brooklyn to other boroughs. Garment manufacturers are also moving into Brooklyn in an attempt to escape the high rents of Manhattan or the efforts of union organizers. Once in Brooklyn, these employers establish new sweatshops, often in former auto repair shops and garages that lack heat and ventilation and feature locked exits.

Because of the growing number of garment workers and shops in Brooklyn, the Union of Needletrades, Industrial and Textile Employees'

(UNITE) Campaign for Justice established a "worker's center" in Brooklyn's Sunset Park neighborhood in 1992. The purpose of the center is to act as a magnet for Chinese garment workers in that community by providing education and a base for organizing and networking. UNITE provides English language and civics classes weekly at a local elementary school, using a curriculum focused on civil rights, health care, labor, and women's issues. Both union and non-union workers enrolled, establishing a base of several hundred who come to the center on a regular basis. As part of the registration for classes, workers are asked to bring in manufacturer's labels, registration numbers, and other information from their workplaces. This is the first step in an education and organizing process aimed at helping workers to understand their position in the global garment "food chain." Within this hierarchy, contracting and subcontracting factories are at the bottom of the chain, fed by their jobbers and by manufacturers who distribute the work through a competitive bidding process. These manufacturers, in turn, take orders from retail giants such as JC Penney, Sears, the Federated, and others at the top of the chain of production.

Worker activists enthusiastically formed a committee to organize through the center. These activists were all rank-and-file immigrant workers, mostly women, and they continue to be the backbone of the Sunset Park Workers Center. Committee members received training and support from APALA, CLUW, the AFL-CIO Organizing Institute, and the Trade Union Women's Summer School. Often through participatory training sessions conducted in their own languages, they learned public speaking, organizing, and leadership skills and acquired an awareness of the U.S. labor movement, its social context, and the current economy. It was a transforming experience for the participants, the union, and the surrounding community.

The center's effect on the community was demonstrated by the organization of a major rally in Sunset Park in June 1995. Rank-and-file leaders formulated the rally's demands and developed a flyer presenting the workers' concerns to the government and to industry manufacturers, retailers, and contractors. The rally, whose purpose was to "fight for fair wages for garment workers and demand an end to sweatshops," took on a life of its own. Workers center activists made telephone calls and home visits to every member of the center's programs, encouraging them to attend the rally and to mobilize others to go. Workers reached out to the community, through the local community board, churches, the senior center, and the Brooklyn Chinese Association (BCA). The BCA, which provides social services and support for small businesses in the area, opened its doors to the rally organizers and served as the central staging area for the rally.

Spanish-speaking workers and organizers of the UNITE Workers Center, located in the Manhattan garment district, mobilized the Spanish-speaking population of Sunset Park. In fact, the workers center office in Manhattan hummed with activity every evening, as dozens of Chinese- and Spanish-speaking garment workers created large colorful posters and placards in English, Spanish, and Chinese. Huge posters depicted the economics of the garment industry—dresses selling for $198 retail that are made by workers paid only $10 for their labor.

There is still a great deal of skepticism about whether immigrant workers can be organized—especially Asian Pacific American immigrants employed by an Asian Pacific American boss. The experience in Sunset Park shows that it is eminently possible, given the proper resources for educating and training worker leaders, hiring and utilizing bilingual union staff, establishing a labor voice in the ethnic community media, and support among community organizations. Local 23-25 of UNITE has organized some 20,000 Chinese immigrant workers in the Chinatown garment industry in New York, and this base of unionized garment workers has provided a strong support mechanism for the non-union sweatshop workers of Brooklyn.

According to the estimates of Chinese community newspapers, more than 1,000 people rallied in Sunset Park, comprising the first massive political rally ever held in that neighborhood. Speakers from the community, local elected officials, workers and union officials echoed the rally's themes. Workers center activists were exhilarated by the turnout. Immigrant workers who had never ventured to a demonstration before brought their families and co-workers. In the week following the rally, Chinese garment factory bosses responded by bringing their payrolls up to date.

Since the rally, the garment industry has faced the exposure of horrifying sweatshop conditions both in the U.S. and abroad, a result of union efforts and the work of the National Labor Committee (NLC) (an activist project sponsored by a number of national unions). The NLC has targeted the working conditions in factories that produce clothing associated with celebrities, like Kathie Lee Gifford, or with high profile companies like Disney. In doing this, they have tarnished the public images so important for marketing these products, and they have shown the public how dependent the garment industry is on sweatshops around the world. Other incidents have dramatically underscored this revelation, such as the freeing of seventy-two immigrant workers from Thailand from slave labor conditions in El Monte, California. These workers, paid $1.60 per hour, worked under prison-like conditions in a compound surrounded by barbed wire. Public awareness of sweatshop labor in the U.S. was greatly heightened by the intense media coverage of these events.

The movement to organize and protest these conditions continues, and includes a growing consumer constituency that demands accountability from large retailers. UNITE, APALA, CLUW, and other labor organizations have joined with consumer groups, women's groups, and the religious community to form a "Partnership for Responsibility" to demand fair treatment for garment workers. The history of early organizing in the American garment industry has shown the importance of industry-wide action combined with an informed and active consumer campaign. Huge retail stores are today's economic engine in the garment industry. Organizing workers in contracting and subcontracting shops, or individual home-workers, must be linked with an aggressive corporate campaign to expose the connections of large retailers to the sweatshop workers producing their garments.

The workers center in Sunset Park has built a steady base among immigrant workers at the bottom, which is the essential foundation for further action. However, there is still a "disconnect" between this community-based organizing foundation and a comprehensive strategy linking union organizing with consumer/corporate campaigns. Asian American and other immigrant garment workers wait hopefully for the organizing rhetoric of APALA, UNITE, and the AFL-CIO to be realized in successful, wide-scale unionization.

CONCLUSION

The changes within the American labor movement since the new leadership was elected in October 1995 are historic and far-reaching. The call to organize the unorganized on an unprecedented scale and scope, the vision to build unions as part of a movement for social justice, and the commitment to greater diversity at every level of the labor movement are all welcome and long overdue changes.

This transformation of the American labor movement, however, must be thorough. Tension still exists between the older, white, and male-dominated leadership of the American labor movement, and the growing "new majority" of workers who are women and people of color. This tension is deeply rooted in labor's history; however, the open acknowledgment of it at the highest levels of leadership within the AFL-CIO bodes well for the necessary structural and ideological changes needed to address inequality within unions.

We must transform not only the leadership, but also the very culture and identity of the labor movement. This requires recruiting organizers who reflect the rich diversity of U.S. workers, and ensuring that union staff also represent changing union membership. Unions must advocate for civil and human rights; worker rights and the right to organize, in turn, must become part of the civil rights agenda.

Constituency groups within the AFL-CIO, who have long served as a voice for people of color and women, are strategic bridges between labor unions and these neglected communities. To serve this function well, constituency groups must be self-critical, and must transform their practices to support and embrace an organizing culture and the new spirit of change within labor.

The struggle for diversity and inclusion within the AFL-CIO is not only a principled and moral fight, it is a battle very much in the self-interest of the labor movement. As the demography of the workforce changes, labor unions must reflect the new reality if they are to survive. In an era of rising racial tension and polarization, the labor movement is one of the few social forces with the capacity to advance an agenda of multiracial unity and progressive social change.

Now is the moment to move from rhetoric into action and to embrace the diversity, foster the inclusion, and build the movement for social justice that is long overdue. It is time for activists with a vision of the future to assume greater leadership within the labor movement.

NOTES

1. *Constitution of the Congress of Industrial Organizations,* adopted in Pittsburgh, PA, November 13, 1938 (copy located in the Kheel Center for Labor-Management Documentation and Archives, School of Industrial and Labor Relations, Cornell University).

Transforming Unions and Building a Movement

Larry Adams

In order for the labor movement to become more inclusive, more of a movement of working class people than of trade union members only, individual workers must begin to understand and articulate their interests, and be willing to fight for them. If trade union activists are to foster and act upon this kind of class consciousness, we must remember our own political histories, and recall what motivated us to commit our energy to the labor movement. We need to share strategies for convincing others to become involved, and recount the experiences that demonstrate our successes in building unions. In this context, my own experiences and those of my union local illustrate both the difficulties and the possibilities for change in the U.S. labor movement.

BECOMING A LABOR ACTIVIST

I am an African American. Like so many of my brothers and sisters I was born into conditions that made life hell and into a community with a 400-year-old tradition of struggle against these conditions. I was raised in a large New Jersey inner city, and some of my relatives were activists in the National Association for the Advancement of Colored People (NAACP).

Because I also came of age in the wake of the civil rights movement and witnessed the massive uprising of people in protest against the Vietnam War, I grew up assuming that it was by finding a place in this struggle that you found your role in life. As I matured, I started to make decisions and choices about what to do with my life, about what the content of life was supposed to be and about how I was going to help transform the world. The overriding question for me became, "How was I, along with my brothers and sisters, going to change the conditions that made people's lives hell?"

When I went to college, I learned to place these questions in a broader, global context. I found examples of how people changed their societies. I was interested in the process of change and in efforts to bring about change that succeeded, as well as those that failed. By the time I graduated, I had come to the conclusion that it would be working people, as a class of people, who would be the agents of social transformation. Having come to this conclusion, I had to decide what contribution I would make to the struggle of the working class to change the world.

In 1976, I got a job in the post office, working with people from a wide variety of backgrounds and communities. Despite our differences, however, we were all tied to the same workplace and the same type of job. We all worked in a large mail factory at the largest post office in the world. We were a militant, diverse workforce with a history of struggle. Prior to the postal workers' strike of 1970, conditions were very bad and mandatory overtime was commonplace. In fact, wages at that time were so low that it was possible for New York City postal workers to work full time and still qualify for food stamps. It was the carriers who initiated the strike.

The workers in my particular shop were approximately sixty percent white and forty percent black. The entire plant was like one large machine, with conveyer belts as in any factory. The organization of work was very authoritarian, very hierarchical; in fact, it was quasi-military. There were a lot of veterans in the plant, because veterans got preference in hiring, and some of the management had been military officers. We used military time and military terms. For example, if you were absent, you were said to be AWOL.

As workers in this rigid system, we learned over time that we also have tremendous potential: our workplace, our company, and our industry has strategic significance. During the strike of 1970, postal workers demonstrated this power. The postal service transports bills and payments;

without them, the economy of twenty years ago was effectively crippled. Post offices exist in every small town, rural area, and large city, and most of the workers in these offices belong to one of the four craft unions in the U.S. Postal Service. It was partly in response to this ability of unionized postal workers to disrupt normal business activity that automated billing and diversified methods of collection were developed. The vulnerability of business to the 1970 postal strike was as important to the union's victory as were the actions of postal workers.

TAKING CONTROL: THE UNION IS US

I am currently president of my union, a local of 6,250 members in the National Postal Mail Handlers Union. Initially, I was very reluctant to take on a position of responsibility within the local. While I intended to be an active member, I felt that the union did not serve the members and did not represent their interests. Rather, the union was the control force for management and a social club for union functionaries. Not only did the leaders of the union fail to organize or educate workers to do anything on their own behalf, they also failed to enforce the contract. Incompetence reigned supreme, so that not even efficient business unionism was in effect. Frustrated and angry, my co-workers and I began to lay plans for change. We brought together rank-and-file members—men and women from different nationalities who, as we said at the time, became "sick and tired of being sick and tired." We chose to support a candidate for union office who we believed would represent our interests. We won, and under the leadership of this individual we began to transform our union. Because the previous leadership was so weak and ineffective, they were not hard to overthrow.

We waged a fight around the job and on the shopfloor about the issues that affect workers on a daily basis. The burning issues were sustained levels of mandatory overtime, light duty denials (particularly for pregnant women), systematic favoritism, and discrimination on the basis of race and nationality. The latter, the issue of white supremacy in the workplace was sensitive, and there was disagreement over whether to put it on the table. It was easier to create unity around women's issues. We presented the denial of requests for light duty by pregnant women as essentially a class, rather than a gender issue. All workers get old, anyone can become disabled. We achieved success by tapping into issues around which members could mobilize, in addition to negotiating with management. We organized pickets of pregnant women and women with strollers in the central business district, attracting the attention of both members and the community at large. We were able to win over members and make demands on their behalf through this kind of mobilization. We thought that unions should represent and reflect all of the workers—black, Latino, white, men, and women.

We also moved from workplace to community issues. We decided to address international issues that were not directly related to the daily terms of our contract, or what we called our "temporary peace treaty with the boss." For example, we brought the struggle against apartheid in South Africa to our workplace; we talked about the workplaces and communities in South Africa and what needed to be done to support workers there. We chose to mobilize around these issues because of the personal commitment of several activist workers to the anti-apartheid movement, as well as the escalation of struggle in South Africa at the time. Consciousness about apartheid was heightened both in South Africa and the United States as a result of actions and daily demonstrations organized by anti-apartheid support groups. As the struggle in South Africa became more intense and as worldwide support for the anti-apartheid movement increased, the role of U.S. unions became more prominent. District 65 of the United Auto Workers of America began to mobilize the labor movement in New York and New Jersey around solidarity with black South Africans. This in turn provided a venue for activists in my shop to act on their personal commitment to oppose apartheid.

We also organized against a toxic dump located near public housing. Our educational efforts focused on the class nature of racist environmental policies.

We had little support for our efforts from higher ranking officers and no support from the international leadership of our union. There were also times when we received little support from our own rank-and-file. It is difficult for people to sustain the amount of time and energy it takes to support these kinds of issues outside of the workplace. Increasingly, people need to work more hours just to make ends meet. When we addressed international issues, for example, there were some who told us that South Africa was not why they elected us. The prior leadership of unions never really brought the issues of racism and international solidarity to workers in a way that helped them to realize the importance that the struggles of black workers in South Africa had to their own lives. This is a historic failure of union leadership, and it explains in part why rank-and-file workers might oppose the participation of their union in international solidarity or anti-racism activities. While some union leaders are aware of the importance of international mobilization, and fight to make it part of union agendas, they are in the minority. Most concentrate on local issues or on internal problems and power struggles, while many do not know or care about labor struggles in other countries. The purge of radicals during the fifties and their replacement with business unionists who were, for the most part, anti-communist and U.S. chauvinists, has made isolation from labor in the rest of the world part of the U.S. union tradition. Currently, there is a range of opinions among unions about how important it is to get involved in these struggles. I believe that it is the responsibility of union leaders to understand the connections between U.S. workers and workers in other parts of the world and to raise consciousness about these connections and about the common global enemies of workers. For the most part, U.S. union leaders have failed to meet this responsibility.

When our union organized workers to oppose apartheid, we did meet with initial resistance. We persisted with educational activities that drew connections between the fight of South African workers and our issues. The result was that we mobilized busloads of members to participate in the largest demonstration in New Jersey against apartheid. We used leaflets, newsletters, slides, and videos, in both the workplace and the surrounding communities, to educate workers and to engage them in discussion. Part of this education process included participating in demonstrations, debating issues in the workplace, and struggling with the connections between the experience of black South Africans and black workers here.

I found that it was more difficult to raise issues of inclusion, community, and global affairs as a union officer then it was when I was a rank-and-file member. Union officers have the daily responsibility of managing the union. While we may also have good ideas, the distance between the rank-and-file and the union apparatus erodes our power to act on these ideas. Closing the gap between the union leadership and our rank-and-file members is a primary goal in the work of our local. We have not been as successful as we need to be in achieving this goal. Our efforts have included scheduling more meetings at a variety of places and times to make it more convenient for workers to attend. We have also worked to improve communications between the leadership and rank-and-file through our local newsletter. We encourage members to write articles and letters, rather than contracting out publication. We try to keep the focus on members, and not fill the paper with photos of officers. Content that reflects issues of debate among workers and contributions by members are the means we use to improve communications within the union and to project an image of the union that is dominated by workers, not officials.

Our leaders also participate in, and encourage members to take part in, activities that are not specific to unions but that reflect the concerns of workers in general. For example, we mobilized members for actions such as Motown 97 in Detroit, in support of striking press workers, and for national labor conferences and meetings. We have also taken rank-and-file activists to AFL-CIO regional conferences. Through these activities, we expand the horizons of our most active members. We need, however, to reach further into the rank-and-file.

In spite of the fact that our union structure mandates appointment of stewards by the local president, our local practices a more democratic process. We promote a straw poll that allows members to indicate their choices, and I then appoint these individuals. This increases accountability to members and enhances democracy.

Education and training is another vehicle we try to use to close the distance between the leadership and rank-and-file. Previously, arbitration was handled by lawyers. Now, our members take advantage of courses at local colleges to train worker advocates. This puts the outcome of procedures that affect co-workers in the hands of workers themselves, demystifies arbitration in the process, and cedes more control of key union functions to the rank-and-file.

Clearly, we have much more to do to achieve our goals of closing the gap between union leaders and members. We look to the Canadian Union of Postal Workers as a model for using training and education as a way to involve and mobilize members. Their training fund, negotiated with management, enables workers to take courses in labor history and political economy. The union has a systematic way to raise consciousness through these classes, which they control. Although the fund is financed by management under the terms of the collective bargaining agreement, the menu of course selections differs politically from that offered by most, although not all, U.S. union education and training funds. The latter emphasize peaceful co-existence and cooperation with management, rather than labor's history of struggle.

In general, the gaps between leaders and rank-and-file members of unions stem from the three-legged stool of industrial relations that dominates not only labor management dynamics but also separates officials from the rest of the union. The three legs of the stool are bosses, workers, and unions. Workers and unions are as separate from each other as bosses from workers in this conception. This distance is reinforced by the income disparity that exists between many union leaders and the workers they claim to represent, as well as by union policies and practices that reduce accountability and democracy.

We have to recognize that the working class has been disarmed because the troops who viewed and led unions as an instrument of class struggle were consciously driven out of the labor movement forty years ago. The right-wing leaders of that time made a decision that unions were to be vehicles, not of class struggle, but of class cooperation. Organizing unionism was put on the back burner, and organizers were expelled from the labor movement. The capacity to fight was seriously reduced; unions, instead of educating and organizing workers into a mighty collective, became a shopping mart of services. Workers became the third leg on the stool, removed from the conflict of workers versus bosses, and made into passive observers. As a result, the muscles of the labor movement atrophied from lack of use. The apparatus of unions, which should provide the basic tools for advancing the interest of workers, became instead the very weapons used against us. Leadership structures became substitutes for mobilized memberships; they negotiated peace with management rather than wage war against exploitation of workers. Working people have suffered the consequences of this strategy for the past forty years and now unions are on the verge of irrelevance.

We must recognize that we are in a class war and in a war of ideas that we are not winning. Working people in the United States do not have money or access to the channels of power in the mass media. Our newspapers and leaflets may reach some people, but our enemies have overwhelming control of the resources for reaching large numbers of people. Because of this, they are defining the debate and winning the hearts and minds of our people. We have been disarmed because of the power of those who oppose us and their ability to market their way of looking at the world.

HOW TO CHANGE UNIONS

Whether or not one agrees that unions no longer represent the working class, and that they have never truly represented the concerns of communities of color, it has become obvious that unions must change if they are to have a vital role in the lives of workers. Constitutional and structural changes, as well as changes in union leadership, changes in the relationship between unions and workers of color, and the political education for members are key to making unions relevant to people of color and to the working class in general.

1. Constitutional and Structural Changes

There is too much power in the hands of the principal officers of unions. One step toward changing this is to have the rank-and-file elect their shop stewards, rather than having officers select them. This is necessary but not sufficient. There are unions with elected shop stewards whose leaders still abuse power.

The constitutions of unions should be reformed to provide for rank-and-file involvement in decision-making, so that workers have a voice in all important issues. An example of the kind of decisions that members should participate in is the debate within union leadership on convention resolutions. If rank-and-file members were involved in choosing issues and taking positions, these resolutions might actually lead to political action. Instead, these proclamations end up forgotten and never result in any changes that affect membership. It is too easy for leaders to make a public statement in support of affirmative action within unions, for example, and it is just as easy to never act on such a statement. Rank-and-file members who have been passed over or excluded because of racism are the best ones to translate these resolutions into policies, constitutional changes, and actions that can make unions more inclusive.

Another important issue for constitutional and structural change within unions is the difference in income between union leadership and the base of members. Leaders of workers should live as workers, not as bosses. If careers as union leaders were not so lucrative, more of the pure of heart and less of the career aspirants would fill these positions. A well known example of existing salary disparity is the leader of a New York building services local who earns $400,000 annually while most members make around $30,000. Among the members of the United Electrical Workers of America, on the other hand, officials make no more than the highest paid worker. Not coincidentally, this union has taken more militantly pro-worker positions than many others. It was instrumental in founding the Labor Party and has contributed resources and personnel to the development of a political party that represents the interests of American workers. It holds annual conventions and passes resolutions that are meaningful and become the basis for action. Annual conventions are a structural way of encouraging broader participation in union decisions.

In addition to giving workers more voice within unions and limiting the income of leadership, unions would benefit from more attention to the dynamic between democracy and centralization of authority within the AFL-CIO and within individual unions. For example, there should be more opportunities for rank-and-file members to participate in local union activities on paid time off from their jobs. Everything cannot be done by volunteers or committees, but the answer need not be to increase the role of paid functionaries. At the same time, national union leadership and the AFL-CIO should be able to use their positions to advocate for internal democracy and not subordinate their politics to the positions of the affiliates. Instead, interfering in the internal affairs of local affiliates to promote democracy has become a taboo and has resulted in cases of members held captive to anti-democratic structures, policies, and practices at the local level. If national union leadership assumes the moral high ground, it can be instrumental in fostering internal changes among affiliates that will attract people of color, and empower and liberate workers. The object is to strike a balance between democracy and central authority both within affiliates and between affiliates and federation leadership. Unions need democracy to assure unity among members and to provide for broad rank-and-file participation in decision-making. They need some measure of central authority to ensure the implementation of these democratic decisions.

One important direction a strong AFL-CIO leadership might take on behalf of workers in this country is to identify those struggles of workers it supports and commit resources to winning these fights. An example of this is the Federation's support for the strawberry workers in California. Historically, labor in the U.S. has crippled itself with its own chauvinism and has failed to build class-based solidarity among unions in the U.S. and with labor movements throughout the world. The degree to which the U.S.

labor movement participated in the anti-apartheid struggle is one measure of its progress toward the development of multinational solidarity. Apartheid was unfettered imperialism, naked exploitation; understanding it as such helped workers here see the connections among racism, capitalism, and U.S. foreign policy.

If the AFL-CIO is to develop international solidarity, it can no longer function as a mouthpiece for U.S. policy, or as a shield for U.S. government intelligence agencies. Taking on the political positions of the U.S. government uncritically has put the labor movement here on the wrong side of the ledger in much of the world. Instead, before taking political positions on movements and events in other countries, labor leaders should seek out and consider the voices of workers and unions in those countries, as well as those of indigenous leaders and people of color in the United States. The majority of the world is comprised of people of color; if the AFL-CIO does not blindly follow the U.S. government when it opposes the struggles of these people for liberation, it will begin to be perceived more favorably by workers of color in the U.S.

2. Changes in the Leadership of Unions and their Institutional Allegiances

The changes that are needed within unions are not only constitutional or structural. Change also depends on the quality of union leadership. Leaders who are determined to preserve their power always find ways to circumvent new rules and structures. Leaders who genuinely desire change are produced in the course of struggle; they are not the loyal followers who are dependent on the regime in power for their jobs or their titles. Unfortunately, much of the current union leadership is based on personal loyalty of this kind, rather than on a commitment to workers and to the working class.

Behind this collusion of anti-worker power and leadership lie the vested material interests of unions. For example, the investments of the health and pension funds of some unions make it unlikely that they would support a single-payer health care system, a change that would benefit working people as a class. A single-payer system would eliminate waste and administrative costs, and would take the profits of insurance companies out of the loop. Existing relationships between unions and health insurance providers separate union members from the rest of the working class. While union-sponsored or union-run benefit funds are clearly preferable to leaving workers uncovered, making health care available for all should be a focus of political struggle for the whole labor movement. Instead, this long term strategic objective is compromised by arrangements such as the one between many union benefit funds and the insurance companies that underwrite them. Unions get income from sponsorship of insurance company operations and come to rely on this income. This dependency, in turn, pits unions against the interest of rank-and-file workers.

By investing their assets in ways similar to finance capitalists, unions ally themselves with the interests of capital. In effect, unions have turned into their own opposition. They represent those exploited by capital, yet they share investment strategies and their consequences with the capitalist class. Leaders of unions put the short term interests of their institutions before the long term interests of working people; in the political arena, they act as business functionaries on behalf of unions rather than of members. Working for a union and being a union leader should not be about promoting individual careers or institutions. Nor should personal loyalty to particular leaders be the criterion for those who serve the union. The business of unions should be class struggle, not making money. This will not be the case if unions continue to rely on investment portfolios rather than member dues.

3. Changing the Relationship between Unions and Workers of Color

Unions need to practice affirmative action as a desirable objective. They need to set numerical goals based on percentages of workers of color within the union and within the industries they represent. More importantly, unions must realize that in order to gain the ground they have lost by organizing workers in large numbers, they must learn to present themselves to communities of color as organizations that welcome, value, and support the perspective of workers of color. Communities of color, after all, are primarily communities of workers. Unions must not only seek to attract workers of color, they must craft plans to advance them to positions of authority within unions. Unions must be conscious of promoting the whole spectrum of their membership, rather than always appointing the same people to leadership positions. The positions and functions for which blacks, Latinos, Asians and women are considered must be wider.

It took unions some time to understand the importance of geographic representation and to see geography as a reasonable way to divide power and select leadership. Unions now need to realize that demography is also a legitimate basis for sharing power among union constituencies, that demographic representation of all workers is as critical as geographic coverage, and that hostility to sharing power based on demographics damages the growth and vitality of unions.

Support for issues that concern communities of color is one way to move inclusion beyond rhetoric and into policy. Identifying such issues shows how far labor has to go if it is to become an ally of people of color. Unions, for example, must be willing to take on the issue of police brutality if they are truly to win over people in these communities. Similarly, they must oppose how the politics of welfare reform manipulate workers against their own interests. A population forced to work for below minimum wage now competes directly with workers for jobs and for low cost child care. A class-conscious union would respond to this issue by demanding full employment at a living wage; socially useful work assignments; support for re-entry into the job market, such as access to quality child care, health care, and education; and worksites with high standards of safety and health. The labor movement's message should be: "They R Us."

It is necessary not only to have leaders who are women and people of color within our workplaces and unions, the labor movement needs to reach out and unite with these communities on issues of common interest. To do this, unions must go beyond their narrow range of interest in contract violations at the workplace and take up issues of social justice in these communities. Unions have to take on the offensive to steal back the sixty years of progress that was won by the civil rights movement, because when we talk about African American, Latino, or Asian communities, we are talking about working class communities. The decision to participate in community struggles should be based on the issues involved, rather than on alliances with particular leaders or organizations.

If unions want to send an immediate clear message to these communities that they want to represent their interests, that they want to reverse the dismal history of relations between unions and workers of color, they could do so by making a firm commitment to organize the South, including farm workers and migrant workers. This, along with dramatic, programmatic changes to demonstrate their support for affirmative action as a workers' issue, would begin to establish a new relationship with workers of color. Although efforts to organize the South have not always been successful, labor needs to use new tactics and strategies to achieve victories in this area. Unions should provide support, development, and training for indigenous leaders, rather than appoint outsiders to run campaigns. Calling for elections based on the numbers of workers interested in unions, rather than following National Labor Relations Board procedures, is an organizing strategy that is working elsewhere in the nation and should be attempted in the South. Taking a long-term approach to organizing, rather than focusing on "hot shops," might be more appropriate to the long, entrenched oppression of workers, particularly black workers, in the South.

4. Unions Should Provide Political Education for their Members

There is an urgent need for political education within unions. Unions should work with their members to identify the important political and economic issues they want to understand and provide education in these areas. Such education should emphasize the history of the labor movement in ways that focus on the struggle against exploitation and the contributions made by all workers. The material should be multicultural, and link U.S. workers with international labor issues and conflicts. Both content and instruction should combine theory and practice, direct and indirect experience. For example, we used the bus trip to Detroit, for Motown 97, to build solidarity by showing political videos and holding discussions of the issues portrayed. The bus became a rolling union meeting.

If unions are institutions of workers, the experience of participation in running them gives us the skill and confidence to run the world. In that participation, our commonalities as workers emerge. Unions teach democracy though the opportunity they provide for people to experience a greater degree of competence and control over their lives. In turn, mobilization and participation of members changes unions, changes how we do things, and how we view things.

The labor movement also needs to develop its own media, using the latest technology, to reach out to working people, as a mechanism of education and training to counter the corporate messages of the mainstream media. Through our own media, we can publicize our history and our struggles. Our media should develop audio and video resources and popularize them, following the example of radio station WBAI in New York, which demonstrates how electronic media and the progressive movement can offer an alternative to mass media.

LOOKING AHEAD

Change is both essential and inevitable. Those who are at the forefront of change in the labor movement will hold positions of leadership; those who do not will ultimately lose power. Without policies and practices that are both democratic and inclusive, unions are doomed to irrelevance. With them, the labor movement has the potential to dramatically change the conditions under which we all live and work.

The program of the New Voice leadership of the AFL-CIO, if implemented, would move us in this direction. While the content of the program endorses the spirit of change, steps must be taken to ensure that real change occurs at a pace responsive to the urgency many workers and union members of color feel. If this happens, over the next five years we should see more people of color in positions of authority in unions, and as a more visible presence throughout the Federation.

Certainly, unions should represent a larger portion of American workers within the next five years. Hopefully, unions will be purged of mob influences, cleaning their own houses and rendering unions less vulnerable to the criticism of conservative politicians. To the degree that organized crime interferes with the legitimate interests of unions, democracy within unions is suppressed, and inclusion is unlikely to occur, because criminal operations within unions require loyal, hand-picked leaders and functionaries. I would hope that unions would be more internationalist in outlook over the next five years. Corporate power is organized across the world; it is up to unions to develop international cooperation among workers as a form of self-defense and solidarity. If all of these things come to pass, labor would threaten monopoly capital far more than it does today, and would be actively engaged in fighting the oppression of women, people of color, and the working class. The labor movement has the potential power to weld and merge the energy present among disparate social movements, and build effective unity among the forces for change.

PART | 4 | PARTIES AND POLITICS

Ever since the inauguration of the New Deal, labor's political effort has focused on maximizing its influence within the Democratic Party, getting out the labor vote to help elect a Democratic president and congress, and then lobbying for its legislative agenda. The strategy has turned out to be too narrow, mechanical, and ineffective. Big business continues to dominate the Democratic Party, unions are having difficulty "delivering" their members to candidates, and the candidates that labor does help to elect often turn their backs on working people once in office. Today, American voter indifference to electoral politics is one of the highest in the Western world. At the same time, the mass media and the money needed to buy media time are playing an ever increasing role in shaping the political landscape. For organized labor, all this makes politics tougher than it used to be. The current leadership of the AFL-CIO has made politics, along with organizing, a top priority and is committing more money and resources to politics than ever before. To what extent should these resources be allocated to improve on old methods or to try new ones? Should organized labor buy more media time, or redefine political goals and strategies? Central to the political debate facing the labor movement is the level of independence from the Democratic Party and the degree to which labor's strategy relies on grassroots efforts.

Pat Lippold and Bob Kirkman begin this section by arguing that a movement seeking to speak to and for the working class will need to use class-based rather than union-based criteria to evaluate its political strategies. They highlight the importance of articulating a vision of a just and decent society, providing issue oriented education, and focusing on issues that speak to the broad, economic realities of class. The authors are encouraged by the steps taken by the current leadership of the AFL-CIO to move organized labor in the direction of class-based politics. They would like to see more campaigns, such as the AFL-CIO's "America Needs a Raise" campaign, that focus on broad economic issues and have an immediate, realizable objective. They identify three key components for developing a new political strategy: the articulation of a vision; the creation of an active corps of rank-and-file organizers; the establishment of a new set of tactics. They offer a host of strategic recommendations toward that end.

Dennis Rivera suggests that politics is the arena where the labor movement can rise above parochialism, aspire to advance the general welfare, and fulfill its role as a nation builder. He calls on organized labor to assume a more independent and aggressive stance in politics. In fact, it was the commitment on the part of the New Voice administration to move in such a direction that convinced Rivera's union to re-affiliate with the AFL-CIO. His emphasis is on independent politics, whether working inside or outside the political mainstream. Rivera is comfortable pursuing two seemingly contradictory tracks simultaneously: his own union works toward revitalizing the Democratic Party at the same time that it aids in the development of third party options. What is important to Rivera is building a movement that will check the power of large corporations and cause sufficient harm to labor's political enemies. He emphasizes the importance of local politics and makes several suggestions: targeting anti-labor incumbents for political defeat; cultivating coalitions; building grassroots political campaigns; developing massive political education programs; and focusing on cities and states where labor is strongest. He also stresses the importance of providing an alternative economic vision, ideological leadership, and greater visibility as the champion of working class interests.

While Tony Mazzocchi praises the steps taken by the current AFL-CIO to gain greater independence from the Democratic Party, he argues that only a political party independent of corporate sponsors can represent and advance the interests of working people. Mazzocchi argues that labor's long and deep support for the Democratic Party has not paid off for workers. This is no surprise, he points out, given that corporations far out-spend labor in support of both Republican and Democratic candidates. He believes that labor's lack of political independence has also prevented working people from developing their own political vision and strategy. He goes on to argue that a political strategy that relies solely on getting "pro-labor" candidates elected will not result in a political sea change. Labor must organize around its own political issues—from the grassroots up—if it is to challenge the status quo and hold its candidates accountable. He outlines the program of the newly created Labor Party and suggests that part of its role is to provide a forum where workers can come together to formulate new ideas and proposals.

Arthur Cheliotes suggests that unions need to pay more attention to public policies affecting our communities. These, he says, often undermine the gains unions make at the collective bargaining table and create hardships for working people. He urges unions to develop policy initiatives that provide vision, answers, and concrete proposals for social change. Cheliotes urges unions to adapt a pro-active strategy for improving community life in such areas as economic development, health care, welfare reform, housing, education, and tax reform. With such a strategy, labor can change the nature of public discourse, exert a leadership role in the community, and effect concrete and meaningful change. In this way labor and its allies can start building more humane, people oriented communities from the bottom up, piece by piece. Cheliotes provides examples from his own local and other unions that can serve as models of union leadership in local communities.

BLOCKING BRIDGES:
Class–Based Politics and the Labor Movement

Patricia Lippold and Bob Kirkman

In their 1995 pre-election debate over the leadership of the AFL-CIO, Tom Donahue attacked his rival candidate, John Sweeney, for "blocking bridges" when, in his opinion, the labor movement needed to "build bridges." Donahue was making reference to the tactics of the Justice for Janitors campaign waged by Service Employees International Union (SEIU), then led by Sweeney. The campaign, a nationwide effort to organize low-wage building service workers, has earned widespread recognition as the kind of strategically smart and politically militant program needed to revitalize the labor movement. In Washington, D.C., Justice for Janitors (J for J) has achieved significant success over the last eight years, and has taken on Oliver Carr, the head of a major real estate empire. Carr has enjoyed substantial tax breaks, as a result of his political connections, during a time when the nation's capital has suffered a major fiscal crisis. In 1994 and 1995, after a long period of militant actions and other activities, J for J blocked two major bridges during rush hour. Each action was intended to protest the fact that Carr uses a secretive appeals procedure to avoid paying fair taxes on his office buildings. This very public engagement of Carr dramatized how he was hurting the city's economy not only through his tax breaks, but also through the sub-standard wages he pays his workers. In one bridge-blocking action, a yellow school bus was used as a "classroom" to educate the public about the political economy of such special deals for those who exploit the city's workers.

Sweeney's response to Donahue's remark about these tactics was that unions were through being "road kill" for corporate America, and that when corporations and their agents in government stop running roughshod over the needs, hopes, and aspirations of workers, labor can begin to talk about building bridges. The mass media presented this exchange as if it were a debate about tactics rather than a discussion about the essence of the movement we need to create. In fact, Sweeney's New Voice campaign used "blocking bridges" as a symbol of its theme of revitalizing the labor movement based on mass member involvement and the clear class-based analysis of issues that affect working class people in America. The challenge is to carry out this vision in practice and in the political arena, as well as in organizing and collective bargaining.

HISTORICAL SHIFTS IN THE POLITICS OF LABOR

Labor's current lack of political influence can be traced to the post-World War II period, when trade unions moved away from the mass-based, often class-conscious activity that had characterized the movement, especially the CIO unions, in the 1930s. During the post-war period, U.S. productive forces of the United States were called upon to rebuild much of the world. With American workers and their products in high demand, the labor movement was in a good position to grow and to influence how the economic pie was to be divided among the classes in U.S. society.

The unions, which represented over one-third of the workforce throughout this period, seemed to "raise the whole ship." The standard of living improved for union and non-union workers alike. Furthermore, the later creation of Medicare and Medicaid and the passage of the Civil Rights Act and the Voting Rights Act were at least partly due to the political power of labor to level the playing field. Today's labor movement, which represents a much smaller share of the workforce, simply does not have the power it needs to better the lives of America's workers. The first lesson of politics, then, is "organize the unorganized!"

In the post-war period, union leaders became complacent—so did some union members. As long as there appeared to be common interests between capital and labor, buttressed by labor's experience of power during the war and post-war years, labor leaders could at least "deliver the goods" to a significant portion of the working class. Those in positions of power in the AFL-CIO either thought that these conditions were permanent or were so enraptured with the new "international responsibilities" they shared with capital that they lost sight of the interests of U.S. workers both inside and outside their organizational base of support.

This was, after all, also a period of racial segregation, national chauvinism, and the suppression of women's rights. Many workers had been left behind when the "whole ship rose." The civil rights movement and opposition to the war in Vietnam did get some institutional support from labor,[1] but unions were divided and ineffectual as a movement in these two struggles. In addition, labor's dependence on the Democratic Party prevented its leaders from recognizing and combating the economic and political changes that would later erode unions and weaken their political influence.

As a result of post-war anti-communist hysteria, the left of the labor movement, communist and non-communist, was marginalized. Coupled with the increasing tendency of labor leaders to support the U.S. government's official positions at home and abroad, this purging and silencing of progressives pushed the politics of labor still further to the right. The plan to organize the South known as Operation Dixie, for example, was abandoned in large part because the campaign was supported and would have been implemented by the left wing of the labor movement.

During the 1980s, these changes dramatized how little political leverage labor had and how conservative its leaders had become. To be sure, there were complaints from labor when good union jobs went to the non-union South and finally to other countries where workers had few rights and would work for a fraction of what American workers earned. There were protests when labor laws were changed to make it more difficult to organize. There was opposition to the deregulation and privatization that would destroy so many good jobs. There was an outcry when the air traffic controllers were fired and their union was crushed in 1981. Nonetheless, all of labor's actions on these fronts were largely ineffective, because there was no movement to question the political decisions that were responsible for so much hardship among U.S. workers *and* union members. Those with a memory of the New Deal seemed to believe that, somehow, someday, the Democrats would come through. They had forgotten how hard workers and their unions had fought to *make* them come through during the New Deal. It seemed to many of us that the leaders of the AFL-CIO were more effective in Poland[2] than they were in the United States.

Recognition of the crisis confronting unions and their leaders had become widespread and permeated every level of labor by the 1990s. Business as usual and survival of the movement could no longer co-exist. Without higher union density in the workforce than it enjoys today, the labor movement does not have the power it needs to effectively improve the lives of America's workers by changing the balance of political and economic power. The weakness of unions at the bargaining table is evidenced by the inability to win many strikes, the decline in real wages, the failure of health reform, and the near demise of labor law reform. This is the crisis that prompted the changes in the leadership and politics of the AFL-CIO in 1995.

CLASS-BASED POLITICS AND THE *NEW* AFL-CIO

Much has happened in labor's political arena since October 1995, when the John Sweeney, Richard Trumka, and Linda Chavez-Thompson slate was elected to head the AFL-CIO. While the mass media and the political right have focussed public attention on how much money the AFL-CIO spent in the 1996 elections, the more significant change in strategy was to allocate most of these funds to educate a broad segment of the population on issues. The issues chosen were not the narrow and technical "labor concerns" as defined by the former leaders of the AFL-CIO, but were instead part of a broad economic populist approach, or class-based politics.

Just months after winning office in 1995, AFL-CIO President John Sweeney initiated a campaign his predecessors would never have attempted, the "America Needs a Raise" campaign. This campaign took aim at CEO salaries and the unequal distribution of wealth and connected them with such issues as tax policy, health care, education, urban issues, and affirmative action. The new leaders of the AFL-CIO called for the organization of town meetings all around the country where workers, union members and non-members alike, testified about their low wages, lack of benefits, and lack of job security. This helped focus public and media attention on these issues and was instrumental in mobilizing the political support for increasing the minimum wage. Within a year, Congress passed a minimum wage increase even with Gingrich Republicans in control of both House and Senate.

The "America Needs a Raise" campaign serves as a model for how labor should reach out to our members and to all working Americans: *"Build it among the people and the politicians will come."* Campaigns like this, based on political issues that speak to the realities of class, should be labor's *Field of Dreams*, not just in Iowa, but in every hamlet, town and city of this country. "America Needs a Raise" was strategically smart because it was based on the correct assessment that support could be built around this issue and that there was an immediate objective, increasing the minimum wage, that was winnable. American workers and American unions needed a victory; after years of drought there was leadership who could help us make rain.

ELEMENTS OF A NEW POLITICAL STRATEGY

Developing a new, class-based political strategy for labor, as exemplified by the "America Needs a Raise" campaign, demands a vision, a plan and the activation of union members. Labor needs to develop a very broad base of support among union members and working people generally for a political program that raises labor's voice for a class-based vision of a just, decent society that works for the vast majority of its people. To do so, the labor movement needs to: 1) clearly articulate this vision in a variety of media and forums; 2) develop an active corps of member political organizers to spread this vision; 3) change union tactics in the political arena: stop behaving like appendages of the Democratic Party or blocking guards for narrow institutional interests and start conducting campaigns on the local and state level that emulate the strategic wisdom of "America Needs a Raise,"and focus on issues that we can garner mass and broad support for and are possible to win; 4) discuss, formulate, and carry out a long-term political plan that changes the current vision, practices, and tactics of unions.

The labor movement should be about raising the standard of living and quality of life for all working people—this is what it means to be a labor movement again, instead of a trade union movement. Unions must look at issues that affect all working people, not just their own members. While unions should continue to motivate their members to act on issues that directly affect their own industries, the labor movement must also educate members about broad economic issues like tax policy, health care, education, and welfare reform.

What else is needed if our movement is to be guided by a class-based vision of a just, decent society? Most importantly, we need what some call "fire in the belly." Working class people are angry. They often are not sure what or who they are angry with and they are often just angry with each other. Labor leaders need to help union members and all working class people to focus their anger on the real problems and the real enemies. We will not be able to do that, even with the best strategies and plans, if we do not feel it. That means we have to be not only *for* the things we have been talking about, but also against the vile and disgusting things that have been ravaging the people we represent and care about. If we are going to be *against* these things, then we have to be *against* the vile and disgusting individuals and class of people that support them, make them happen, and benefit from them.

STRATEGIES FOR ADVANCING CLASS-BASED POLITICS

The labor movement needs to spend its time and money on changing the minds and focusing the anger of working people—not on convincing politicians to support our positions.

Labor has focused its attention on buying access and lobbying politicians on the virtue of our issues. Instead, labor ought to focus on changing the minds of the electorate to whom legislators must respond. Labor's base is its members and other working class people whose interests are essentially the same as those of union members. We do not underestimate how difficult it will be to win the hearts and minds of America's working people. It will require a long-term commitment. There are no real solutions if unions do not deepen and broaden their support among working people.

The union movement can make headway on this front immediately. The "America Needs a Raise" campaign is a good example of this. If unions focus on issues that they can win broad support for, conduct campaigns that tap the creativity and anger of working people, and project intermediate objectives that are winnable, labor can increase its credibility and build its base of support.

The key to any new political strategy is increasing membership support and involvement.

The Service Employees International Union's (SEIU) "Committee on the Future"[3] provides this useful guidance:

...support (for the union's political program) can be built only if members clearly understand that our political activity is based on their interests and not on affiliation with any political party....Member education about the importance of political action needs to be part of all union activities, especially new member education, steward training and lifelong trade union education programs....Increasing the level of support among leaders is also important....too few secondary leaders recognize the importance of political action...all leadership training needs to have a focus on political action.

SEIU has decided to develop an active corps of member political organizers who can participate in campaigns, do grassroots lobbying, and raise money for political activities. At the SEIU convention in April 1996, the newly elected president, Andy Stern, asked "...every leader at every level of this union—from the international president to the rank-and-file member—to devote five working days this year to political action." In support of this effort, the union has begun a pledge program and has asked its local unions to set goals for participation levels and assign staff to coordinate this work. SEIU's goal is to have 10,000 educated and active member political organizers by the year 2000 with a minimum of 35 members making up a political action team in each of the approximately 300 congressional districts where the union has a significant base.

Organized labor needs to build on the successful labor-neighbor strategy.
Practiced in various cities across the country, this strategy has rank-and-file members at the precinct or election district level take the lead in forming grassroots activist committees in their neighborhoods to work on broad progressive, pro-worker projects and local issues that affect workers and their families. On the local level there are many centers of power—school boards, town councils, and committees of local government—where members can achieve victories and gain political experience. This is one area where we have much to learn from the Christian Coalition. Everyone likes to repeat former Massachusetts Congressman Tip O'Neill's adage that "all politics are local," but the union movement has yet to demonstrate that it has the stomach to carry it out in practice. This will take organization, resources, and planning on the part of local unions with the support and guidance of their national unions. It will also require involvement of central labor bodies and state federations.

The AFL-CIO needs to revitalize its central labor bodies and encourage them to take greater initiative and leadership in the political arena on the local level.

In this area, the new AFL-CIO leaders have hit the ground running. Sweeney's New Voice team actively sought support from central labor bodies during the campaign to win the 1995 AFL-CIO election. Many people thought this emphasis was foolish because each central labor body had only one vote at the AFL-CIO convention while each national union could vote the number of its members. But the effort was about building a sense of movement and signaling the importance central bodies would have, especially in the arena of politics. Since the convention, central labor body leaders from around the country have met and formed a task force to develop revitalization plans.

Most local unions are relatively small, and even the largest locals usually do not have the numbers to effectively cover whole communities. Central labor bodies are the logical vehicles for developing "Labor to Neighbor" programs and carrying out political campaigns. They are less dominated by the particular concerns that each local union has to focus on. These bodies are the natural instruments for the development of a progressive populist political agenda and can often take the lead in coalescing with other forces. The AFL-CIO needs to help these central labor bodies develop political education programs and learn how to create and carry out local strategic political plans. All indications are that this is just what the Sweeney team intends to do.

Labor needs to change at all levels to attract the activists it will need for the struggle ahead.

That means creating an organization that looks and sounds like the people we are trying to lead and whose interests we claim to represent. Regardless of the color of their skin, their choice of partner, their language, country of origin, their age or gender, all should be welcomed, encouraged, and supported at all levels in organized labor.

Despite good intentions, union leaders are often clueless about how to carry this out in practice. National and international unions need to develop education programs to demonstrate why unions need diversity programs and show how to create them. First, national and local leaders need to be won to the importance of this initiative. Through 'train the trainer' programs, they can then educate their stewards, active members, and rank-and-file members. Diversity and equality are about justice, but they are also fundamentally questions of power. We must enlist all our potential forces and create a more united movement if we are to amass the power we need to win.

Unions need to do more to build coalitions with progressive political organizations.

Progressives continually kill themselves fighting over minutia instead of acting in unity around a common agenda. The labor movement has enough "mass" to be a center of gravity and help keep progressives together around the interests of the broad majority of the people. If we keep our "eye on this prize," we can organize for power to advance our common interests. Jobs with Justice coalitions have been a useful vehicle for this work in many areas. Labor organizations can often take the lead in building coalitions but we also need to be able to take leadership from others.

Some coalitions are limited, based on temporary confluence of interests and expediency, while others are permanent. For example, we may unite with an employer group around an issue, but our basic interests are opposed. Some alliances, such as those with community organizations or social justice groups, are more permanent. These we might call our natural allies. Our work with all coalition partners must be based on honesty and we need to follow through on our particular commitments. We also need to educate our base as to the reasons and importance of these alliances. Labor organizations engage in multifaceted activity and it would be naive to think that everything we do can be fully and adequately explained to our members. But it would be a mistake to continue the practice that exists in many parts of our movement of only "coalescing at the top" and never involving the base. With our natural allies we need to maintain our commitment to coalitions even when our most direct concerns are not at the top of the agenda. Because of our membership base and resources we can and should provide stability and leadership in building progressive coalitions.

The labor movement must be more selective about its endorsements of candidates and take a hard look at its electoral strategy.

For example, consider the national AFL-CIO endorsement process, which is remarkably similar to the endorsement process in state federations, local labor councils, and most international unions. Labor seems to feel compelled to make an endorsement in every district, thus we are constantly holding our noses and going with the "lesser of two evils." Instead, labor endorsements should be sacred, bestowed only on those candidates who support labor and a pro-worker economic course in this country. We should forget about endorsing the "lesser of two evils" and instead focus our energy on defeating the evil entirely. If the labor movement only endorsed and funded those candidates who take the lead in fighting for progressive issues, we would be able to fund more campaigns to educate and motivate the electorate. The labor movement would have more resources available to defeat candidates that take the lead against us.

Some labor leaders argue that this strategy would lead to greater control by enemies of labor. But in fact, "endorsing a horse in every race" is itself a reason for labor's political losses. Although candidates endorsed by labor lost in the 1994 GOP election sweep, labor has not enjoyed a majority for working Americans even when the Democrats controlled one or both houses of Congress. Despite the fact that the 1996 elections did not sweep the Republicans from power in the Congress, some of the worst reactionaries targeted by the AFL-CIO were defeated and we came very close to changing the balance of power. The trade union movement is recognized as more of a power than it has been in decades and there is a sense that the Federation's more aggressive and targeted approach is a part of our resurgence.

Specifically, we need to set new criteria for how the AFL-CIO Committee on Political Education (COPE) makes endorsement recommendations to the AFL-CIO Executive Board. All too often, recommendations are based on gaining access, or support for a single industry issue, or on whether or not elected officials will throw labor a vote now and then. We should only endorse candidates who will vote in support of labor issues and will fight for them. We must set higher standards for labor support and hold politicians accountable. If we want to speak to and for the working class, we must use class-based rather than union-based criteria to evaluate politicians.

The labor movement needs to wield political sticks rather than holding out political carrots.

Despite the recent public relations debacle of the National Rifle Association, it was one of the organizations that politicians, candidates or incumbents, feared most. Few progressive or moderate politicians ever voted with the NRA to seek their support. Rather, they voted with the NRA so that they would not be targeted for defeat. The NRA's high tech direct mail, media, and grassroots campaigns against candidates were effective and powerful, sometimes moving polling numbers eight to ten points and defeating pro-working class, progressive candidates. The AFL-CIO was right to have targeted right-wing Republicans in the 1996 election. The fact that the "America Needs a Raise" campaign changed some votes on the minimum wage is testament to the success of this strategy.

The money the labor movement spends on direct candidate contributions, political parties, and political fundraising dinners should be used to create education programs that challenge corporate America's vision of the way the world should work.

This would allow the labor movement to control the debate, and to project an active, rather than reactive, message. We watched in horror one election year as an AFL-CIO endorsed candidate pledged to reduce the federal deficit and cut back on the bloated government bureaucracy in Washington. This candidate not only received labor's endorsement, the vast majority of his funding came from labor, including from our own union, which represents many public sector workers! Our money would have been better spent educating the electorate on how corporate America, not hard working public sector employees, created this monster called the budget deficit. We could have used the funds to sponsor forums and hold events that addressed the direction of U.S. tax policy and how it rewards only the very rich. We could have produced our own commercials to highlight the results and benefits of publicly funded social programs. This would encourage members to vote on issues, not candidates.

Finally, every international union, local union, central labor body, and state federation needs to develop a long term political plan.

These plans have to be constructed with the involvement of all the appropriate leaders and active members at each level of organization, as well as coordinated with the AFL-CIO's new approach to politics. To do this, every union, from a large international to a small local union, must have good communication that is organized, systematic and two-way (e.g. leadership-base-leadership; officers-executive board-officers). Second, the union needs to have goals and objectives. Goals tend to be broader and long term, like increasing the union's political power and increasing member support and involvement in a political program that they help to create. Objectives are often sub-sets of goals. They are usually geared to the short and intermediate term. Both must have target dates or deadlines and be measurable, but the more general goals may not be as easy to quantify.

Plans need to have detailed stages of implementation and evaluation. This is important so that all participants can assess and change the plan if needed. It is essential, especially in beginning this work, that objectives be realistic and achievable. Successes and victories, however small, will build this work, while frustration with impossible targets will only derail it. Finally, it should be recognized that a clear plan, developed with participation of every level of an organization, becomes everyone's property and makes them feel invested in it. Such a plan and planning process is profoundly democratizing for an organization at the same time as it demonstrates the value of leadership. It is a tool and an essential element for implementing a class-based approach.

CONCLUSION

The new leadership of the AFL-CIO is relying on union members and working class people to be the engines that will drive a new political program for a "new labor movement." This is the key to the class-based approach that we advocate. We need to build an educated activist core that can be the main organizational link to this broad base of support. This calls for a major shift in resources toward educating this core and also toward getting the progressive populist message out to our members and working class families. Labor must continue the work it has begun to change the terms of the debate. Working people's interests can never be defended, let alone advanced, unless the corporatist vision is challenged by a working class, populist, and progressive vision.

Working people need victories. Obviously unions and their allies cannot win every struggle, and some battles must be fought, win or lose. But when labor has strategic choices, it is often better to focus on smaller objectives (sometimes in smaller arenas) than to throw all resources into the larger and longer term struggles that we do not have the power or resources to win.

Finally, labor's political independence is central to every point in the strategies discussed above. Whatever political organization, alliance or affiliation the labor movement takes part in, unions, and the AFL-CIO in particular, must independently speak for and seek to represent the interests of working class Americans. The crisis of the labor movement that helped bring forward the new leadership of the AFL-CIO has not been resolved. There are, however, signs of resurgence, including the increasing flow of ideas as activists debate new directions for the movement.

NOTES

1. The UAW, 1199, District 65, and the West Coast Longshoremen were some of the many unions that championed these causes.

2. Lane Kirkland was widely credited with having been very effective in marshaling support from the U.S. Government and the international community for the Solidarity Movement in Poland.

3. "A New Voice for SEIU Members," the fifth and final report of "The SEIU Committee on the Future." This report was presented and adopted by the seventy-fifth Anniversary Convention of SEIU held in April 1996. It reflected four years of work by a group of SEIU Local Union leaders who were charged by the 1992 Convention with studying and reporting on the strengths and weaknesses of the organization and making recommendations on the future direction of SEIU. These leaders met with members in their workplaces all over the United States and Canada. Polls and surveys were conducted and an assessment of the union disseminated, discussed, and debated throughout the organization.

Labor's Role in the Political Arena

Dennis Rivera

Politics is the process of contesting for government power. As such, it is the arena in which the crystallization of broad economic interests occurs. It is the space in which those who work for the post office and those who work in hospitals, those who work with hammers and those who work with computers, are most likely to see their interests converge. It is also the arena in which corporate interests are united across sectoral, industrial, and geographic lines.

Politics has this status because the government sets the framework in which the creation and distribution of wealth takes place. The fight, then, for government power—politics—is primarily a fight over economics. Of course, in our society nothing is ever as clear as that. There are a multiplicity of issues, perceptions, and interests that blur the economic fault lines. Workers can, at one and the same time, have a common interest as employees, but divergent interests as homeowners or renters. They can also see their interests differ on the basis of race or nationality, as men and women, or on the basis of religious belief.

LABOR AND POLITICS

In this cauldron of confusion the labor movement can define its historic role; here, it can rise above parochialism and aspire to advance the general welfare. Politics is where labor can play its role as a nation builder, as the last line of defense against the hyper-mobility of capital and its disregard for the needs of society.

Labor cannot adequately advance the political interests of union members without doing so for working people as a whole. Construction workers, hospital workers, garment workers, and computer programmers can find their commonality in the political arena. But they can only do so with a politically vigorous and united labor movement that sees as its mission the uplift of all who work and, by extension, the improvement of society in general.

THE AFL-CIO

Upon his election, John Sweeney asked our union, the 1199 National Health and Human Service Employees Union (1199), to rejoin the AFL-CIO as a national union and we accepted.

There were a number of reasons that we rejoined the Federation, but first among them was our commitment to advancing the interests of our members and working people in general in the political arena. We believed that the new leadership shared a view consistent with ours about the role of labor in the political life of the country. We also rejoined because we believed that the new leadership had a conception of labor as more than the sum of the parts making up the Federation—a conception that saw the AFL-CIO as a movement. The initiatives of the new leadership since its election convince me that our decision was correct: the AFL-CIO has placed the rejuvenation of the political role of labor at the center of its activity.

Instead of operating as a lowest-common-denominator organization, an institutional clearinghouse of diverse sectional interests, the new leadership has successfully reunited the labor movement in a short period of time around an aggressive program of political action whose twin objectives were to recapture Democratic control of the House of Representatives in the 1996 elections, and to conduct a massive member- and public issues-oriented education program.

This change at the AFL-CIO was the direct result of the watershed election of 1994 in which the Republicans took control of the House and Senate. While many in the top leadership of the AFL-CIO saw the need for change, the 1994 election and Lane Kirkland's non-response galvanized the consensus that a major shift in labor's political operations was required.

We saw this shift in labor's 1996 political campaign. The AFL-CIO committed $35 million to political education and mobilization, more money than at any time in its history. But more importantly, these funds were not being funneled through the Democratic National Committee or handed out to candidates, but rather were part of the independent expenditures of the labor movement. This money was spent on high profile, issue-oriented advertising campaigns, on putting organizers on the ground in key congressional districts, and on providing crucial information to unions—in the form of report cards—on where labor's opponents stood on key issues.

This approach is significant for a number of reasons. First, it allows labor to maintain a clarity of message throughout the campaign and therefore raise the level of class consciousness among both its members and working people in general. Second, it means that labor is not simply an adjunct of the Democratic Party, but rather is developing its own independent political operation, giving it more leverage in the future both in the electoral and legislative arenas. Third, it raises the visibility of labor as a champion of the interests of working people in general, which will enhance its future credibility in organizing and political activity.

While the national media focused on the AFL-CIO's 1996 advertising campaign, it ignored its grassroots "America Needs a Raise" campaign. In my view, the "America Needs a Raise" campaign is as significant as the millions spent on advertising in congressional districts, because it is the beginning of political organization and consciousness building around the basic class divide in our society. The pressure created by the campaign brought a very real victory for working people: the first minimum wage increase since 1991, despite a Republican-controlled congress. For the first time since the 1930s, the labor movement as a whole is engaged in a national campaign to reach out to all working people on the issue that drives American politics—the distribution of income and wealth. For the first time in its history, the AFL-CIO is acting not as a loose federation of independent affiliates, but rather as a united factor in the political life of the country.

This approach to politics combines a conviction to promote an independent agenda for labor capable of inspiring working people and their allies, with a commitment to clearly assess and expand the boundaries of current political possibilities. This marriage of a principled, long-term agenda with real efforts to enlarge present possibilities also informs the political work of our union.

At its core, 1199 seeks to create the broad social agenda and progressive coalition that will enable labor and its allies to shape the social, political, and economic institutions of our nation in the interests of working people, their families, and communities. Simultaneously, the union endeavors to protect the interests of its members and their communities based on an assessment of the current balance of power, the extent to which our members and their allies are willing to fight, and how much further the union will be able to inspire them to fight. These efforts require the marriage of long-term goals with an accurate, understanding of current political conditions. These concerns have informed the union's decisions to work toward the revitalization of the Democratic Party, as it is currently doing in coalition with other unions in New York State, and, at other times, to aid in the development of third party options.

ALL POLITICS IS LOCAL

The effort of the national AFL-CIO to jump start labor's political activity is a welcome and needed step in the rejuvenation of the labor movement in America and in the process of advancing the economic and political interests of working people in our society. There is no doubt in my mind that it is having a significant trickle-down effect on local unions and state and central labor bodies. But the ultimate driver of American politics is not in Washington, but in communities across the nation where real people with real problems live and work.

This is where I see the biggest work ahead. Because, while the overall prestige of the Democrats has risen in response to the extremes of the Gingrich-led House, we do not yet see a significant shift in the political climate in the country. The fundamental ideas that have been the Republican stock-in-trade continue to gain ground. Indeed, there appears to be a national consensus around free-market principles, the need for less government and lower taxes, support for the rights of individuals over the needs of the community, and disregard for the most disadvantaged among us. The pressure on President Clinton to sign the pre-1996 election welfare "reform" bill was but a flagrant example of this shift to the right. And this national consensus derives its strength from the problems confronted by working people in local areas in the face of mobile capital, downsizing, budget deficits, job insecurity and layoffs, declining wages, and rising tax burdens.

One of the basic laws of politics is that people pursue their self-interest within the context given to them. Absent a realistic alternative political-economic vision and movement, the imperatives of simple survival make working people prey to reactionary ideas and policies. Because people reject proposed Republican cuts in Medicare, for example, does not mean that they are also ready to jettison free-market and individualistic ideology and policies in general.

Working people develop their conceptions of politics and political possibility out of their day-to-day experience. And, as that experience grows more difficult, the sense of what is possible is also restricted. Temporary electoral advantage—the swinging pendulum of American politics—is an insufficient barometer for gauging the fundamental shifts in American politics. This is the hard task of politics and it can only be achieved by a concentrated and long-term grassroots strategy.

1199 is committed to changing both the national and local political landscape. We have devoted enormous resources, both human and financial, to both tasks. While we are very concerned about the path politics takes in Washington, particularly since our members' jobs are so heavily dependent on federal dollars, we understand that, if we cannot shift the political balance in New York City and New York State, anything we do at the national level is short-lived.

Changing the political balance of forces is a question of power. In order to gain power, one must be able to change the political cost-benefit equation. We have been able to do that with relative success over the last year-and-a-half through campaigns against the Governor's budget cuts in specific electoral districts by targeting incumbents and providing air and ground support for our Democratic allies in budget and electoral fights. This has allowed us to acquire a degree of power that we did not have before. Both Democrats and Republicans must factor 1199's activity into their cost-benefit equation. Although we have not been able to stop the cuts— because we are not strong enough to alter the overall political-economic equation—we have been able to reduce them substantially.

While it is gratifying to us to be able to play a significant role, we are not satisfied with our position. We are still weak as a union and as a labor movement when measured against the overall direction of the State political economy. We have not been able to stop the wave of tax cutting and budget cuts. We have not been able to stop the drive to deregulate the health care industry and other industries. We have not been able to change the overall economic equation where largesse to big business and the wealthy is understood as the central factor in economic development. In a word, we are still fundamentally in a defensive battle, trying simply to hang on and preserve what we have. Our victories are limited by the options presented. They are circumscribed by a political economy that is arrayed against the interests of the working class more than ever before.

While the labor movement is more united nationally, and our state and central bodies are trying harder to keep labor together, there is the inevitable run-for-cover, scarcity-crunch-time reality, where each union tries to protect its own interests and the interests of its members, often at the expense of the interests of working people in general.

This is where the easy and hard work of politics meet. It is easy to spend money and mobilize members to affect short-term electoral and legislative outcomes. We have achieved victories in this arena even in this conservative climate. But the climate is still conservative and the range of options limited as never before in the post-Depression history of our country.

If labor's political power is to be rebuilt, it must first be rebuilt at the sources of its current strength. For example, in New York State close to one-third of the workforce is unionized. The same holds true in New York City. This compares to a fifteen percent rate nationally. If we cannot restore labor's political power in New York, we cannot do it in Washington.

In each state where labor has the potential to transform the political-economic equation we need to develop a plan for doing so. Big business takes this precise approach in its effort to turn back pro-worker legislation. It starts where it is strongest and builds a national movement. Whether the issue is workers' compensation or regulatory reform or cuts in welfare, business forces first go to where labor and its allies are weakest and then come to the strong labor states last. We need to start in the other direction. We need to inoculate strong labor states against the worst aspects of the free market consensus. But in order to do this we must develop a viable alternative vision of what our society should look like. And we must then develop a campaign to build mass support for that alternative.

LOCAL POLITICS START AT HOME

We have ignored our base for too long. If labor is to rebuild its political clout it cannot do so without educating and involving union members. It is nice to reach out to the general public, but this is only as effective as the involvement and commitment of our members. This political process, of course, is part-and-parcel of the larger task of reinventing our unions into true social organizations which attain the status of one of the top social identifications of our members. Class consciousness is tough to have if one is not also union conscious. Our goal is to build class consciousness and unity. This must start with our members first.

This means organizing our members on a political basis as well as on an employer basis—at the assembly, electoral, and congressional district levels. This means constant education and involvement in activities—from demonstrations, to lobbying, to letter-writing campaigns, in electoral as well as non-electoral political-action campaigns. This means spending a larger percentage of our dues on the political education of our members. It also means persuading members to directly support the union's political action work by agreeing to make financial contributions through political action check-off.

From 1989 to the present, 1199 has experimented in these areas with the goal of qualitatively and quantitatively increasing the participation of our members in politics. To begin with, we needed to gain accurate information regarding the percentage of our members that were registered to vote, as well as the districts in which they were registered. We discovered that, in fact, large numbers of our members lacked citizenship. This led the union to embark upon a citizenship campaign, which included organizing citizenship classes for hundreds of our members who requested them. Voter registration is also an on-going activity of the union that reaches members, their families, and communities.

In an effort to increase our ability to engage in more sophisticated campaigns, the union leadership took up the challenge of promoting political action check-off. This requires that we educate and inspire the membership sufficiently to persuade them to "put their money where their mouth is," and as such, it provides a serious indicator of membership political consciousness and commitment to the political action work of the union.

To this end, the union engages regularly in one-on-one member education, mail campaigns, and setting up literature tables in 1199 hospitals and institutions. In any given month, approximately thirty percent of the union's 117,000 membership choose to make this political action check-off.

The union's increased resources for political action have allowed it to use the media more effectively for the purpose of educating members about key issues, and deepening their identification with the union and the labor movement. This effort requires increasingly sophisticated media research and media usage. The AFL-CIO's considerable success in this area points the way for local unions and central and state labor bodies.

1199 is also interested in developing strategies which will enable it to deepen its roots in the communities where our members live and vote. Get-out-the-vote efforts in members' districts at election time yield limited results when unions do little to educate and activate community members between elections. An approach likely to bear more fruit would be for unions or central labor bodies to identify communities with high union member concentrations and establish year-round education and political action centers in those areas. Efforts like this hold the potential for enabling unions to enrich the lives of workers in their communities, develop grassroots activists, and gain the understanding and trust which prove crucial during campaigns.

The difficult work of forming durable, strategic alliances with groups outside of the labor movement, and developing common, long-term agendas for state and local labor movements will prove fundamental to altering the balance of power in favor of workers in this country. Here, state and central labor bodies have a crucial contribution to make. It is their role to unite workers in a given jurisdiction across union affiliations and to join in broader class-based action. This is the significance of the "America Needs a Raise" campaign and other activities rooted in the central labor councils.

This also means engaging union members not as a mass to be led, but as leaders of working people in their neighborhoods. It means generating the confidence among our own members that they can make a difference and that this is their country and their community, and that they are qualified to speak out for their neighbors. It is as simple as starting a movement among different unions to run union members as candidates for office. The central labor councils or the state federations, for example, could set goals for a certain number of union members to run for office with the united backing of the labor movement.

Central and state labor bodies, particularly in regions where labor is strongest, have a crucial role to play in supporting the development of state and citywide political agendas for labor. These bodies could assist unions in tracking members' voter registration, provide resources for member phone-banking on political issues and campaigns, and aid in the development of more sophisticated, coordinated media campaigns. The AFL-CIO's Labor-Neighbor project, which canvassed union members and their families in targeted electoral districts and provided issues-oriented information, presents a model for further efforts which could be extended to issue-based campaigns, as well as electoral campaigns.

IDEAS MATTER

It will be hard to change the institutional and political-economic arrangement that presents us with the limited options that we must currently choose from. But this should be the objective of labor's political activity. And the first step in this process is a broad, public discussion of ideas.

For example, the following bi-partisan articles of faith need to be challenged:

- that taxes cannot be raised, regardless of the income or wealth,

- that unrestricted markets are the best way to organize economic activity,

- that corporations are more efficient than government,

- that there should be no limits on income and wealth of individuals,

- that the best way to create jobs is to cut the costs of doing business,

- that we should accept what global markets present to us as economic options,

- that regulating corporate activities is economically inefficient,

- that high taxes and government spending are the cause of economic insecurity.

Challenging these and other concepts needs to be done on a national level. But it needs to start on a local level, where whipsawing by corporations and capitulation by government are the norm. We need to challenge corporate prerogatives and win victories locally in order to build the base to do so nationally.

In order for this to happen, however, leadership from the national AFL-CIO is necessary. In this regard, we need to push for the development of a labor vision of American society and a long-range labor program. Only a program that contains a stark critique of the status-quo can initiate the political realignment that is required for the labor movement to flourish again. Labor needs more than a series of good tactical initiatives to regenerate itself: it needs a new vision with which to enter the battle of ideas—a progressive populist vision which unites the broadest number of working Americans.

That vision needs to start with a critique of the source of the problem: corporate power and the greed that can be personalized in the form of the new high-tech/high finance robber barons. Americans need to know that the market does not make decisions about resource allocation—capitalists with names and faces do. Wages and jobs are not a function of some invisible hand, but are the result of the decisions of individuals who now make an average of 225 times what the ordinary American worker makes and who are responsible for the movement of billions of dollars a day in capital around the world.

Like its counterparts in Europe and Canada, the AFL-CIO needs to put together a comprehensive alternative economic agenda for publication and mass distribution as a tool for educating and mobilizing members and influencing public opinion.

REAL POWER IS THE ABILITY TO IMPOSE COSTS

Real power means developing the political strength sufficient to check the power that the financial markets and large corporations have over the economic and political life of the nation. Only a social movement capable of imposing sufficient costs on the political and economic elite can achieve this objective. This can mean a variety of different things, from electoral power to social upheaval.

In my view, all of the negative features of politics in America today also hold out the possibility for a progressive shift in the political arena. Right now, according to numerous recent polls, we are seeing a growing class awareness in America. As the notion that we have one dominant political party with two names becomes common, we are seeing the proliferation of third party alternatives, some of a progressive character like the New Party and Labor Party.

That shift will only come, however, when people are in motion in combination with a direct challenge to the philosophical framework that dominates economic policy at all levels of government in our society. The only institution that has the resources, constituency, and national reach to lead this shift is the labor movement. This means a conscious effort to produce a large-scale public challenge to the basic precepts of corporate market economics and corresponding public support for the idea that social objectives, not market subservience, should drive public policy.

Until the labor movement is recognized by most Americans as the central defender of economic democracy and American living standards in the face of corporations who know no flag, its decline will continue. But in order to be so identified, labor needs to break from its traditional role as the transmission belt of resources and shock troops for a lifeless Democratic Party and move into a more public, independent, aggressive, and focused role as the last line of defense between corporate greed and the American standard of living. Developing an effective grassroots movement to defend the American wage base is a good start in the necessary process of unifying working Americans and defeating the shift to the right on all other issues.

BUILDING A PARTY OF OUR OWN

Tony Mazzocchi

In August 1996, just a few months after the Labor Party was founded, President Bill Clinton signed a piece of legislation that perfectly illustrates why working people need a political party of their own: he enacted "welfare reform." After twelve years of Republican rule in the White House, it was a Democrat who rolled back this basic federal protection.

The problem is not that we were betrayed by a particular Democrat. The problem is that the whole framework of public debate and public policy is skewed, and has been for decades. We live in a nation (and a world) where corporate interests dominate, and there is virtually no counterweight to their power. The corporate vision is developed by corporate-supported think tanks, promulgated by corporate-owned media, and enacted by politicians from two corporate-supported parties that have become increasingly indistinguishable. Correctly sensing that they have no voice and no power in this closed world, the vast majority of Americans have disengaged from the political process.

As a result, working people do not see many political victories these days. Even more tragically, we are not even able to develop a vision of how things could be different. Without a chance to develop our agenda and our own vision of the future, those of us who are not totally alienated from the wider political world are continually drawn into defensive and ultimately losing battles like the one over welfare reform. Rather than debating the pros and cons of welfare, we should be talking about the changing nature of work, and figuring out how everyone in this society can lead full and productive lives. Instead, we are convinced by corporate interests that we are living in a period of scarcity, when those lucky enough to have decent jobs must pit themselves against those who do not in a struggle for resources. So long as we attempt to hitch our wagon to the two parties, we will lack vision, direction, inspiration, and militancy.

That is why, in June 1996, nearly 1,400 elected union and community activists representing over a million working people came together in Cleveland, Ohio, to create a labor party. The convention included everyone from rail workers, nurses, farm workers, oil workers, and machinists, to grad students and community activists. In the years to come, we hope to build the Labor Party into a powerful force that can challenge the burgeoning power of corporations and the wealthy in this country.

If we are to rebuild the labor movement in this country, we need the Labor Party. It has become all too clear to unionists everywhere that fighting in the plant or the office just is not enough to win anymore: We need political power to win—political power to change the anti-worker laws, to restrain corporations from trampling on our rights, to ensure that there is a social safety net so that employers cannot pit the unemployed against the employed, to guarantee that "free trade" is not just a way for corporations to evade workers' rights and environmental protections. In the long run, the labor movement just cannot win without amassing much greater power in the broader political arena. The Democrats have proven they are not up to the job. And that is why the labor movement needs the Labor Party.

We find that union members are already convinced of this. In fact, when we first began to organize for a labor party years ago, our most powerful organizing tool was a workers' poll. We asked union leaders to survey their members about creating a labor party—and the results almost always surprised them. In union after union, it turned out, workers said they wanted a political party of their own. That the present political system is controlled by corporate interests came as no surprise to the unionists we surveyed. During our years of organizing as Labor Party Advocates, our perception was confirmed again and again: Working people are ready to form a party of their own.

But it was not until our founding convention that we actually drew up a program and a constitution to give shape to the Labor Party. After addressing, and in some cases incorporating, hundreds of suggestions and proposals from the elected delegates at the convention, we adopted a sixteen-point "Call for Economic Justice." The program is built on the belief that our country can and should ensure a decent standard of living for everyone. Most fundamentally, we call for a constitutional amendment guaranteeing everyone a job at a living wage—at least ten dollars an hour. This demand is the basis of our first coordinated national campaign.

The convention delegates, after much debate, also decided that our newly created party would hold off on participating in electoral politics for at least two years. Instead, we decided to adopt "an organizing model of politics." Our aim is to develop creative grassroots means of bringing substantive issues to working people—through their unions and communities. In fact, the main goal of the Labor Party is to radically shift the political debate in this country.

LABOR'S POLITICAL STRATEGIES HAVE NOT WORKED

Every election year, organized labor shells out millions of dollars in direct and indirect contributions to help elect Democrats. We knock on doors, we staff the phone banks, we sponsor get-out-the-vote drives. Sometimes the candidates we support get elected.

Yet each year, we lose political ground. And all too often, even the candidates we have supported vote against us. The North American Free Trade Agreement (NAFTA), budgetary austerity, corporate subsidies, cuts in benefits to poor and working people: These measures have had significant bipartisan support. Politicians from both parties are interested in privatizing Social Security, expanding "workfare," and propping up a system of health care that most of us abhor. They can agree that the private sector can do almost everything better, and so we are as a nation stepping up support for private hospitals, private schools, private prisons. Meanwhile, labor's own political priorities—like changing labor laws so that workers can once again have a good shot at organizing unions—remain forever on the back burner.

For decades, working people have gone without effective political representation, and as a result, the whole face of our nation has changed. The

United States has slipped to the bottom of the industrialized world when it comes to pay and benefits and our general level of economic security. Working people are appalled that their children can expect to lead lives that are less prosperous, less secure than their own.

What workers have lost, the rich have gained: The U.S. has become the most stratified industrialized country in the world—the wealthiest one percent of American households owns nearly forty percent of the nation's wealth. In fact, the Census Bureau reported recently, income disparity is higher now than at any time since World War II. And electing Democrats to the White House has not helped: The first two years of Clinton's administration saw the income disparity widen more rapidly than during the Reagan years.

The period of 1992–94 is instructive: At last, after twelve years, labor had its wish: a Democratic president and a Democratic congress. But the result was highly disappointing. A couple of extremely modest measures were passed, including the Family and Medical Leave Act (which makes the U.S. the only highly industrialized country that only guarantees parents unpaid leave, and only if their employer has more than fifty employees). Clinton's early promise to make a significant "social investment" fell by the wayside. Our elected Democrats could not even muster the will to increase the outrageously low minimum wage. It was not until 1996, when Republicans were in control, that Congress passed an (utterly inadequate) minimum wage hike.

Part of the problem is that, as much as we contribute and as hard as we work to support Democrats, we can never outspend corporations, the main sponsors of the Democratic Party. In the 1994 congressional elections, for instance, business and corporate political action committees out-gave labor by a ratio of 3 to 1. When you add in contributions from wealthy individuals, we are outnumbered 7 to 1. According to Common Cause and the Federal Elections Commission, the Democratic Party raised $75 million in soft money between 1991 and 1994, and more than seventy percent of it came from corporate donors. In the 1996 elections, the biggest soft-money donors to both parties were executives and corporations from Wall Street, and the insurance and real estate industries. The telecommunications and tobacco industries were also generous.

So it stands to reason that corporate-supported Democrats and Republicans vote the interests of corporations. The two parties are wholly owned subsidiaries, and what they do should come as no surprise to us. We believe it is time to bring an end to this thankless job of slaving for politicians who proceed to turn their backs on us.

Granted, there are a handful of Democrats out there who do their best to represent working people. But they are hopelessly surrounded. The pro-corporate flank grows ever more militant and powerful, while the pro-worker flank shrivels, robbed of creativity and the will to fight.

The AFL-CIO leadership elected in 1995 has made some important moves to gain greater independence from the Democratic Party. In the 1996 elections, the Federation invested most of its political action dollars not in direct contributions to candidates, but in TV and radio ads that pushed labor's agenda. In 1997, the AFL-CIO, for the first time, aired spots critical of Democrats—not just Republicans—who had sold out working people. A fundamental problem however remains: The Democratic Party realizes that organized labor literally has nowhere else to go.

We created the Labor Party because we believe we cannot turn things around without banding together as a class. As unionists, we know this instinctively. In fact, the point of having a union is to come together with people whose interests we share, to determine our collective goals, and to strategize about how to win them. Ideally, a union is a place where working people can shape their own sense of identity and beliefs, and find camaraderie with one another. All working people—not just unionists—need a place to figure out what we want and how to fight for it effectively in the political arena—and that place is the Labor Party.

WE HAVE TO BUILD A MOVEMENT—NOT JUST A MACHINE

It has been a long time since labor and progressive forces built a powerful mass movement to change economic and political realities in this country. But that is what it takes. We did not win Social Security, unemployment insurance or other basic social guarantees because Franklin Roosevelt was a nice guy: It took a mass movement to extract those concessions. Richard Nixon was no do-gooder, but his administration supported economic and environmental legislation that Bill Clinton would not dream of signing. Why? Because civil rights, anti-war, environmental, and women's movements had heated up the political climate.

The same is true today. We cannot expect, with our largely alienated, discouraged electorate, to magically bring scores of pro-worker candidates to office. If we could, we could not hold them to their promises. As unionists, we can never forget that all our power comes from below—without a mobilized membership, we cannot expect any favors from the employer. Without a broad base of energized supporters, the Labor Party cannot expect to achieve its goals in the electoral arena either. That is why the Labor Party postponed running or endorsing candidates. The first step is to organize our base and to cement relationships with all our potential allies—and there are many.

Organized labor is uniquely positioned to reach millions of ordinary people on the basis of their class interests. Union members are a cross-section of Americans whose names we know and whose interests we already represent. What is more, unions have resources: real budgets, staff, and infrastructure we need if we are to build a mass movement. Our Labor Party has already won the support of nine national unions representing a wide range of workers, plus hundreds of local unions and labor bodies. In the coming years, the Labor Party will be working to bring many more local, national, and regional labor bodies into this struggle.

The idea of a "labor party" may not be very familiar in this country, but obviously, this is no strange new invention. European social democracies were virtually built by labor parties. The superior social supports European workers have won is directly related to the political power they hold through labor-based parties.

If there has been a weakness to the European labor parties and to Canada's labor-sponsored New Democratic Party (NDP), it has been the extent to which they have moved away from their labor base. Some Canadian activists complain bitterly about the compromised politics of the NDP, and they link it directly to the waning ability of unions to hold the party to its role of representing the distinct interests of working people. Our Labor Party hopes to avoid this pitfall by structurally insuring that unions have a say in the party's governance.

But if it is to become a powerful force, the Labor Party will have to do more than gain endorsements and institutional support: We need to reach workers themselves. That is why, under the Labor Party's constitution, unions that want to be represented on the party's leadership body must actually meet a quota—they have to recruit a certain number of their own members in order to lead the Party. In this way, we hope to bring hundreds of thousands of individuals into the Labor Party.

Although the Labor Party is built on the foundation of unions, if it is to vie for power it will have to reach far beyond the nation's sixteen million organized workers. We have structured the Labor Party to invite participation by unorganized individuals and by non-union community-based organizations, and created a structure to involve people through local and statewide party organizations. Ultimately, the Labor Party must forge alliances with other political movements to build a real alternative to the dominant two parties. But our first step has to be to organize our own base. A "coalition" made up of groups that only represent a few thousand people barely deserves the name.

We know we cannot build a movement that can force dramatic change with just a handful of paid staffers. We have got to find a way to educate masses of people to themselves become educators and organizers. We have to employ new ways of teaching and learning that actively involve the participants in thinking for themselves. The Labor Party is proposing to eventually train 1,000 rank-and-file unionists and community activists to themselves become trainers, helping other workers explore and discuss the basic political and economic issues we face.

To undertake the organizing job before us, we know we will have to relearn some of the skills many of us have lost in our atomized, desocialized society. Because we are trying to build a party of working people, and not just an organization of already-committed activists, we have to learn how to reach out to and co-exist with people who disagree with us on some issues. And we must develop a democratic organization that allows our disparate voices to be heard.

FORGING A POLITICAL AGENDA

There is a very common misunderstanding about the Labor Party among many activists on the left—that it is a gathering of "progressives" in the labor movement. Of course, many of us who are involved in the Labor Party do consider ourselves to be progressive. But a lot of the people we are inviting to join the Labor Party would not describe themselves that way. We are, in fact, trying to draw into the Labor Party anyone who agrees with our basic economic analysis: That corporations and the wealthy have too much power in this country, and working people do not have enough. Beyond that, much is up for debate and discussion in our Labor Party. This was clear at our founding convention, where delegates got into a lengthy and emotional debate about abortion. The delegates eventually adopted a position that calls for "unimpeded access to a full range of family planning and reproductive services," but that did not include specific mention of the word "abortion."

While trying to organize such a broad base of people is likely to be tough and contentious, we believe we have the best possible starting point for building a program that has substance and broad appeal: our goal is to promote the interests of working people. The Labor Party's stand on the 1996 welfare reform bill is a case in point. In a statement released after the bill's signing, the Labor Party called the legislation "a rollback of the social insurance programs all working people pay into and benefit from in times of need." We called attention to the way Democrats and Republicans alike have scapegoated immigrants and the poor as a way to divide working people against each other. The new welfare law, we pointed out, will not only deprive millions of people of necessary benefits, but intensify the wage squeeze on the rest of us. In New York City, union leaders who have endorsed the Labor Party have been in the forefront of building an alliance with "workfare" employees. By keeping our eye on our broad class interests, we can present an alternative to the kind of scapegoating that is devouring us today.

In this era of hopelessness, most of us have been conditioned to expect very little from our society. But it is time to expand our sense of possibility again—a task that is next to impossible so long as our political expressions are limited to the horizons of the Democratic Party. Our first national campaign, for a constitutional amendment guaranteeing everyone a job at a living wage, is intended to broaden our horizons. We want to bring this concept door-to-door and workplace-to-workplace: Why is it that the wealthiest nation in the world cannot afford to keep all its people employed?

The fact is, the idea of a guaranteed job was not considered the least bit far-fetched in 1946, when both Democratic and Republican presidential candidates called for it. Americans knew that full employment was possible: in the course of the war, the U.S. mobilized fifteen million troops (as many people as were unemployed in the height of the depression), and at home, six million unemployed people found jobs in the defense industry or in other industries prospering because of the defense boom. What is more, wages were high. Personal and corporate taxes were at record highs, but after-tax incomes rose even more. Productivity was way up. Even corporations could not complain—they saw their after-tax profits rise. Low unemployment helped give rise to a powerful wave of union organizing (unions gained four million members during the war) and brought up labor standards for everyone.

So it was not surprising that the Democrats, in their 1944 platform, promised to establish and maintain peace, guarantee full employment, and provide prosperity. In 1945, the House passed the Full Employment Act, which would have guaranteed that all Americans able to work and seeking work have the right to useful, remunerative, regular, and full-time employment. Although the bill was immensely popular, the version that was finally passed was heavily diluted, as a result of frantic lobbying by business interests. But the lesson should not be lost: When the nation mobilizes its resources, it can stamp out unemployment and raise wages dramatically.

We welcome the recent extremely modest increase of the minimum wage to $5.15 an hour. But it is no secret that it does not constitute a "living wage." We would like to restore the minimum wage to something that might actually support a small family—at least $10 an hour. We also believe the wage should be indexed to inflation, so it is never again allowed to become a poverty wage. Indexing has been proposed again and again, and never passed in Congress. We would like to put it in the constitution.

There have been repeated attempts to pass legislation requiring full employment or better wages. But inevitably, the legislation fails or is watered down to the point of near uselessness. That is why we are now constructing a campaign to build support for a constitutional amendment to establish this basic right. Once such an amendment is passed, it would be the duty of congress to pass laws to implement it. These laws might take a myriad of forms, since there are many ways we, as a nation, can ensure that everyone has a job at a living wage. The Labor Party's goal is to establish the right in the first place.

This is a big organizing job, and we know it. But there is no way around the slow, bottom-up job of winning millions of Americans to our point of view. Constitutional amendments must be ratified by three-quarters of state legislatures. The process lends itself to the kind of grassroots, door-to-door campaign the Labor Party is committed to.

Among the other basic planks in the Labor Party's program: We want to require employers to pay laid-off workers two months' severance pay for every year of service, and provide the community that must sustain the layoffs with $25,000 per laid-off employee. We want to restore workers' rights to organize, bargain, and strike. We call for an end to bigotry and the scapegoating of immigrants, and for affirmative action. We demand guaranteed universal, single-payer health care for everyone. We call for paid family leave, subsidized child care and elder care for all who need it, mandatory minimum pensions, and a guaranteed basic income for all. We call for national financing of all public education, free college and university education, and funding to support a student-teacher ratio of 15 to 1 in public schools. We call for strong international labor and environmental standards, and for international solidarity and cooperation with labor movements in other nations. We want an "end to corporate welfare as we know it." We want to make the wealthy pay their fair share of taxes. We want to rebuild the public sector. We call for campaign spending reform, including full and equal public financing of all candidates with proven popular support. We want national legislation that would mandate that workers be trained and deputized to be health and safety inspectors on the job—there is no other way to guarantee a safe workplace for all. We call for a labor-based, publicly-funded commission on democratizing technology—so that workers have more of a say in how new technology is developed and used.

WE NEED FRESH THINKING

We do have a sixteen-plank program, but we do not have all the answers. Partly because the corporate-controlled media has so long dominated discussion, and because we have had no viable national class-based movement in this country in decades, we need to begin to carve out a space for working people to have a discussion about the challenges we face and how to confront them.

We know that our political and economic circumstances are dramatically different from those we confronted in 1926, 1946 or 1966. Profound changes that none of us completely understand are shaping the way we live today. Rather than falling back on the solutions labor or progressives offered in 1966 or 1946, we have got to collectively increase our understanding of what is happening to us, and craft new demands that reflect these realities.

For instance: As members of my union know all too well, technology has utterly revolutionized the workplace. An oil refinery that used to employ thousands of workers now needs only a couple hundred to do the same amount of work. This ought to be great news for working people—we can produce everything we need in less time. No one really wants to spend forty hours a week in an oil refinery anyway. The problem is, we do not have control over how this new leisure is distributed. It now takes the form of family-wrecking overtime for some and hopeless unemployment for others.

In recognition of this reality, the Labor Party is calling for a thirty-two-hour workweek at no loss of pay. European workers have had some success moving toward shorter workweeks; we should stop underselling our fellow workers in Europe and follow suit. We want European-length vacations as well: The Labor Party calls for a guaranteed four-week vacation for all. We also believe that all workers—not just university professors—should have a chance to recharge their batteries with sabbaticals: We call for a year paid leave for every seven years worked.

In this era, we have to rethink what we even mean when we talk about "work," and what constitutes a "job." For instance, it may be that for many people the most important and beneficial "work" we can provide is the opportunity to get a full college education at no cost (also part of the Labor Party's program). It is now widely acknowledged that the post-war GI Bill of Rights was one of the best social investments this nation ever made. Millions of working class people gained free access to a good education—plus housing and living expenses. Today, we are still reaping the benefits of that social decision. We need a Labor Party to mine our experiences from the past and come up with innovative new solutions to chronic problems like unemployment and alienation.

There are other fundamental new realities we have to address. Our society is on a collision course with nature. The whole structure of our economy and our economic system drives us toward more and more production and endless growth that our planet simply cannot sustain. Corporations have a vested interest in seeing to it that we do not address this crisis.

Our Labor Party program calls for a "just transition movement" that will force corporations to finance the rocky transition away from polluting industries. We have to ensure that workers do not bear the brunt of the pain, that they are guaranteed income if they are laid off as a result of environmental change. That is an important first step. But the environmental crisis poses very fundamental questions about the way we live that we have to begin to address more broadly. And that is a task for the Labor Party.

In the years I spent flying around the country organizing for the Labor Party, I became very familiar with people's questions and concerns about the movement we were proposing to build. Over and over, people would raise their hands and start out by saying "But won't it be hard to…" or "Don't you think you'll have problems…." Many of us have had experiences that have taught us to be cautious or to expect failure. Our worries and fears are real: this is an uphill battle, and it will take time. We do anticipate risks, battles, powerful enemies, and organizational problems, but we cannot allow ourselves to be defeated before we begin. We have to be prepared to stay with it, even when we face opposition, when we are divided, or when we lose an argument. We have to ban hopelessness and cynicism—they lead nowhere.

Trying to build the Labor Party might be hard work, but it is also fun. In fact, it is not unlike running a campaign against your employer. It is scary and usually exhausting. But you do get a thrill when you see that the fight has inspired creativity in people you did not know had it in them, when you discover new friends and allies in unexpected corners—and when you begin to feel that you and your co-workers actually do have the power to build something together.

THE POLITICS OF LEADERSHIP:
THE ROLE OF UNIONS IN DEVELOPING POLICY INITIATIVES

Arthur Cheliotes

The American labor movement has paid a heavy price for its failure to speak on behalf of the majority of U.S. workers. The eighty-five percent of U.S. workers who are not union members see little reason to support our strikes and corporate campaigns. Rather, they see us as fighting for more money, job security, and benefits only for our own members. This is particularly true for public sector unions, whose members' paychecks come from tax dollars. After all, most workers are electing politicians who promise tax cuts because it is a way to increase their take-home pay.

It is our task to change this perception of the selfish unionized worker. Unions must demonstrate that our struggle is for justice, not privilege. We can do this by engaging in public policy debates on issues that affect all working people and their families—issues like quality public education, universal health care, fair tax policies, and affordable housing. A government by and for the people requires an organized and active public demanding justice. Only the labor movement can commit the resources, experience, and skills necessary to put the needs of the American people ahead of the profits of corporations. It is up to unions to offer a vision of a humane and just society where the economy is a means to a better life for the entire society and not an end in itself. We must do this not only in the workplace, but block by block, neighborhood by neighborhood, and town by town.

THE NEED FOR RADICAL CHANGE IN THE LABOR MOVEMENT

It is not hard to see why labor needs to be involved in public policy. It has been decades since the labor movement was able to substantively improve job conditions or the standard of living for working people in this country. The statistics are all too familiar: the percentage of families that need two incomes to preserve a middle class standard of living has risen from thirty-six percent in 1975 to fifty-eight percent in 1993. The eroding purchasing power of the minimum wage means that workers who currently earn the minimum must work more than seventy hours per week to raise their families above the poverty line. The benefits and protections U.S. workers used to enjoy have been diminished. Employers have weakened workers' compensation and limited unemployment insurance.

Our government's policies have supported employers' efforts to reduce labor costs. The North American Free Trade Agreement (NAFTA) and the General Agreement of Tariffs and Trade (GATT), two prime examples, treat human labor as a commodity, no different than oil or pork bellies, on sale in the international marketplace to the lowest bidder. As a result, American corporations ship jobs that formerly paid U.S. workers a living wage to economies where labor costs are minimal. The threat of plant relocation hangs over our contract negotiations, enhancing employers' ability to negotiate give-backs and to blame unions for declining job opportunities.

Welfare reform is another government policy that undermines wages and conditions for all workers. The already saturated low-wage job market will be flooded with public assistance recipients seeking work, causing wages to drop. Some economists estimate that wages could fall as much as seventeen percent in large cities such as New York and Los Angeles. Many workers supported welfare reform because they were angry that their tax dollars were used to support people whom they believed chose not to work—a perception encouraged by headlines that communicated the message of welfare reform as "Get a Job." The question workers and unions should be asking is: "Whose job at what wage?" Under the requirements of workfare, which stipulate that public assistance recipients must earn their checks, the unemployed are forced into many jobs that formerly paid a living wage with benefits. Nor are there enough jobs outside of workfare to employ those receiving public assistance and unemployment insurance. In New York City, for example, a study of entry-level jobs in Harlem documented that there was only one job for every fourteen applicants.

In addition to forced labor through workfare and reduced labor costs through exporting jobs, prison labor has become a key strategy for lowering wages and defeating the power of labor. Billions of dollars are made through industries whose work is performed by prisoners at a pittance. In New York, for example, office furniture used in state and local government offices is made by prison labor, while skilled furniture workers in private industry who formerly bought consumer goods and paid taxes have lost jobs.

It is unfortunate but telling that the largest employer in the United States today, with over 550,000 employees, is Manpower, Inc., a temporary agency that pays $6.50 an hour as its average wage. The overwhelming majority of workers at Manpower are part-time, and seventy-five percent have no benefits. Imagine a spouse and children that depend on a worker making $6.50 an hour, even one who works sixty hours a week and whose spouse also works part-time at a similar rate of pay. With the cost of housing, health care, food, transportation, and utilities, that family will be hard-pressed to do anything other than meet minimal expenses. Yet the Federal Reserve insists on a six percent unemployment rate, and raises interest rates whenever it fears there are "too many jobs." How can we accept government policies that force public assistance recipients to work and yet oppose full employment?

As these examples demonstrate, in a democracy, the power to regulate capital does not rest in a union contract but in government policies. Currently, these policies are crafted to sustain good conditions for employers—conditions that create profit regardless of their impoverishing effect on workers. In the early part of this century, when the power of capital and government was similarly allied against workers, labor was a leader in the fight for social and economic justice. The history of our struggles and victories should inspire us with hope for what we can accomplish now and in the future. We must learn from our past and use the power of unions to take back what is ours and create a government by and for the people.

STRATEGIES FOR CHANGE

How can organized labor address the worsening conditions described above? How can labor's response be a catalyst for stemming labor's decline?

How can we push unions to the forefront of the struggle for the future of our movement, our communities, and our country? These are the questions labor must address.

1. Develop a National Media Strategy

A critical step toward reclaiming the nation for labor is to understand the power of the media and to use that power for our ends. Mass media— television, radio, and print—have rendered unions irrelevant to the public discourse by ignoring our existence and our concerns. As a result, unions are perceived as anachronisms at best or collections of murdering mobsters at worst. Corporate media will continue to define unions in a way that alienates us from most workers. Therefore, labor must present its own image if it is to develop credibility with U.S. workers. The resources of the labor press include many outstanding editors, writers, researchers, and others with the kinds of skills that would support a media offensive. The fifteen to twenty million households of union members and retirees with relatively high wages and pensions could attract advertising revenues to cover the costs of publication. Public-access cable shows, radio talk shows, the Internet, and other audio and video communication channels can help us circumvent the power of corporate networks and transmit news across the country from a labor perspective. A national media strategy for labor could begin with a national daily labor newspaper.

2. Redefine Labor's Constituency

The union movement must change the concept of who is a union member. For too long, many unions have defined their relationship to workers in terms of particular jobs or industries. We must transcend this narrow, bureaucratic notion of membership if unions are to grow in numbers and power. The existing definition of a union member allows employers to select our members, and is particularly inappropriate in an economic context of downsizing and contingent employment. Unions need to expand their relationships to workers so that they transcend employment in organized workplaces and include, instead, laid-off workers, retired workers, part-time and temporary workers, family members of union members, and others. To do so, unions must consider developing a variety of ways for workers to belong to unions, including associate membership status that is not dependent on working in a unionized shop.

3. Moving Labor Beyond the Workplace

Organized workers and unorganized workers change places frequently, live in the same communities, and face the same problems. As unions become more inclusive, they will, of necessity, become involved in public policy on a wide range of issues. The wages negotiated by union contracts are evaluated by workers in light of the cost of housing, tuition for themselves and their children, health care, etc. If unions do not speak to these basic needs, they become irrelevant to the organized and the unorganized alike. But if unions stand up for workers' rights to housing, education, and health care, they help build a culture of trade unionism, a labor movement that encompasses all working people. The vision of our local is that unions could one day provide union-sponsored housing, union-provided health care facilities, union-sponsored training and education, and union-hosted social and cultural events. This notion of unions is part of our history. Many unions provided these services for their members in the past. Such endeavors would help build class consciousness and counter the efforts by politicians and employers to divide us by race, gender and nationality. Examples of efforts made by Local 1180 to address community issues are described in detail below.

There is, however, a limit to the services unions can provide for their members. To ensure that working people have access to the necessities of life and to opportunities for individual and collective advancement, unions must become involved in policy issues that go beyond the concerns of unionized workplaces and that affect working class communities of all kinds. Health care, housing, education, and other vital aspects of the social wage constitute the social/economic climate within which collective bargaining takes place. The value of what we win for workers depends greatly on public policy, on how much power communities are allowed to exert over corporations. As unions become more involved with policy issues, as we broaden our political agenda, our appeal to workers increases. As unions define their membership more inclusively, community concerns become union concerns.

LABOR AND POLITICS

Decisions affecting the economic and social lives of workers and their families are made every hour of every day by government officials, heads of banks, corporate elites, and other wealthy and powerful individuals who represent their own interests. By advocating for working people on issues of public policy and corporate responsibility, unions can do more to improve our members' standard of living than any collective bargaining agreement we could negotiate. In fact, union leaders who operate under the assumption that the bargaining table and grievance procedure are the only arenas in which they can fight for their members will not hold office for long. Organized labor in a democratic society has a responsibility to speak for its constituency in every forum that affects the lives of workers and their families.

In the United States, unions' political role is limited to supporting candidates perceived as sympathetic. All other political initiatives by labor are seen as wielding unfair influence. But in other industrial democracies, labor's policy role is broader, institutionalized, and effective. In Europe, labor's representation in decision-making bodies of government and industry was seen as a mechanism for protecting democracy after the defeat of fascism in World War II. In France, for example, the working class which made up much of the resistance to the Nazis came to power after the war, giving worker representatives a voice in shaping national economic policy. Labor representatives sit on the boards that govern social security, public utilities, and nationalized industries, and participate in decisions regarding how these entities and other public services function. As a result, France enjoys national health insurance, a national pension system, free education through university levels, access to child care, and family leave with a stipend to raise children. In Germany and in Japan, the average full-time worker gets more time off than the U.S. worker, and far more comprehensive benefits. It is ironic that the very safeguards and mechanisms that our country helped establish in former fascist and imperial nations were not institutionalized in our own society.

The unfortunate reality of working people today is that predatory corporate power has taken control of both the political parties that claim to represent our interests. This is why the bulk of the tax burden falls on the working people while the corporate share of taxes and the portion paid by the very rich has shrunk. It also explains the trend toward privatization, which moves services and resources away from communities and the arena of democratic decision-making and into the hands of private businesses. Increasingly, we have to fight for what we used to take for granted, like quality public schools, and pay for what we used to count on government to provide, like drinkable water.

The hegemony of corporate employer interests in U.S. politics reduces labor to choosing between the lesser of two evils. The Democrats are not really representing us, but if the Republicans get in it will be worse. Organized labor, in this scenario, will always be the battered spouse in relation to the Democratic Party. We offer our support unconditionally and demand little in return for turning out our members' votes. The wing of the Democratic Party that has corporate backing compromises our proposals before they ever become the subject of battle between Democrats and Republicans. This dynamic has profoundly alienated working people, and should be the impetus for the formation of a political party of our own. Toward that end, I attended the founding convention of the Labor Party, continue to be active in its New York state branch and encourage our members to join and become involved in the Labor Party.

Labor must raise its own political voice, break from its abusive relationship to the Democrats, and lead the rank-and-file workers of this country in a party that represents the majority of the people. Currently, we are a long way from meeting this challenge. We need to begin by addressing the issues that concern workers in their communities at the local level and by contributing a labor perspective to local and national debates.

EXAMPLES OF A POLICY APPROACH TO POLITICS AT THE LOCAL LEVEL: THE CASE OF LOCAL 1180

To reverse its membership decline, organized labor will have to win back the hearts and minds of working people, including many of those already organized into unions. To do so, organized labor needs to exert leadership and demonstrate that it can provide a vision, an agenda, and a set of concrete proposals for improving the lives of working people both in the workplace and in the community. Labor can provide the initiative for real change by proposing and then fighting for the implementation of carefully thought out, well researched, and innovative policy recommendations. Such an approach to policy increases labor's potential for capturing positive media attention. Taking the initiative in policy debates breaks the mold that casts unions as narrow, parochial, reactive organizations interested only in workplace issues. By inserting itself in these debates, labor refurbishes its image as a fighter for working people, both organized and unorganized.

Developing a policy approach to politics and an active strategy for improving community life will help organized labor counter the cynicism and negative thinking that is so rampant among working people. It provides a political agenda and links these ideas to a broader, pro-labor, democratic vision. In addition to shifting public debate, helping to build a movement within our communities, and effecting concrete change in the lives of working people, a policy-oriented strategy provides an opportunity for labor and its allies to start rebuilding society and our communities from the bottom up, piece by piece.

Local 1180 represents about 7,500 public sector workers, primarily supervisory and administrative staff in virtually every city agency. Most of our members work for the Department of Social Services, the Health and Hospitals Corporation, or the Board of Education. Eighty percent are women. My conviction that we should become involved in policy emerged from my experiences as a rank-and-file member of Local 1180. As a supervisor responsible for the administration of welfare, I saw firsthand how workers were blamed for the problems of our system of public assistance to poor people. To those who receive city services, we were the enemy, the representatives of the government they hated. I began to question why working and poor people hated government, and concluded that they resent the tax policies that burden them while failing to improve the quality of services they receive. When our union began to explore how tax policies were crafted and whom they benefitted, we saw that our task was to encourage working people to reclaim what is theirs, to take back political control over taxes and public services. We wanted to be able to deliver the message that this was possible, to challenge the illusion that global forces render economic policy beyond the control of the average person. We want to provide evidence that we have the power to change policies that are anti-worker; we have done it historically and we can do it now.

As a public sector union, Local 1180 has chosen to enter local policy debates for several reasons. Although as city workers we are often blamed when public services deteriorate, we are keenly aware of the reasons for such deterioration, and we need a forum to express our understanding of the way services are delivered and how they can be improved. As public workers, our members are directly affected by policies that reduce city services. In order to negotiate contracts and protect jobs in a climate of budget cuts and privatization, we needed to understand the policies of city government. More importantly, we needed to be able to propose viable alternatives to cutting public services, reducing the quality of life in New York City, and laying off our members. For public sector unions, involvement in policy is analogous to the research done by private sector unions on company assets and CEO salaries. Forming alliances with community groups around alternatives to current policy is our version of corporate campaign strategy.

1. Initiating an Economic Development Plan

A public sector union might begin its involvement in policy by asking, "How do we protect our members and their jobs?" Because city governments base their negotiations with the union on the lack of public funds, unions should become informed about how city government is funded and how it makes decisions about the uses of public money. When Local 1180 did this, we learned that working people disproportionately carry the burden of financing government, thus engendering resentment of government among workers. Unions, in this scenario, need to become advocates for democracy, which is supposed to be a form of government that equalizes power between the rich and everyone else. For Local 1180, this meant becoming a proponent of a fair tax structure and of alternative economic development that is in the interests of the majority of people in New York City. The city's existing economic development plans protected the financial, insurance, and real estate interests and were not conducive to prosperity for working people. Our local supported research which helped us develop a plan for rebuilding New York, one that would create a climate in which working people and their families could thrive.

We began by looking at the assets and advantages of the city. For example, New York has a natural harbor but does not link the harbor effectively to other transportation systems. Our plan to revitalize New York includes rail connections to encourage manufacturing and create jobs that would enable workers without skills or education to earn a living wage. As our researcher, Bob Fitch, points out in his book, *The Assassination of New York*, the largest single export shipped out of New York harbor at the present time is waste paper. This is because past policies have failed to maximize the harbor's potential. However, a port and rail infrastructure is vital to regaining manufacturing capacity in New York. Estimates of the number of jobs created by the port in the 1950s range from 90,000 in manufacturing alone to a total of 400,000. Although modern ports require fewer workers, it is reasonable to expect a minimum of 50,000 jobs as a result of a revival of New York's harbor. In 1996, Rudolph Giuliani, New York's

Republican mayor, called for development of transportation links to support such a revival, demonstrating that proposals that support jobs and that are in labor's interests are not merely visionary rhetoric. If we research and develop sound policies and proposals, there will be support for them among our own constituency and also possibly from unexpected corners.

Based on our research, Local 1180 developed a booklet highlighting strategies for reviving New York. The goal of these strategies is to create jobs—specifically to raise the labor force participation among New York's youth to the national average, and to raise the city's employment/population ratio to the national average for cities. Our plans included building 50,000 housing units annually, creating both much-needed housing stock and jobs in the construction industry. We also call for raising the wages of New York City industrial workers to the national average, and for retaining New York's existing industries and industrial land. To build a city with a diversified economy and equal access to skilled jobs requires a change in land use, zoning laws, and tax policies, as well as funding institutions that support job creation and community development.

We publicized our plan by organizing a conference on the issues it raises and by speaking out at community events. As a result of these efforts, we were quoted in the mass media as something other than a drain on the taxpayers or a protected group of not-very-hard-working people. The reputation of our local was enhanced and the image of public workers was improved. Afterwards, we returned to our original question: how would the city get money to finance such a plan? Our next step was to develop a tax reform proposal.

2. Tax Reform

At the local level, unions should establish relationships with community organizations, progressive politicians and others who support our efforts to promote policies that favor working people. Our union participates frequently in public hearings and community and political events with our members and our allies, as a way of both building solidarity and communicating our political positions on issues. The union takes the time to research its positions, to package its main points, and to anticipate and respond to critics of our perspective on policy issues.

For example, we put together and widely disseminated a paper called "Don't Blame Us!" which confronts the myths about public sector workers.

The paper not only defends our members against these attacks, but also raises questions about what is really behind the inadequate funding and poor quality of many public services. As New Yorkers who are on the front-line of delivering public services, our members are doubly concerned about the city's social and economic problems. This concern gave rise to our participation in the campaign to revitalize New York and led us to develop a tax reform policy.

Our tax reform policy recognizes that our members are not just municipal workers, they are also consumers, taxpayers, and community members. After all, what good is a generous pension if old age is spent without adequate police protection, affordable housing or access to parks and public libraries? Salary gains won through collective bargaining can be eroded by increases in city sales, income or real estate taxes. During New York City's financial crisis in the 1970s, the city turned to "solutions" that hurt workers, such as layoffs, pension deferrals, and "productivity measures," resulting in hardships for our members and exclusion from debate of proposals for progressive tax policies.

Our proposal for tax reform emphasizes five basic points. First, we call for a truly progressive income tax, at a rate of 5.5 percent for those with incomes between $100,000 and $499,000, 6.5 percent for those earning $500,000 to $999,999, and 7.5 percent for those whose incomes surpass one million dollars annually. In contrast, the maximum current tax rate is 3.91 percent for individuals with incomes over $60,000. Second, we call for a tax on business services, not consumer necessities. We propose phasing out the sales tax on items like clothing and low-cost restaurant meals and replacing them with a four percent tax on such services as advertising, public relations, consulting, and legal and financial services, which would generate considerable revenue. Third, we recommend a differential tax that falls more heavily on land than on improvements to buildings. Recommended by the New York City Tax Study Commission (appointed by former Mayor Koch to examine tax policies in the city), this kind of tax promotes greater equity, lowers housing costs, and generates new construction jobs. Local 1180's proposal favors the elimination of the Industrial and Commercial Incentives Program, a tax incentive program developed by the Koch administration to encourage industrial development that, in our view, became a boondoggle for corporations, as well as of luxury tax exemptions and abatement programs which result in approximately $5 billion in lost revenue.

According to our estimates, phasing out these programs would realize an annual saving to the city of about half-a-billion-dollars per year. Finally, the union recommends taxing private universities (something other cities are already doing), and elite non-profits. This could result in more than $100 million in tax revenue.

Our union financed the research and development of this plan. We also initiated a campaign to publicize an alternative tax policy that would increase the burden on corporations and the rich and reduce the share that working people contribute. Historically, income tax was paid only by the upper classes. It is the labor movement's job to restore balance and a sense of history to the discussion of tax reform. Our tax reform proposal states that working people are carrying too much of the tax burden of New York City, and it demonstrates how that burden can be shifted to those who reap the greatest profits—the financial and real estate industries, for example. Initiatives like our tax reform proposal change the public perception that unions simply protect the wages and contracts of their members. We showed that as a public sector union, our members can offer ideas and an understanding of city government and services that can benefit all working New Yorkers.

3. Challenging Welfare Reform

The welfare reform legislation passed during 1996 speaks to the heart of how the labor movement defines its interests and its constituency. From labor's perspective, poverty and unemployment arise from policy rather than from aberrant behavior by the poor. Thus, as union members, we believe the solution lies in policies that support full employment, living wages, and benefits for all workers. From this perspective, WEP (the Work Experience Program), New York City's version of workfare, is an urban atrocity and we actively oppose it. Therefore, our union has been involved in exposing and opposing this key aspect of welfare reform in New York City. Together with the Community Food Resource Center, we chair a coalition of labor, community, and religious groups that support WEP workers organizing around their conditions of work, and that keeps the abuses of workfare in the public eye.

Along with other members of this coalition, Local 1180 has endorsed "principles of unity" that call for real job training and job opportunities for those on public assistance, and for changes in New York City's existing welfare-to-work programs. These principles are based on the fact that WEP workers are entitled to the same benefits, wages, and conditions that others doing the same work receive. Our coalition has learned, for example, that many WEP workers do not receive protective clothing, safety equipment or training to deal with the hazards they face on the job. Moreover, WEP workers commonly are paid at a level of minimum wage or below, which violates the law and impairs the city's economic health. The coalition also supports the right of those on public assistance to obtain the education and training they need to get a job that can sustain a family.

As workers and as citizens, our members are deeply affected by workfare. The interests of all New Yorkers are tied fundamentally to the interests of city workers. While workfare is presented as if it were a training program leading to jobs, it functions instead as a punitive action against the poor that simultaneously adds a subgroup of unpaid laborers to the city's workforce. Workfare supporters defend it as a way to increase city services, shrink the budget, and avoid the pitfalls of public assistance. We do not see it that way. Although WEP workers do contribute to city services, they do so largely as replacements for city workers. This actually perpetuates the problems of unemployment and poverty that drive people to seek public assistance in the first place, because it reduces the number of jobs for workers who pay taxes and who earn viable wages with benefits.

Our members, as public workers, often work with or supervise WEP workers. For example, an 1180 member met a WEP worker at her job who had worked for the Human Resources Administration (the agency that oversees public assistance in New York City), took a buyout, was unable to find work, and was now emptying waste baskets and cleaning bathrooms in another city agency. Our member commented:

> I admired the way she [the WEP worker] went about her work, but it demeaned her skills. We tried to make the work situation as comfortable for her as possible. What happened to her could happen to any of us. WEP is not the answer. The answer is a meaningful job that utilizes the skills that workers have acquired in their lifetime.

Such experiences illustrate the close connections between those on welfare and those who are currently working. Our members have become acquainted with WEP workers who desperately want to continue their education or to work at the level of their previous employment. Instead, their skills, ambition, and experience are wasted in a program designed only to force them to work for their check. In the process of working with WEP participants, our members can see how their own interests lie in fighting for decent jobs for all working people.

4. The Urban Leadership Program

The purpose of the Urban Leadership Program is to develop a perspective on policy issues that comes from front-line workers, a "bottom-up" perspective that is missing in public discourse. This program, developed by CWA 1180 in cooperation with Queens College, enables members to organize themselves into task forces that work on policy issues from the viewpoint of public sector workers. Because such workers often have to implement policies that they have had no voice in designing, and their perspective is informed by the daily practice of public service, they constitute a unique source of expertise and informed knowledge on issues of public interest. In this program, workers themselves craft a policy approach for unions. They identify community problems and propose solutions that promote interests of working people. In the process, they democratize both public and union discourse on the social issues they confront daily. So far, task forces have addressed such topics as health care, economic development, housing, welfare, education, and criminal justice.

The Urban Leadership Program expands the union's voice in public policy while involving members in developing alternative solutions to urban problems. The program provides the opportunity for policy initiatives to emerge from the union's rank-and-file membership, rather than from the professional union staff. Members who participate in this program also earn the college credits they need to help them advance on the job. Thus, the Urban Leadership Program enhances educational opportunities for Local 1180 members. Undergraduate and graduate courses are designed to encourage information sharing, discussion, and collective problem solving under the guidance of faculty members. Students examine relevant literature, hear from guest speakers and policy experts, and produce a collective position paper. In the process, students sharpen their professional skills, acquire greater knowledge and understanding of city government and public administration, improve their written and oral communication, and obtain academic credentials.

The Urban Leadership Program is premised on the belief that alternative approaches to urban issues have not been fully explored, and that the city has failed to tap its own workforce in seeking solutions to the city's problems. Instead, the media projects city workers as part of the problem of city government. However, those on the front line of city services have much to contribute, both in evaluating agency operations and recommending changes in policy and practice. Professional development that increases the voice of workers in city government improves morale, productivity, and public service, and helps the advancement of women and people of color who predominate among city workers. The Urban Leadership Program also helps the union, as it identifies those rank-and-file members who have ideas to contribute and who see the union as a way to disseminate their perspective. These members become the spokespersons for the union in public hearings and forums, where they can speak with knowledge, confidence, and experience on policy issues.

A recent task force report prepared by workers in the program examined welfare reform. The task force members interviewed members from the Financial Information Services Agency, the New York City Board of Education, an Income Support Center in Harlem, and the Department of Sanitation, all of whom presently work with or supervise public assistance recipients assigned to their job sites as part of the Work Experience Program. The task force also researched related issues, such as income disparity in the United States, corporate welfare, and immigration. The task force report made recommendations in the areas of: women on Aid to Families with Dependent Children (AFDC) and welfare reform, child support, immigration, workfare, housing and homelessness, general assistance, behavior modification, immigration, and corporate welfare. On welfare reform, the report called for the creation of secure and well-paying jobs in the private sector, and for support of community-based employment that allows job seekers to contribute to their communities. The task force called attention to the problems of domestic violence and recommended expanding counseling, safe houses, and other support for women fleeing domestic violence. The recommendations clearly stem from what task force members have learned (through research and on the job) about why people seek public assistance in the first place. They conclude their remarks on welfare reform by stating that work should be for wages, not "to work off welfare benefits and displace other full-time workers." The task force supported the right to full-time education, and opposed the practice of refusing benefits to families with a spouse or partner living in the household. They noted the failure of training programs to match participants to jobs, while citing the success of women who continue their education in college programs.

The report, entitled "They Came for the Poor," aligns the interests of workers, public assistance recipients and the nation in its conclusion:

> The Task Force concluded its deliberations with a call to CWA Local 1180 and its allies in the labor, faith-based and activist communities to correct the current welfare legislation and at the same time restore welfare benefits to the entitlement status they have enjoyed for the last 60 years. Members challenge the focus of the nation and local leaders on the victims of poverty instead of its structural roots in increasing inequality, abetted by government programs. Citing the impact of entitlement programs and public benefits crafted over the last 60 years, the Task Force noted that millions of Americans were lifted from poverty, including the elderly, disabled, women and children and working people. Current government policy is designed to reverse 60 years of struggle for equal justice, redistribution of wealth and social equality. Task Force members warned that without such efforts, the nation may well enter the 21st Century in the same state in which it entered this one.

The work of this group exemplifies how the Urban Leadership program supports the active involvement of Local 1180 and its members in public policy, and how this involvement in turn enlarges the vision of the constituency and goals of the labor movement.

CONCLUSION

The conditions facing workers and unions today cry out for the voice of labor to publicize them, explain their causes, and propose solutions. Instead, the mainstream media interprets the economy from a corporate employer's perspective, and discourages white workers from seeking unity with others who share their problems. Our union is eighty percent women, fifty percent African American, fifteen percent Latino, and five percent Asian. The interests of our members lie with the diverse community of New Yorkers and the increasingly diverse membership of unions. However, mainstream labor and the AFL-CIO have been notoriously slow to recognize the concerns and potential of this diversity. The directions we proposed above will raise the voices of women and people of color, as bottom-up leadership is fostered and developed, and as the concerns of communities become those of labor.

If the labor movement is to grow in size and importance, it must change, change radically, and change now. A media counter-offensive, a redefinition of labor's constituency, and a strong role in public policy are all necessary, but these initiatives will only succeed if they are based on workers' ideas and interests. The current AFL-CIO leadership recognizes the need for political education at all levels within our unions. This can provide an impetus for us to begin honing and articulating a workers' perspective on important policy issues.

Labor must have its own political voice, its own political party. The time has come to end our abusive relationship with the two-party system, bring our own political organizations to maturity, and strategize to have a powerful impact on national and global politics. If we are to do this, if we are to lead rank-and-file workers into the political arena, we must first establish a labor presence in the world in which they live, rather than in the virtual reality inside Washington's beltway. By engaging in community struggles around health care, education, environmental issues, and other concerns that affect workers, we demonstrate our commitment not just to union members, but to all working people, and to all those who want to work. By using labor's resources to research, understand, and develop viable policy alternatives to the market-driven economic development currently favored by government, we present a vision of what work could be. By taking on politicians and demanding that they represent the majority of people in our cities, towns, states, and nation, we exercise the power of an energized, mobilized labor movement. We can begin by addressing the issues of workers in their communities and by articulating a labor perspective in the debates that matter most to them. As we do this, we rebuild not only our unions, but democracy itself.

PART | 5 | INTERNATIONAL AFFAIRS

Engaging in international activities is no longer a choice for organized labor. Today, the U.S. economy is dominated by transnational corporations with no national boundaries that shift production to wherever they can find the cheapest labor and the fewest restrictions on their operations. This has severely thwarted union efforts at the collective bargaining table and dramatically undercut the gains made by workers over the last three decades. In the past, the dominant labor policy was alternately driven by cold war anti-communist ideology, a belief that prosperity was dependent on foreign markets for U.S. products, and a protectionism that sought to prevent the importation of foreign products. Each of these approaches, in their own way, supported U.S. corporate interests. But now that workers and unions are combating employers that are multinational, organized labor is forced to organize against capital on a global scale. Consequently, the current AFL-CIO has turned decidedly internationalist in perspective. The new economic order demands an international strategy that restricts the ability of corporations to pursue sub-minimum wages, anti-union environments, and lax—or non-existent—health and safety regulations. Contributors to this section discuss recent world economic trends and their impact on the future of international labor activities. All focus on how to stem the power of transnational corporations.

In the lead article of this section, Barbara Shailor and George Kourpias relate how the industrialized nations of the world have been rapidly dismantling their welfare states and deregulating their economies—a phenomenon that has led to the breaking of the post-war social contract that provided workers with the promise of prosperity and economic security. Furthermore, these nations have transmitted these policy changes to the rest of the world through their dominance of international trade and finance. The enormous growth of multinational corporations and the inability of the governments to control capital within their borders have given rise to increased inequality in the U.S. and rising unemployment in Europe, despite a continuing boom in international trade and finance. They proscribe a program whereby labor organizes workers on an international level, compels governments to regulate global capital, establishes a global council of union representatives for each transnational corporation, and develops multinational codes of conduct and monitoring systems for all the world's major corporations. Unions, the authors argue, have a political and moral responsibility to bring these issues to the collective bargaining table and build them into basic labor contracts.

Labor's ability to pursue a company or an industry globally, writes Andy Banks, will often mean the difference between good and safe union jobs or low wage, non-union employment (and a high unemployment) at home. Transnational corporations have become increasingly dominant in the global economy and their ability to move operations to non-union areas of the world have had an impact on all the basic functions of trade unions—bargaining, organizing, negotiating, and grievance handling. Banks urges the labor movement to create international structures to match the structures of employers. The new global economy requires that labor unions develop the institutional structures and engage in organizational activities that will link them to unions representing workers in the same transnational corporations and industries in other parts of the world. Banks describes the experience of European unions which, faced with economic integration of the continent through the European Union, established international industry-wide bargaining councils, developed a structure for negotiating minimal social standards for all countries, and created government mandated Works Councils for each company that operates in more than one European country. Unions in less wealthy regions viewed this as a way to raise their standards, while unions in the more developed countries saw this as a way to prevent the erosion of their higher level of social benefits. Banks urges the AFL-CIO to assist the international trade secretariats, help organize transnational companies which have bargaining relationships with AFL-CIO affiliates, turn to member unions to finance its international activities, and provide affiliates with concrete service that enhance their abilities to organize, bargain, and campaign against multinational corporations.

Héctor Figueroa reviews the Federation's current international strategy as it seeks to focus international policy on the interests of U.S. workers, organize and coordinate international activities along industrial lines, monitor and counterbalance the behavior of multinationals, and establish trade conditions that protect worker rights and living standards. While viewing these efforts favorably, he suggests that the "pursuit of American workers' self-interest" approach may prompt suspicion amongst trade unionists in other parts of the world. Overcoming that suspicion may not be so easy given labor's checkered history of international activities, differences in philosophies and practices, and competing economic interests that often turn workers from different countries against each other. U.S. labor, suggests Figueroa, must somehow resist economic nationalism without abandoning the struggle for more jobs and increasing living standards at home. Central to this effort will be cooperative activities across geographical, cultural, and political boundaries to take wages and working conditions out of global competition. U.S. labor will have to rebuild a relationship with trade unionists in other countries and with human rights activists, environmental groups, and policy centers around the world. To this end, it must win the trust of trade unionists abroad and consciously depart from the worst aspects of the Federation's cold war legacy to promote a new culture of international solidarity as both a moral imperative and an economic necessity.

Ron Blackwell warns that as long as there are impoverished and oppressed people in the world, domestic jobs and working conditions are at risk. At the same time, he suggests that labor cannot and should not try to stop the integration of the world economy. Instead he urges organized labor to ensure that workers benefit from the growth and prosperity that results from this integration. He calls for a practical, non-ideological, non-partisan, member-based approach to international union work and draws on the experience of the needle trades unions, which have long dealt with the problem of capital flight, to outline a strategy for the contemporary period. He suggests that unions help workers in other countries organize by developing reciprocal relations with movements in those countries; work with employers who respect the rights of workers and encourage them to develop a "high road" competitive strategy (i.e., quality products produced by a highly skilled and motivated workforce); "get between" the employer and their customer base with negative publicity campaigns and consumer boycotts when they do not respect workers' rights; and change the rules of international commerce so that companies are prevented from crossing international borders in search of labor unless they produce goods in a manner that respects fundamental worker rights and is compatible with the upward movement of labor standards. The Federation and unions, Blackwell argues, must stand behind workers, organizations, and locals that are engaged in international work.

DEVELOPING AND ENFORCING INTERNATIONAL LABOR STANDARDS

Barbara Shailor and George Kourpias

The current leadership of the AFL-CIO came to office in 1995, in large measure because of its commitment to strengthening labor's ability to meet current global challenges with new strategies, innovative actions, and a new generation of international labor activists who will take on the forces that pit workers in different countries against each other. This leadership knows that it is not enough to wage a struggle within Washington, D.C., or Brussels or Geneva. The AFL-CIO needs to create a culture and capacity to educate its members and all working people about the realities of today's global economy. Our unions have to establish and strengthen bonds between U.S. workers and workers around the world. It is clear that the realities of the global economy dictate that we can only secure and strengthen American workers' "right to organize" by extending the "right to organize" to workers the world over. This international strategy is an integral part of building labor's power in the U.S. The AFL-CIO and all its affiliates are uniquely positioned to provide leadership and vision for the international labor movement. The time for change has never been riper.

THE INTERNATIONAL CHALLENGES FACING THE LABOR MOVEMENT

The U.S. labor movement faces monumental challenges as it enters the twenty-first century. We are living and laboring in a world that has been transformed. Over the past two decades we have seen multinational corporations circling the globe in search of cheap labor. Today, jobs are on the move as never before. In the U.S., engineering jobs are moving to Mexico; garment jobs are going to Central America; data processing jobs are switching to Ireland; aerospace jobs are now on their way to China. But, it is not just jobs from the industrial world which are leaving. The same thing is happening even in developing economies. This job mobility is accompanied by increasing exploitation, falling wages, worsening working conditions, and growing worker insecurity. Across the world workers are increasingly unorganized and increasingly vulnerable. When they try to do something about it they face harassment, intimidation, and even murder. In 1995, 378 workers were murdered for their trade union activities, 1,900 seriously injured, 5,000 arrested and detained, and 68,000 dismissed. We have seen economic inequality return unlike any recent period in American history.

In the past two decades we have witnessed the restructuring of work process, the internationalization of capital markets, and the decline and offshore relocation of manufacturing. We have also witnessed the birth and enormous growth of the modern transnational corporations, 37,000 of which, along with their subsidiaries, now control seventy-five percent of all world trade. Such companies account for one third of all foreign direct investment and one third of all output, and control at least 150 million jobs worldwide. In the industrial world sixty-one million workers are now directly employed by the transnationals.

In contrast the 1950s and 1960s were characterized by a period when the industrialized countries followed economic and social policies based on an unwritten but generally accepted social contract, aiming to promote full employment and provide social protection for all citizens. For a quarter century or more after the end of World War II, there was widespread social solidarity in the U.S. and in most other advanced industrial societies. Most people lived by and benefited from a set of common values and shared understandings. Business, labor, and government assumed that working people were entitled to a fair share of the wealth they produced. Unions and business grew strong together. Rich and poor alike benefited from economic growth. Living standards rose. Since the oil shocks of the 1970s, the recessions of the 1980s, and a series of financial debt crises, the industrial nations have been dismantling their welfare states and deregulating their economies. The effect has been to break the post-war social contract.

Moreover, the industrialized nations have transmitted these policy changes to the rest of the world through their dominance of international trade and finance. The power of creditor countries, particularly the U.S. and Britain, increased even more because of the massive debts developing countries acquired during the 1970s and 1980s. All this happened just as the U.S. and British governments were being taken over by reactionary politicians promoting free market ideologies.

With the end of the cold war in the late 1980s and early 1990s, transnational corporate power and the neoliberal ideologies it has generated became truly global. Today, transnational corporations enjoy immensely increased power and a practically uncontrolled ability to move their capital around the globe. The growing power of the corporations has also meant that national governments find it increasingly difficult to control capital, even within their borders through legislation or other political measures.

For generations, we were told that increasing trade and investment, coupled with advances in technology, would drive national productivity and create wealth. Yet over the past decade, despite a continuing boom in international trade and finance, inequality in the United States and unemployment in Europe has worsened. In the U.S. this has produced anxious and angry workers as well as political opportunists of the Right. In Europe it has produced right-wing politicians who play on the real fears of workers all over the continent. It should be crystal clear to the economists and the politicians: if we have twenty-first century global rights for capital with weak twentieth century national rights for labor, we will end up with brutal nineteenth century capitalism for workers all over again.

This is the context in which we have to look at the consequences of globalization. Globalization is here to stay, but the neoliberal model of globalization is not preordained. In fact, it is within organized labor's collective ability and responsibility to radically change the dangerous course we are now on. Labor has no choice but to educate our ranks about globalization, demand regulation of the global capital market, and organize the global labor market.

EDUCATING AND CHANGING OURSELVES

The election of new leadership to the AFL-CIO was crucial not only for the U.S. labor movement, but for the revitalization of the labor movement around the world. AFL-CIO President John Sweeney clearly describes our reality and challenge: "Before we can change the world, we must change ourselves." We can no longer be satisfied to represent dwindling shares of the workforces in our own countries. We can no longer be content to represent our members only on wages, hours, and working conditions while letting our employers determine whether, where, and how they will invest the wealth that we produced. And no longer can we fool ourselves, or let anyone else fool us, into believing that the quality of goods we produce and the services we provide are not our business.

Of course, labor cannot stand up to global power abroad if workers are on their knees at home. Rebuilding labor's strength within our borders is essential. But the U.S. labor movement must also fight to help workers extend their rights abroad. As national economies fold into a new global economy, big governments, rich banks, and multinational companies are moving to ensure that new global laws protect the rights of capital. But global action should not be the narrow preserve of these powerful entities. Consumers and environmental organizations who coined the slogan, "think global; act local" will have to add a third refrain: "organize internationally." Labor must lead this global organizing and assert its place at the table in the new world economy.

Workers around the world are beginning to understand that their own government's austerity programs are but a part of the global neoliberal realities that are affecting workers the world over. During the December 1995 strikes, French workers were hailed by some as "the first wave of revolt against the New World Order." Over the course of several months, French public workers brought their nation to a standstill. They were protesting government plans to privatize services and cut health care and pension benefits, the same policies that are bedeviling workers in the U.S. and around the globe. We need to demonstrate the connection between these struggles and our members whenever they occur.

Labor is beginning to do just that. When the Brazilian workers recently called for a general strike in Brazil, there were demonstrations, protests, and picketing at the Brazilian embassy in Washington, D.C. and five other cities across the United States. Within hours of the Korean government's attempt to pass repressive labor legislation, American trade unionists were on the streets protesting in front of the Korean embassy and consulates in cities across the country. In Austria, Argentina, Mexico, and Germany workers are increasingly confronted with demands from their employers to accept the "American economic model"—the flexible, neoliberal model. The U.S. labor movement needs to support the efforts of workers in other countries to maintain all the hard-fought gains they achieved through years of union organizing. We should not be asked to choose between a model that offers growth and jobs at the cost of wages and security, or a model that offers security and decent wages at the cost of jobs and growth. Neither of these models is sustainable over the long run. Neither has answers for the fundamental crisis of a global economy characterized by growing inequality, endemic poverty, and widespread unemployment.

Organized labor needs to create energy in the movement at home, educate its members on the movements abroad, and then get down to the practical work of mobilizing union members on the shop floors in all industries across the world.

ESTABLISHING GLOBAL WORKERS' RIGHTS AND PRO-WORKER TRADE STANDARDS

Too often in the past the international stage was dominated by the arguments and differences of the cold war. We are just beginning to refocus on company and industrial strategies. Many meetings are routine and without effective focus. To date most international campaigns have centered on the resolution of disputes involving strikes, collective bargaining or trade union recognition. Corporate campaigning has been a response to a crisis. With notable exceptions, international solidarity is more often talked about than actually practiced.

As President Sweeney declared at the International Confederation of Free Trade Unions (ICFTU) Congress, "We must do more than talk to each other, pass fine resolutions, and go home. We must create clear and measurable goals and design campaigns to accomplish them." More aggressive direct action at an international level is needed. That is why the AFL-CIO must lead the fight to dramatically strengthen and enforce workers' rights around the world. AFL-CIO unions represent more workers employed by multinational companies operating around the globe than any other labor federation in the world.

We have the practical necessity and the moral responsibility to connect the workers bargaining at General Electric in Cincinnati with the struggle of workers at General Electric in Indonesia, workers prohibited from bargaining and jailed for organizing. We need to connect the bargaining strategy for our members at Boeing in Seattle with the struggle of 35¢-an-hour workers producing airplanes in Xian, China. We need to follow the Guess Company from San Francisco to Mexico City and the Zenith Corporation from Iowa to the *maquiladoras*.

No worker in the world should be exploited by any multinational within the reach of a U.S.-based union. This also means that we need to convince unions in the rest of the industrialized world to do the same. German, Swedish, British, French, and Japanese unions have a political and moral responsibility to fight for worker rights wherever their companies operate.

The more specific, more concrete, and closer to the ground our work becomes, the easier and more understandable the fight for "worker rights" will become for our members, for our unions, for the press, for the politicians, and, yes, even for the companies.

It is the companies, in fact, not just the governments, that are driving this unregulated global integration. We need to strategically organize companies, industries, and entire sectors of the global economy. For this, we must be clear that our unions are operating independently of the foreign policy considerations that so dominated the cold war period across the globe. For international labor to organize across borders, a trust between workers and their unions must develop that will allow the sharing of information, economic data, and company plans. What is good for GM may be good for GM, but what is good for American auto workers is a strong international labor movement.

We need to address, head on, the criticism that "worker rights" in trading agreements are just a new form of protectionism designed only to keep jobs in the U.S. or to prevent goods produced in the developing world from being sold in developed markets. Democratic governments and trade unions who refuse to come to the defense of universally recognized labor rights become accomplices of those ruling classes which remain in power through oppression and terror. The labor movement simply cannot take the view that worker rights are the domestic concern of individual countries. This approach would abandon workers in repressive countries, such as China, Indonesia or Burma, and would suggest the most fundamental aspirations of human beings for dignity and self-expression are only to be reserved for the advanced economies. Hundreds of wildcat strikes take place every day across the developing world. A fledgling labor movement is struggling to be born, and American trade unionists must see the other end of the global trading systems not as a threat, but as workers sharing a common self-interest. The struggle for democratic rights and for trade union rights is the clearest expression of true international labor solidarity. No economy should benefit from impoverishing its working men and women. No nation should benefit by exploiting, rather than educating its children. In the race to the bottom, there are no winners, only losers.

Ensuring worker rights in trade agreements would recognize that many nations are at an earlier stage of development, but that an international campaign for worker rights would create the conditions in the developing world where workers could organize their way to greater prosperity through collective action.

Labor cannot wait for governments, diplomats, or politicians. Together, workers must develop and coordinate the ways and means to enforce the "right to organize" on all the world's major corporations, and to secure from the companies a commitment to respect modern democratic rights in the workplace.

ORGANIZING THE GLOBAL LABOR MARKET—WHAT DOES IT MEAN?

A global strategy of organizing key industries would be a fine start. Such a strategy requires a planned approach that focuses on increasing trade union presence in the subsidiaries of key transnational companies. It could include establishing global councils of union representatives in each of the main transnationals. It might involve securing global "framework" agreements with companies or bargaining with companies to adopt codes of conduct covering labor practices. Such organizing cannot be left to individual unions. Instead, organizing must become the centerpiece of trade union activity at every level—local, national, and international.

Strategy and planning are essential for the success of any organizing campaign. This has heightened importance when the target is operating transnationally. American trade union presence needs to be strengthened in all the International Trade Secretariats (ITS). The ITSs are in a key position to develop the planning and execution of a global strategy. Adopting a whole-company approach can clarify the objectives of the campaign, establish whether these are realistically obtainable, identify what forms of leverage can be brought to bear on the targeted company, and determine the likely resource requirements. Specific international regions need to be targeted as we now target regions within the United States. The most obvious targets are the Free Trade Zones which have, in reality, become, union-free zones. This involves a complex action plan involving not just traditional organizing but using trade-related pressure through the Generalized System of Preferences (GSP), corporate pressure through consumer campaigns, and extensive and intense union-to-union support.

At the global level the necessity for developing social/industrial counterpart relationships becomes increasingly pressing. European Union social legislation requires companies with more than 1,000 employees and operating in more than one member state of the Union to establish works councils involving workers' representatives from each of their operations for the purpose of consultation. Almost 200 U.S. multinationals are now required under European law to provide workers with a structure and process unheard of in the United States. Hundreds of such councils have now been established. In many cases the meetings involve union representatives from the company's global operations.

The creation of global company councils within all leading transnationals would greatly facilitate coordinated organizing and bargaining across the whole company structure. Implementing company codes of conduct with independent monitoring and the acceptance of the right to organize and to bargain collectively would provide a very powerful tool for increasing trade union representation within the company. The making of such agreements with retailers, merchandisers, and transnationals is now a priority for a number of unions and consumer groups. If written into contracts as a matter of course, such codes could be used to eliminate a considerable part of the exploitation currently rampant, particularly in sub-contracting operations.

Major changes are taking place in the international trade union movement. The emphasis is rapidly moving towards aggressive involvement in organizing and bargaining. The American strategy of targeting regions has been the catalyst for such change. Our unions must be prepared to play a leading role in every ITS and must demand that companies and regions be targeted internationally in the same way they are being targeted domestically. We must insist that the ITSs adopt an international global organizing strategy, and we must be prepared to provide the resources and talent needed for a successful global organizing effort.

We, in the U.S. labor movement, must get to work. If workers are not empowered, if they do not struggle for and gain their rights, then the powerful will not hesitate to reap all the profits they can and exact all the pain people are prepared to suffer.

This is an age-old struggle, and now the struggle is truly global.

NEW VOICES, NEW INTERNATIONALISM

Andy Banks

For too many years ideology has been the chief export of the AFL-CIO when it comes to international affairs. We've changed that and now the chief export and import of the department will be a far more precious and relevant commodity, one called "international solidarity"... we are now devoting all of our time and energy and staff to mobilizing worldwide in support of organizing and bargaining.

—Richard Trumka[1]

AN INTERNATIONAL LABOR TROUBADOUR

Kelly Eddington drives a Wonder Bread truck, but what he really likes to do is sing. Some of Kelly's fellow Teamsters, who also drive for Continental Bakeries around the Buffalo, New York, area, think it is a bit odd that someone with Kelly's seniority would bid for routes that cover longer distances between stops. But it is not odd to Kelly. He prefers the longer hauls because it gives him a chance to work new melodies and lyrics out in his head. On his days off, Kelly can often be found in his basement sound studio recording all the instrumental and vocal tracks of his latest creations.

Kelly writes music about what he knows best: his family, his community, his job, his union.

One day, the CEO of Royal Ahold, a major Netherlands-based conglomerate, was driving to Schiphol Airport in Amsterdam to catch a plane to New York. This CEO was in a bad mood. The purpose of his trip was to meet with a group of American labor, religious, and community activists who were angry about his company's treatment of workers at Royal Ahold's six U.S-based supermarket chains. He could anticipate that this would not be a pleasant experience. To distract himself, he turned on the radio, and was dismayed to hear the voice of Kelly Eddington singing to the tune of Harry Belafonte's banana boat song. But the words were different: "Ahold Comes and the Jobs Go Away," sang the Teamster from Buffalo, on Dutch radio. This did not improve the Dutch CEO's mood.

Kelly and a growing number of union activists are becoming a new type of global labor crusaders, playing an important role in redefining how the Teamsters and the rest of American labor look at international relations. Kelly and these others are attempting to help American workers hang onto the American working class dream of prosperity and security. To do this, they have found it necessary to look beyond their country's borders for solutions to the problems that arise from working in a global economy.

American workers are increasingly focusing their attention internationally. Their concerns are not over threats of war or foreign political domination (if anything, these concerns seem to have diminished since the fall of the Iron Curtain). Their own daily reality gives rise to more concrete international threats: runaway shops, foreign investment by American-based transnational employers which creates greater insecurity at home, and foreign-based transnational employers snatching up local companies, and making coldly calculated decisions that often spell disaster to the local workforce and their communities.

The experiences of these trade unionists are not unique in America to the Teamsters, nor for that matter to unionists in this country. The future of American labor, and labor throughout the world, will be determined by these global economic forces. Right now those forces are controlled mostly by transnational corporations free to operate unfettered by international regulation. This "freedom" allows them to force citizens, workers, and sovereign nations to engage in a global bidding war, producing a downward competitive spiral in people's standard of living, conditions of work, and even their most basic human rights. What can and should the AFL-CIO do to restructure its international policy to help American labor survive in this thing we call the global economy?

The AFL-CIO will only see its international work embraced by meeting the needs of those doing the everyday trade union work of its affiliates—collective bargaining, organizing, negotiating, and grievance handling. To the degree that these basic trade union functions are affected by international forces, the AFL-CIO must create policies and programs which help its member unions fight internationally. Kelly Eddington has, in his own way, taken steps to advance his union's everyday work by looking beyond the U.S. borders and going global. It is from his experiences and those of others of this new breed of labor activists that the AFL-CIO and American labor must forge their new international strategies.

AMERICAN LABOR BILATERALISM AND THE GLOBAL POLITICS OF THE COLD WAR

For the last thirty-five years, global politics dominated international relations worldwide and the AFL-CIO's international policy and programs. At the center was a global political chess game between the Soviet Union and the United States, with both superpowers seeking allies in every corner of the world. The game was played in international political structures such as the International Labor Organization, the World Health Organization, United Nations Children's Fund, and other United Nations bodies.

The AFL-CIO was crucial to the U.S. Government's cold war competition, and State Department funds flowed abundantly to the Federation to support those elements in foreign trade unions deemed most likely to support American foreign policy objectives. At one point in the 1980s, half of the AFL-CIO's total budget was provided by the State Department. Critics have claimed that at the AFL-CIO, international affairs, cold war-style, was the tail wagging the dog.

U.S. government money financed large AFL-CIO international structures in the developing world: the American Institute for Free Labor Development in Latin America, the Asia-American Free Labor Institute in Asia, the African American Labor Center in Africa, and, after the lifting of the Iron Curtain, the Free Trade Union Institute in Eastern and Central Europe.

This massive international structure was the face of American trade unionism overseas. Through the AFL-CIO institutes, the U.S. government funded scores of AFL-CIO country directors and staff throughout the world. The fact that much of this overseas staff had little or no trade union background was largely irrelevant to their mission to collect information on trade unions in their assigned country and provide financial and technical assistance. The AFL-CIO sometimes helped organize and finance breakaway factions within a nation's dominant labor organization. It was a controversial policy to some union leaders and activists back home. But if the AFL-CIO's international trade unionism during this period was politics-driven, the Federation was not alone in this. Most trade union central federations from other western nations aligned with the AFL-CIO in this geopolitical unionism under a common banner, the Brussels-based International Confederation of Free Trade Unions (ICFTU).

Though generally in agreement over the cold war goals of international unionism, many ICFTU member federations objected to the extent to which the AFL-CIO pursued the foreign policy goals of the U.S. Government. They objected to the Federation's close relationship with the U.S. State Department, and its go-it-alone or bilateral approach to working overseas. This bilateralism is most clearly demonstrated by the fact that the AFL-CIO, alone among all the national trade union federations, maintains its own multicountry international structure overseas.

Other national central unions in the ICFTU conducted their international activities multilaterally, through independent, international, multinational trade union structures governed by its member unions. These multilateral structures were the ICFTU and the International Trade Union Secretariats, federations of national trade unions grouped by industry. For example, transportation unions around the world joined together under the transportation industry secretariats, the Transport Workers Federation. Before 1989, when the Berlin Wall fell, the secretariats generally took a back seat to the ICFTU because the political work of fighting the cold war much better reflected the strengths and purpose of the ICFTU and its member organizations, the national trade union central federations. The secretariats were better structured to pursue the economic industrial union work of their affiliates, national trade unions.

During this period, the AFL-CIO's international work went unnoticed by most U.S. labor leaders, activists, and rank-and-file members. This is understandable, since fighting the cold war was not central to the economic goals of the trade unions which make up the AFL-CIO. The core work of American trade unions—organizing, collective bargaining, grievance handling, and political action—took place inside our nation's borders.

CONFRONTING GLOBAL ECONOMIC POWER AND THE NEW LABOR INTERNATIONALISM

By the end of the cold war, unions at home experienced serious problems in obtaining their traditional economic goals. The global corporation had increasingly come to dominate economic activity, posing serious problems for unions. Liberalization of the world's economy, an improved global transportation system, and computerized banking transactions all facilitated overseas investment. Manufacturing fled the high-wage countries of the North to seek bargain wages in developing countries. There, national governments, eager to attract outside investment, would often help curtail one of the largest barriers to maintaining a low-wage workforce: the right to form independent trade unions.

The fall of the Berlin Wall brought a new era, with the struggle between the superpowers giving way to the reign of the global corporation, global competition, and the global economy. Transnational companies found that opening non-union operations overseas made it easier to deal with their American unions, even in industries that were predominantly unionized in North America. In industry after industry, company after company, unions were discovering that national borders did little to protect their members if the industry had not been unionized globally.

To add insult to injury, foreign-based companies would also buy out American firms here in the U.S., often wreaking havoc on workers and their communities by spinning off all but the most profitable pieces, and introducing new work methods without regard to the larger social impact. Foreign-based multinational companies, long accustomed to social partnerships with strong unions back home in Europe, were quick to pick up on American corporate union-busting techniques and rapidly adopted anti-union, anti-community standards which the citizens in the home countries of these companies would never accept.

Unions in America found that strategies that had been implemented successfully on a national level now often came up short when tested against a global corporation. If a union were to successfully strike a unionized company here in the U.S., the company's ability to shift work overseas enabled them to continue production throughout the strike. For example, during the United Auto Workers' valiant but unsuccessful strike against Caterpillar, the company was able to prevail, in great part, because its almost totally unionized U.S. operations only represented twenty-eight percent of its global manufacturing capacity, and the union could not halt the shift of production overseas.

This example, and many others like it, began to force the American labor movement to find ways to follow their work overseas. At the same time, unions overseas in the same industries and the same companies were experiencing similar problems. The basic premise that started the industrial union movement 100 years ago is still true today: workers' ability to successfully engage in collective bargaining is directly determined by their degree of organization in their industry and their company. If an industry or company has a significant operation outside the U.S., American unions must discover ways to coordinate their activities with unions at overseas operations and to unionize those operations if they are non-union.

To be effective in today's global economy, unions must operate internationally. National pride and independence rule out the possibility that American unions will directly organize into their ranks workers in other countries or that unions from the highly organized parts of Europe would be able to organize in the U.S. Instead, international industrial unionism will require American unions to develop cooperative relationships with unions in other countries in the same industries and the same companies. It will require sponsoring and supporting unionization in overseas operations at these companies. And it will require getting unions overseas to support our organizing efforts to organize companies in the U.S. which are already unionized there.

NEW UNION STRUCTURES IN THE NEW WORLD ORDER

For political leaders around the world, negotiating trade agreements and lifting investment barriers now often take precedence over mutual defense treaties and political alignments. The global economic expansion of transnational corporations is no longer the servant but the master of global politics. And so it is for labor: the bilateral, go-it-alone days of the cold war are over. What we now need are strong, permanent multilateral trade union structures that can help national unions to join together internationally to coordinate bargaining, to organize their companies and industries, and to conduct global corporate campaigns.

And labor already has a structure that can do this: the international trade union federations—the secretariats which are organized on a sectoral or industry basis. These international trade union federations directly affiliate the national unions in their respective industries worldwide. Though most of their members come from European affiliates, many of the major American unions have already affiliated (at least partially) with the appropriate secretariats for their industry. Some general unions, like the Teamsters, have affiliated with several secretariats because their members work in a number of different industries.

Most secretariats are now going through intense restructuring, shedding their cold war role as secondary players to the ICFTU and the national central unions. They are now claiming their new pivotal role: together they form the international structures that will allow unions to organize and bargain collectively within industries, sectors, and companies. But the secretariats face a formidable task. Only a few have the staff necessary to pull off global bargaining, and unions from the developing nations are underrepresented in most secretariats.

Under the cold war model of international unionism, unions in the Southern hemisphere were pawns in a larger geopolitical game dominated by the relatively rich and powerful national trade union centrals of the North. But now, to effectively represent their members at home, trade unions in the North must have strong partners in the South. This became apparent to the Teamsters Union when it tried to fight the implementation of the North American Free Trade Agreement trucking provisions, which would allow Mexican truck drivers making eight dollars per day to carry and pick up loads throughout the U.S. and Canada. The Teamsters were stunned to discover that in Mexico there were only a few tiny unions in the embryonic stages of building an independent national truckers union.

In Europe workers have been forced to build European-wide industrial union structures because of the impending integration of the European economy under the auspices of the European Parliament and the European Commission (the government bodies of the European Union). The European Union (EU) process has threatened to make each national bargaining law irrelevant—just as if in the United States there were only state bargaining laws, and unions in one state could not have bargaining relationships in another state. Basic things that unions take for granted, such as national agreements and pattern bargaining, would become nearly impossible. Companies could pick and choose which state they would locate in based on labor legislation most favorable to business, and that would ignite a round of concession fever. The European-wide economic integration has forced European unions to move much quicker than their American or Japanese counterparts to create international structures capable of dealing with global corporations (although the structures only include unions operating in the European region). Perhaps the European experience holds some of the answers for building new international union structures for the global economy.

EUROPEAN ECONOMIC INTEGRATION AND THE BIRTH OF EUROPEAN WORKS COUNCILS

More than twenty years ago it became apparent to labor leaders in Western Europe that eventually most of their countries would unite under a single set of trade agreements, investment, customs, and currency standards. The European trade unions knew this would pave the way for national companies—with which the unions had strong bargaining relationships—to move easily into other countries within the European Union. Unionists were concerned that workers in one EU country could be pitted against their counterparts in other EU countries in a downward spiraling bidding war. To avert this, European union leaders developed a long term strategy to create European legislation that would mandate Europe-wide bargaining structures.

EU trade unions also realized that social standards such as minimum wage laws, worker safety regulations, national health care systems, and unemployment benefits influenced corporate decisions to shift work and investments. European labor committed itself to include within the economic integration process a social dialogue through which unions, business associations, and government would jointly negotiate uniform standards for European social benefits and standards.

The European labor movement's twin goals of creating international industry-wide bargaining councils for the region and a structured dialogue for negotiating minimum social standards for all countries now drives international unionism in Western Europe. Unions from less wealthy European countries saw this as a way to raise their standards, while unions from Scandinavian and Northern European countries viewed it as essential to prevent erosion of their higher level of social benefits. Permanent region-wide trade union structures had to be created to iron out these internal differences between national union movements and to allow labor to present a strong, united voice to the other emerging European institutions.

Two such structures were formed. One was a united federation for all European labor, the European Trade Union Congress. This Congress pushed away from cold war politics and instead pressed for passage of European-wide legislation to create mechanisms for collective bargaining. A second organization was created to facilitate industry-wide bargaining across Europe, the European Industrial Committees, composed of all national unions within a given industry.

The move toward legislation creating European-wide collective bargaining was hotly resisted by European employer federations and by American transnational companies, which kept a well-financed lobbying machine in Brussels. But labor, government, and industry forged a compromise, and legislation was passed which mandated the creation of a European Works Council for each company that operates in more than one EU country, and has at least 150 employees, and more than 1,000 European employees overall.

The European Works Councils fall far short of the unions' original goal of legislating European-wide bargaining structures for each industry. First, the legislation does not mandate collective bargaining nor union representation on the councils. Second, councils are company-based, not industry-based. The legislation sets up procedures for worker representation from each country. Representation on a council for a qualifying company could come from national trade unions, already existing company works councils, or from a combination of the two.[2]

Under the legislation, the nature of representation would be determined company by company. It is estimated that over 1,200 companies, many of them American- and Japanese-based transnationals, qualify for coverage by this legislation. The European Industrial Federations fear that it will be nearly impossible to organize this large a number of European works councils. European Trade Union Congress policy states that the European Industrial Federations should be the recognized coordinator of works council activity on the workers' side. Leaders of national unions in Europe and their international bodies clearly see the councils as only an intermediate step in the process of European industry-wide bargaining. Their intent is to transform the councils first into company-wide and then industry-wide bargaining councils.

European unions have already negotiated some structures which make the industrial federation for that particular industry the recognized administrative arm for the workers' side. In specially organized pre-meetings to the joint worker-employer meetings of councils, the European Industrial Federation brings together the workers' representatives. The workers' representatives can discuss joint strategies ranging from dealing with workplace issues, such as safety and health, to larger industry issues, such as the coordination of bargaining demands and organizing campaigns. The labor pre-meetings could also provide a forum for unions to plan strategic campaigns against particularly recalcitrant companies in their industry.

There have been many problems for European unions trying to take advantage of the European works councils: worker representatives are not always trade union representatives, building union structures to monitor and implement works councils in over 1,200 companies is hardly practical for any of the European Industrial Federations, and the tendency for such a strong focus on Europe may divert European labor from seeing the strategic sense in extra-European labor alliances in some important instances. It is hopeful that these are just growing pains in the world's largest effort at establishing transnational bargaining structures.

The development of European Works Councils can be instructive to American and other unions outside Europe that wish to develop strategies to deal with global corporations. Barring the unlikely scenario in the near future of international regulation mandating global bargaining or works councils, unions in the U.S. and elsewhere are free to build international structures to enable them to assist one another in organizing and bargaining in targeted companies and industries—worldwide union councils. This cannot be done ad hoc or without permanent international structures.

The European unions discovered that strong international union structures had to be created before international bargaining was legislated. Just as the regional arms of the secretariats were the foundation for what eventually became the European Industrial Federations, the International Trade Union Secretariats provide the only global union structures capable of laying the basis for unions to organize and bargain with the global corporation and to set industry standards that function beyond any single nation's borders.

NEW VOICE FOR WORKERS—NEW INTERNATIONAL STRATEGY FOR AMERICAN LABOR

Now we return to the Netherlands-based CEO of Royal Dutch Ahold's North American Division who was on his way to meet with a group of religious, labor, civil rights, and environmental leaders to talk about Ahold's corporate behavior in the United States. Ahold had tried for nearly a year to avoid any such meeting, preferring instead to direct complaints from Americans back to the headquarters of each of its eight different regional grocery chains in America. By quietly buying up regional chains, Ahold's Dutch executives had made Holland's largest retailer the third largest supermarket chain in America and the largest in the Eastern U.S. With over 80,000 workers in America, Royal Ahold now had more American employees than it had Dutch. Ahold was making money hand over fist.

Ahold managers had successfully translated into the American supermarket industry certain of the economies it had developed through a new technology-driven, just-in-time distribution system for its huge Albert Heijn chain of supermarkets in the Netherlands. Instead of each store receiving dozens of deliveries each day from a wide variety of food, beverage, and dry goods vendors, Ahold transmitted to the product supplier the inventory information generated by the product bar codes from each cash register of each store. The supplier then created custom-made mixed pallets of products based on the bar code information and delivered these pallets to one of four gigantic regional distributions centers in Holland. At the distribution center, Ahold employees transferred the pallets to the truck designated for each store, never needing to warehouse any products at the distribution centers nor at the stores. Deliveries to each Albert Heijn store, made by Ahold trucks only, were reduced from as many as forty per day under the old vendor-delivery system to only two deliveries per day under this new system known as cross-docking.

Leaders of Teamsters Local 264 in Buffalo, New York, became suspicious when managers of Ahold's Western New York chain, Tops Markets, announced plans to build a massive 28-acre cross-docking distribution center on a 160-acre site in rural Lancaster, just outside of

Buffalo. Local 264 members primarily work for vendors that provide local grocery merchants with their products such as beer, soda, bread, snacks, and dairy products, while warehouse workers at Tops in Buffalo are represented by Teamsters Local 558. Local 264 soon realized that if Tops, which enjoys a sixty-seven percent share of the Buffalo grocery sales, switched to cross-docking, many of its members would be thrown out of work. Moreover, efficiencies created for Tops by cross-docking would force its larger competitors to follow suit, and its mom-and-pop neighborhood store competitors to close down. When Tops management refused to meet over this issue, leaders of Local 264 turned to the Teamsters Office of Strategic Campaigns.

The Teamsters commissioned a Cornell University study on cross-docking and its potential effects on Teamsters members and their communities. With help from the Midwest Center for Labor Research in Chicago and the Dutch transnational corporate research group, SOMO, Cornell professor Gordon McClelland pieced together a frightening picture of the costs to workers and the community when a transnational company can freely decide to behave as a good corporate citizen in some countries and a bad one in others. In the Netherlands, its home country, Ahold had taken full responsibility for the social impact of its cross-docking restructuring by guaranteeing full employment to all its workers. In the U.S., Ahold claimed it had no intention of doing anything to help workers laid off as a result of its cross-docking.

According to the Midwest Center for Labor Research, Local 264 could expect that eighty-one percent of its Buffalo area members who drove delivery trucks would lose their jobs as a result of Royal Ahold's cross-docking at Tops. Because they were not Tops employees, these workers would receive no compensation from Ahold for this drastic dislocation. Research showed a very different picture of Ahold in the Netherlands, where the 2,000 Ahold workers displaced by cross-docking were all guaranteed full employment with the company.

In Buffalo, Ahold infuriated local residents of Lancaster, inner-city residents of Buffalo, and environmentalists when it decided to place the new mega-distribution center on environmentally fragile wetlands rather than utilize the abundance of free industrially-zoned property available in high unemployment areas of the inner city. Political leaders of Buffalo's African American community were also quick to point out that when cross-docking forced the closure of small minority-owned neighborhood stores in the inner city, there would be no other source of groceries for many residents, because Tops had not maintained a single supermarket in a 100,000-person legislative district composed mostly of blacks and immigrant minorities.

The study also showed how the vast Ahold empire was wreaking similar havoc in its other operations in the Eastern United States. It shut down its warehouse in Connecticut and forced 500 Teamster workers there to sign a gag order preventing them from publicly criticizing the company actions if they wanted to receive their meager severance package. Six months later, Ahold reopened the warehouse with non-union workers by subcontracting the operations to the notoriously anti-union C&S Wholesalers from Vermont. The Cleveland Workers' Rights Board held worker abuse hearings against Ahold's cross-docking there. They issued a statement condemning the practice and calling for protections for the workers and the community. When Buffalo's Teamsters Local 558 tried to organize a Tops freezer warehouse, they were hammered by a slick anti-union campaign by Ahold—something unheard of in the Netherlands.

With help from organizations such as Jobs with Justice, Friends of the Earth, and civil rights and church leaders from across the Eastern U.S., the Teamsters were able to mount a credible public awareness program and demand that Ahold negotiate with this coalition over its corporate responsibilities to American workers and their communities. The Teamsters even sent a representative to organize publicity and support from religious, consumer, environmental, and labor groups in the Netherlands. Things got so heated for Ahold over its practices in America that it finally agreed to meet with the Teamsters' coalition in America.

It was with these problems in mind that the Ahold executive was traveling to New York in March 1996. What was he going to do? He would tell them that Ahold had good relations with similar groups in Dutch society. On the other hand, some of these same Dutch groups were supporting the Teamsters' demands that Ahold negotiate a corporate code of conduct to regulate its behavior in the United States. The Ahold executive knew this trip to New York was not going to be easy—and Eddington's song, which lampoons Ahold's cross-docking, was not making it any easier.

The New York meeting did not go well, and no agreement was reached between Ahold and the Teamsters' coalition. In May, the union purchased shares of Ahold stock and announced its intention to attend the shareholders meeting in Amsterdam. Ahold invited the Teamsters and their coalition partners to meet with them in Holland.

At this meeting, the two sides hammered out an agreement for Ahold's conduct in the U.S. They agreed on six points: (1) they would study ways in which Ahold could effectively change from sub-contracting their warehouse work; (2) they agreed to cooperate in a study to find ways to ameliorate the impact of cross-docking; (3) Ahold would recognize the value of collective bargaining and strive to improve their relationship with Teamster locals; (4) Ahold would use Friends of the Earth as a resource in determining the environmental impact of building new distribution centers; (5) Ahold would consult with community groups and would work with local government to select inner-city areas for opening new supermarkets; and (6) this process would be monitored and jointly reviewed with the Teamsters once a year.

Though proud of its accomplishments in securing the first ever such corporate code of conduct covering U.S. operations by a foreign-based multinational company, the Teamsters-led coalition feels there has been serious backsliding by Ahold since the agreement was signed. Ahold has also toughened its stand with its Dutch unions while expanding its operations dramatically into East Asia, Brazil, and Central Europe. As a result, the Teamsters joined with the United Food and Commercial Workers, which represents tens of thousands of Ahold USA employees, and asked the secretariats for commercial workers to create a World Ahold Union Council. In August 1996, Ahold unions held their first organizational meeting in Washington, with representatives from America, the Czech Republic, Holland, and Singapore. A committee with representatives from the Teamsters, the United Food and Commercial Workers, and the Dutch Commercial Workers Union was formed to draft a model agreement in the World Ahold Union Council's campaign to get recognition from the company.

The point to this pretty amazing story is that local trade union work for the Teamsters necessitated an international effort. Community activists and union members such as Kelly Eddington were motivated to join in this international campaign because it was part of a concrete struggle seriously affecting their lives. The Teamsters campaign made much progress, but afterwards, when the company thought it could renege, it was essential that the Ahold unions came together worldwide under the auspices of an existing secretariat international structure to facilitate communication, information sharing, and strategizing on bargaining and organizing for Ahold unions everywhere.

INTERNATIONAL WORK IS UNION WORK—STRATEGIC IMPLICATIONS FOR THE AFL-CIO

The story of the Teamsters and Royal Ahold bears out a key conclusion that emerged from a recent international conference on labor and the global economy held at the University of California at Berkeley. The conference endorsed the notion that the relative success of all union work is contingent upon how well organized labor can muster and apply power vis-à-vis the employers with whom they must interact. Labor's ability to pursue a company or an industry globally will often mean the difference between good and safe union jobs or a non-union, low-wage, and high unemployment existence for union members at home.

The Berkeley conference participants welcomed the changes taking place in the AFL-CIO's international departments because, like the Teamsters, they know that international work is trade union work. They outlined three ways the AFL-CIO can assist its affiliates in doing international work. First, AFL-CIO affiliates increasingly need help in implementing the international components of campaigns emanating from tough bargaining situations or corporate restructurings. These campaigns also involve foreign-based companies doing business in the U.S. or American companies that have overseas markets or operations. Second, the AFL-CIO unions will need the same type of assistance in organizing campaigns against U.S. and foreign-based transnational companies. And finally, AFL-CIO affiliates need help in making sure their respective industries and companies are organized overseas so they can increase their bargaining power in the U.S.

Just as the union push for European bargaining structures became the driving force of the European Trade Union Congress and its national center members, the expansion of the AFL-CIO affiliates' ability to organize, bargain, and conduct strategic campaigns must become the single most important objective of the AFL-CIO's international policy. There are already some promising indications that the AFL-CIO International Affairs Department may go in this direction.

The AFL-CIO's cold war organizations are no longer needed by the U.S. government, and signs are that soon this revenue stream will dry up or will be reduced to a fraction of its current size. Whatever remaining funding the AFL-CIO receives, it should be used to assist international trade union secretariats in their efforts to help unions in developing countries to organize transnational companies which have bargaining relationships with AFL-CIO affiliates.

But because the demands for international assistance in corporate campaigns, bargaining, and organizing will only increase as the global economy matures, the AFL-CIO leadership must eventually turn to its member unions to finance its international activities, just as it has in political action and in organizing. That support will come only if the affiliates perceive that the AFL-CIO can provide them with concrete services that enhance their abilities to organize, bargain, and campaign against multinational companies.

The AFL-CIO can also help its affiliates by strategically directing its remaining resources to assist its member unions to organize and bargain in key industries and companies overseas, and to create international union councils (these can be regional for the Americas or worldwide as in the case with Ahold and United Parcel Service for the Teamsters). The AFL-CIO should encourage this activity within the multilateral structures of the secretariats and, in turn, encourage the secretariats to identify and overcome barriers to helping American and non-European affiliates to organize. The AFL-CIO should actively encourage full affiliation to the appropriate secretariat by each of its member unions.

It is also important that the AFL-CIO push for the enactment of domestic and international legislation which will allow unions to organize and thrive everywhere. Workers in much of the developing world still do not enjoy authentic trade union rights. There is a crying need for the new leaders of the AFL-CIO to demonstrate to the world that they are committed to building strong unions here and abroad. The AFL-CIO should use its bully pulpit to help pull together an authentic global coalition of North and South unions, development organizations, religious activists, women's, and human rights organizations to announce a campaign to adopt labor rights protections at the World Trade Organization, the World Bank, and the International Monetary Fund.

This new international strategy for the AFL-CIO means reforming the International Confederation of Free Trade Unions, from its policy orientation left over from the cold war, toward an industrial union action orientation which is now dictated by the primacy of the global economy. As the largest affiliate of the confederation, the AFL-CIO can begin by pushing for full representation on the confederation executive committee by the secretariats, which are still, with all their weaknesses, the most important international structures available for advancing and coordinating real trade union work.

INTERNATIONAL STRENGTH THROUGH INCLUSION

Building union power began as a local effort hundreds of years ago in the fledging craft unions formed out of the old guilds. As the economy grew to inter-city and then national levels, trade unions had to adapt by creating national union structures that matched the structures of the employers. The nearly breathtaking speed at which the economy is now being dominated by global companies makes it obvious that the great task facing unions today is to build dynamic international trade union structures.

Some people argue that while this is important, we must first focus on building strong local and national union structures. But this analysis, however well intentioned, ignores the new reality of the global economy. Formerly strong local and national union structures are weakened today by an inability to aggressively challenge global corporations. By effectively incorporating a global component into its bargaining, organizing, and corporate campaign strategies, unions can help make national and local union structures stronger. To successfully build strong local and national unions, today's unions must learn how to act globally.

We must figure out ways to involve our national and local unions here with overseas unions in joint expressions of solidarity in struggles against global corporations. But solidarity is not charity. Too often international solidarity has a cycle of paternalism and dependency: the expectation was that the North gave and the South received. This was a bad deal for unions on both sides of the equator. The transition from an era of geopolitical international unionism to a new era of international industrial unionism struggling in the global economy dictates that, though unions in the South will need assistance in their efforts to organize in strategic sectors, it is a two-way street: Southern unions' strength in key strategic enterprises also allow them to offer solidarity to union struggles in the North.

The trade union and social justice movements in the developing world have been on the front line, fighting against the most powerful forces mustered by global capital. In some purely remarkable instances, such as the defeat of apartheid in South Africa, these union movements have given working people their biggest victories in decades. The strategies developed by these unions need to be shared and, where appropriate, adopted globally. World labor has to pursue an aggressive policy demanding the full participation in international union structures from the unions in the South. Specifically, the national trade union centers in Brazil, in South Africa, and in South Korea should be encouraged to lead in organizing a Third World bloc to participate in international multilateral bodies.

It would be a strategic error for unions in the North to continue giving only lip service to building international trade union structures which provide full participation and address the unique concerns of the unions in the South. It would be equally wrong for international trade unionism to remain the exclusive domain of union international affairs departments and international trade union bureaucracies headquartered in Brussels or Geneva. We must build our international trade union strategy on the full participation and sharing of experiences from trade unionists who are actively organizing and bargaining at the national and local level—particularly those in the South. Only then will we be able to say along with Kelly Eddington and his fellow Teamsters at Wonder Bread, "International Work is Union Work." Who knows? Maybe he will even write us a song.

NOTES

1. Trumka's speech was given at the University of California at Berkeley, at a conference on "Labor and the Global Economy," November 22, 1996.

2. With the significant exceptions of the Nordic countries, Ireland and Great Britain, most European countries have—in addition to regular collective bargaining laws—legislated works council systems, which enable workers in each plant to choose a representative council of their peers to deal with employment conditions. Unions run lists of their candidates for these spots, as well as engage in collective bargaining, through structures independent of the works councils. The European Works Councils legislation is independent of these national works councils and bargaining structures.

INTERNATIONAL LABOR SOLIDARITY IN AN ERA OF GLOBAL COMPETITION

Héctor J. Figueroa

The change in leadership at the AFL-CIO has generated a great deal of expectation among progressive trade unionists. The New Voice leadership has brought in some of the best staff in the labor movement to direct its organizing, legal, political, field mobilization, research, and strategy operations as well as its international program. In the past, trade unionists at home and abroad who have been active in international solidarity work often found themselves at odds with the Federation's operations and its anti-communist bias. However, there is now hope that the new AFL-CIO's approach to international labor issues will make way for a more effective, coherent, and strategic international program.

To succeed, the Federation's international program must increase labor's industrial and political power. It must also help unite international labor to protect worker rights, improve working conditions, and increase living standards for all union and non-union workers in both the advanced and the less developed world. Increased organizational power and commitment to labor unity and social justice are needed if the American labor movement is to counter the growing power of multinational companies in an increasingly integrated world. The reason is simple enough: our ability to rebuild the house of labor is greatly affected by increased international competition.

Multinational companies and institutions have turned the world into a vast labor market where workers of all nationalities are made to compete against one another in an effort to maximize corporate profits and expand the market economy. As a result, U.S. labor can no longer take wages and working conditions away from business competition by acting solely at the national level. The relentless increase in the flow of capital, trade, and people across national borders and the almost universal acceptance of neoliberal capitalist economic policies have radically altered labor relations. Unions can no longer afford to ignore the impact of globalization on their members and employers.

U.S. labor needs to do better and more international work than in the past. This requires not only programmatic changes on the part of the AFL-CIO and greater involvement of union leaders and rank-and-file members in international work, but also a deeper understanding of the threats and opportunities that an emerging global economy offers. Subordinating international solidarity to the defense of American workers' self-interest must not turn away from defending the interest of workers abroad—whether from the North, South, East, or West. Building stronger unions at home must be supported by a program that builds stronger unions abroad if we are to make multinational companies and national governments more responsive to the interests of working people.

REDEFINING THE SELF-INTEREST OF AMERICAN WORKERS

The new AFL-CIO leadership believes that labor's international program must be firmly grounded on defending the interest of American workers. The Federation has increased its support for organizing and contract campaigns that involve the overseas operations of companies; linking trade agreements to protect worker rights, and fair trade policies that create American jobs as an alternative to "free trade." It is also moving away from its previous cold war anti-communist orientation, showing greater disposition to work with strong and militant trade unions abroad—like the Central Única Dos Trabalhadores in Brazil and the Congress of South African Trade Unions in South Africa—regardless of their political or ideological orientation.

An honest search for a "new" strategic international solidarity is a step forward for the American labor movement. Organizing is the top priority of the new AFL-CIO, and if labor's international program is to have any meaning, it must support labor's organizing efforts at home. The biggest challenge, however, for the new AFL-CIO, is to demonstrate that a new international program, centered on organizing principles, is not only needed for the resurgence of U.S. labor, but that it is also in the interest of organized labor abroad. Promoting international solidarity that puts "American workers' interests" first may well prompt curiosity or even suspicion from our brothers and sisters overseas.

This is not a trivial matter: international solidarity is a two-way street. Unless workers abroad see the pursuit of "American workers' self-interest" as a reflection, at least partially, of their own interests, our international efforts will amount to little more than diplomacy and short-term coordinated actions. This is easier said than done, though. At a first glance, and despite two centuries of interaction among labor organizations and working people from different countries, the development of the working class and the labor movement has been shaped by different national economic and political institutions, different trade union paths and experiences. International competition among companies and governments often turns workers in one country against workers in another country.

Under the current circumstances, an international labor community with common goals and interests can only develop through a conscious and organized effort on the part of trade unionists. This requires education about labor abroad and involvement of organized workers in the international programs of their own unions and the Federation. International labor cooperation can only be built through constant interaction around specific issues such as common employers and common industrial problems. It also requires participation in the same international labor organizations that deal with general issues such as international labor rights and international labor standards.

Given the central role the U.S. plays in the world market, both economically and politically, the U.S. labor movement must take greater responsibility in building international labor cooperation with unions abroad on issues deemed of interest to both. To do this effectively the AFL-CIO must educate leaders, international staff, and members about the importance of understanding the conditions that workers and trade unions face abroad. It should also encourage them to engage trade unionists abroad in international campaigns that utilize the Internet, labor conferences, and the labor press. The objective would be to develop common responses to global challenges such as building union membership, enhancing union power, upgrading living standards, and removing wages and working conditions from international competition.

REBUILDING LABOR'S INTERNATIONAL PROGRAM

The AFL-CIO and its affiliates have started to forge new alliances with unions overseas and develop more strategies to effectively counter multinational employers. Historically, the Federation's priority has been forging alliances—particularly with trade unions considered to be friendly to U.S. foreign policy interests. Given this history, the AFL-CIO is beginning to transform its existing international affairs operation, developing the organizational structure that is necessary to overcome the constraints, and seize the opportunities that multinationals and the new global economy bring about.

In addition to implementing organizational changes, the Federation and its affiliates must also focus its international work on the need to counter international competition with international solidarity. That is, it must center its international work on how organized labor can cooperate across geographical, cultural, and political differences to take wages and working conditions out of global competition. It must resist economic nationalism without abandoning the struggle for more jobs and increasing living standards at home. Although protecting American jobs and standards has to remain a priority, labor should not share the illusion that whatever makes American-based companies more competitive in the world market necessarily translates into employment or income gains for American workers.

The Federation also needs to reevaluate its relationships with labor federations and international labor organizations, human rights, and other non-governmental organizations. This process needs to be guided by this basic principle: U.S. labor should relate to those abroad who have a genuine and proven record of actively defending workers' interests, whatever their political or ideological positions. It should naturally relate to those trade unions with whom affiliates already have or want to have a relationship, to those labor organizations that represent a majority of workers in the country, and to any union that is engaged in organizing employees of U.S.-based multinational companies or their subcontractors or clients. The Federation also needs to tighten its relationship with international labor bodies like the International Secretariats at the global and regional level, and seek both bilateral and multilateral relationships with unions abroad.

Another major challenge for U.S. labor is to overcome its cold war heritage and to sever its funding from the U.S. State Department. Labor must systematically build its own international capacity and find better ways to economically sustain its international program. The AFL-CIO needs to establish educational programs that clearly define the strategic need for international solidarity among members, staff, and union officers. Having international solidarity as a distinctive area of labor activity, separate from all others, has actually diminished its importance in the eyes of most trade unionists. "International solidarity" needs to overcome its bad reputation among the many rank-and-file, staff, and officers who view international work as little more than "labor diplomacy" and an excuse for staff and high-ranking officers to travel abroad.

CATCHING UP WITH A CHANGING GLOBAL ECONOMY

American unions have always engaged in some form of international solidarity work. The immigrant origins of our workforce, America's complex relationship to the world economy, and our capitalistic economic system have all driven U.S. labor to deal with international issues. The real question is not whether we do international work, but how, why, and how much we should do it.

The global economy is radically altering the way American workers relate to one another and to their bosses and the way bosses compete here or abroad. Central to building a more effective international program is a clear understanding of how the new global economy affects our ability to organize, secure good contracts, and engage in independent politics.

Such an understanding requires more than just an analysis of U.S. international trade and investment policies, of how the U.S. economy "competes" within the global economy, or of how U.S. multinational companies conduct their business. We must also understand how the relative power between employers and workers, in the U.S. and abroad, contribute to the global economy's effect on the American labor movement. The competitive drive in the world market, while unavoidable and relentless, is not producing the positive results described in economic textbooks lauding this phenomenon.

The new global economy fosters increased concentration of income and wealth among fewer and fewer companies, exacerbates income inequality across and within nations, and drives working conditions, wages, and living standards to the lowest denominator. It is now common for companies to relocate production to less developed regions where wages are lower, and to contract out work to local or foreign companies in an effort to lower wages and avoid unions. The U.S. has been relinquishing hard-won environmental and safety and health regulations, lowering corporate taxes, and opposing organizing drives in an effort to attract capital investments. This daily reality is also being "sealed" by international trade and investment agreements such as the North American Free Trade Agreement (NAFTA) and the General Agreement on Tariffs and Trade (GATT).

In this context, we must distinguish between the internationalization of the economy and the emergence of the global economy. The two are related but distinct. Internationalization refers to the fact that textiles, steel or banking services can all be produced in multiple countries. Globalization occurs when, for example, IBM integrates the financing, design, production, and marketing of computers across several countries. Internationalization refers to global trade. Globalization refers more to a functional integration of production, distribution, and finance by multinational companies. Under globalization, production decisions are made by companies who own and manage production and distribution sites in different countries, producing a commodity or service for the world market. Internationalization is an old phenomenon, going back to the beginnings of the Industrial Revolution if not earlier. Globalization is more recent. While multinational companies have existed for two centuries, they have become a dominant form of doing business since the end of World War II.

Distinguishing between internationalization and globalization is important for labor activists. Historically, internationalization has helped build a common identity among workers in similar industries who have a similar work experience. Indeed, the first international labor bodies, the current International Trade Secretariats, are organizations where unions in similar trades come together to help each other, exchange information, and develop common policies. Globalization is forcing workers and international labor bodies along industrial lines to develop an even deeper identity, one built around the fact that we now have common or greatly interconnected employers. As the logic of international competition compels capital formations to evolve into "globalization," the potential also grows for workers to find a common link.

Economists like to paint a picture of a world economy in which countries "specialize" and "compete" based on their endowments of natural resources, labor, and capital. Free trade is said to benefit all because countries with abundant labor will specialize in producing labor intensive products, and those with abundant capital specialize in the production of capital intensive ones. Companies in both groups of countries are compelled by the market to produce those goods where they have a comparative advantage and everybody is better off. Unfortunately, the real world operates very differently, as most workers know.

In the world market, companies, not countries, compete. Companies that have the lowest costs per product ultimately have a distinct advantage over their competitors, regardless of whether they produce in a labor- or a capital-abundant country. They can either enjoy higher profits by selling at the going price or increase their share of the market by selling at lower prices, driving competitors who cannot match their lower costs out of competition. Companies can lower costs by adopting new technology and new organizational methods, by relocating to sites where they can save on transportation or labor costs or by cutting wages or making workers produce more per hour. Of course, companies always seek to attain an absolute cost advantage by all these methods. The reality of absolute cost advantages is that international trade can have devastating consequences to workers since, when left unregulated, companies will try to lower costs by lowering wages and increasing productivity, dragging countries into a race to the bottom instead of an optimal exchange of goods. Working people also need to understand this concept of "absolute cost advantages" and all of its implications.

Still, trade unionists need not exaggerate the extent to which globalization creates an international, interdependent labor market. The globalization of the economy is a powerful, albeit contradictory and uneven trend. While the world is becoming integrated, we are far from having a borderless economy. Rather, distinct regions around three core economies—North America, Europe, and Japan—are emerging. Although international competition is affecting wages and working conditions, these are still largely determined by local and national conditions, including the price of local products, the existing mandatory benefits, work standards, and unionization levels.

Local labor conditions, regulations, and institutions still help explain, to a great extent, why a worker in Montreal may earn more than a worker in Atlanta or Bogotá doing the same kind of work—especially if you include benefits and access to social services. The employer's profitability in the domestic market also matters. So does a region's unemployment level.

Workers in countries where unemployment levels are high will be under pressure to accept lower wages or worse working conditions, especially if unions are weak. What happens at the local, regional, and national level matters, not only to the workers in that locality but in other places. If labor's international work is to be effective, it must increase trade union power at both the regional and national level and pursue an aggressive progressive political agenda at home. Such work must take into consideration the more limited role the state has in regulating multinational companies in a globalized economy. But whatever minimized capacity there is for local, national, and regional regulation of capital, it must be pursued and extended to the global arena if labor is to counter the power of multinational companies. Multinational companies still need state intervention to secure profits.

Corporations have tried to improve their profits during this age of slow growth by engineering a massive redistribution of income from working people—at the workplace and at the level of the state. They have literally launched an assault on all workers, American and foreign. Corporations are increasingly more inclined to compete by reducing wages and implementing labor-saving technology, and engaging in mergers, acquisitions and financial speculation. They try to increase their competitiveness at the expense of workers, reducing wages and union strength as a means of lowering costs. They attempt to replace workers with machines, keeping investment in new equipment as low as possible. When expanding, corporations increasingly rely on hiring an army of part-time, temporary, and contract employees who get low pay and no benefits. These practices force the remaining full-time workers to work harder and longer at lower wages to keep their living standards from falling.

Corporations are conducting this assault on labor at all levels, and globalization is one of its most visible aspects. In the U.S., corporations export jobs by outsourcing or relocating production abroad. More than one-third of U.S. trade consists of "sales" between multinationals and their foreign subsidiaries. A similar trend is now becoming evident in Western Europe and Asia. The practice of outsourcing and relocation of production is creating major regional trade blocks in North America, Europe, and the Pacific Rim. The desire of U.S. multinationals to secure their own regional supply of cheap labor and to dominate regional markets is the real motive behind the U.S.-Canada Free Trade Agreement (FTA), the Caribbean Basin

Initiative (CBI) and NAFTA. The global consensus around such strategies is evident in the provisions of GATT.

Workers' wages are kept in check by employer opposition at the bargaining table and the workplace, by banks and investment companies, which insist that corporations become "lean and mean," and by an almost fanatic commitment by international financial markets to fiscal austerity and tight monetary policies. In the U.S., such policies are kept in place by the Federal Reserve; in other countries by their respective central banks, the International Monetary Fund, and the World Bank. These policies give priority to the repayment of public debt through fiscal austerity (balanced budgets), privatization, and other measures that contribute to a contraction of total demand, and thus maintain slow growth and unemployment.

While the world market has been expanding production, distribution and finance have become internationalized throughout this century, and the emergence of the global economy has accelerated at a particularly difficult time for American workers and for workers around the globe. The globalization of the economy coincided with the end of the unprecedented economic expansion of the 1960s.

During the "golden age" of 1947 to 1966, the world economy experienced fast economic growth, fiscal and financial stability, increased employment levels, increasing real wages, and improvements in living standards for most people. Industrial capacity was high and expanded with strong rates of private investment. Economic equality increased, and women and minorities fared better in the labor market. Meanwhile cold war politics and support for "free trade unions" dominated U.S. labor overseas operations. Since opening foreign markets to U.S. companies was an important aspect of U.S. foreign policy, the U.S. labor movement was generally supportive of free trade initiatives.

It was not until the golden age ended that globalization began to take an important place in labor's radar. Slower economic growth became apparent during the late sixties and early seventies. This coincided with a deterioration of capitalism's fundamentals: declining rates of return on investment, declining or slowly growing total profits, and financial fragility. During the phase of slower growth (which continues today for most of the world, despite the apparent recovery of the U.S. economy), the U.S. and the rest of the world saw a marked deceleration of growth and capital investment. Three major recessions hit the economy, the first in 1974-75, followed by 1981-82, and 1990-91. Each recession was marked by a significant fall in the relative level of the private investment, an increase in the "natural" level of unemployment, a decline in real wages and in family earnings, and a marked increase in income inequality in favor of higher income groups. At the international level, recession and slow growth exacerbated the U.S. trade deficit, weakened the dollar as a world currency, and prompted U.S. companies to face more intense competition at home and abroad.

This change of fortune, along with the pervasive anti-union sentiments of employers, eventually undermined the system of industrial relationships in the U.S. and many other countries in the advanced and developing world. The tacit "social contract" that prevailed between capital and labor came under attack, in the private and the public sector. Partly as a result of such slow-growth policies, economies stagnate and become increasingly vulnerable to economic recessions. Unemployment forces more workers to accept lower wages. It also undermines union strength by providing corporations with a readily available pool of workers to be hired—and fired—when needed. Ironically, while the corporate agenda is aimed to keep labor costs low to increase profits, it has itself prevented most of the world economy from growing at a healthy rate. Multinational corporations increasingly operate in an environment of slowly growing or even shrinking markets.

In their attempt to boost profits by squeezing workers, corporations have found a willing ally in national governments and international bodies. Whether we call it conservative economic policy, neoliberalism, or austerity politics, the emerging conventional wisdom is to use rising budget deficits as an excuse to reduce public services. In the process, consumer spending is lowered, further contributing to slow growth and more unemployment. Neoliberalism also seeks tax policies that redistribute income from the poor to the rich, from workers to corporations. These neoliberal policies are making recessions longer and economic recoveries weaker than they used to be. For example, the 1990-91 recession lasted longer than originally anticipated. High debt, low investment, and mass layoffs that began well before the recession, started accounted for the lowest rate of growth in the world economy since the Great Depression. The recession was widespread and affected both the three main economies—the U.S., Europe, and Japan— and with a few exceptions, much of the developing world.

The economic expansion that followed the world economic crisis of the early nineties, and which is still underway, has concentrated mostly in North America, where companies have managed to increase profits and resume corporate accumulation and expansion. But in most of Europe, Japan, and the developing world, slow growth and high unemployment are still a major problem. Even in the expanding U.S. economy, economic growth has translated into few income gains for the majority of workers. On balance, unemployment continues to hurt workers throughout the world, as corporations and austerity politicians make sure that job gains—where they occur—do not result in higher wages. In fact, underemployment and low wage jobs have come to characterize employment growth. Labor's new international efforts may have to face economic conditions more reminiscent of the nineteenth century's "Victorian Age" than of the post-war "Golden Age."

Many of the private sector new jobs are part-time and temporary. Many companies are also finding it cheaper to rely on overtime work rather than hire new employees. In fact, if workers went back to the same amount of overtime they did a decade ago, three million new jobs would be created. Real per capita and median family incomes are declining for the first time since World War II, and the number of poor people is increasing.

Frenzied global competition and austerity policies have combined to create a sort of global "casino economy," which makes countries even more vulnerable to recessions and international competition. Company buy-outs left a legacy of high debt, bankruptcies, and falling real estate values. This triggered many bank failures and bail-outs, leaving less money available for social programs. In Japan, the nineties have witnessed a spiral of debt and restructuring, while in the less developing countries, national debt, capital flight, weak currencies, and the fragility of the financial system have wiped out any hopes of catching up with the advanced capitalist countries.

The dominant role of multinationals and international banks in the global economy limits the ability of unions to improve conditions through national governments. Banks and stock and bond holders oppose increased public spending and lower interest rates by threatening to shift their investments to countries whose governments are more compliant. Multinationals undermine labor, environmental, and business legislation and taxation of corporate income by threatening to move to countries that offer a "friendlier" environment. In the U.S., spending on needed social programs has been cut under the excuse of reducing the size of government debt. Despite these cuts, government deficits continue to increase, thanks to corporate income tax breaks, falling wage income, rising health care costs, and still increasing military spending. Interest payments on mounting public debt have also transferred working people's income—through taxes—to rich bondholders, banks, and corporations.

NEED FOR A LABOR ALTERNATIVE

The global nature of the corporate agenda and neoliberalism clearly demonstrate the need for an alternative labor agenda. The AFL-CIO should work with labor federations in other countries and with pro-labor policy analysts to advance such an agenda—one that would seek to stimulate a stagnant global economy, promote stronger, more democratic economies, and more humane societies. Global labor could advocate for full employment, more equitable income distribution, and increasing growth by upping public investment. Labor should demand lower interest rates, a stiff progressive income tax, and bank reform to discourage short-sighted speculation. The AFL-CIO must also frame its call for increased U.S. competitiveness in a way that finds common ground with trade unions overseas, gives emphasis to control and regulation of transnational capital movements, imposes "universal" codes of conduct to multinationals, and empowers communities and workers by giving them a voice on how capital investments (start-ups and closings) are conducted, and how their assets (pension funds) are used by multinationals.

International labor should seek greater control of the workplace, and force employers to apply "high road," human-centered management strategies that enhance workers' involvement in decision-making without undercutting wages and working conditions. We must fight for an international "working day" to reduce working hours without sacrificing pay, and improve working conditions for the growing "contingent" and underground workforce.

On the trade front, the AFL-CIO must continue to reject the principles of corporate protection and oppose existing free trade agreements, such as NAFTA and GATT, because they undermine worker rights and living standards. At the same time, the Federation should call for the inclusion of internationally-recognized worker rights in trade agreements. We need to support policies that forgive third world debt, and oppose the use of foreign aid to maintain low wages abroad. International labor solidarity—a moral imperative—is also an economic necessity.

Building industrial power is the most urgent international solidarity work for most U.S. trade unionists. The decline in "union density" and labor's loss of strength at the bargaining table is almost a universal phenomenon that calls for new fighting strategies. More and more, U.S. unions have gained support from unions overseas in organizing and contract fights. U.S. unions have supported local and cross-border organizing of common employers and sectors and cooperated with unions abroad in their own solidarity efforts. Examples include the Union of Needletrades, Industrial and Textile Employees' organizing initiatives among garment workers in Central America and the Dominican Republic; Communications Workers of America's (CWA) work with European unions representing Telecom workers; CWA's work with Mexican unions during the Sprint campaign; and the United Mine Workers' ties with counterparts in Colombia. Working together, unions have gotten companies to adopt codes of conduct that require respect for worker rights and labor standards. The Service Employees International Union (SEIU) has learned that even in industries oriented to local markets, such as building service and health care, cooperation with international trade unions can be important. SEIU's successful Justice for Janitors campaign against Apple Corporation a few years back involved ISS, the European-based cleaning company.

Exchanging information and conducting strategic research on multinational employers is essential. Even unions in sectors which were outside the process of globalization are now giving greater attention to international organizing. For instance, cleaning services are becoming more "global" as several global cleaning companies are increasing their presence and market share. Multinational real estate companies own and manage a greater number of commercial office real estate than in the past.

International solidarity is the traditional area of work for most trade unionists involved in international affairs. The U.S. labor movement needs to collaborate with the International Trade Secretariat (ITS), yet seek to strengthen and promote direct bilateral and multilateral union-to-union relationships. Industry organizing and bargaining campaigns can be centered around such union-to-union and ITS relationships.

In addition to organizing to build industry power and union capabilities, general demands could also be part of the work of the broadest international union bodies, such as the regional federations and the International Confederation of Free Trade Unions Congress. A labor program needs to be shaped at that broader level, one that helps shape perceptions of issues as diverse as protecting worker rights, banning child and forced labor, developing alternatives to neoliberal policies, standardizing and reducing the length of the working day, ending racism and discrimination in the workplace, and promoting capital strategies tied to the use of pension funds. Several U.S. unions gained experience doing this as part of the anti-NAFTA campaign.

The NAFTA campaign revitalized the discussion about the need to develop strategic alliances that serve the mutual interests of workers across the border. Cross-border worker actions between the Teamsters and Mexican unionists played an important role in highlighting the problems NAFTA poses for transportation workers.

We now have a great opportunity to show our commitment to worker rights by working in collaboration with trade unions, North and South, East and West. This work can also resonate at home. For instance, the global campaigns to ban child labor have clear implications to the reemergence of child labor and sweatshops in the U.S. Defending worker rights can also be tied to improving labor standards to minimize the social costs of global competition. The AFL-CIO can play an important role in promoting worker rights and the harmonization of standards upwards, not downwards, in ways that are not perceived as the North imposing standards on the South, but rather establishing mutual minimum standards for workers.

Promoting international worker rights has to include defending previous gains that are now under threat. The attacks on social security, national pension systems, national health care systems, and public spending on education ultimately cripple labor's ability to organize and bargain effectively. While these attacks occur at the national level, the outcome of the fight in one country affects the outcome in another, and the economic policies justifying these attacks are being implemented around the globe.

Labor should articulate its general demands within a similar framework across borders. A more clearly articulated fight against neoliberalism and the corporate agenda would strengthen our counterparts' ability to support our struggles. This could be an area for collaboration between different departments of the AFL-CIO, such as the international, education, and policy departments.

The need for more effective international work is all the more urgent because other alternatives to protect our members are not as effective as they once were. For example, trade policies intended to protect jobs through limiting imports have lost much of their effectiveness. Because companies themselves increasingly produce overseas and import their products back to the internal domestic market, they are less willing to demand trade protections as a general policy principle. In addition, the mobility of capital and technology to low-wage areas results in unit labor-costs low enough to overcome even significant tariffs, that is, the absolute cost advantages to producers overseas can ultimately overcome them. Companies are also quick to violate protective measures. This is not to suggest that managed trade is not worth pursuing to protect jobs and standards; it only suggests that relying on trade policies, without addressing the need to take wages out of competition internationally, cannot be effective over the long term.

Demands for solidarity actions will continue to drive some of the Federation's international work. Solidarity actions present an opportunity to raise issues like worker rights, discrimination, and labor standards here in the U.S. For example, the fight against apartheid in South Africa, against the violation of human rights in Central America, and the campaign against NAFTA, all resulted in a renewed appreciation by unions for coalition work around issues of worker rights and social justice at home. Solidarity efforts on issues related to free trade and economic integration have also given labor more experience in working with non-governmental organizations, immigrant worker groups, environmentalists, and others.

LOOKING AHEAD

The new AFL-CIO is trying to reorient its international program towards more strategic undertakings within a traditional international affairs structure. The Federation leadership may opt to emphasize support for international solidarity work that fosters the organizing, bargaining, and policy efforts of its affiliates. However, if the AFL-CIO's international efforts are to increase labor's power, vis-à-vis global employers, over the long term, it must resist the temptation to see international work as part of American labor's effort to increase membership and fight contract concessions or plant shutdowns. While U.S. labor must bring about much needed victories in organizing, job protection, contract campaigns, and U.S. trade policy, if it is to be of any use to its affiliates, the AFL-CIO must be a step ahead. It must attempt to rebuild the web of relationships between U.S. labor and trade unionists in other countries, and between U.S. labor and human right activists, environmentalists, and policy centers. It must win the trust of trade unionists abroad and depart from the worst aspects of the Federation's cold war legacy, while rediscovering the best traditions of international solidarity that have characterized the American labor movement. The AFL-CIO must develop an international program that not only serves the immediate interests of American workers but also promotes a new culture of international solidarity based on mutual respect and assistance.

BUILDING A MEMBER-BASED INTERNATIONAL PROGRAM

Ron Blackwell

It is incumbent on us all to be fairly modest when we talk about the labor movement's efforts in the area of international labor solidarity. Measuring our effect in the world against the enormity of the problems we face, it is clear that we have a long, long way to go. In the United States real wages have been falling since 1973, and they are currently at levels unseen in this country since the 1950s. Young American workers today are the first generation in our history who can expect to earn less in their lifetime than their parents did.

The declining standard of living is not just an American problem. The effect of global economic integration—that is, trade with other countries and the free flow of foreign investment—is causing problems for workers in the developing world as well as in the United States. Indeed, there are very few working people in the world who are not experiencing a dramatic assault on their living standards. There is no labor movement that is not under attack.

We must be clear about the challenge before us. The United States, the world's only super power, has a comparatively closed economy: we are still relatively well-sheltered from the force of the world market. Nonetheless, the United States is more integrated with the world economy—through trade, investment, and immigration—than ever before. This has changed labor's position in the economy and dramatically altered the meaning of international solidarity.

The U.S. economy has not been growing very rapidly recently. International trade, especially with the developing world, has been growing much faster than domestic economic activity. International investment is growing faster than trade. In fact, in dollar terms, it is larger than the international trade in goods.

What is driving the increase in investment and trade? Mainly, it is the globalized production that takes place within multinational firms. These firms, many of them American, are using their capacity to locate their operations anywhere in the world to weaken the power of labor and to attack workers everywhere. These international corporations, operating outside effective national regulatory structures, are responsible for the race to the bottom that so many workers find themselves in today.

We in the United States, along with our brothers and sisters in other lands, have to find a way to engage the multinational companies. The future of international economic relations will be determined in the struggle with these companies. If we are successful, we will redefine what globalization means to the vast majority of the world's people.

A CRITERION FOR ACTION

It will not be easy. Unions and national labor movements are groping for ways to respond adequately to the challenge of globalization. As we do this, we have to compare our experiences, criticize each other openly and fairly, stay united, and move forward. Any effort that does not help workers to collectively resist the assault on their living standards is unnecessary—at best, a distraction, and at worst, a barrier.

Our international solidarity work needs to be a practical, non-ideological, emphatically non-partisan effort to build the collective power of workers to resist the assault on their living standards. The challenge is so immediate, we cannot afford theological discussion about which flag people happen to be flying, the name of a union, or any other distraction.

Those of us who represent United States workers must recognize that as long as impoverished and oppressed people exist in the world, domestic jobs and working conditions are at risk. We cannot stop the integration of the world economy. Rather, our mission is to ensure that workers benefit from the growth and prosperity that result from economic integration. Unless workers in less developed countries prosper, U.S. workers cannot prosper either. In the private sector, especially in manufacturing, it is impossible to defend our jobs, wages, and living conditions unless we are able to help workers in other countries defend theirs.

International solidarity must, therefore, become an organic part of our strategy for defending the interests of American workers. Our notion of solidarity can no longer be purely ceremonial. It can no longer be in the service of American geopolitical interests. It can no longer be in the spirit of "saviors" of people of color around the world. It must be more member-based than we have ever succeeded in making it. It must be directed at building reciprocal relationships with movements in other countries for the common cause of reversing unionism's retreat around the world.

LESSONS FROM OUR HISTORY: FASHIONING THE NEW JERSEY STRATEGY

The challenge we face is unprecedented. Workers, however, have a heritage of struggle that unions can build upon. In the Union of Needletrades Industrial and Textile Employees (UNITE), we learned some valuable lessons over the years. The problem of mobile capital, for instance, is not a new one to workers in the needle trades. We have always faced the threat of employers who run away from unions in their quest for cheap labor.

Apparel makers have always relied on labor-intensive production techniques. This gives them flexibility: it is easy to hire or lay-off workers with changes in the market. It also creates a problem. Because wages are a relatively large share of their costs, manufacturers are particularly sensitive to wage increases. All this makes for footloose employers. They have the ability and a strong incentive to move their factories to low-wage areas, which they have been doing for nearly a century.

Two of UNITE's predecessor unions, the International Ladies' Garment Workers' Union (ILGWU) and the Amalgamated Clothing Workers, were forged in 1900 and 1910 out of bitter strikes by shirtwaist makers and cloak makers in New York City, and by men's clothing workers in Chicago. These cities were the major centers of the apparel industry at the time. The workers, most of them young immigrant women, just left their sewing machines and hit the street. Their picket lines were attacked mercilessly by the police and thugs hired by the companies. They fought back. Although many of them were hurt or killed, they remained determined. Ultimately they were successful; they founded a union.

Almost from the time the unions were established, they were involved in an "international" struggle. The first thing that the employers did when they were forced to sign a union contract to improve pay and working conditions, was to search for cheaper and more compliant labor. Many New York employers ran away to what were then known as "foreign zones," in Hackensack, Passaic, and Trenton, New Jersey.

The union pursued a three-pronged strategy in response to corporate flight. I call it the "New Jersey strategy." First the union went to New Jersey and organized the workers there. Second, the union did everything it could to encourage employers to compete with one another in ways that did not depend on exploiting their workers—ways that were compatible with workers' rights to organize and bargain collectively. Third, the union sought to establish rules for interstate commerce. Unregulated trade between the states allowed companies to avoid labor regulations by shipping goods from states with low or no labor standards to consumers in states with higher standards. The struggle culminated in the 1930s with the Fair Labor Standards Act. That federal legislation established, for the first time, national labor standards: the minimum wage, premium pay for overtime, and a ban on child labor. It also made it illegal to ship goods that were produced under substandard conditions across state borders.

Of course, the companies did not stop in New Jersey. They went to what was called the "Siberia" of the clothing industry—Philadelphia. The unions followed the New Jersey strategy and organized the apparel makers there. The companies kept moving. That is why much of the U.S. clothing industry and the bulk of our textile industry are now found in the South and Southwest where some of the most dynamic contemporary organizing efforts are taking place. Meanwhile, the employers have moved on to Asia and the Caribbean Basin: the Dominican Republic, Central America, and Mexico.

UPDATING THE NEW JERSEY STRATEGY

The union's New Jersey strategy is essentially what it is pursuing today, though under very changed circumstances. While it cannot go to another country and organize the way it did in New Jersey, it can still help workers in other countries to organize. The competitive strategies of the companies are different today then they were decades ago. The Union has found ways to work with employers who respect the rights of workers, or "get between" employers and their customer base when they do not. Changing the rules of international commerce is certainly more difficult than changing the rules of interstate commerce. Nonetheless, trade agreements can include enforceable labor standards and workers' rights.

Following the Work Across International Borders

UNITE has joined with workers in other countries as they struggle for decent wages and working conditions. Several years ago, the Amalgamated Clothing and Textile Workers Union (ACTWU) forged a working partnership with its sister union in South Africa, the South African Clothing and Textile Workers Union (SACTWU). When the American-owned Tidwell Company opened a plant in the Ciskei, one of apartheid's "homelands," SACTWU called on ACTWU to help coordinate pressure on the company. Because unions were banned in the former "homeland," SACTWU demanded that the plant be closed. ACTWU coordinated a campaign by labor, church, and civil rights organizations that forced Tidwell to shut the plant down. The South African brothers and sisters also found ways to help U.S. workers. When ACTWU was engaged in an organizing drive at a Courtaulds (a multinational textile firm) plant in Martinsville, Virginia, South African Courtaulds workers protested the company's anti-union stand by refusing to work overtime.

A recent victory for workers in one of the Dominican Republic's free-trade zones illustrates how different union bodies can be coordinated to apply pressure on employers across international borders. The Republic's free-trade zones have been a union-free haven for U.S. multinationals for a quarter century. After three years of struggle, workers at the Bibong Apparel Corporation won the zone's first collective bargaining agreement.

They got help on the ground from both ACTWU and the ILGWU, as well as the AFL-CIO's American Institute for Free Labor Development, which provided training to organizers of the Federation of Free Zone Workers. An international trade union secretariat, the Inter-American Regional Organization of Textile, Garment, Leather, and Shoe Workers, coordinated the solidarity activities of the U.S. unions with the unions in the Dominican Republic. ACTWU and the ILGWU pressured Bibong's U.S. customers to cancel their contracts unless it signed with the union. The

AFL-CIO petitioned the U.S. trade representative to deny the Dominican Republic duty-free trade benefits. The latter threat finally prompted action by the Dominican government. The Labor Minister stepped into the dispute, first requesting the suspension of Bibong's license to export and then extending legal recognition to the union. Coordinated activity was possible because everyone involved put the interests of the workers ahead of other considerations.

Encouraging High Road Competitive Strategies

Unions want their companies to be competitive. But there are different ways to compete and they result in different standards of living. Companies can compete by sweating people or by producing quality products. For example, in the early 1980s, the Xerox Corporation—one of UNITE's largest employers—faced stiff competition from Japanese photocopy machine manufacturers. Yet, the corporation did not recapture market share from its Japanese competitors by finding cheap workers to make copy machines. Rather than outsource its production, Xerox reached an agreement with the union to establish a joint study team to look for cost-saving improvements. The team was able to identify changes in the organization of work flow, work area design, and equipment, which convinced management that it could compete without resorting to low-wage labor. Continued cooperation between ACTWU and the corporation meant that Xerox built its new xerographic toner plant in Rochester, New York and not the South. ACTWU helped Xerox to compete on the basis of quality. It now makes the best copiers in the world, with union labor.

Another one of UNITE's employers, Levi Strauss and Company, recognized that establishing outsourcing guidelines was good business. It will not outsource work to companies in countries that do not meet certain democratic standards, and it will not engage business partners that do not respect basic labor standards. Levi Strauss did this voluntarily because it did not want its name to be associated with exploitative practices overseas.

Companies that demand basic worker rights and labor standards from their international business partners follow a high-road business strategy. It is one the union wants to encourage. The union has worked with those employers who respect the rights of their employees to compete on the basis of quality and customer service. That strategy depends on a highly skilled and motivated workforce. At both Xerox and Levi Strauss, ACTWU worked with management to improve product quality and worker productivity.

Employers are not always so enlightened. Where the carrot of cooperation fails, the union has found a stick. Companies whose brand name is on a garment have invested millions to create a good image for their product. That makes them vulnerable to negative publicity about the blind eye they turn toward their suppliers' abuses of workers' rights. When necessary, the union has exposed retailers and manufacturers who shirk their responsibility for the working conditions under which their products are made. Recently, for example, the Union engaged in a successful campaign to highlight the conditions of workers in El Salvador making apparel for The Gap, a well-known retail chain. Under the pressure of negative publicity and the threat of a consumer boycott, The Gap agreed to a code of conduct for its suppliers which will be monitored by Salvadoran church, human rights, and labor organizations.

This kind of aggressive public exposure has set the stage for the next step in the fight against sweatshop conditions which now exist on both sides of the U.S. border. Unions, employers, human rights organizations, and consumer groups have met—under the auspices of a presidential task force—to create a comprehensive agreement which will establish voluntary standards, and a means to monitor them, in the areas of worker rights, minimum wages, maximum hours, and child labor.

Our hope is that these negotiations will forge an industry-wide compact which will establish a basic level of fair wages and working conditions for apparel workers around the world. The compact will help workers here and abroad. And it will be good for business; corporations which comply with these standards will have the right to put "no sweat" labels on their clothes, informing customers that their products have been made without sweatshop labor.

Regulating International Commerce

Even with such codes, organized labor will still have to change the rules of international commerce. Voluntary standards cannot guarantee universal compliance. We will also need a global equivalent of the Fair Labor Standards Act. That equivalent will have to recognize the distinction between worker rights and labor standards. Worker rights include the right to speak openly, to associate freely, to organize unions, and to act collectively in defense of their interests. These fundamental civil rights must exist regardless of a country's level of development, and must not be abridged simply because a country is poor.

Labor standards include the minimum-wage level and maximum-hours laws, health and safety, and child labor provisions. Labor standards cannot be the same in all countries. Whether the minimum wage is high or low and whether people work longer or shorter hours depends on a country's level of development. Therefore, some means need to be established to ensure that labor standards rise as productivity and development permit. It will be a challenge to find an effective mechanism for enforcing worker rights and to harmonize labor standards upward so that workers everywhere benefit from economic growth. For this to happen, U.S. international trade and investment laws must include workers' rights provisions as there is no supranational entity or state to pass an international fair labor standards act. A company should not be allowed to cross international borders in search of labor unless it produces goods in a manner that respects fundamental worker rights and is compatible with the upward harmonization of labor standards.

U.S. trade laws and multilateral trade agreements, like the Generalized System of Preferences, the Caribbean Basin Initiative, and the North American Free Trade Agreement (NAFTA) side-agreements, have incorporated a number of clauses which recognize—in principle, if not in practice—this long-standing objective of the labor movement. The labor movement must build on this approach. Labor will need stronger protections and more effective enforcement mechanisms that can operate on the widest international scale if we are to have broad-based, just, and sustainable development around the world.

The United States should not simply set labor standards and then dictate them to the rest of the world. The standards of the United Nation's International Labor Organization (ILO) are the most comprehensive in the world, and they were negotiated on a multilateral, tripartite basis. They do not have to be ratified by the U.S. Congress to be used as guidelines for any agreement that the United States signs on trade, investment, or aid. If ILO standards are not used, however, labor standards should be established on a negotiated basis with the countries involved in an international agreement. These standards should be enforceable. Chapter 17 of NAFTA has some practical provisions for enforcing intellectual property rights. Human rights are surely as important as intellectual property rights, and their enforcement is no more difficult.

CONCLUSION: INTERNATIONAL SOLIDARITY MUST BE MEMBER-BASED

Where does the AFL-CIO fit into this updated version of the New Jersey strategy? There are some rather obvious and very practical contributions the Federation can make to strengthen the ability of the affiliates to engage employers across borders. The Federation can facilitate the work of affiliates in the international trade secretariats and foster the further development of bilateral contacts between U.S. unions and their counterparts abroad. The AFL-CIO is well-positioned to expand and coordinate the flow of information unions need to organize in a globalized economy. The Federation can support long-run, strategic planning for internationally coordinated organizing and collective bargaining campaigns.

The needle trades experience, however, suggests that the principle organizers of international solidarity must be the individual unions rather than the Federation. Individual workers, groups of workers, locals, and regional boards inside unions should set the agenda for international solidarity. That is where the front line is. Those are the people who are fighting the multinational companies. It is the job of national and international unions—as well as the Federation and the secretariats—to support them and stand behind them. Workers themselves are the leading edge in fighting for their living standards everywhere in the world. Their success can shape the future of the world's economy.

| Afterword

John J. Sweeney

This book is a product of—and a valuable contribution to—the new spirit of open debate and aggressive action that is revitalizing American labor.

In the early summer of 1995, activists from every level of the labor movement launched a campaign to bring new energy, new ideas, and new leadership to the AFL-CIO. We were concerned that most Americans' living standards were stagnating and that the only institution that expressly represents them—the labor movement—was losing membership strength, political power, and public esteem. Our goal was not just to win the election, but to renew the labor movement by involving union members across the country and attracting the attention of unrepresented workers, the news media, and potential allies throughout society.

Never before had there been a contested election for the leadership of the labor federation, and, as with many large institutions, there was a reluctance to criticize established ways of doing things.

Those of us in the "New Voice" campaign believed the AFL-CIO would benefit from free discussion and even self-criticism. That is why I ended virtually every speech with a call for open debate: "My idea of a perfect labor movement is one which consistently re-examines itself and corrects its own imperfections."

Throughout that campaign—and during the two years since Rich Trumka, Linda Chavez-Thompson, and I were elected—I have been encouraged and inspired by the growing interest, involvement and exchange of ideas about how to revitalize the labor movement. This excitement has spread from union meetings and picket lines to church halls and college classrooms.

In fact, on the eve of the October 1995, AFL-CIO convention in New York City, there was a conference at the Queens College Labor Resource Center on how to take the labor movement into the twenty-first century. And now, the center's director, Gregory Mantsios, has edited and published a collection of essays, *A New Labor Movement for the New Century*, based on the presentations at this conference.

These essays address labor's challenges: organizing unrepresented workers; inspiring the involvement of all workers, especially women and people of color; building a stronger political presence in this country; and promoting solidarity among working people throughout the world as we all struggle to survive in the harsh new global economy.

The questions these essays raise—and many of the ideas they offer— exemplify the thinking labor activists need as we strive simultaneously to build and change our movement. While I may not agree with *the substance* of every idea, I heartily endorse *the spirit* in which they are offered. What shines through from these papers is the unshakable commitment of so many unionists, academics, and other activists to find new and effective ways to organize and mobilize working Americans for economic justice in our workplaces and social justice in our nation.

Lord knows, the labor movement needs this combination of restless, intelligent, and reinvigorated activism. In fact, since these papers were presented, we have hired four of the authors for staff positions at the AFL-CIO: International Affairs Director Barbara Shailor, Education Director Bill Fletcher, Corporate Affairs Director Ron Blackwell, and Assistant Organizing Director Stephen Lerner.

While I find many ideas to agree with in these essays—and also some to dispute—I would suggest three main points of my own: First, nobody has all the answers about how to revitalize the labor movement. Second, very often the only way to find out if an idea will work is to try it out. And, third, we can and should try many different kinds of ideas in different unions, different industries, different communities, and different sectors of the workforce.

In other words, we should act in the spirit of that gifted innovator, Franklin D. Roosevelt, who once offered America "bold persistent experimentation," explaining: "It is common sense to take a method and try it. If it fails, admit it. But, above all, try something."

In that spirit, let me address some of the most important issues raised in these essays.

ORGANIZING

In different ways, Stephen Lerner, Steve Early, Janice Fine, and Josephine LeBeau and Kevin Lynch address the most important issue of all—rebuilding the ultimate source of our movement's strength, our membership base.

As their essays explain, we need to address this challenge in many ways: generating new resources at every level of the labor movement, recruiting and training new organizers, involving rank-and-file members, devising more effective strategies, and building a culture of organizing throughout the movement.

At the AFL-CIO, we have created an organizing department for the first time in the Federation's history. We are devoting approximately thirty percent of our resources to organizing. And we are helping unions at every level—national, regional, and local—put more resources into organizing and organize more effectively.

Much of our effort is devoted to working with regional and local unions, since, as LeBeau and Lynch report, these are often the most effective mechanisms for organizing workers in their own communities. Through the Elected Leader Task Force, we are drawing upon the experience of local and regional unions that are shifting their resources toward organizing—and organizing strategically and successfully. We are spreading their message through regional "Changing to Organize" conferences, holding a dozen of these meetings during the summer of 1997 alone.

In order to help national, regional, and local unions find effective organizers, we are stepping up our efforts at recruitment, training, and placement through the Organizing Institute. While Early correctly stresses the importance of "membership-based organizing," those who share his concerns should know that most of the organizers who are trained by the institute come from working class backgrounds, many are union members themselves, and quite a few go to work for regional offices of national unions, union regions, or local unions. Just as importantly, the AFL-CIO helps unions at every level train and mobilize rank-and-file members as volunteer organizers whose efforts are indispensable to campaigns.

Through our organizing fund, we are also helping unions develop and coordinate organizing strategies similar to those Lerner describes, targeting entire industries and communities. These efforts include the United Farm Workers' campaign for strawberry workers in California and the building trades' unions campaign for construction workers in Las Vegas. There is also much to be learned from the efforts at community unionism that Janice Fine describes, such as the Union of Needletrades, Industrial and Textile Employees' service centers for immigrant workers.

Just as we must strengthen our presence in American workplaces, we must also strengthen our presence in American cities, suburbs, and small towns. That is the goal of our new "Union Cities" efforts to build stronger community labor councils. We are working with these councils—which represent local unions in their communities—to encourage them to take on tasks including: enrolling local unions in the Changing to Organize program; building active support for workers' struggles through mobilization committees; and conducting grassroots legislative and political action and broad-based community interest campaigns.

Meanwhile, at the local and national levels, we are calling attention to how corporate America is violating the letter and the spirit of federal laws guaranteeing working Americans the right to organize unions. More than 10,000 workers are illegally fired each year, just for trying to organize unions. But the real scandal is what is legal: routine corporate harassment and intimidation of workers who even dare to murmur the word "union." From community protests against corporations that browbeat workers who organize, to efforts to persuade the local, state, and federal governments to stop doing business with union-busters, we are trying to make the right to organize the civil rights issue of the 1990s and beyond. And we are laying the groundwork for future efforts at labor law reform.

While we are building for the future, our efforts have already begun to pay off with victories among state employees in Maryland, asbestos workers in New York, mechanics at Continental Airlines, and health care, clothing and textile, and retail workers across the country, among others.

But, just to maintain our current percentage of the workforce, we must grow by 300,000 members a year. This sobering reality reminds us that we must think and act more ambitiously than ever.

PROMOTING PARTICIPATION AND DIVERSITY

Elaine Bernard, Bill Fletcher, Ruth Needleman, José La Luz and Paula Finn, and Kent Wong and May Chen all offer important pointers for how the labor movement can inspire the involvement of more workers, particularly those whom unions have too often overlooked.

In our "New Voice" campaign and at the AFL-CIO, we have called for making the faces of labor's leadership reflect the faces of Americans at work, and we have made some progress. Rich Trumka, now forty-seven, is the youngest full-time national officer of the AFL-CIO. Linda Chavez-Thompson is a person of color. Twenty-seven percent of the members of the new executive council are women or people of color. And, at the AFL-CIO, we now have the first Working Women's Department in the Federation's history, headed by Karen Nussbaum, founder of the working women's association, 9 to 5, and former director of the Women's Bureau of the Labor Department.

All this is good, but not good enough. We need to do more to reach out to the new American workforce.

That is why the Working Women's Department conducted a major outreach effort in 1997, appropriately entitled "Ask a Working Woman." The effort included: a national tour by Chavez-Thompson, Nussbaum, and AFL-CIO Vice President Gloria Johnson, with dozens of meetings with women at their worksites; a scientific survey of a cross-section of working women, including union members and unrepresented workers; and questionnaires returned by nearly 50,000 union and unrepresented women from every walk of life. Their views are guiding our work on issues women tell us are high priorities, including equal pay, child care, family leave, and health insurance.

BUILDING POLITICAL POWER

In different ways, Dennis Rivera, Tony Mazzocchi, Arthur Cheliotes, Gregory Mantsios, and Patricia Lippold and Bob Kirkman all make important points about the need for labor to be political watchdogs, not political lapdogs.

American labor is beginning to build a political presence that mobilizes working people, raises their issues in public debate, and brings their concerns before public officials—every year and all year round. In 1996, we took working families' issues to the airwaves, with TV and radio spots supporting Medicare, Medicaid, education, job safety, and health and pension protections against attacks in Congress. In particular, we zeroed in on raising the minimum wage, with messages broadcast in thirty key congressional districts. We mobilized public opinion and, against the odds, helped persuade a hostile Congress to raise the minimum wage. And, throughout the year, grassroots volunteers kept union members informed about how their representatives had acted—or failed to act—on issues of concern to working families.

These efforts signal a change from the old days, when unions too often did little more than endorse candidates and give them—and their party machinery—campaign contributions. And we are going to do lots more to build an independent political presence: recruiting union members to run for office themselves; training many more grassroots political activists; and organizing new networks for worker-to-worker communications on legislative and political issues, from their worksites to their communities.

BUILDING INTERNATIONAL SOLIDARITY

My response to most of the ideas offered in the essays on international affairs can best be summed up with one word: "Amen!"

In particular, the paper by George Kourpias, the recently retired president of the Machinists (and chair of the AFL-CIO's international affairs committee), and Barbara Shailor (our new international affairs director) offers insights into our efforts to build solidarity with working people and their unions throughout the world.

Increasingly, working Americans understand that it is a threat to their job security and living standards if working people anywhere on earth are forced to do the same jobs for poverty wages. In this age of global trade and instant communications, this is true not only for manufacturing workers but for clerical and professional employees as well, from data input operators to software writers.

And our concerns are moral as well as material: It is wrong when China exports products made by political prisoners. It is wrong when Indonesia imprisons its trade union leaders. It is wrong when Pakistan relies on child labor in its factories. And, just as American unionists did in our efforts to support the Solidarity trade union movement in Poland and the movement against apartheid in South Africa, we are answering injustice with action.

That is why we are fighting for workers' rights clauses in every international trade agreement, so that global trade lifts all working people up, instead of dragging us all down. Now that the cold war is over, we are working with labor unions and labor federations throughout the world, and our watchword is solidarity, not ideology.

From our workplaces to the world economy, working Americans are finding new ways to make their voices heard through their unions. The essays in this book should stimulate the thinking and inspire the efforts of everyone who is striving to build "a new labor movement for the new century."

ABOUT THE CONTRIBUTORS

Larry Adams is president of Local 300 of the National Postal Mail Handlers Union. As one of four craft unions in the U.S. Postal Service, Local 300 represents 6,600 mail handlers in New York, New Jersey, and Southern Connecticut. A union activist since entering the postal service, Adams was fired in the 1978 contract dispute and work stoppage. Upon reinstatement he served as steward, chief steward, and then local vice president. He was elected local president in 1991. A strong advocate of rank-and-file democracy and activism, Adams has led the local to affiliate with the Labor Party, emphasize internal organizing, and engage in external labor and community solidarity activities. He also functions in the leadership of Workers For One Postal Union.

Andy Banks has coordinated international activities for the Teamsters' Office of Strategic Initiatives and Corporate Affairs. Prior to that, he was the education officer of the Public Service International (PSI), the international trade union federation of public sector unions around the world. Between 1977 and 1992, Banks was the associate director for Labor Education of the Center for Labor Research and Studies at Florida International University in Miami. He holds an advanced degree in Labor Studies, was a long time editorial board member of *Labor Research Review*, and has written a number of articles on labor union topics.

Elaine Bernard is executive director of the Trade Union Program at Harvard University. Before moving to Boston in 1989, Bernard taught at Simon Fraser University in Vancouver, British Columbia, and was president of the British Columbian wing of Canada's labor party, the New Democratic Party. Bernard is a popular lecturer, has published on a wide variety of labor-related topics, and has conducted courses on labor, technological and organizational change, politics, and international comparative industrial relations for a wide variety of trade unions, community groups, universities, and government departments in the United States, Canada, Australia, South Africa, and Europe. She holds a Ph.D. in history.

Ronald Blackwell was chief economist for the Union of Needletrades, Industrial and Textile Employees (UNITE) when he wrote his essay for this volume and was subsequently appointed director of the AFL-CIO's new Corporate Affairs Department. At the AFL-CIO he is responsible for developing programs to support unions in their direct relations with employers at levels ranging from capital strategies, corporate ownership, and governance, to collective bargaining, to workplace reform and technological change. Previously, as chief economist for UNITE, he advised union leadership on public policy and union strategy. Before joining the labor movement, Ron Blackwell was an associate dean in the Seminar College of the New School for Social Research, where he taught economics. He holds an advanced degree in economics from the New School for Social Research.

Jeremy Brecher is the author of eight books on labor and other social movements. A revised, twenty-fifth anniversary edition of his first book, *Strike!* was recently released by South End Press. He has also received three Emmy awards and the Edgar Dale screenwriting award for his work as a documentary video scriptwriter. The most recent products of Brecher's twenty-year collaboration with Tim Costello include *Building Bridges: The Emerging Grassroots Coalition of Labor and Community* and *Global Village or Global Pillage: Economic Reconstruction from the Bottom Up*.

Arthur Cheliotes is president of Local 1180 of the Communications Workers of America (CWA), a union representing administrative employees throughout New York City and the largest public sector local in the CWA. Under his leadership, the union has launched a progressive tax campaign to maintain city services and bring equity to the New York City tax structure, served as the home of the Labor Committee Against Apartheid, and has been a vocal advocate for worker education, pay equity, and enforcement of civil service laws. Cheliotes also serves as vice chair of the New York City Municipal Labor Committee, president of the Greek American Labor Council, board member of the New York

State Public Employees Conference, and chair of the City University of New York and Queens College Labor Advisory Boards.

May Ying Chen is the assistant manager of Local 23-25 Union of Needletrades, Industrial and Textile Employees (UNITE). Her local is the largest in UNITE and represents 20,000 members, mostly Chinese immigrant women, working in the New York City garment industry. Having worked for the International Ladies' Garment Workers' Union (ILGWU) and then UNITE since 1984, she has been involved with programs to educate and mobilize union members around such issues as immigration rights, sweatshops, day care, voter registration, and women's rights. Chen brings a background of community organizing to the labor movement, and seeks to sensitize community organizers and activists to issues and concerns of workers. Chen is also active in the Coalition of Labor Union Women (CLUW) and serves on the national board of the Asian Pacific American Labor Alliance (APALA).

Tim Costello is director of Northeast Action's Campaign on Contingent Workers in Boston. He has been a workplace activist for more than twenty years and a union representative for the Service Employees International Union Local 285 in Boston for four years. He has collaborated with Jeremy Brecher on a number of books including *Building Bridges: The Emerging Grassroots Coalition of Labor and Community* and *Global Village or Global Pillage: Economic Reconstruction from the Bottom Up.*

Steve Early is the international representative of the Communications Workers of America (CWA) for District 1. He joined the staff of CWA in 1980, assisting in the successful drive to organize 40,000 New Jersey State workers. He later assisted in the victorious 1989 strike at NYNEX by 60,000 telephone workers. In his twenty-five years of activism in the labor movement, he has served as a labor educator, attorney, organizer, and journalist. He is Boston-based and a longtime participant in the Massachusetts Jobs with Justice campaigns. Prior to his involvement with unions, he was active in the campus-based anti-war movement.

Héctor Figueroa is assistant research director for the Building Service Division of the Service Employees International Union (SEIU) where he coordinates research for the union's "Justice for Janitors" organizing campaign. Prior to joining SEIU, Figueroa worked as a research associate for the Amalgamated Clothing and Textile Workers Union, and was actively involved in the union's international solidarity work and NAFTA campaign. Figueroa is completing his Ph.D. in economics at the New School for Social Research and has written several articles on labor and economic issues. He is an activist within the Puerto Rican civil rights movement.

Janice Fine is the organizing director of Northeast Action, a network of statewide labor/community coalitions across the northeast which works to train grassroots organizers and leaders. Fine founded the New England Money and Politics Project at Northeast Action which recently played a leading role in passing the country's first system of voluntary total public financing in Maine and Vermont. She is a doctoral candidate in political science at the Massachusetts Institute of Technology writing about workers, unions, and state and local politics in the United States. Fine is a member of the United Auto Workers Local 376.

Paula Finn is the associate director of the Queens College Labor Resource Center and co-editor of the center's journal, *New Labor Forum.* Previously she served as the director of education for 1199 Health and Human Service Employees Union and as associate national director of education for the Amalgamated Clothing and Textile Workers Union. Finn has worked with unions to develop curriculum, train teachers, establish bilingual educational programs, and organize international exchanges. She holds an advanced degree in English from New York University, teaches, and writes poetry.

Bill Fletcher, Jr. was serving as director of field services for the Service Employees International Union (SEIU) when he wrote his essay for this volume and was subsequently appointed director of education for the AFL-CIO. Previous to his work with SEIU, Fletcher was an organizer for District 65 of the United Auto Workers and administrative director of the National Postal Mail Handlers Union. He writes on numerous issues, including questions facing the labor movement, for a wide variety of publications.

Bob Kirkman has been involved in the union movement for over twenty-five years as a rank-and-file activist, shop steward, union education director, field representative, and labor educator. He is the N.Y./N.J. regional coordinator of the Service Employees International Union (SEIU). Prior to joining SEIU, Kirkman served as director of education for the United Auto Workers District 65. He has been involved in a wide variety of coalition work in the New York area and is on the administrative committee of New York Jobs with Justice. He holds an advanced degree in Labor Studies from Rutgers University.

George Kourpias was president of the International Association of Machinists and Aerospace Workers until his recent retirement. In that capacity he also served on the Executive Council of the AFL-CIO and was the delegate who nominated John Sweeney for the presidency at the 1995 convention. He has played an active role in politics and government, serving on the Democratic National Committee, the National Advisory Commission on Worker Based Learning, the Overseas Private Investment Corporation, and the National Advisory Council on Social Security. Kourpias also serves as the vice president of the National Council of Senior Citizens. He served the members of his union for nearly forty years.

José La Luz has been a worker-educator and union organizer for the past twenty-five years. He has practiced his craft in various unions, including the garment and clothing workers unions (now merged as UNITE), the hotel and restaurant workers union (HERE), and more recently with American Federation of State, County, and Municipal Employees (AFSCME), where he has served as associate director of education and currently directs a large-scale organizing drive among public service workers in the Commonwealth of Puerto Rico.

Stephen Lerner is the assistant director of organizing for the AFL-CIO and directs the federation's activities with both the strawberry workers in California and the construction workers in Las Vegas. Lerner has been a union organizer for over twenty years. He first started as an organizer for the United Farm Workers' (UFW) grape boycott and then went on to organize in the South for the International Ladies' Garment Workers' Union. As organizing director for the Building Services Department of the Service Employees International Union, he launched and directed Justice for Janitors—a national campaign that organized over 35,000 janitors.

Patricia Lippold has worked for the Service Employees International Union (SEIU) for ten years, serving in various capacities including political field director, director for the eastern region in New York, and currently as assistant to the executive vice president for the midwest region. Before joining SEIU, she worked in numerous political campaigns on behalf of progressive candidates in a number of senatorial and congressional races. She also served as a union organizer for the machinist union (IAM) and the United Food and Commercial Workers (UFCW).

Kevin P. Lynch served as director of political action and organization for District Council 1707, AFSCME during the 1995-96 period when the union successfully organized 1,800 workers and helped elect five pro-labor candidates to the New York State Legislature. He now works for District 15, International Association of Machinists and Aerospace Workers, organizing limousine and car service drivers, mechanics, and physicians.

Josephine LeBeau is the executive director of District Council 1707 of the American Federation of State, County, and Municipal Employees (AFSCME) which represents 23,000 members employed in non-profit social service agencies. She is the first African American and first woman to hold this position. LeBeau is also the national vice president of the Coalition of Labor Union Women (CLUW), served as an officer of the New York Coalition of Black Trade Unionists (CBTU), and is on CBTU's National Executive Council. Prior to her involvement with District Council 1707, LeBeau was senior assistant to the dean of graduate faculty at Bank Street College.

Gregory Mantsios is the director of worker education at Queens College. In this capacity he is responsible for the college's campus-based degree program for working adults (Labor Education and Advancement Project), its Worker Education Extension Center in mid-Manhattan, and its Labor Resource Center. He also developed a new bachelor's degree program in Applied Social Science that is designed to prepare students for public service and advocacy. Previously, he taught at William Paterson College, served as an officer of the American Federation of Teachers Local 1796, and worked as a community organizer for the ACTION program. He holds a Ph.D. in sociology, teaches labor studies, and writes on poverty, inequality, labor, and education.

Tony Mazzocchi has served the Oil, Chemical, and Atomic Workers (OCAW) in a number of capacities over the course of forty-five years. These included international vice president, secretary-treasurer, legislative director, health and safety director, and president of Local 8-149. He currently holds the position of presidential assistant. He has been the prime mover in forming the recently established Labor Party and serves as its interim national organizer. Mazzocchi has also been very active in the occupational and environmental health movement and, after the death of Karen Silkwood, with whom he worked, campaigned to make public the truth about her case. He is publisher of *New Solutions*, a journal of environmental and occupational health policy.

Ruth A. Needleman is associate professor of labor studies at Indiana University. Her program provides college-degree and training programs for workers and unions in northwest Indiana. She has worked in the labor movement as a rank-and-file organizer, editor of the United Farm Workers' newspaper and, more recently, education director of the Service Employees International Union. Her research focuses on women workers, leadership development, race and gender issues, and organizing, with recent articles on "Organizing Low-Wage Workers," "Space and Opportunity: Developing Leaders for Labor's Future," and "Raising Visibility, Reducing Marginality: A Labor Law Reform Agenda for Working Women of Color." She holds a Ph.D. in Spanish and Latin American literature from Harvard University.

Dennis Rivera has served as president of 1199 National Health and Human Service Employees Union, AFL-CIO since April 1989. The 117,000-member union is the largest health care union in the United States and represents service, professional, technical, and clerical workers employed in non-profit voluntary hospitals and nursing homes, as well as home care workers, employees of community health centers, and retail drug stores. In 1994, Rivera negotiated a contract with the League of Voluntary Hospitals that created the largest group of workers in America with absolute guarantees of jobs and incomes. He was one of the founders of the National Union of Health Care Workers of Puerto Rico and of the Municipal Employees Union of the City of San Juan. He also serves as co–vice chairperson of the New York State Democratic Party.

Barbara Shailor was serving as director of International Affairs for the International Association of Machinists and Aerospace Workers (IAM) when she co-authored her essay for this anthology and was subsequently appointed director of the AFL-CIO International Affairs Department. She is an expert on international trade, a frequent lecturer, and a television and radio commentator. She serves on the Executive Committee of the International Confederation of Trade Unions (ICFTU), the U.S. Labor Department's Advisory Committee, and the boards of the International Labor Rights Fund and the Alliance for Responsible Trade. She has earned international recognition for her work on behalf of economic, social, and political rights for workers in the U.S. and throughout the world.

John Sweeney was elected president of the AFL-CIO in October 1995. Previously he led the Service Employees International Union, which during a period when the labor movement was in steep decline, grew from 625,000 to 1.1 million members. Known for his militant championing of the poorest and least powerful segments of the workforce, Sweeney has also served on the National Committee on Employment Policy and in the International Labor Organization. He is author of *America Needs a Raise* and co-author of *Solutions for the New Work Force*.

Kent Wong has served as president of the Asian Pacific American Labor Alliance, AFL-CIO since its founding convention in 1992. He is the director of the Labor Center at the University of California, Los Angeles, and teaches Asian American Studies and Labor Studies there. Wong previously worked for six years as staff attorney for Local 660 of the Service Employees International Union and also served as the first staff attorney of the Asian Pacific American Legal Center of Southern California. He has litigated several major sex and race discrimination cases representing government workers.

INDEX